TREASURES OLD & NEW

Daily Readings From the Greek and Hebrew Scriptures and the Lutheran Confessions

John C. Jeske

NORTHWESTERN PUBLISHING HOUSE
Milwaukee, Wisconsin

Cover illustration: ShutterStock, Inc.
Art Director: Karen Knutson
Designer: Pamela Dunn

Library of Congress Control Number: 2009934424
Northwestern Publishing House
1250 N. 113th St., Milwaukee, WI 53226-3284
www.nph.net

Published 2009
Printed in the United States of America
ISBN 978-0-8100-2259-1

26 27 28 29 30 31 32 33 34 35 14 13 12 11 10 9 8 7 6 5

Editor's Preface

This volume is the labor of love of the Rev. John Jeske, longtime professor of Old Testament at Wisconsin Lutheran Seminary and one of my own mentors. For many years Prof. Jeske's daily devotions included the use of Heinrich Bitzer's *Light on the Path*, which contained a daily Old Testament selection in Hebrew and a New Testament selection in Greek, each with basic lexical notes for the reader. Jeske's contact with former students convinced him of the usefulness of such daily work in the original languages for the busy pastor. Without it, the years spent honing language skills often gave way to ministries in which those skills were eventually lost.

While Prof. Jeske frequently encouraged students to purchase and use Bitzer's volume and its successor, *More Light on the Path*, he also noted several weaknesses. The Hebrew passages selected were often unusually difficult. Too often scriptural gems were ignored and less common passages used. He often looked for greater emphasis on the specific message of the liturgical church year. Finally, Prof. Jeske wished for more passages with a gospel emphasis, so that the selections would not be speaking merely to a language scholar but to a child of God.

During one period when the original volume was out of print, Prof. Jeske conceived the idea of a replacement volume that would address some of these weaknesses, while keeping the general format. Upon his retirement from the seminary, he began work on the project by identifying 366 Old Testament passages of note. He then matched these with appropriate New Testament passages, having similar content wherever possible. Grammatical and lexical helps were then prepared for each section.

About ten years ago, an attempt was made to turn Prof. Jeske's typed and handwritten notes into a published volume. For a number of reasons, the project never came to fruition. In mid-2008, I was asked for advice on seeing the project through to completion. Discussions with Northwestern Publishing House soon led to a concrete proposal, and the results are now before you.

One major element of the present book was added to Prof. Jeske's manuscript—a small daily excerpt from the Lutheran Confessions. Since the book's audience was envisioned as Lutheran pastors, and since I have often heard complaints that pastors do not have enough time for regular reading of the Confessions, this was deemed a worthy addition. The present editor is responsible for the selections made. These have often, but not always, been chosen to fit the theme of the passages. We thank Concordia Publishing House for allowing the use of citations from their modern-English "reader's version" of the confessions: *Concordia: The Lutheran Confessions—A Reader's Edition of the Book of Concord* by Paul Timothy McCain. The numbering given with the Confession passages is that found in the reader's edition, which is consistent with the Kolb-Wengert edition of *The Book of Concord* as well.

All quotations from the Old Testament are taken from *Biblia Hebraica Stuttgartensia*. New Testament quotations are taken from the standard text shared by the 4th edition of the UBS and the 27th edition of the Nestle-Aland Greek New Testament. The authors and editors thank Linguist's Software, Inc. for their help with font issues. The Hebrew and Greek fonts used are *New Jerusalem* and *Graeca II* respectively.

The person most responsible for the timely publication of this work is seminary student Jacob Behnken, my research assistant during the past year. Jacob did the entire input of Prof. Jeske's typescript into the various ancient fonts and helped with the selection of *The Book of Concord* passages. His attention to detail and patience with the font problems have been invaluable. A grant from Prof. Jeske's family and the ongoing financial support of the Fischer Family Foundation have funded Jacob's work on the project. Special thanks are due to Dr. Seth Erlandsson, and to Professors John Schmidt and Thomas Nass of Martin Luther College for their knowledgable assistance in proofreading the Hebrew and Greek. In addition, Prof. Nass made numerous helpful suggestions reflected in the volume. Curt Jahn of Northwestern Publishing House has also been instrumental at every stage—from the idea to its publication.

But above all, this is the fruit of Prof. Jeske's many years of biblical study and teaching. The publisher and editors pray that this volume might carry on his legacy of love for the Scriptures for many years.

Glen L. Thompson
Professor of History
Wisconsin Lutheran College

Notes to the User

The notes to the passages should present no problem to the average user. Although most abbreviations should be intuitively understood, a complete list is given below. Some of the daily readings provide only part of the verse, but it was felt that it was not necessary to note this. The indices of Bible and Confession passages will allow the reader to locate specific selections.

Normally the general meaning of a word is provided in the notes, but more specific meanings are given to assist in translating the passage at hand. This is especially true in the case of Hebrew verbs since the meaning often changes in their various formations.

For the Hebrew, the text has been simplified by the removal of most of the accent marks, but the *atnach* (֑), the accent that marks a verse's main division, and the *silluq* (ֽ), the accent that marks the verse's end, have been retained. Also, to encourage the oral reading of the Hebrew text, a carat (˂) has been inserted in Hebrew words where the accent is on the *penult* (the second-to-last syllable) instead of its usual place on the *ultima* (the last syllable). In a few cases we also note the alternative readings which lie behind the Greek translations of the Septuagint (LXX) or behind early translations into other languages (Versions). When the Hebrew text has a ketiv and qere, the ketiv with its appropriate vowel pointing is put first, followed by the qere in brackets. In the Greek passages, we have retained the words which the UBS editors have bracketed as possible readings. In the passages from the Lutheran Confessions, words in angle brackets are found in only the German or Latin texts, and bracketed words in italics are our additions, providing the context for our short excerpts.

Abbreviations

abs	*absolute*
acc	*accusative*
act	*active*
adj	*adjective*
adv	*adverb*
aor	*aorist*
coh	*cohortative*
coll	*collective*
conj	*conjunction*
cst	*construct*
dat	*dative*
dep	*deponent*
du	*dual*
f	*feminine*
gen	*genitive*
hiph	*hiphil*
hithp	*hithpael*
hoph	*hophal*
impf	*imperfect*
imv	*imperative*
ind	*indicative*
inf	*infinitive*
inf abs	*infinitive absolute*
inf cst	*infinitive construct*
interj	*interjection*
interrog	*interrogative*
juss	*jussive*
LXX	*Septuagint*
m	*masculine*
MT	*Masoretic Text*
mid	*middle*
n	*neuter*
neg	*negative*
niph	*niphal*
nom	*nominative*
pass	*passive*
pf	*perfect*
pi	*piel*
pl	*plural*
plpf	*pluperfect*
prep	*preposition*
pres	*present*
pron	*pronoun*
pu	*pual*
ptcp	*participle*
qal	*qal*
sf	*suffix*
sg	*singular*
v-c	*vav-consecutive*
voc	*vocative*

JANUARY 1

Deuteronomy 31:8

וַיהוָה הוּא הַהֹלֵךְ לְפָנֶיךָ הוּא יִהְיֶה עִמָּךְ לֹא יַרְפְּךָ
וְלֹא יַעַזְבֶךָּ לֹא תִירָא וְלֹא תֵחָת׃

לְפָנֵי (2 sg sf): before – רָפָה (hiph impf 3 sg + 2 sg sf): abandon – עָזַב (qal impf 3 sg + sf): forsake – יָרֵא (qal impf 2 sg): be afraid – חָתַת (qal impf 2 sg): be dismayed, discouraged

Matthew 28:20

διδάσκοντες αὐτοὺς τηρεῖν πάντα ὅσα ἐνετειλάμην ὑμῖν· καὶ ἰδοὺ ἐγὼ μεθ’ ὑμῶν εἰμι πάσας τὰς ἡμέρας ἕως τῆς συντελείας τοῦ αἰῶνος.

διδάσκω (pres ptcp pl): teach – τηρέω (pres inf): obey – ἐντέλλω (aor mid dep): command – συντελεία: end – αἰών (gen sg): age

Formula of Concord SD VIII 78

Christ has received this majesty, according to His humanity, at the right hand of God's majesty and power. So also, according to His received human nature and with the same, He can be, and also is, present where He wants to be. He is present especially in His Church and congregation on earth as Mediator, Head, King, and High Priest.

JANUARY 2

Joshua 1:5

לֹא־יִתְיַצֵּב אִישׁ לְפָנֶיךָ כֹּל יְמֵי חַיֶּיךָ כַּאֲשֶׁר הָיִיתִי
עִם־מֹשֶׁה אֶהְיֶה עִמָּךְ לֹא אַרְפְּךָ וְלֹא אֶעֶזְבֶךָּ׃

יָצַב (hithp impf 3 sg): stand up against – חַיִּים: life – רָפָה (hiph impf 1 sg + 2 sg sf): abandon – עָזַב (qal impf 1 sg + 2 sg sf): forsake

---

Matthew 6:30

εἰ δὲ τὸν χόρτον τοῦ ἀγροῦ σήμερον ὄντα καὶ αὔριον εἰς κλίβανον βαλλόμενον ὁ θεὸς οὕτως ἀμφιέννυσιν, οὐ πολλῷ μᾶλλον ὑμᾶς, ὀλιγόπιστοι;

> χόρτος (acc sg): grass – ἀγρός (gen sg): field – σήμερον (adv): today – αὔριον (adv): tomorrow – κλίβανος: oven – βάλλω (pres pass ptcp): thrown – ἀμφιέννυμι (pres ind): clothe – ὀλιγόπιστος (adj): of little faith

---

Large Catechism II 24

For here we see how the Father has given Himself to us, together with all creatures, and has most richly provided for us in this life. We see that He has overwhelmed us with unspeakable, eternal treasures by His Son and the Holy Spirit, as we shall hear.

January 3

Deuteronomy 7:9

וְיָדַעְתָּ כִּי־יְהוָה אֱלֹהֶיךָ הוּא הָאֱלֹהִים הָאֵל הַנֶּאֱמָן שֹׁמֵר הַבְּרִית וְהַחֶסֶד לְאֹהֲבָיו וּלְשֹׁמְרֵי מִצְוֹתוֹ [מִצְוֹתָיו] לְאֶלֶף דּוֹר׃

אָמַן (niph ptcp): faithful – שָׁמַר (qal ptcp): keep – בְּרִית: covenant – אָהֵב (qal ptcp + 3 sg sf): love – מִצְוָה (qere: pl + 3 sg sf): command – אֶלֶף: thousand – דּוֹר: generation

1 Corinthians 1:9

πιστὸς ὁ θεός, δι' οὗ ἐκλήθητε εἰς κοινωνίαν τοῦ υἱοῦ αὐτοῦ Ἰησοῦ Χριστοῦ τοῦ κυρίου ἡμῶν.

πιστός (adj): faithful – καλέω (aor pass 2 pl): called – κοινωνία (acc sg): fellowship

Smalcald Articles III XII 2

Thank God, ‹today› a seven-year-old child knows what the Church is, namely, the holy believers and lambs who hear the voice of their Shepherd [John 10:11-16].

JANUARY 4

Deuteronomy 7:6

כִּי עַם קָדוֹשׁ אַתָּה לַיהוָה אֱלֹהֶיךָ בְּךָ בָּחַר יְהוָה
אֱלֹהֶיךָ לִהְיוֹת לוֹ לְעַם סְגֻלָּה מִכֹּל הָעַמִּים אֲשֶׁר
עַל־פְּנֵי הָאֲדָמָה׃

קָדוֹשׁ: holy – בָּחַר (qal pf 3 sg) + בְּ: choose – סְגֻלָּה: valued property, treasured possession – אֲדָמָה: earth

---

1 Peter 2:9

ὑμεῖς δὲ γένος ἐκλεκτόν, βασίλειον ἱεράτευμα, ἔθνος ἅγιον, λαὸς εἰς περιποίησιν, ὅπως τὰς ἀρετὰς ἐξαγγείλητε τοῦ ἐκ σκότους ὑμᾶς καλέσαντος εἰς τὸ θαυμαστὸν αὐτοῦ φῶς·

γένος: people, nation – ἐκλεκτός: chosen – βασίλειος: royal – ἱεράτευμα: priesthood – ἔθνος: nation – ἅγιος: consecrated – λαός: people – περιποίησις: possession, property – ἀρετή: praise, moral excellence (his holiness, but above all his grace) – ἐξαγγέλλω (aor subj 2 pl): proclaim – σκότος: darkness – θαυμαστός: wonderful – φῶς: light

---

Power and Primacy 69

Finally, Peter's statement also confirms this, "You are . . . a royal priesthood" [1 Pet 2:9]. These words apply to the True Church, which certainly has the right to elect and ordain ministers, since it alone has the priesthood.

January 5

Psalm 119:105

נֵר־לְרַגְלִי דְבָרֶךָ וְאוֹר לִנְתִיבָתִי׃

נֵר: lamp – רֶגֶל (1 sg sf): foot – אוֹר: light – נְתִיבָה (1 sg sf): path

---

John 6:63

τὸ πνεῦμά ἐστιν τὸ ζῳοποιοῦν, ἡ σὰρξ οὐκ ὠφελεῖ οὐδέν· τὰ ῥήματα ἃ ἐγὼ λελάληκα ὑμῖν πνεῦμά ἐστιν καὶ ζωή ἐστιν.

πνεῦμα: Spirit – ζῳοποιέω (pres ptcp): make alive, give life – σάρξ: flesh – ὠφελέω (pres ind 3 sg): help, benefit – ῥῆμα (pl): word – λαλέω (pf act ind 1 sg): speak – ζωή: life

---

Formula of Concord Ep Summary 1

We believe, teach, and confess that the only rule and norm according to which all teachings, together with ‹all› teachers, should be evaluated and judged [2 Tim 3:15-17] are the prophetic and apostolic Scriptures of the Old and New Testament alone. For it is written in Ps 119:105, "Your word is a lamp to my feet and a light to my path."

JANUARY 6

Isaiah 60:3-4

3 וְהָלְכוּ גוֹיִם לְאוֹרֵךְ וּמְלָכִים לְנֹגַהּ זַרְחֵךְ׃
4 שְׂאִי־סָבִיב עֵינַיִךְ וּרְאִי כֻּלָּם נִקְבְּצוּ בָאוּ־לָךְ
בָּנַיִךְ מֵרָחוֹק יָבֹאוּ וּבְנֹתַיִךְ עַל־צַד תֵּאָמַנָה׃

גּוֹי (pl): nation – אוֹר (2 sg sf): light – מֶלֶךְ (pl): king – נֹגַהּ: brightness – זֶרַח (2 sg sf): dawn – עַיִן (pl + 2 sg sf): eye – קָבַץ (niph pf 3 pl): assemble – בֵּן (pl + 2 sg sf): son – רָחוֹק: afar – בַּת (pl + 2 sg sf): daughter – צַד: side – אָמַן (niph impf 3 pl): be carried

---

Matthew 2:10-11

10 ἰδόντες δὲ τὸν ἀστέρα ἐχάρησαν χαρὰν μεγάλην σφόδρα.
11 καὶ ἐλθόντες εἰς τὴν οἰκίαν εἶδον τὸ παιδίον μετὰ Μαρίας
τῆς μητρὸς αὐτοῦ, καὶ πεσόντες προσεκύνησαν αὐτῷ, καὶ
ἀνοίξαντες τοὺς θησαυροὺς αὐτῶν προσήνεγκαν αὐτῷ δῶρα,
χρυσὸν καὶ λίβανον καὶ σμύρναν.

ἰδόντες (aor act ptcp pl of ὁράω): see – ἀστήρ: star – χαίρω (aor 3 pl): rejoice – χαρά: joy – σφόδρα: greatly – ἐλθόντες (aor ptcp pl of ἔρχομαι): come – παιδίον: child – πίπτω (aor ptcp pl): fall – προσκυνέω (aor ind): worship – ἀνοίγω (aor ptcp): open – θησαυρός: treasure – προσφέρω (aor ind): bring out – λίβανος: frankincense – σμύρνα: myrrh

---

Augsburg Confession III 1

Our churches teach that the Word, that is, the Son of God [John 1:14], assumed the human nature in the womb of the Blessed Virgin Mary.

JANUARY 7

Isaiah 9:1

הָעָם הַהֹלְכִים בַּחֹשֶׁךְ רָאוּ אוֹר גָּדוֹל
יֹשְׁבֵי בְּאֶרֶץ צַלְמָוֶת אוֹר נָגַהּ עֲלֵיהֶם׃

הָלַךְ (qal ptcp pl): walk – חֹשֶׁךְ: darkness – אוֹר: light – גָּדוֹל: great – יָשַׁב (qal ptcp pl): dwell – צַלְמָוֶת: the shadow of death – נָגַהּ (qal pf 3 sg): shine

---

Matthew 4:13-16

13καὶ καταλιπὼν τὴν Ναζαρὰ ἐλθὼν κατῴκησεν εἰς
Καφαρναοὺμ τὴν παραθαλασσίαν ἐν ὁρίοις Ζαβουλὼν
καὶ Νεφθαλίμ· 14ἵνα πληρωθῇ τὸ ῥηθὲν διὰ Ἠσαΐου τοῦ
προφήτου λέγοντος· 15γῆ Ζαβουλὼν καὶ γῆ Νεφθαλίμ,
ὁδὸν θαλάσσης, πέραν τοῦ Ἰορδάνου, Γαλιλαία τῶν
ἐθνῶν, 16ὁ λαὸς ὁ καθήμενος ἐν σκότει φῶς εἶδεν μέγα,
καὶ τοῖς καθημένοις ἐν χώρᾳ καὶ σκιᾷ θανάτου φῶς
ἀνέτειλεν αὐτοῖς.

καταλείπω (aor ptcp): leave behind – ἐλθών (aor act ptcp of ἔρχομαι): go – κατοικέω (aor ind): live – παραθαλασσία: by the lake – ὅριον: region – πληρόω (aor pass subj): fulfill – ῥηθέν (aor pass ptcp of λέγω/εἶπον): spoken – πέραν (adv): on the other side – ἔθνη (gen): Gentiles – κάθημαι (pres ptcp): live – σκοτία: darkness – σκιά: shadow – ἀνατέλλω (aor ind 3 sg): to dawn

---

Formula of Concord Ep VIII 6

We believe, teach, and confess that the divine and human natures are not mingled into one substance, nor is one changed into the other.

January 8

Isaiah 60:1-2

1קוּמִי אוֹרִי כִּי בָא אוֹרֵךְ וּכְבוֹד יְהוָה עָלַיִךְ זָרָח׃
2כִּי־הִנֵּה הַחֹשֶׁךְ יְכַסֶּה־אֶרֶץ וַעֲרָפֶל לְאֻמִּים
וְעָלַיִךְ יִזְרַח יְהוָה וּכְבוֹדוֹ עָלַיִךְ יֵרָאֶה׃

קוּם (qal imv f): arise – אוֹר (qal imv f): shine – כָּבוֹד: glory – זָרַח (qal pf 3 sg/qal impf 3 sg): rise – עֲרָפֶל: thick darkness – לְאֹם: nation – רָאָה (niph impf 3 sg): be seen

---

Ephesians 5:8-10

8ἦτε γάρ ποτε σκότος, νῦν δὲ φῶς ἐν κυρίῳ· ὡς τέκνα φωτὸς
περιπατεῖτε 9 – ὁ γὰρ καρπὸς τοῦ φωτὸς ἐν πάσῃ
ἀγαθωσύνῃ καὶ δικαιοσύνῃ καὶ ἀληθεία – 10δοκιμάζοντες
τί ἐστιν εὐάρεστον τῷ κυρίῳ . . .

σκότος: darkness – φῶς: light – περιπατέω (pres imv 2 pl): live, conduct oneself – καρπός: fruit – ἀγαθωσύνη: goodness – δικαιοσύνη: uprightness – ἀλήθεια: truth – δοκιμάζω (pres act ptcp): try to learn – εὐάρεστος: pleasing

---

Formula of Concord Ep VIII 9

The two natures are united personally (i.e., in one person). Therefore, we believe, teach, and confess that this union is not the kind of joining together and connection that prevents either nature from having anything in common with the other personally (i.e., because of the personal union). It is not like when two boards are glued together, where neither gives anything to the other or takes anything from the other.

January 9

Isaiah 42:1

הֵן עַבְדִּי אֶתְמָךְ־בּוֹ בְּחִירִי רָצְתָה נַפְשִׁי
נָתַתִּי רוּחִי עָלָיו מִשְׁפָּט לַגּוֹיִם יוֹצִיא׃

עֶבֶד (1 sg sf): servant – תָּמַךְ (qal impf 1 sg): uphold – בָּחִיר (1 sg sf): chosen one – רָצָה (qal pf 3 sg f): delight – רוּחַ: Spirit – מִשְׁפָּט: God's judicial pronouncement – יָצָא (hiph impf 3 sg): bring

---

John 1:32-34

32Καὶ ἐμαρτύρησεν Ἰωάννης λέγων ὅτι τεθέαμαι τὸ πνεῦμα
καταβαῖνον ὡς περιστερὰν ἐξ οὐρανοῦ καὶ ἔμεινεν ἐπ'
αὐτόν. 33κἀγὼ οὐκ ᾔδειν αὐτόν, ἀλλ' ὁ πέμψας με βαπτίζειν
ἐν ὕδατι ἐκεῖνός μοι εἶπεν· ἐφ' ὃν ἂν ἴδῃς τὸ πνεῦμα
καταβαῖνον καὶ μένον ἐπ' αὐτόν, οὗτός ἐστιν ὁ βαπτίζων
ἐν πνεύματι ἁγίῳ. 34κἀγὼ ἑώρακα καὶ μεμαρτύρηκα ὅτι
οὗτός ἐστιν ὁ υἱὸς τοῦ θεοῦ.

μαρτυρέω: testify – θεάομαι (pf): see – καταβαίνω: descend – περιστερά: dove – μένω: remain – ᾔδειν (plpf of οἶδα with impf meaning): know – ἴδῃς (aor subj of ὁράω): see – ὁράω (pf ind): see

---

Formula of Concord Ep VIII 10

We believe, teach, and confess that God is man and man is God. This could not be true if the divine and human natures had (in deed and truth) absolutely no communion with each other.

Isaiah 61:1-2

1 רוּחַ אֲדֹנָי יְהוִה עָלָי יַעַן מָשַׁח יְהוָה אֹתִי
לְבַשֵּׂר עֲנָוִים שְׁלָחַנִי לַחֲבֹשׁ לְנִשְׁבְּרֵי־לֵב
לִקְרֹא לִשְׁבוּיִם דְּרוֹר וְלַאֲסוּרִים פְּקַח־קוֹחַ׃
2 לִקְרֹא שְׁנַת־רָצוֹן לַיהוָה

רוּחַ: Spirit – יַעַן: because – מָשַׁח (qal pf 3 sg): anoint – בָּשַׂר (pi inf cst): proclaim good news – עָנָו (pl): poor – חָבַשׁ (qal inf cst): bind up – שָׁבַר (niph ptcp cst pl): broken-hearted – קָרָא (qal inf cst): proclaim – שָׁבָה (qal pass ptcp pl): captives – דְּרוֹר: liberty – אָסַר (qal pass ptcp): prisoners – פְּקַח־קוֹחַ: opening, release – שָׁנָה (cst): year – רָצוֹן: favor

---

Luke 4:18,21

18 πνεῦμα κυρίου ἐπ᾽ ἐμὲ οὗ εἵνεκεν ἔχρισέν με
εὐαγγελίσασθαι πτωχοῖς, ἀπέσταλκέν με κηρύξαι
αἰχμαλώτοις ἄφεσιν καὶ τυφλοῖς ἀνάβλεψιν, ἀποστεῖλαι
τεθραυσμένους ἐν ἀφέσει . . . 21 ἤρξατο δὲ λέγειν πρὸς
αὐτοὺς ὅτι σήμερον πεπλήρωται ἡ γραφὴ αὕτη ἐν τοῖς
ὠσὶν ὑμῶν.

οὗ εἵνεκεν: because – χρίω: anoint – πτωχός: poor – ἀποστέλλω (pf): send – κηρύσσω (aor inf): preach – αἰχμάλωτος: captive – ἄφεσις: freedom – τυφλός: blind – ἀνάβλεψις: restoration of sight – ἀποστέλλω (aor act inf): send out – θραύω (pf pass ptcp): shatter – σήμερον: today – πληρόω: fulfill – οὖς: ear

---

Formula of Concord SD VIII 72

He has not received His gifts with limits as other saints. For on Christ the Lord, according to His received human nature, rests "the Spirit of wisdom and understanding . . . "

January 11

Isaiah 49:6

וַיֹּאמֶר נָקֵל מִהְיוֹתְךָ לִי עֶבֶד לְהָקִים אֶת־שִׁבְטֵי יַעֲקֹב
וּנְצִירֵי [וּנְצוּרֵי] יִשְׂרָאֵל לְהָשִׁיב וּנְתַתִּיךָ לְאוֹר גּוֹיִם
לִהְיוֹת יְשׁוּעָתִי עַד־קְצֵה הָאָרֶץ׃

קָלַל (niph pf 3 sg): be small – קוּם (hiph inf cst): raise up, restore – שֵׁבֶט (cst pl): tribe – נָצַר (qere: qal pass ptcp): the kept ones, the remnant – אוֹר: light – גּוֹיִם: Gentiles – יְשׁוּעָה (1 sg sf): salvation – קָצֶה (cst sg): end

---

Revelation 5:9

καὶ ᾄδουσιν ᾠδὴν καινὴν λέγοντες· ἄξιος εἶ λαβεῖν τὸ βιβλίον καὶ ἀνοῖξαι τὰς σφραγῖδας αὐτοῦ, ὅτι ἐσφάγης καὶ ἠγόρασας τῷ θεῷ ἐν τῷ αἵματί σου ἐκ πάσης φυλῆς καὶ γλώσσης καὶ λαοῦ καὶ ἔθνους . . .

ᾄδω (pres ind 3 pl): sing – ᾠδή: song – καινός: new – ἄξιος: worthy – λαμβάνω (aor inf): take – βιβλίον: scroll – ἀνοίγω (aor inf): open – σφραγίς (acc pl): seal – σφάζω (aor pass 2 sg): slay – ἀγοράζω (aor ind 2 sg): buy – φυλή: tribe – γλώσση: tongue – λαός: people – ἔθνος (gen sg): nation

---

Formula of Concord SD V 24

These two doctrines *[Law and Gospel]*, we believe and confess, should always be diligently taught in God's Church forever, even to the end of the world. They must be taught with the proper distinction of which we have heard: (a) through the preaching of the Law and its threats in the ministry of the New Testament the hearts of impenitent people may be terrified, and (b) they may be brought to a knowledge of their sins and to repentance.

January 12

1 Kings 17:22-24

22וַיִּשְׁמַע יְהוָה בְּקוֹל אֵלִיָּהוּ וַתָּשָׁב נֶפֶשׁ־הַיֶּלֶד עַל־
קִרְבּוֹ וַיֶּחִי׃ 23וַיִּקַּח אֵלִיָּהוּ אֶת־הַיֶּלֶד וַיֹּרִדֵהוּ מִן־
הָעֲלִיָּה הַבַּיְתָה וַיִּתְּנֵהוּ לְאִמּוֹ וַיֹּאמֶר אֵלִיָּהוּ רְאִי חַי
בְּנֵךְ׃ 24וַתֹּאמֶר הָאִשָּׁה אֶל־אֵלִיָּהוּ עַתָּה זֶה יָדַעְתִּי כִּי
אִישׁ אֱלֹהִים אָתָּה וּדְבַר־יְהוָה בְּפִיךָ אֱמֶת׃

שׁוּב (qal v-c impf 3 sg f): return – קֶרֶב: inward part = to him – חָיָה (qal v-c impf 3 sg): live – יָרַד (hiph v-c impf 3 sg): carry down – עֲלִיָּה: upper room – אֵם: mother – רָאָה (qal imv sg f): see – פֶּה (2 sg sf): mouth – אֱמֶת: truth

---

Luke 7:13-15

13καὶ ἰδὼν αὐτὴν ὁ κύριος ἐσπλαγχνίσθη ἐπ᾽ αὐτῇ καὶ εἶπεν
αὐτῇ· μὴ κλαῖε. 14καὶ προσελθὼν ἥψατο τῆς σοροῦ, οἱ δὲ
βαστάζοντες ἔστησαν, καὶ εἶπεν· νεανίσκε, σοὶ λέγω,
ἐγέρθητι. 15καὶ ἀνεκάθισεν ὁ νεκρὸς καὶ ἤρξατο λαλεῖν,
καὶ ἔδωκεν αὐτὸν τῇ μητρὶ αὐτοῦ.

ὁράω (aor ptcp): see – σπλαγχνίζομαι (aor pass 3 sg): feel sympathy – κλαίω (pres imv sg): weep – προσέρχομαι (aor act ptcp): come – ἅπτομαι (aor 3 sg): touch – σορός: coffin – βαστάζω (pres ptcp pl): carry – ἵστημι (aor 3 pl): stand – νεανίσκος: young man – ἐγείρω (aor pass imv): get up – ἀνακαθίζω (aor 3 sg): sit up – νεκρός: dead – ἄρχομαι (aor mid dep 3 sg): begin – λαλέω (pres inf): speak – δίδωμι (aor 3 sg): give – μητήρ: mother

---

Formula of Concord Ep VIII 15

We believe, teach, and confess that the Son of Man really is exalted . . . according to His human nature to the right hand of God's almighty majesty and power.

Psalm 8:4-6

4כִּי־אֶרְאֶה שָׁמֶיךָ מַעֲשֵׂי אֶצְבְּעֹתֶיךָ יָרֵחַ וְכוֹכָבִים אֲשֶׁר
כּוֹנָנְתָּה׃
5מָה־אֱנוֹשׁ כִּי־תִזְכְּרֶנּוּ וּבֶן־אָדָם כִּי תִפְקְדֶנּוּ׃
6וַתְּחַסְּרֵהוּ מְּעַט מֵאֱלֹהִים וְכָבוֹד וְהָדָר תְּעַטְּרֵהוּ׃

מַעֲשֶׂה (cst pl): work – אֶצְבַּע (pl + sf): finger – יָרֵחַ: moon – כּוֹכָב: star – כּוּן (polel pf 2 sg): set in place – אֱנוֹשׁ: man – פָּקַד (qal impf 2 sg + 3 sg sf): care for – חָסֵר (pi v-c impf 2 sg + 3 sg sf): cause to lack – מְעַט: a little – הָדָר: honor – עָטַר (pi impf 2 sg + 3 sg sf): crown

Hebrews 2:6-8

6διεμαρτύρατο δέ πού τις λέγων· τί ἐστιν ἄνθρωπος ὅτι μιμνῄσκῃ αὐτοῦ, ἢ υἱὸς ἀνθρώπου ὅτι ἐπισκέπτῃ αὐτόν;
7ἠλάττωσας αὐτὸν βραχύ τι παρ᾽ ἀγγέλους, δόξῃ καὶ τιμῇ ἐστεφάνωσας αὐτόν, 8πάντα ὑπέταξας ὑποκάτω τῶν ποδῶν αὐτοῦ. ἐν τῷ γὰρ ὑποτάξαι [αὐτῷ] τὰ πάντα οὐδὲν ἀφῆκεν αὐτῷ ἀνυπότακτον. Νῦν δὲ οὔπω ὁρῶμεν αὐτῷ τὰ πάντα ὑποτεταγμένα·

ἐπισκέπτομαι (pres ind 2 sg): be concerned about – ἐλαττόω (aor 2 sg): make lower – βραχύς: little – στεφανόω (aor 2 sg): crown – ὑποτάσσω (aor 2 sg/aor act inf): subordinate – ὑποκάτω: under – ἀφίημι (aor 3 sg): leave – ἀνυπότακτος: not made subject

Formula of Concord SD VIII 70

For although God is in the saints with all the fullness of His Godhead that He has everywhere with Himself, He does not dwell in them bodily. Nor is He personally united with them as in Christ.

Isaiah 65:1

נִדְרַשְׁתִּי לְלוֹא שָׁאָלוּ נִמְצֵאתִי לְלֹא בִקְשֻׁנִי
אָמַרְתִּי הִנֵּנִי הִנֵּנִי אֶל־גּוֹי לֹא־קֹרָא בִשְׁמִי׃

דָּרַשׁ (niph pf 1 sg): let oneself be consulted = I revealed myself – שָׁאַל (qal pf 3 pl): ask – מָצָא (niph pf 1 sg): be found – בָּקַשׁ (pi pf 3 pl + 1 sg sf): seek – קָרָא (pu pf 3 sg): be called; Versions read קֹרֵא (qal act ptcp): that did not call upon my name

---

Luke 10:21

ἐν αὐτῇ τῇ ὥρᾳ ἠγαλλιάσατο [ἐν] τῷ πνεύματι τῷ ἁγίῳ καὶ εἶπεν· ἐξομολογοῦμαί σοι, πάτερ, κύριε τοῦ οὐρανοῦ καὶ τῆς γῆς, ὅτι ἀπέκρυψας ταῦτα ἀπὸ σοφῶν καὶ συνετῶν καὶ ἀπεκάλυψας αὐτὰ νηπίοις· ναὶ ὁ πατήρ, ὅτι οὕτως εὐδοκία ἐγένετο ἔμπροσθέν σου.

ἀγαλλιάομαι (aor 3 sg): be overjoyed – ἐξομολογέομαι (pres 1 sg): praise – ἀποκρύπτω (aor 2 sg): hide – σοφός: wise – συνετός: intelligent – ἀποκαλύπτω (aor 2 sg): reveal – νήπιος: infant – εὐδοκία: good pleasure – ἔμπροσθεν: in the sight of

---

Large Catechism II 38-39

So that this treasure might not stay buried, but be received and enjoyed, God has caused the Word to go forth and be proclaimed. In the Word He has the Holy Spirit bring this treasure home and make it our own. Therefore, sanctifying is just bringing us to Christ so we receive this good, which we could not get ourselves [1 Pet 3:18].

January 15

Proverbs 2:6

כִּֽי־יְהוָה יִתֵּן חָכְמָה מִפִּיו דַּעַת וּתְבוּנָה׃

נָתַן (qal impf 3 sg): give – חָכְמָה: wisdom – פֶּה (3 sg sf): mouth – דַּעַת: knowledge – תְּבוּנָה: understanding

Colossians 2:2

ἵνα παρακληθῶσιν αἱ καρδίαι αὐτῶν συμβιβασθέντες ἐν ἀγάπῃ καὶ εἰς πᾶν πλοῦτος τῆς πληροφορίας τῆς συνέσεως, εἰς ἐπίγνωσιν τοῦ μυστηρίου τοῦ θεοῦ, Χριστοῦ.

παρακαλέω (aor pass subj 3 pl): encourage – συμβιβάζω (aor pass ptcp pl): unite – πλοῦτος: riches – πληροφορία: full assurance – σύνεσις: understanding – ἐπίγνωσις: knowledge – μυστήριον: mystery

Augsburg Confession I 1-3

Our churches teach with common consent that the decree of the Council of Nicaea about the unity of the divine essence and the three persons is true. It is to be believed without any doubt. God is one divine essence who is eternal, without a body, without parts, of infinite power, wisdom, and goodness. He is the maker and preserver of all things, visible and invisible [Neh 9:6]. Yet there are three persons, the Father, the Son, and the Holy Spirit [Matt 28:19]. These three persons are of the same essence and power.

Isaiah 35:4

אִמְרוּ לְנִמְהֲרֵי־לֵב חִזְקוּ אַל־תִּירָאוּ
הִנֵּה אֱלֹהֵיכֶם נָקָם יָבוֹא
גְּמוּל אֱלֹהִים הוּא יָבוֹא וְיֹשַׁעֲכֶם׃

אָמַר (qal imv pl): say – מָהַר (niph ptcp cst pl): be fearful – חָזַק (qal imv pl): be strong – יָרֵא (qal juss 2 pl): fear – נָקָם: vengeance – גְּמוּל: retribution – יָשַׁע (hiph impf 3 sg + 2 pl sf): save

---

Matthew 11:2-5

2 Ὁ δὲ Ἰωάννης ἀκούσας ἐν τῷ δεσμωτηρίῳ τὰ ἔργα τοῦ
Χριστοῦ πέμψας διὰ τῶν μαθητῶν αὐτοῦ 3 εἶπεν αὐτῷ· σὺ
εἶ ὁ ἐρχόμενος ἢ ἕτερον προσδοκῶμεν; 4 καὶ ἀποκριθεὶς ὁ
Ἰησοῦς εἶπεν αὐτοῖς· πορευθέντες ἀπαγγείλατε Ἰωάννῃ
ἃ ἀκούετε καὶ βλέπετε· 5 τυφλοὶ ἀναβλέπουσιν καὶ χωλοὶ
περιπατοῦσιν, λεπροὶ καθαρίζονται καὶ κωφοὶ ἀκούουσιν,
καὶ νεκροὶ ἐγείρονται καὶ πτωχοὶ εὐαγγελίζονται·

δεσμωτήριον: prison – ἐρχόμενος: the coming one – προσδοκάω (pres subj 1 pl): look for – πορεύομαι (aor ptcp pl): go – ἀπαγγέλλω (aor imv 2 pl): report – τυφλός: blind – ἀναβλέπω (pres ind 3 pl): gain sight – χωλός: lame – περιπατέω (pres ind 3 pl): walk – καθαρίζω (pres pass ind 3 pl): cleanse – κωφός: deaf – νεκρός: dead – ἐγείρω (pres pass ind 3 pl): raise – πτωχός: poor – εὐαγγελίζω (pres pass ind 3 pl): preach the good news

---

Large Catechism II 31

Let this, then, be the sum of this *[second]* article: the little word *Lord* means simply the same as *redeemer.* It means the One who has brought us from Satan to God, from death to life, from sin to righteousness, and who preserves us in the same.

January 17

Genesis 28:12-13

12וַיַּחֲלֹם וְהִנֵּה סֻלָּם מֻצָּב אַרְצָה וְרֹאשׁוֹ מַגִּיעַ הַשָּׁמָיְמָה
וְהִנֵּה מַלְאֲכֵי אֱלֹהִים עֹלִים וְיֹרְדִים בּוֹ׃ 13וְהִנֵּה יְהוָה
נִצָּב עָלָיו וַיֹּאמַר אֲנִי יְהוָה אֱלֹהֵי אַבְרָהָם אָבִיךָ וֵאלֹהֵי
יִצְחָק הָאָרֶץ אֲשֶׁר אַתָּה שֹׁכֵב עָלֶיהָ לְךָ אֶתְּנֶנָּה
וּלְזַרְעֶךָ׃

חָלַם (qal v-c impf 3 sg): dream – סֻלָּם: ladder, stairway – נָצַב (hoph ptcp): set up – רֹאשׁ: top – נָגַע (hiph ptcp): touch, reach – מַלְאָךְ (cst pl): angel – נָצַב (niph ptcp sg): stand – שָׁכַב (qal ptcp sg): lie

---

John 1:50-51

50ἀπεκρίθη Ἰησοῦς καὶ εἶπεν αὐτῷ· ὅτι εἶπόν σοι ὅτι εἶδόν σε ὑποκάτω τῆς συκῆς, πιστεύεις; μείζω τούτων ὄψῃ.
51καὶ λέγει αὐτῷ· ἀμὴν ἀμὴν λέγω ὑμῖν, ὄψεσθε τὸν οὐρανὸν ἀνεῳγότα καὶ τοὺς ἀγγέλους τοῦ θεοῦ ἀναβαίνοντας καὶ καταβαίνοντας ἐπὶ τὸν υἱὸν τοῦ ἀνθρώπου.

ὑποκάτω: under – συκή: fig tree – μείζω (acc pl n): greater – ὄψῃ (fut dep ind 2 sg of ὁράω): see – ἀνοίγω (pf ptcp): standing open

---

Formula of Concord Ep VIII 16

Christ always had this majesty according to the personal union. Yet He abstained from using it in the state of His humiliation, and because of this He truly increased in all wisdom and favor with God and men.

January 18

Psalm 34:8-9

8 חֹנֶה מַלְאַךְ־יְהוָה סָבִיב לִירֵאָיו וַיְחַלְּצֵם׃
9 טַעֲמוּ וּרְאוּ כִּי־טוֹב יְהוָה אַשְׁרֵי הַגֶּבֶר יֶחֱסֶה־בּוֹ׃

חָנָה (qal ptcp): encamp – מַלְאָךְ: angel – סָבִיב: around – יָרֵא (qal ptcp pl + 3 sg sf): fear – חָלַץ (pi v-c impf 3 sg + 3 pl sf): rescue – טָעַם (qal imv pl): taste – רָאָה (qal imv pl): see – אֶשֶׁר (cst pl): happiness, blessed is – גֶּבֶר: man – חָסָה (qal impf 3 sg): seek refuge

---

Acts 12:11

Καὶ ὁ Πέτρος ἐν ἑαυτῷ γενόμενος εἶπεν· νῦν οἶδα ἀληθῶς ὅτι ἐξαπέστειλεν [ὁ] κύριος τὸν ἄγγελον αὐτοῦ καὶ ἐξείλατό με ἐκ χειρὸς Ἡρῴδου καὶ πάσης τῆς προσδοκίας τοῦ λαοῦ τῶν Ἰουδαίων.

γίνομαι (aor ptcp) + ἐν ἑαυτῷ: came to himself – ἀληθῶς: truly – ἐξαποστέλλω (aor ind 3 sg): send out – ἐξαιρέω (aor mid 3 sg): rescue – χείρ: hand – προσδοκία: expectation – λαός: people

---

Large Catechism II 19

Now, all that we have, and whatever else is in heaven and upon the earth, is daily given, preserved, and kept for us by God. Therefore, it is clearly suggested and concluded that it is our duty to love, praise, and thank Him for these things without ceasing [1 Thess 5:17-18].

Psalm 91:10-11

10 לֹא־תְאֻנֶּה אֵלֶיךָ רָעָה וְנֶגַע לֹא־יִקְרַב בְּאָהֳלֶךָ׃
11 כִּי מַלְאָכָיו יְצַוֶּה־לָּךְ לִשְׁמָרְךָ בְּכָל־דְּרָכֶיךָ׃

אָנָה (pu impf 3 sg): be allowed to meet, befall – רָעָה: evil – נֶגַע: plague – קָרַב (qal impf 3 sg): come near – אֹהֶל (2 sg sf): tent – מַלְאָךְ (pl + 3 sg sf): angel – צָוָה (pi impf 3 sg): command – שָׁמַר (qal inf cst + 2 sg sf): guard – דֶּרֶךְ (pl + sf): way

---

Romans 8:28

Οἴδαμεν δὲ ὅτι τοῖς ἀγαπῶσιν τὸν θεὸν πάντα συνεργεῖ εἰς ἀγαθόν, τοῖς κατὰ πρόθεσιν κλητοῖς οὖσιν.

ἀγαπάω (pres act ptcp dat pl): love – συνεργέω (pres ind 3 sg): work together with – ἀγαθός: good – πρόθεσις: plan, purpose – κλητός: called – οὖσιν (ptcp of εἰμί): being

---

Large Catechism II 23

We ought, therefore, daily to recite this *[first]* article. We ought to impress it upon our mind and remember it by all that meets our eyes and by all good that falls to us. Wherever we escape from disaster or danger, we ought to remember that it is God who gives and does all these things. In these escapes we sense and see His fatherly heart and His surpassing love toward us [Ex 34:6]. In this way the heart would be warmed and kindled to be thankful, and to use all such good things to honor and praise God.

Isaiah 55:1-2

1 הֹוי כָּל־צָמֵא לְכוּ לַמַּיִם וַאֲשֶׁר אֵין־לֹו כָּסֶף לְכוּ
שִׁבְרוּ וֶאֱכֹלוּ וּלְכוּ שִׁבְרוּ בְּלֹוא־כֶסֶף וּבְלֹוא מְחִיר יַיִן
וְחָלָב׃ 2 לָמָּה תִשְׁקְלוּ־כֶסֶף בְּלֹוא־לֶחֶם וִיגִיעֲכֶם בְּלֹוא
לְשָׂבְעָה שִׁמְעוּ שָׁמֹועַ אֵלַי וְאִכְלוּ־טֹוב וְתִתְעַנַּג בַּדֶּשֶׁן
נַפְשְׁכֶם׃

הֹוי (interj): ah! – צָמֵא: thirsty – כֶּסֶף: silver – שָׁבַר (qal imv pl): buy grain – בְּלֹוא: without – מְחִיר: price – חָלָב: milk – יְגִיעַ (2 pl sf): labor – שָׂבְעָה: satiety + בְּלֹוא לְ: what does not satisfy – שָׁמַע (qal imv pl/inf abs): listen, listen! – אָכַל (qal imv pl): eat – עָנַג (hithp impf 3 sg f): delight – דֶּשֶׁן: richest of foods

---

John 4:13-14

13πᾶς ὁ πίνων ἐκ τοῦ ὕδατος τούτου διψήσει πάλιν· 14ὃς δ' ἂν πίῃ ἐκ τοῦ ὕδατος οὗ ἐγὼ δώσω αὐτῷ, οὐ μὴ διψήσει εἰς τὸν αἰῶνα, ἀλλὰ τὸ ὕδωρ ὃ δώσω αὐτῷ γενήσεται ἐν αὐτῷ πηγὴ ὕδατος ἁλλομένου εἰς ζωὴν αἰώνιον.

πίνω (pres ptcp sg/aor subj 3 sg): drink – διψάω (fut 3 sg): thirst – πάλιν: again – δίδωμι (fut 1 sg): give – πηγή: spring – ἅλλομαι (pres ptcp): spring up

---

Apology VII-VIII (IV) 15

But the Gospel brings not merely the shadow of eternal things, but the eternal things themselves: the Holy Spirit and righteousness. By the Gospel we are righteous before God.

Psalm 45:8

אָהַבְתָּ צֶּדֶק וַתִּשְׂנָא רֶשַׁע
עַל־כֵּן מְשָׁחֲךָ אֱלֹהִים אֱלֹהֶיךָ שֶׁמֶן שָׂשׂוֹן מֵחֲבֵרֶיךָ׃

אָהֵב (qal pf 2 sg): love – צֶדֶק: righteousness – שָׂנֵא (qal v-c impf 2 sg): hate – רֶשַׁע: wickedness – מָשַׁח (qal pf 3 sg + 2 sg sf): anoint – שֶׁמֶן: oil – שָׂשׂוֹן: gladness – חָבֵר (pl + 2 sg sf): companion

Acts 10:38

Ἰησοῦν τὸν ἀπὸ Ναζαρέθ, ὡς ἔχρισεν αὐτὸν ὁ θεὸς πνεύματι ἁγίῳ καὶ δυνάμει, ὃς διῆλθεν εὐεργετῶν καὶ ἰώμενος πάντας τοὺς καταδυναστευομένους ὑπὸ τοῦ διαβόλου, ὅτι ὁ θεὸς ἦν μετ' αὐτοῦ.

ὡς: how – χρίω (aor ind 3 sg): anoint – διέρχομαι (aor ind 3 sg): go about – εὐεργετέω (pres ptcp sg): do good – ἰάομαι (pres ptcp): heal – καταδυναστεύω (pres pass ptcp): oppress, dominate – διάβολος: devil

Large Catechism I 189

Second, a person who does evil to his neighbor is not the only one guilty under this *[fifth]* commandment. It also applies to anyone who can do his neighbor good, prevent or resist evil, defend, and save his neighbor so that no bodily harm or hurt happen to him—yet does not do this [Jas 2:15-16].

January 22

Proverbs 23:26

תְּנָה־בְנִי לִבְּךָ לִי וְעֵינֶיךָ דְּרָכַי תִּרְצֶנָה [תִּצֹּרְנָה]׃

נָתַן (qal imv sg): give – לֵב (2 sg sf): heart – עַיִן (pl + 2 sg sf): eye – דֶּרֶךְ (pl + 1 sg sf): way – תִּרְצֶנָה (ketiv: qal impf 3 pl of רָצָה): be pleased with – תִּצֹּרְנָה (qere: qal impf 3 pl of נָצַר): guard, keep to my ways

---

1 John 5:3

αὕτη γάρ ἐστιν ἡ ἀγάπη τοῦ θεοῦ, ἵνα τὰς ἐντολὰς αὐτοῦ τηρῶμεν, καὶ αἱ ἐντολαὶ αὐτοῦ βαρεῖαι οὐκ εἰσίν.

αὕτη: this – ἐντολή (acc pl): command – τηρέω (pres subj 1 pl): obey – βαρύς (adj pl f): hard, heavy, burdensome

---

Large Catechism I 311

Now we have the Ten Commandments, a summary of divine teaching about what we are to do in order that our whole life may be pleasing to God. Everything that is to be a good work must arise and flow from and in this true fountain and channel. So apart from the Ten Commandments no work or thing can be good or pleasing to God, no matter how great or precious it is in the world's eyes.

January 23

Psalm 40:13-14

13 כִּי אָפְפוּ־עָלַי רָעוֹת עַד־אֵין מִסְפָּר
הִשִּׂיגוּנִי עֲוֺנֹתַי וְלֹא־יָכֹלְתִּי לִרְאוֹת
עָצְמוּ מִשַּׂעֲרוֹת רֹאשִׁי וְלִבִּי עֲזָבָנִי׃
14 רְצֵה יְהוָה לְהַצִּילֵנִי יְהוָה לְעֶזְרָתִי חוּשָׁה׃

אָפַף (qal pf 3 pl): surround – רָעָה (pl): trouble – אַיִן (cst): nonexistence, without – מִסְפָּר: number – נָשַׂג (hiph pf 3 pl + 1 sg sf): overtake – עָוֺן (pl + 1 sg sf): sin (as guilt) – יָכֹל (qal pf 1 sg): be able – רָאָה (qal inf cst): see – עָצַם (qal pf 3 pl): be numerous – שַׂעֲרָה (pl): hair – עָזַב (qal pf 3 sg + 1 sg sf): forsake, fail – רָצָה (qal imv sg): be pleased – נָצַל (hiph inf cst): deliver, save – עֶזְרָה (1 sg sf): help – חוּשׁ (qal imv sg): come quickly

Matthew 9:2

καὶ ἰδοὺ προσέφερον αὐτῷ παραλυτικὸν ἐπὶ κλίνης βεβλημένον. καὶ ἰδὼν ὁ Ἰησοῦς τὴν πίστιν αὐτῶν εἶπεν τῷ παραλυτικῷ· θάρσει, τέκνον, ἀφίενταί σου αἱ ἁμαρτίαι.

προσφέρω (impf 3 pl): bring to – κλίνη: mat – βάλλω (pf pass ptcp): placed – ὁράω (aor act ptcp): see – θαρσέω (pres imv 2 sg): have courage – ἀφίημι (pres 3 pl): be forgiven – ἁμαρτία (pl): sin

Apology IV (II) 5

All Scripture ought to be distributed into these two principal topics: the Law and the promises. For in some places Scripture presents the Law, and in others the promises about Christ.

January 24

Leviticus 20:26

וִהְיִ֤יתֶם לִי֙ קְדֹשִׁ֔ים כִּ֥י קָד֖וֹשׁ אֲנִ֣י יְהוָ֑ה וָאַבְדִּ֥ל אֶתְכֶ֛ם
מִן־הָֽעַמִּ֖ים לִהְי֥וֹת לִֽי׃

הָיָה (qal v-c pf 2 pl/qal inf cst): be – קָדוֹשׁ: holy – בָּדַל (hiph v-c impf 1 sg): set apart – עַם (pl): people, nation

---

Titus 2:14

ὃς ἔδωκεν ἑαυτὸν ὑπὲρ ἡμῶν, ἵνα λυτρώσηται ἡμᾶς ἀπὸ πάσης ἀνομίας καὶ καθαρίσῃ ἑαυτῷ λαὸν περιούσιον, ζηλωτὴν καλῶν ἔργων.

δίδωμι (aor ind 3 sg): give – λυτρόω (aor mid subj 3 sg): redeem – ἀνομία: wickedness – καθαρίζω (aor subj 3 sg): purify – λαός: people – περιούσιος: chosen, special – ζηλωτής: person who is zealous – ἔργον: work

---

Apology IV (II) 80

For Christ has been set forth as an Atoning Sacrifice, so that for His sake, the Father may be reconciled to us. But Christ is not received as a Mediator except by faith.

January 25

Genesis 41:51-52

51וַיִּקְרָא יוֹסֵף אֶת־שֵׁם הַבְּכוֹר מְנַשֶּׁה כִּי־נַשַּׁנִי
אֱלֹהִים אֶת־כָּל־עֲמָלִי וְאֵת כָּל־בֵּית אָבִי׃ 52וְאֵת
שֵׁם הַשֵּׁנִי קָרָא אֶפְרָיִם כִּי־הִפְרַנִי אֱלֹהִים בְּאֶרֶץ עָנְיִי׃

קָרָא (qal v-c impf 3 sg): call – שֵׁם: name – בְּכוֹר: firstborn – נָשָׁה (pi pf 3 sg + 1 sg sf): make forget – עָמָל (1 sg sf): trouble – בַּיִת (cst sg): house – שֵׁנִי: second – פָּרָה (hiph pf 3 sg + 1 sg sf): make fruitful – עֳנִי (1 sg sf): suffering, misery

---

1 Peter 1:6-7

6ἐν ᾧ ἀγαλλιᾶσθε, ὀλίγον ἄρτι εἰ δέον [ἐστὶν] λυπηθέντες
ἐν ποικίλοις πειρασμοῖς, 7ἵνα τὸ δοκίμιον ὑμῶν τῆς
πίστεως πολυτιμότερον χρυσίου τοῦ ἀπολλυμένου διὰ
πυρὸς δὲ δοκιμαζομένου, εὑρεθῇ εἰς ἔπαινον καὶ δόξαν
καὶ τιμὴν ἐν ἀποκαλύψει Ἰησοῦ Χριστοῦ·

ἀγαλλιάομαι (pres mid 2 pl): be overjoyed – ὀλίγον: for a little while – εἰ δέον: if it must be – λυπέω (aor pass ptcp): become sad – ποικίλος: of various kinds – πειρασμός: trial – δοκίμιον: testing – πολυτιμότερος: of greater worth – χρυσίον: gold – ἀπόλλυμι (pres mid ptcp): pass away – πῦρ: fire – δοκιμάζω (pres pass ptcp): refine – εὑρίσκω (aor pass subj 3 sg): find – ἔπαινος: praise – δόξα: glory – τιμή: honor – ἀποκάλυψις: revelation

---

Apology IV (II) 85

Therefore, let not good minds allow themselves to be forced from the conviction that we receive forgiveness of sins for Christ's sake, through faith alone. In this they have sure and firm consolation against the terrors of sin, against eternal death, and against all the gates of hell.

JANUARY 26

Psalm 32:1-2

[1]אַשְׁרֵי נְשׂוּי־פֶּשַׁע כְּסוּי חֲטָאָה׃
[2]אַשְׁרֵי אָדָם לֹא יַחְשֹׁב יְהוָה לוֹ עָוֹן וְאֵין בְּרוּחוֹ רְמִיָּה׃

אֶשֶׁר (cst pl): blessedness – נָשָׂא (qal pass ptcp cst): forgive – פֶּשַׁע: sin (as rebellion) – כָּסָה (qal pass ptcp cst): cover – חֲטָאָה: sin (as missing the mark) – חָשַׁב (qal impf 3 sg): count against, reckon to – רוּחַ (3 sg sf): spirit – רְמִיָּה: deceit

---

1 John 2:1-2

[1]Τεκνία μου, ταῦτα γράφω ὑμῖν ἵνα μὴ ἁμάρτητε. καὶ ἐάν
τις ἁμάρτῃ, παράκλητον ἔχομεν πρὸς τὸν πατέρα Ἰησοῦν
Χριστὸν δίκαιον· [2]καὶ αὐτὸς ἱλασμός ἐστιν περὶ τῶν
ἁμαρτιῶν ἡμῶν, οὐ περὶ τῶν ἡμετέρων δὲ μόνον ἀλλὰ καὶ
περὶ ὅλου τοῦ κόσμου.

τέκνιον: child – ἁμαρτάνω (aor subj 2 pl/3 sg): sin – παράκλητος: intercessor, one who appears in another's behalf – δίκαιος: righteous – ἱλασμός: atoning sacrifice – ἁμαρτία: sin – ἡμέτερος: our – ὅλος: whole – κόσμος: world

---

Apology IV (II) 76-77

To receive the forgiveness of sins is to be justified, according to Ps 32:1, "Blessed is the one whose transgression is forgiven." By faith alone in Christ—not through love, not because of love or works.

January 27

Psalm 19:13

שְׁגִיאוֹת מִי־יָבִין מִנִּסְתָּרוֹת נַקֵּנִי׃

שְׁגִיאָה (pl): error – בִּין (qal impf 3 sg): understand – סָתַר (niph ptcp f): hidden – נָקָה (pi imv sg + 1 sg sf): forgive

---

Romans 7:18-20

18Οἶδα γὰρ ὅτι οὐκ οἰκεῖ ἐν ἐμοί, τοῦτ᾽ ἔστιν ἐν τῇ
σαρκί μου, ἀγαθόν· τὸ γὰρ θέλειν παράκειταί μοι, τὸ δὲ
κατεργάζεσθαι τὸ καλὸν οὔ· 19οὐ γὰρ ὃ θέλω ποιῶ ἀγαθόν,
ἀλλὰ ὃ οὐ θέλω κακὸν τοῦτο πράσσω. 20εἰ δὲ ὃ οὐ θέλω [ἐγὼ]
τοῦτο ποιῶ, οὐκέτι ἐγὼ κατεργάζομαι αὐτὸ ἀλλὰ ἡ οἰκοῦσα
ἐν ἐμοὶ ἁμαρτία.

οἰκέω (pres ind 3 sg): dwell – σάρξ: sinful nature – ἀγαθός: good – θέλω (pres inf): will – παράκειμαι: be at hand – κατεργάζομαι (pres inf): carry it out – καλόν: what is good – ποιέω (pres ind 1 sg): do – πράσσω: do – ἁμαρτία: sin

---

Augsburg Confession XI 1-2

Our churches teach that private Absolution should be retained in the churches, although listing all sins is not necessary for Confession. For, according to the Psalm, it is impossible. "Who can discern his errors?" (Ps 19:12).

JANUARY 28

Isaiah 44:6

כֹּה־אָמַר יְהוָה מֶלֶךְ־יִשְׂרָאֵל וְגֹאֲלוֹ יְהוָה צְבָאוֹת
אֲנִי רִאשׁוֹן וַאֲנִי אַחֲרוֹן וּמִבַּלְעָדַי אֵין אֱלֹהִים׃

גֹּאֵל (qal act ptcp + 3 sg sf): kinsman-redeemer – צָבָא (pl): army, host – רִאשׁוֹן: first – אַחֲרוֹן: last – מִבַּלְעֲדֵי: apart from me – אַיִן (cst sg): is not

Hebrews 4:16

προσερχώμεθα οὖν μετὰ παρρησίας τῷ θρόνῳ τῆς χάριτος, ἵνα λάβωμεν ἔλεος καὶ χάριν εὕρωμεν εἰς εὔκαιρον βοήθειαν.

προσέρχομαι (pres subj 1 pl): approach – παρρησία: boldness, confidence – χάρις: grace – λαμβάνω (aor subj 1 pl): receive – ἔλεος: mercy – εὑρίσκω (aor subj 1 pl): find – εὔκαιρος: well-timed, suitable – βοήθεια: help

Apology V (III) 42

Christ remains Mediator, and we should always be confident that for His sake we have a reconciled God, even though we are unworthy. Paul clearly teaches this when he says, "I am not aware of anything against myself, but I am not thereby acquitted" (1 Cor 4:4).

January 29

Psalm 28:9

הוֹשִׁיעָה אֶת־עַמֶּךָ וּבָרֵךְ אֶת־נַחֲלָתֶךָ
וּרְעֵם וְנַשְּׂאֵם עַד־הָעוֹלָם׃

יָשַׁע (hiph imv sg): save – עַם (2 sg sf): people – בָּרַךְ (pi imv sg): bless – נַחֲלָה (2 sg sf): inheritance – רָעָה (qal imv sg + 3 pl sf): be a shepherd – נָשָׂא (pi imv sg + 3 pl sf): carry – עוֹלָם: eternity + עַד: forever

---

Galatians 4:7

ὥστε οὐκέτι εἶ δοῦλος ἀλλὰ υἱός· εἰ δὲ υἱός, καὶ κληρονόμος διὰ θεοῦ.

> οὐκέτι: no longer – εἰμί (pres ind 2 sg): be – δοῦλος: slave – υἱός: son – κληρονόμος: heir

---

Apology V (III) 61

From this it is clear that we are justified before God through faith alone. Through faith alone we receive forgiveness of sins and reconciliation, because reconciliation or justification is a matter promised for Christ's sake, not for the Law's sake. Therefore, it is received through faith alone, although, when the Holy Spirit is given, the fulfilling of the Law follows.

January 30

Psalm 13:2,5-6

2 עַד־אָנָה יְהוָה תִּשְׁכָּחֵנִי נֶצַח עַד־אָנָה תַּסְתִּיר
אֶת־פָּנֶיךָ מִמֶּנִּי׃
5 פֶּן־יֹאמַר אֹיְבִי יְכָלְתִּיו צָרַי יָגִילוּ כִּי אֶמּוֹט׃
6 וַאֲנִי בְּחַסְדְּךָ בָטַחְתִּי יָגֵל לִבִּי בִּישׁוּעָתֶךָ
אָשִׁירָה לַיהוָה כִּי גָמַל עָלָי׃

עַד־אָנָה: how long? – שָׁכַח (qal impf 2 sg + 1 sg sf): forget – נֵצַח: perpetuity, forever – סָתַר (hiph impf 2 sg): hide – פֶּן: lest – אוֹיֵב (1 sg sf): enemy – יָכֹל (qal pf 1 sg + 3 sg sf): overcome – צַר (pl + 1 sg sf): foe – גִּיל (qal impf 3 pl): rejoice – מוֹט (niph impf 1 sg): be shaken, fall – בָּטַח (qal pf 1 sg): trust – שִׁיר (qal coh 1 sg): sing – גָּמַל (qal pf 3 sg): deal bountifully with

---

2 Corinthians 5:4-5

4 καὶ γὰρ οἱ ὄντες ἐν τῷ σκήνει στενάζομεν βαρούμενοι, ἐφ'
ᾧ οὐ θέλομεν ἐκδύσασθαι ἀλλ' ἐπενδύσασθαι, ἵνα καταποθῇ
τὸ θνητὸν ὑπὸ τῆς ζωῆς. 5 ὁ δὲ κατεργασάμενος ἡμᾶς εἰς
αὐτὸ τοῦτο θεός, ὁ δοὺς ἡμῖν τὸν ἀρραβῶνα τοῦ πνεύματος.

σκῆνος: tent (of one's body) – στενάζω (pres ind 1 pl): groan – βαρέω (pres pass ptcp): burdened – ἐφ' ᾧ: because – ἐκδύω (aor mid inf): be unclothed – ἐπενδύομαι (aor mid inf): put on in addition – καταπίνω (aor pass subj): swallow up – κατεργάζομαι (aor ptcp): fashion – δίδωμι (aor act ptcp): give – ἀρραβών: deposit

---

Apology V (III) 44

We never satisfy the Law! So we must always run back to the promise. Our infirmity must be recognized in this matter. We must regard it as certain that we are counted righteous for the sake of Christ, "who . . . is interceding for us" (Rom 8:34).

Genesis 32:27

וַיֹּאמֶר שַׁלְּחֵנִי כִּי עָלָה הַשָּׁחַר וַיֹּאמֶר לֹא אֲשַׁלֵּחֲךָ כִּי אִם־בֵּרַכְתָּנִי׃

שָׁלַח (pi imv sg + 1 sg sf): let go – עָלָה (qal pf 3 sg): rise – שַׁחַר: dawn – שָׁלַח (pi impf 1 sg + 2 sg sf): let go – כִּי אִם: unless – בָּרַךְ (pi pf 2 sg + 1 sg sf): bless

---

James 1:6-7

6αἰτείτω δὲ ἐν πίστει μηδὲν διακρινόμενος· ὁ γὰρ
διακρινόμενος ἔοικεν κλύδωνι θαλάσσης ἀνεμιζομένῳ
καὶ ῥιπιζομένῳ. 7μὴ γὰρ οἰέσθω ὁ ἄνθρωπος ἐκεῖνος ὅτι
λήμψεταί τι παρὰ τοῦ κυρίου . . .

αἰτέω (pres imv 3 sg): ask – διακρίνομαι (pres ptcp): doubt, waver – ἔοικα (pf 3 sg with pres meaning): resemble, be like – κλύδων: rough water, waves – ἀνεμίζω (pres pass ptcp): be moved by the wind – ῥιπίζω (pres pass ptcp): blown here and there – οἴομαι (pres mid imv 3 sg): think, suppose – λαμβάνω (fut ind): receive

---

Apology IV (II) 55-56

Therefore, whenever mercy is mentioned, we must keep in mind that faith, which receives the promise of mercy, is required there. Again, whenever we speak about faith, we want an object of faith to be understood, namely, the promised mercy. For faith justifies and saves, not because it is a worthy work in itself, but only because it receives the promised mercy.

Psalm 84:2-3

2 מַה־יְּדִידוֹת מִשְׁכְּנוֹתֶיךָ יְהוָה צְבָאוֹת׃
3 נִכְסְפָה וְגַם־כָּלְתָה נַפְשִׁי לְחַצְרוֹת יְהוָה
לִבִּי וּבְשָׂרִי יְרַנְּנוּ אֶל אֵל־חָי׃

יָדִיד: lovely – מִשְׁכָּן (pl + 2 sg sf) dwelling place – צָבָא (pl): army, host – כָּסַף (niph pf 3 sg f): long for – כָּלָה (qal pf 3 sg f): waste away – חָצֵר (pl): court – רָנַן (pi impf 3 pl): cry out – אֵל: God – חַי: living

---

Luke 2:49

καὶ εἶπεν πρὸς αὐτούς· τί ὅτι ἐζητεῖτέ με; οὐκ ᾔδειτε ὅτι ἐν τοῖς τοῦ πατρός μου δεῖ εἶναί με;

τί ὅτι: why? – ζητέω (impf 2 pl): look for – οἶδα (plpf 2 pl with impf meaning): know – δεῖ: it is necessary

---

Large Catechism II 51

But this is the meaning and substance of this addition *["the communion of saints"]:* I believe that there is upon earth a little holy group and congregation of pure saints, under one head, even Christ [Eph 1:22].

FEBRUARY 2

Psalm 103:10-13

10 לֹא כַחֲטָאֵינוּ עָשָׂה לָנוּ וְלֹא כַעֲוֺנֹתֵינוּ גָּמַל עָלֵינוּ׃
11 כִּי כִגְבֹהַּ שָׁמַיִם עַל־הָאָרֶץ גָּבַר חַסְדּוֹ עַל־יְרֵאָיו׃
12 כִּרְחֹק מִזְרָח מִמַּעֲרָב הִרְחִיק מִמֶּנּוּ אֶת־פְּשָׁעֵינוּ׃
13 כְּרַחֵם אָב עַל־בָּנִים רִחַם יְהוָה עַל־יְרֵאָיו׃

גָּמַל (qal pf 3 sg): repay – גָּבַהּ (qal inf cst): be high – גָּבַר (qal pf 3 sg): be strong – חֶסֶד: faithful love – יָרֵא (qal ptcp pl + sf): fear – רָחַק (qal inf cst): be distant – מִזְרָח: east – מַעֲרָב: west – רָחַק (hiph pf 3 sg): remove – פֶּשַׁע (pl + 1 pl sf): sin (as rebellion) – רָחַם (pi inf cst/pi pf 3 sg): have compassion on

---

Luke 15:20

καὶ ἀναστὰς ἦλθεν πρὸς τὸν πατέρα ἑαυτοῦ. Ἔτι δὲ αὐτοῦ μακρὰν ἀπέχοντος εἶδεν αὐτὸν ὁ πατὴρ αὐτοῦ καὶ ἐσπλαγχνίσθη καὶ δραμὼν ἐπέπεσεν ἐπὶ τὸν τράχηλον αὐτοῦ καὶ κατεφίλησεν αὐτόν.

ἀνίστημι (aor ptcp): get up – μακράν: far – ἀπέχω (pres ptcp): be far away – σπλαγχνίζομαι (aor pass dep 3 sg): feel sympathy – δραμών (aor ptcp of τρέχω): run – ἐπιπίπτω (aor ind 3 sg): throw oneself on – τράχηλος: neck – καταφιλέω (aor ind 3 sg): kiss

---

Formula of Concord Ep III 4

We believe, teach, and confess that our righteousness before God is this: God forgives our sins out of pure grace, without any work, merit, or worthiness of ours preceding, present, or following.

FEBRUARY 3

Exodus 3:7

וַיֹּ֣אמֶר יְהוָ֔ה רָאֹ֥ה רָאִ֛יתִי אֶת־עֳנִ֥י עַמִּ֖י אֲשֶׁ֣ר בְּמִצְרָ֑יִם
וְאֶת־צַעֲקָתָ֤ם שָׁמַ֙עְתִּי֙ מִפְּנֵ֣י נֹֽגְשָׂ֔יו כִּ֥י יָדַ֖עְתִּי
אֶת־מַכְאֹבָֽיו׃

עֳנִי: affliction – עַם: people – צְעָקָה (3 pl sf): outcry – מִפְּנֵי: because of – נָגַשׂ (qal ptcp pl + 3 sg sf): taskmaster – יָדַע (qal pf 1 sg): know, be concerned about – מַכְאוֹב (pl + 3 sg sf): suffering

---

John 11:33-35

33 Ἰησοῦς οὖν ὡς εἶδεν αὐτὴν κλαίουσαν καὶ τοὺς
συνελθόντας αὐτῇ Ἰουδαίους κλαίοντας, ἐνεβριμήσατο
τῷ πνεύματι καὶ ἐτάραξεν ἑαυτὸν 34 καὶ εἶπεν· ποῦ
τεθείκατε αὐτόν; λέγουσιν αὐτῷ· κύριε, ἔρχου καὶ ἴδε.
35 ἐδάκρυσεν ὁ Ἰησοῦς.

κλαίω (pres act ptcp f): weep – συνέρχομαι (aor ptcp): come with – ἐμβριμάομαι (aor 3 sg): be deeply moved – ταράσσω (aor 3 sg): shake + ἑαυτόν: shake oneself, be troubled – τίθημι (pf 2 pl): place – ἔρχομαι (pres imv 2 sg): come – ὁράω (aor imv 2 sg): see – δακρύω (aor 3 sg): weep

---

Small Catechism Address of the Lord's Prayer

Our Father who art in heaven.

What does this mean?

Answer: By these words God would tenderly encourage us to believe that He is our true Father and that we are His true children, so that we may ask Him confidently with all assurance, as dear children ask their dear father.

FEBRUARY 4

Psalm 90:1-3

1אֲדֹנָי מָעוֹן אַתָּה הָיִיתָ לָּנוּ בְּדֹר וָדֹר׃
2בְּטֶרֶם הָרִים יֻלָּדוּ וַתְּחוֹלֵל אֶרֶץ וְתֵבֵל וּמֵעוֹלָם
עַד־עוֹלָם אַתָּה אֵל׃
3תָּשֵׁב אֱנוֹשׁ עַד־דַּכָּא וַתֹּאמֶר שׁוּבוּ בְנֵי־אָדָם׃

מָעוֹן: dwelling place – דֹּר: generation – בְּטֶרֶם: before – הַר: mountain – יָלַד (pu pf 3 pl): be born – חוּל (polel v-c impf 2 sg): bear – תֵּבֵל: world – עוֹלָם: eternity – שׁוּב (hiph impf 2 sg): turn back – אֱנוֹשׁ: man – דַּכָּא: dust

Revelation 14:13

Καὶ ἤκουσα φωνῆς ἐκ τοῦ οὐρανοῦ λεγούσης· γράψον· μακάριοι οἱ νεκροὶ οἱ ἐν κυρίῳ ἀποθνῄσκοντες ἀπ' ἄρτι. ναί, λέγει τὸ πνεῦμα, ἵνα ἀναπαήσονται ἐκ τῶν κόπων αὐτῶν, τὰ γὰρ ἔργα αὐτῶν ἀκολουθεῖ μετ' αὐτῶν.

ἀκούω (aor 1 sg): hear – φωνή: voice – γράφω (aor imv 2 sg): write – μακάριος: blessed – νεκρός: dead – ἀποθνῄσκω (pres ptcp): die – ἀπ' ἄρτι: from now – ναί: yes – ἀναπαύω (fut pass dep): rest – κόπος: labor – ἀκολουθέω (pres ind 3 sg): follow

Augsburg Confession XVII 1

Our churches teach that at the end of the world Christ will appear for judgment and will raise all the dead [1 Thess 4:13–5:2].

FEBRUARY 5

2 Samuel 22:29

כִּֽי־אַתָּ֥ה נֵירִ֖י יְהוָ֑ה וַיהוָ֖ה יַגִּ֥יהַּ חָשְׁכִּֽי׃

נֵר: lamp – נָגַהּ (hiph impf 3 sg): enlighten, turn into light – חֹשֶׁךְ (1 sg sf): darkness

---

John 8:12

Πάλιν οὖν αὐτοῖς ἐλάλησεν ὁ Ἰησοῦς λέγων· ἐγώ εἰμι τὸ φῶς τοῦ κόσμου· ὁ ἀκολουθῶν ἐμοὶ οὐ μὴ περιπατήσῃ ἐν τῇ σκοτίᾳ, ἀλλ' ἕξει τὸ φῶς τῆς ζωῆς.

λαλέω (aor ind 3 sg): speak – φῶς: light – ἀκολουθέω (pres ptcp sg): follow – περιπατέω (aor subj 3 sg): walk + οὐ μή: will not walk – σκοτία: darkness – ἕξει (fut of ἔχω): have – ζωή: life

---

Apology IV (II) 15-16

We see books published in which certain sayings of Christ are compared with the sayings of Socrates, Zeno, and others. It's as though Christ had come to deliver certain laws through which we might merit forgiveness of sins, as though we did not receive this freely because of His merits. Therefore, if we here accept the teaching of the adversaries—that by the works of reason we merit forgiveness of sins and justification—there will be no difference between righteousness of philosophers (or certainly of Pharisees) and of Christians.

FEBRUARY 6

Numbers 23:19

לֹא אִישׁ אֵל וִיכַזֵּב וּבֶן־אָדָם וְיִתְנֶחָם
הַהוּא אָמַר וְלֹא יַעֲשֶׂה וְדִבֶּר וְלֹא יְקִימֶנָּה׃

כָּזַב (pi impf 3 sg): lie – אָדָם: man – נָחַם (hithp impf 3 sg): change one's mind – קוּם (hiph impf 3 sg + sf): fulfill

Hebrews 10:23

κατέχωμεν τὴν ὁμολογίαν τῆς ἐλπίδος ἀκλινῆ, πιστὸς γὰρ ὁ ἐπαγγειλάμενος . . .

κατέχω (pres subj 1 pl): hold fast – ὁμολογία: confession – ἐλπίς: hope – ἀκλινής: without wavering – πιστός: faithful – ἐπαγγέλλομαι (aor ptcp): promise

Apology IV (II) 53

Whenever we speak of justifying faith, we must keep in mind that these three objects belong together: the promise, grace, and Christ's merits as the price and atonement. The promise is received through faith. Grace excludes our merits and means that the benefit is offered only through mercy. Christ's merits are the price, because there must be a certain atonement for our sins.

FEBRUARY 7

Psalm 113:3

מִמִּזְרַח־שֶׁמֶשׁ עַד־מְבוֹאוֹ מְהֻלָּל שֵׁם יְהוָה׃

מִזְרָח (cst sg): rising – שֶׁמֶשׁ: sun – מָבוֹא (3 sg sf): place where it sets – הָלַל (pu ptcp): is to be praised – שֵׁם: name

Luke 2:29-32

29νῦν ἀπολύεις τὸν δοῦλόν σου, δέσποτα, κατὰ τὸ ῥῆμά σου
ἐν εἰρήνῃ· 30ὅτι εἶδον οἱ ὀφθαλμοί μου τὸ σωτήριόν σου,
31ὃ ἡτοίμασας κατὰ πρόσωπον πάντων τῶν λαῶν, 32φῶς
εἰς ἀποκάλυψιν ἐθνῶν καὶ δόξαν λαοῦ σου Ἰσραήλ.

ἀπολύω (pres ind 2 sg): dismiss – δοῦλος: servant – δεσπότης: master– ῥῆμα: word – ὀφθαλμός: eye – σωτηρίον: means of deliverance – ἑτοιμάζω (aor ind 2 sg): prepare – πρόσωπον: face – ἀποκάλυψις: revelation – δόξα: glory

Apology IV (II) 67

But God cannot be interacted with, God cannot be grasped, except through the Word. So justification happens through the Word, just as Paul says in Rom 1:16, "[The Gospel] is the power of God for salvation to everyone who believes." Likewise, he says in 10:17, "Faith . . . comes from hearing." Proof can be derived even from this: faith justifies because, if justification happens only through the Word, and the Word is understood only by faith, it follows that faith justifies.

February 8

Exodus 34:5-7

[5] וַיֵּרֶד יְהוָה בֶּעָנָן וַיִּתְיַצֵּב עִמּוֹ שָׁם וַיִּקְרָא בְשֵׁם יְהוָה׃
[6] וַיַּעֲבֹר יְהוָה עַל־פָּנָיו וַיִּקְרָא יְהוָה יְהוָה אֵל רַחוּם
וְחַנּוּן אֶרֶךְ אַפַּיִם וְרַב־חֶסֶד וֶאֱמֶת׃ [7] נֹצֵר חֶסֶד
לָאֲלָפִים נֹשֵׂא עָוֺן וָפֶשַׁע וְחַטָּאָה וְנַקֵּה לֹא יְנַקֶּה פֹּקֵד
עֲוֺן אָבוֹת עַל־בָּנִים וְעַל־בְּנֵי בָנִים עַל־שִׁלֵּשִׁים
וְעַל־רִבֵּעִים׃

עָנָן: cloud – יָצַב (hithp v-c impf 3 sg): take one's stand – קָרָא (qal v-c impf 3 sg): call, proclaim – עָבַר (qal v-c impf 3 sg): pass – רַחוּם: compassionate – חַנּוּן: merciful – אֶרֶךְ (cst): long + אַפַּיִם: slow to anger – רַב: great, abounding in – חֶסֶד: faithful love – אֱמֶת: faithfulness – נָצַר (qal ptcp): keep, maintain – אֶלֶף (pl): thousand – נָשָׂא (qal ptcp): lift up, forgive – נָקָה (pi inf abs/pi impf 3 sg): leave unpunished – פָּקַד (qal ptcp): punish – שִׁלֵּשִׁים: pertaining to the third generation – רִבֵּעִים: pertaining to the fourth generation

Romans 11:22

ἴδε οὖν χρηστότητα καὶ ἀποτομίαν θεοῦ.

χρηστότης: kindness – ἀποτομία: severity

Apology V (III) 208

In the Lord's Prayer the saints ask for the forgiveness of sins. Therefore, even the saints have sins.

FEBRUARY 9

Psalm 26:8

יְהוָה אָהַבְתִּי מְעוֹן בֵּיתֶךָ וּמְקוֹם מִשְׁכַּן כְּבוֹדֶךָ׃

אָהֵב (qal pf 1 sg): love – מָעוֹן (cst sg): dwelling – מָקוֹם: place – מִשְׁכָּן: dwelling – כָּבוֹד (2 sg sf): glory

---

Luke 19:45-47

45Καὶ εἰσελθὼν εἰς τὸ ἱερὸν ἤρξατο ἐκβάλλειν τοὺς
πωλοῦντας 46λέγων αὐτοῖς· γέγραπται· καὶ ἔσται ὁ οἶκός
μου οἶκος προσευχῆς, ὑμεῖς δὲ αὐτὸν ἐποιήσατε σπήλαιον
λῃστῶν. 47Καὶ ἦν διδάσκων τὸ καθ' ἡμέραν ἐν τῷ ἱερῷ.

εἰσέρχομαι (aor ptcp): enter – ἱερόν: temple – ἄρχομαι (aor 3 sg): begin – ἐκβάλλω (pres inf): throw out – πωλέω (pres ptcp): sell – γράφω (pf pass): write – προσευχή: prayer – σπήλαιον: den – λῃστής: robber – διδάσκω (pres ptcp): teach – τὸ καθ' ἡμέραν: day by day

---

Large Catechism I 86

This is the simple meaning of the *[third]* commandment: People must have holidays. Therefore, such observances should be devoted to hearing God's Word so that the special function of this day of rest should be the ministry of the Word for the young and the mass of poor people [Neh 8:2-3,8]. Yet the resting should not be strictly understood to forbid any work that comes up which cannot be avoided.

Isaiah 66:2

וְאֶל־זֶה אַבִּיט אֶל־עָנִי וּנְכֵה־רוּחַ וְחָרֵד עַל־דְּבָרִי׃

נָבַט (hiph impf 1 sg): esteem – עָנִי: humble – נָכֶה (cst): contrite – רוּחַ: spirit – חָרֵד (adj): trembling

---

1 Peter 5:6

Ταπεινώθητε οὖν ὑπὸ τὴν κραταιὰν χεῖρα τοῦ θεοῦ, ἵνα ὑμᾶς ὑψώσῃ ἐν καιρῷ . . .

ταπεινόω (aor pass imv 2 pl): humble yourselves – καραταιός: mighty – χείρ: hand – ὑψόω (aor subj 3 sg): lift up – καιρός: proper time

---

Formula of Concord Ep I 4

God created the body and soul of Adam and Eve before the fall. But He also created our bodies and souls after the fall. Even though they are corrupt, God still acknowledges them as His work.

Psalm 91:4

בְּאֶבְרָתוֹ יָסֶךְ לָךְ וְתַחַת־כְּנָפָיו תֶּחְסֶה
צִנָּה וְסֹחֵרָה אֲמִתּוֹ׃

אֶבְרָה (3 sg sf): feathers – סָכַךְ (hiph impf 3 sg): screen, cover – כָּנָף (pl + 3 sg sf): wing – חָסָה (qal impf 2 sg): find refuge – צִנָּה: shield – סֹחֵרָה: means of protection, rampart – אֱמֶת (3 sg sf): faithfulness

---

Mark 4:39-41

39καὶ διεγερθεὶς ἐπετίμησεν τῷ ἀνέμῳ καὶ εἶπεν τῇ
θαλάσσῃ· σιώπα, πεφίμωσο. καὶ ἐκόπασεν ὁ ἄνεμος καὶ
ἐγένετο γαλήνη μεγάλη. 40καὶ εἶπεν αὐτοῖς· τί δειλοί
ἐστε; οὔπω ἔχετε πίστιν; 41καὶ ἐφοβήθησαν φόβον μέγαν
καὶ ἔλεγον πρὸς ἀλλήλους· τίς ἄρα οὗτός ἐστιν ὅτι καὶ
ὁ ἄνεμος καὶ ἡ θάλασσα ὑπακούει αὐτῷ;

διεγείρω (aor pass ptcp): awaken – ἐπιτιμάω (aor ind 3 sg): rebuke – ἄνεμος: wind – θάλασσα: sea – σιωπάω (pres act imv 2 sg): be quiet – φιμόω (pf pass imv 2 sg): be silent – κοπάζω (aor ind 3 sg): abate – γαλήνη: calm – μέγας: great – δειλός: afraid – οὔπω: not yet – φοβέομαι (aor ind 3 pl): be afraid – ἀλλήλων: one another – ὑπακούω (pres ind 3 sg): obey

---

Large Catechism I 2

A god means that from which we are to expect all good and in which we are to take refuge in all distress. So, to have a God is nothing other than trusting and believing Him with the heart. I have often said that the confidence and faith of the heart alone make both God and an idol.

Exodus 34:29

וַיְהִי בְּרֶדֶת מֹשֶׁה מֵהַר סִינַי וּשְׁנֵי לֻחֹת הָעֵדֻת בְּיַד־מֹשֶׁה
בְּרִדְתּוֹ מִן־הָהָר וּמֹשֶׁה לֹא־יָדַע כִּי קָרַן עוֹר פָּנָיו
בְּדַבְּרוֹ אִתּֽוֹ׃

יָרַד (qal inf cst/qal inf cst + 3 sg sf): come down – הַר: mountain – לוּחַ (pl): tablet – עֵדוּת: testimony – קָרַן (qal pf 3 sg): be radiant – עוֹר: skin – דָּבַר (pi inf cst + 3 sg sf): speak

---

Matthew 17:2

καὶ μετεμορφώθη ἔμπροσθεν αὐτῶν, καὶ ἔλαμψεν τὸ πρόσωπον αὐτοῦ ὡς ὁ ἥλιος, τὰ δὲ ἱμάτια αὐτοῦ ἐγένετο λευκὰ ὡς τὸ φῶς.

μεταμορφόω (aor pass ind 3 sg): be transfigured – ἔμπροσθεν: before, in the sight of – λάμπω (aor ind 3 sg): shine – πρόσωπον: face – ἥλιος: sun – ἱμάτιον (pl): garment – λευκός: white – φῶς: light

---

Formula of Concord SD VIII 49

Regarding the divine nature in Christ, in God there is no change (Jas 1:17). His divine nature, in its essence and properties, suffered no subtraction or addition by the incarnation. It was not, in or by itself, either diminished or increased by it.

FEBRUARY 13

Job 1:21

וַיֹּאמֶר עָרֹם יָצָתִי [יָצָאתִי] מִבֶּטֶן אִמִּי וְעָרֹם אָשׁוּב שָׁמָּה
יְהוָה נָתַן וַיהוָה לָקָח יְהִי שֵׁם יְהוָה מְבֹרָךְ׃

עָרֹם: naked – יָצָא (qal pf 1 sg): come out – בֶּטֶן: womb – אֵם (1 sg sf): mother – שׁוּב (qal impf 1 sg): return – הָיָה (qal juss 3 sg): may it be – בָּרַךְ (pu ptcp): be blessed

James 1:17

πᾶσα δόσις ἀγαθὴ καὶ πᾶν δώρημα τέλειον ἄνωθέν ἐστιν καταβαῖνον ἀπὸ τοῦ πατρὸς τῶν φώτων, παρ’ ᾧ οὐκ ἔνι παραλλαγὴ ἢ τροπῆς ἀποσκίασμα.

δόσις: gift – ἀγαθός: good – δώρημα: gift – τέλειος: perfect – ἄνωθεν: from above – καταβαίνω (pres ptcp): come down – φῶς: light – ἔνι = ἔνεστιν: there is – παραλλαγή: change – τροπή: turning – ἀποσκίασμα: shadow

Large Catechism I 247

Beware of this: The poor man will come to you (there are so many now). He must buy things with the penny of his daily wages and live upon it. When you are harsh to him, as though everyone lived by your favor, and you skin and scrape him to the bone, and when you turn him away with pride and arrogance to whom you ought to give things without payment, he will go away wretched and sorrowful. Since he can complain to no one else, he will cry and call to heaven [Ps 20:6; 146:8-9]. Then beware (I say again) as of the devil himself.

February 14

Psalm 51:3-4

3 חָנֵּנִי אֱלֹהִים כְּחַסְדֶּךָ כְּרֹב רַחֲמֶיךָ מְחֵה פְשָׁעָי׃
4 הַרְבֵּה [הֶרֶב] כַּבְּסֵנִי מֵעֲוֺנִי וּמֵחַטָּאתִי טַהֲרֵנִי׃

חָנַן (qal imv sg + sf): have mercy – חֶסֶד: faithful love – רֹב: greatness – רַחֲמִים: mercies – מָחָה (qal imv sg): blot out – פֶּשַׁע: sin (as rebellion) – הַרְבֵּה (ketiv: hiph inf abs of רָבָה as adv): completely – כָּבַס (pi imv sg + sf): wash – עָוֹן: sin (as guilt) – חַטָּאת: sin (as missing the mark) – טָהֵר (pi imv sg + sf): cleanse

Romans 5:8-9

8 συνίστησιν δὲ τὴν ἑαυτοῦ ἀγάπην εἰς ἡμᾶς ὁ θεός, ὅτι
ἔτι ἁμαρτωλῶν ὄντων ἡμῶν Χριστὸς ὑπὲρ ἡμῶν ἀπέθανεν.
9 πολλῷ οὖν μᾶλλον δικαιωθέντες νῦν ἐν τῷ αἵματι αὐτοῦ
σωθησόμεθα δι' αὐτοῦ ἀπὸ τῆς ὀργῆς.

συνίστημι (pres ind 3 sg): demonstrate – ἁμαρτωλός: sinner – εἰμί (pres ptcp): be – ἀποθνῄσκω (aor ind 3 sg): die – δικαιόω (aor pass ptcp pl): justify – αἷμα: blood – σῴζω (fut pass 1 pl): save – ὀργή: wrath

Apology II (I) 3

We teach that those who are born according to the fleshly nature have concupiscence. This means people not only lack fear and trust in God, but also do not even have the power or gifts to produce fear and trust in God. . . . So when we mention concupiscence, we understand not only the acts or fruit, but also the constant inclination of the nature.

FEBRUARY 15

Psalm 118:6

יְהוָה לִי לֹא אִירָא מַה־יַּעֲשֶׂה לִי אָדָם׃

לִי: with me – יָרֵא (qal impf 1 sg): fear – עָשָׂה (qal impf 3 sg): do – אָדָם: man

---

Hebrews 13:5-6

5αὐτὸς γὰρ εἴρηκεν· οὐ μή σε ἀνῶ οὐδ᾽ οὐ μή σε
ἐγκαταλίπω, 6ὥστε θαρροῦντας ἡμᾶς λέγειν· κύριος ἐμοὶ
βοηθός, [καὶ] οὐ φοβηθήσομαι, τί ποιήσει μοι ἄνθρωπος;

εἴρηκα (used as pf of λέγω/εἶπον): say – οὐ μή: strong negative – ἀνίημι (aor act subj 1 sg): abandon – ἐγκαταλείπω (aor act subj 1 sg): forsake – ὥστε: so that – θαρρέω (pres act ptcp): be confident – βοηθός: helper – φοβέομαι (fut dep 1 sg): be afraid

---

Large Catechism I 13-15

A person's entire heart and all his confidence must be placed in God alone and in no one else. For to "have" God, you can easily see, is not to take hold of Him with our hands or to put Him in a bag ‹like money› or to lock Him in a chest ‹like silver vessels›. Instead, to "have" Him means that the heart takes hold of Him and clings to Him. To cling to Him with the heart is nothing else than to trust in Him entirely.

Jeremiah 23:16

כֹּה־אָמַר יְהוָה צְבָאוֹת אַל־תִּשְׁמְעוּ עַל־דִּבְרֵי הַנְּבִאִים הַנִּבְּאִים לָכֶם מַהְבִּלִים הֵמָּה אֶתְכֶם חֲזוֹן לִבָּם יְדַבֵּרוּ לֹא מִפִּי יְהוָה׃

צָבָא (pl): army, host – **שָׁמַע** (qal juss 2 pl): listen to – **נָבִיא** (pl): prophet – **נָבָא** (niph ptcp pl): prophesy – **הָבַל** (hiph ptcp pl): fill with false hopes – **חָזוֹן** (cst sg): vision – **לֵב** (sg + 3 pl sf): heart – **פֶּה** (cst): mouth

Romans 16:17

Παρακαλῶ δὲ ὑμᾶς, ἀδελφοί, σκοπεῖν τοὺς τὰς διχοστασίας καὶ τὰ σκάνδαλα παρὰ τὴν διδαχὴν ἣν ὑμεῖς ἐμάθετε ποιοῦντας, καὶ ἐκκλίνετε ἀπ' αὐτῶν·

παρακαλέω (pres ind 1 sg): urge – σκοπέω (pres inf): watch out for – διχοστασία: dissension – σκάνδαλον: enticement to apostasy – παρά: contrary to – διδαχή: teaching – μανθάνω (aor ind 2 pl): learn – ποιέω (pres ptcp): cause – ἐκκλίνω (pres imv 2 pl): turn away from

Large Catechism I 54

But the greatest abuse *[of God's name]* occurs in spiritual matters. These have to do with the conscience, when false preachers rise up and offer their lying vanities as God's Word [Jonah 2:8].

FEBRUARY 17

Jeremiah 17:13

מִקְוֵה יִשְׂרָאֵל יְהוָה כָּל־עֹזְבֶיךָ יֵבֹשׁוּ
יְסוּרַי [וְסוּרַי] בָּאָרֶץ יִכָּתֵבוּ כִּי עָזְבוּ מְקוֹר מַיִם־חַיִּים
אֶת־יְהוָה׃

מִקְוֶה (cst sg): hope – עָזַב (qal ptcp pl + 2 sg sf): forsake – בּוֹשׁ (qal impf 3 pl): be put to shame – סוּר (qere: qal pass ptcp pl + 1 sg sf): turn away from – אֶרֶץ: earth, dust – כָּתַב (niph impf 3 pl): be written, recorded – עָזַב (qal pf 3 pl): forsake – מָקוֹר (cst sg): spring – חַי (pl): living

Luke 10:20

πλὴν ἐν τούτῳ μὴ χαίρετε ὅτι τὰ πνεύματα ὑμῖν ὑποτάσσεται, χαίρετε δὲ ὅτι τὰ ὀνόματα ὑμῶν ἐγγέγραπται ἐν τοῖς οὐρανοῖς.

πλήν: however – χαίρω (pres imv 2 pl): rejoice – πνεῦμα (pl): spirit – ὑποτάσσω (pres pass 3 sg): become subject – ὄνομα (pl): name – ἐγγράφω (pf pass 3 sg): write in

Apology IV (II) 40

By their own strength, people cannot fulfill God's Law. They are all under sin, subject to eternal wrath and death. Because of this, we cannot be freed by the Law from sin and be justified. But the promise of forgiveness of sins and of justification has been given us for Christ's sake, who was given for us in order that He might make satisfaction for the sins of the world. He has been appointed as the Mediator and Atoning Sacrifice.

February 18

Isaiah 59:21

וַאֲנִי זֹאת בְּרִיתִי אוֹתָם אָמַר יְהוָה רוּחִי אֲשֶׁר עָלֶיךָ
וּדְבָרַי אֲשֶׁר־שַׂמְתִּי בְּפִיךָ לֹא־יָמוּשׁוּ מִפִּיךָ וּמִפִּי זַרְעֲךָ
וּמִפִּי זֶרַע זַרְעֲךָ אָמַר יְהוָה מֵעַתָּה וְעַד־עוֹלָם׃

בְּרִית (1 sg sf): covenant – אוֹתָם = אִתָּם: with them – רוּחַ (1 sg sf): Spirit – דָּבָר (pl + 1 sg sf): word – שִׂים (qal pf 1 sg): put – פֶּה (2 sg sf/cst): mouth – מוּשׁ (qal impf 3 pl): depart – זֶרַע (2 sg sf): seed, children – מֵעַתָּה: from this time – עַד־עוֹלָם: forever

---

Ephesians 1:17-18

17ἵνα ὁ θεὸς τοῦ κυρίου ἡμῶν Ἰησοῦ Χριστοῦ, ὁ πατὴρ
τῆς δόξης, δώῃ ὑμῖν πνεῦμα σοφίας καὶ ἀποκαλύψεως ἐν
ἐπιγνώσει αὐτοῦ, 18πεφωτισμένους τοὺς ὀφθαλμοὺς τῆς
καρδίας [ὑμῶν] εἰς τὸ εἰδέναι ὑμᾶς τίς ἐστιν ἡ ἐλπὶς τῆς
κλήσεως αὐτοῦ, τίς ὁ πλοῦτος τῆς δόξης τῆς κληρονομίας
αὐτοῦ ἐν τοῖς ἁγίοις . . .

δίδωμι (aor subj 3 sg): give – σοφία: wisdom – ἀποκάλυψις: revelation – ἐπίγνωσις: knowledge – φωτίζω (pf pass ptcp): enlighten – οἶδα (pf inf with pres meaning): know – ἐλπίς: hope – κλῆσις: calling – πλοῦτος: riches – κληρονομία: inheritance – ἅγιος: holy one, saint

---

Formula of Concord SD II 18

The natural or fleshly free will in St. Paul and in other regenerate people strives against God's Law, even after regeneration.

FEBRUARY 19

Isaiah 41:17

הָעֲנִיִּים וְהָאֶבְיוֹנִים מְבַקְשִׁים מַיִם וָאַיִן לְשׁוֹנָם
בַּצָּמָא נָשָׁתָּה
אֲנִי יְהוָה אֶעֱנֵם אֱלֹהֵי יִשְׂרָאֵל לֹא אֶעֶזְבֵם׃

עָנִי (pl): poor – אֶבְיוֹן (pl) needy – בָּקַשׁ (pi ptcp pl): search for, seek – מַיִם: water – אַיִן: nonexistence – לָשׁוֹן (3 pl sf): tongue – צָמָא: thirst – נָשַׁת (qal pf 3 sg f): be parched – עָנָה (qal impf 1 sg): answer – עָזַב (qal impf 1 sg + 3 pl sf): forsake

---

John 4:10

ἀπεκρίθη Ἰησοῦς καὶ εἶπεν αὐτῇ· εἰ ᾔδεις τὴν δωρεὰν τοῦ θεοῦ καὶ τίς ἐστιν ὁ λέγων σοι· δός μοι πεῖν, σὺ ἂν ᾔτησας αὐτὸν καὶ ἔδωκεν ἄν σοι ὕδωρ ζῶν.

οἶδα (plpf 2 sg with impf meaning): know – δωρεά: gift – δίδωμι (aor act imv 2 sg): give – πίνω (aor inf): drink – αἰτέω (aor ind 2 sg): ask – δίδωμι (aor ind 3 sg): give – ὕδωρ: water – ζάω (pres act ptcp acc sg n): live

---

Large Catechism IV 77

Our Baptism abides forever. Even though someone should fall from Baptism and sin, still we always have access to it. So we may subdue the old man again.

Isaiah 11:2-3

2 וְנָחָה עָלָיו רוּחַ יְהוָה רוּחַ חָכְמָה וּבִינָה
רוּחַ עֵצָה וּגְבוּרָה רוּחַ דַּעַת וְיִרְאַת יְהוָה׃
3 וַהֲרִיחוֹ בְּיִרְאַת יְהוָה

נוּחַ (qal v-c pf 3 sg f): rest – רוּחַ: Spirit – חָכְמָה: wisdom – בִּינָה: understanding – עֵצָה: counsel – גְּבוּרָה: power – דַּעַת: knowledge – יִרְאָה (cst sg): fear – רִיחַ (hiph inf cst): delight in

---

Mark 12:35-37

35 Καὶ ἀποκριθεὶς ὁ Ἰησοῦς ἔλεγεν διδάσκων ἐν τῷ ἱερῷ·
πῶς λέγουσιν οἱ γραμματεῖς ὅτι ὁ χριστὸς υἱὸς Δαυίδ
ἐστιν; 36 αὐτὸς Δαυὶδ εἶπεν ἐν τῷ πνεύματι τῷ ἁγίῳ· εἶπεν
κύριος τῷ κυρίῳ μου· κάθου ἐκ δεξιῶν μου, ἕως ἂν θῶ τοὺς
ἐχθρούς σου ὑποκάτω τῶν ποδῶν σου. 37 αὐτὸς Δαυὶδ λέγει
αὐτὸν κύριον, καὶ πόθεν αὐτοῦ ἐστιν υἱός; Καὶ [ὁ] πολὺς
ὄχλος ἤκουεν αὐτοῦ ἡδέως.

διδάσκω (pres ptcp): teach – ἱερόν: temple – γραμματεύς: scholar versed in the law, scribe – κάθημαι (pres imv 2 sg): sit – ἐχθρός: enemy – ὑποκάτω: under – πόθεν: how? – ἡδέως: gladly

---

Formula of Concord SD VIII 72

We believe, teach, and confess that God the Father has given His Spirit to Christ, His beloved Son, according to the received humanity. (Because of this He is called also *Messiah;* i.e., the Anointed.) He has not received His gifts with limits as other saints.

Psalm 51:12

לֵב טָהוֹר בְּרָא־לִי אֱלֹהִים וְרוּחַ נָכוֹן חַדֵּשׁ בְּקִרְבִּי׃

לֵב: heart – טָהוֹר: pure – בָּרָא (qal imv): create – רוּחַ: spirit – כּוּן (niph ptcp): steadfast – חָדַשׁ (pi imv): renew – קֶרֶב (1 sg sf): inward part = within me

Matthew 15:19-20

19ἐκ γὰρ τῆς καρδίας ἐξέρχονται διαλογισμοὶ πονηροί, φόνοι, μοιχεῖαι, πορνεῖαι, κλοπαί, ψευδομαρτυρίαι, βλασφημίαι. 20ταῦτά ἐστιν τὰ κοινοῦντα τὸν ἄνθρωπον, τὸ δὲ ἀνίπτοις χερσὶν φαγεῖν οὐ κοινοῖ τὸν ἄνθρωπον.

καρδία: heart – διαλογισμός: thought – πονηρός: evil – φόνος: murder – μοιχεία: adultery – πορνεία: unchastity – κλοπή: theft – ψευδομαρτυρία: false witness – βλασφημία: slander – κοινόω (pres ptcp/pres ind 3 sg): make impure – ἄνιπτος: unwashed – χείρ (dat pl): hand – φαγεῖν (aor inf of ἐσθίω): eat

Formula of Concord SD II 60

God does not force a person to become godly. (Those who always resist the Holy Spirit and persistently oppose the known truth are not converted, as Stephen says about the hardened Jewish people [Acts 7:51].) Yet God the Lord draws the person whom He wants to convert [John 6:44]. He draws him in such a way that his darkened understanding is turned into an enlightened one and his perverse will into an obedient one. This is what the Scriptures call creating a clean heart [Ps 51:10].

February 22

Psalm 10:17

תַּאֲוַת עֲנָוִים שָׁמַעְתָּ יְהוָה תָּכִין לִבָּם תַּקְשִׁיב אָזְנֶךָ׃

תַּאֲוָה (cst sg): desire – עָנָו (pl): afflicted – שָׁמַע (qal pf 2 sg): hear – כּוּן (hiph impf 2 sg): establish + לֵב (sg + 3 pl sf): heart = encourage – קָשַׁב (hiph impf 2 sg): incline – אֹזֶן (sg + 2 sg sf): ear

1 Peter 5:5

πάντες δὲ ἀλλήλοις τὴν ταπεινοφροσύνην ἐγκομβώσασθε, ὅτι [ὁ] θεὸς ὑπερηφάνοις ἀντιτάσσεται, ταπεινοῖς δὲ δίδωσιν χάριν.

ταπεινοφροσύνη: humility – ἐγκομβόομαι (aor imv 2 pl): clothe oneself – ὑπερήφανος: proud – ἀντιτάσσω (pres mid 3 sg): oppose – ταπεινός: humble

Apology V (III) 71

We think this way also about every good work in the humblest callings and in private affairs. Through these works Christ celebrates His victory over the devil, just as the distribution of alms by the Corinthians (1 Cor 16:1) was a holy work, a sacrifice and battle of Christ against the devil, who labors so that nothing may be done to praise God.

FEBRUARY 23

Isaiah 43:1-3

1וְעַתָּה כֹּה־אָמַר יְהוָה בֹּרַאֲךָ יַעֲקֹב וְיֹצֶרְךָ יִשְׂרָאֵל
אַל־תִּירָא כִּי גְאַלְתִּיךָ קָרָאתִי בְשִׁמְךָ לִי־אָתָּה׃
2כִּי־תַעֲבֹר בַּמַּיִם אִתְּךָ־אָנִי וּבַנְּהָרוֹת לֹא יִשְׁטְפוּךָ
כִּי־תֵלֵךְ בְּמוֹ־אֵשׁ לֹא תִכָּוֶה וְלֶהָבָה לֹא תִבְעַר־בָּךְ׃
3כִּי אֲנִי יְהוָה אֱלֹהֶיךָ קְדוֹשׁ יִשְׂרָאֵל מוֹשִׁיעֶךָ

יָצַר (qal ptcp + 2 sg sf): form – יָרֵא (qal juss 2 sg): fear – גָּאַל (qal pf 1 sg + 2 sg sf): redeem – שָׁטַף (qal impf): overwhelm – בְּמוֹ = בְּ: in – כָּוָה (niph impf): be burned – לֶהָבָה: flame – בָּעַר (qal impf): burn – קָדוֹשׁ: the holy one

---

Galatians 1:3-5

3χάρις ὑμῖν καὶ εἰρήνη ἀπὸ θεοῦ πατρὸς ἡμῶν καὶ κυρίου
ʼΙησοῦ Χριστοῦ 4τοῦ δόντος ἑαυτὸν ὑπὲρ τῶν ἁμαρτιῶν
ἡμῶν, ὅπως ἐξέληται ἡμᾶς ἐκ τοῦ αἰῶνος τοῦ ἐνεστῶτος
πονηροῦ κατὰ τὸ θέλημα τοῦ θεοῦ καὶ πατρὸς ἡμῶν, 5ᾧ ἡ
δόξα εἰς τοὺς αἰῶνας τῶν αἰώνων, ἀμήν.

δίδωμι (aor act ptcp): give – ἐξαιρέω (aor mid subj): rescue – αἰών: age – ἐνίστημι (perf ptcp): be present – πονηρός: evil – δόξα: glory – αἰών τῶν αἰώνων: eternity

---

Small Catechism Seventh Petition

But deliver us from evil.

What does this mean?

Answer: We pray in this petition, as in a summary, that our Father in heaven would deliver us from all kinds of evil, of body and soul, property and honor.

FEBRUARY 24

Psalm 61:2-3

2 שִׁמְעָה אֱלֹהִים רִנָּתִי הַקְשִׁיבָה תְּפִלָּתִי׃
3 מִקְצֵה הָאָרֶץ אֵלֶיךָ אֶקְרָא בַּעֲטֹף לִבִּי
בְּצוּר־יָרוּם מִמֶּנִּי תַנְחֵנִי׃

שָׁמַע (qal imv): hear – רִנָּה (1 sg sf): cry – קָשַׁב (hiph imv): listen to – תְּפִלָּה (1 sg sf): prayer – קָצֶה (cst sg): end – קָרָא (qal impf 1 sg): call out – עָטַף (qal inf cst): be/grow feeble, faint – צוּר: rock – רוּם (qal impf 3 sg): be high – מִן (1 sg sf): than I – נָחָה (hiph impf 2 sg + 1 sg sf): lead

---

Luke 18:7-8

[7]ὁ δὲ θεὸς οὐ μὴ ποιήσῃ τὴν ἐκδίκησιν τῶν ἐκλεκτῶν
αὐτοῦ τῶν βοώντων αὐτῷ ἡμέρας καὶ νυκτός, καὶ
μακροθυμεῖ ἐπ' αὐτοῖς; [8]λέγω ὑμῖν ὅτι ποιήσει τὴν
ἐκδίκησιν αὐτῶν ἐν τάχει.

οὐ μή: expects an affirmative answer in a question – ποιέω (aor subj 3 sg): bring about – ἐκδίκησις: justice – ἐκλεκτός: chosen one – βοάω (pres ptcp gen pl): cry out – μακροθυμέω (pres ind 3 sg): delay – ἐν τάχει: quickly

---

Large Catechism II 67

From this you see that the Creed is a doctrine quite different from the Ten Commandments. For the Commandments teach what we ought to do. But the Creed tells what God does for us and gives to us.

FEBRUARY 25

Psalm 103:8-9

8 רַחוּם וְחַנּוּן יְהוָה אֶרֶךְ אַפַּיִם וְרַב־חָסֶד׃
9 לֹא־לָנֶצַח יָרִיב וְלֹא לְעוֹלָם יִטּוֹר׃

רַחוּם: compassionate – חַנּוּן: gracious – אֶרֶךְ אַפַּיִם: slow to anger – חֶסֶד: faithful love – לָנֶצַח: forever – רִיב (qal impf 3 sg): accuse – נָטַר (qal impf 3 sg): keep, maintain

2 Corinthians 5:19

ὡς ὅτι θεὸς ἦν ἐν Χριστῷ κόσμον καταλλάσσων ἑαυτῷ, μὴ λογιζόμενος αὐτοῖς τὰ παραπτώματα αὐτῶν καὶ θέμενος ἐν ἡμῖν τὸν λόγον τῆς καταλλαγῆς.

ὡς ὅτι: how that, namely – κόσμος: world – καταλλάσσω (pres ptcp): reconcile – λογίζομαι (pres ptcp): count – παράπτωμα: false step, sin – τίθημι (aor mid ptcp): give – καταλλαγή: reconciliation

Apology IV (II) 45

This special faith (by which an individual believes that for Christ's sake his sins are forgiven him, and that for Christ's sake God is reconciled and sees us favorably) gains forgiveness of sins and justifies us. In repentance, namely, in terrors, this faith comforts and encourages hearts. It regenerates us and brings the Holy Spirit so that we may be able to fulfill God's Law: to love God, truly fear God, truly be confident that God hears prayer, and obey God in all afflictions. This faith puts to death concupiscence and the like.

Psalm 95:6-7

6 בֹּאוּ נִשְׁתַּחֲוֶה וְנִכְרָעָה נִבְרְכָה לִפְנֵי־יְהוָה עֹשֵׂנוּ׃
7 כִּי הוּא אֱלֹהֵינוּ וַאֲנַחְנוּ עַם מַרְעִיתוֹ וְצֹאן יָדוֹ

בּוֹא (qal imv pl): come – שָׁחָה (hithp coh 1 pl): worship – כָּרַע (qal coh 1 pl): bow down – בָּרַךְ (qal coh 1 pl): kneel – עָשָׂה (qal ptcp + 1 pl sf): Maker – עַם: people – מַרְעִית (3 sg sf): pasture – צֹאן: sheep, flock – יָד: hand

---

Romans 11:33-36

33 Ὦ βάθος πλούτου καὶ σοφίας καὶ γνώσεως θεοῦ· ὡς
ἀνεξεραύνητα τὰ κρίματα αὐτοῦ καὶ ἀνεξιχνίαστοι αἱ ὁδοὶ
αὐτοῦ. 34 τίς γὰρ ἔγνω νοῦν κυρίου; ἢ τίς σύμβουλος αὐτοῦ
ἐγένετο; 35 ἢ τίς προέδωκεν αὐτῷ, καὶ ἀνταποδοθήσεται
αὐτῷ; 36 ὅτι ἐξ αὐτοῦ καὶ δι' αὐτοῦ καὶ εἰς αὐτὸν τὰ πάντα·
αὐτῷ ἡ δόξα εἰς τοὺς αἰῶνας, ἀμήν.

βάθος: depth – πλοῦτος: riches – σοφία: wisdom – γνῶσις: knowledge – ἀνεξεραύνητος: unfathomable – κρίμα: judgment – ἀνεξιχνίαστος: incomprehensible – ὁδός: way – γιγνώσκω (aor 3 sg): know – νοῦς: mind – σύμβουλος: advisor – προδίδωμι (aor 3 sg): give in advance – ἀνταποδίδωμι (fut pass 3 sg): repay – αἰών: eternity

---

Large Catechism I 16

See, here *[in the First Commandment]* you have the meaning of the true honor and worship of God, which pleases God, and which He commands under penalty of eternal wrath. The heart knows no other comfort or confidence than in Him. It must not allow itself to be torn from Him. But, for Him, it must risk and disregard everything upon earth.

FEBRUARY 27

Psalm 127:1

אִם־יְהוָה לֹא־יִבְנֶה בַּיִת שָׁוְא עָמְלוּ בוֹנָיו בּוֹ
אִם־יְהוָה לֹא־יִשְׁמָר־עִיר שָׁוְא שָׁקַד שׁוֹמֵר׃

בָּנָה (qal impf 3 sg/qal ptcp pl + 3 sg sf): build – בַּיִת: house – שָׁוְא: emptiness, in vain – עָמַל (qal pf 3 pl): toil – שָׁמַר (qal impf 3 sg/qal ptcp): watch over – עִיר: city – שָׁקַד (qal pf 3 sg): stand guard

---

Matthew 7:24-25

24Πᾶς οὖν ὅστις ἀκούει μου τοὺς λόγους τούτους καὶ
ποιεῖ αὐτούς, ὁμοιωθήσεται ἀνδρὶ φρονίμῳ, ὅστις
ᾠκοδόμησεν αὐτοῦ τὴν οἰκίαν ἐπὶ τὴν πέτραν· 25καὶ
κατέβη ἡ βροχὴ καὶ ἦλθον οἱ ποταμοὶ καὶ ἔπνευσαν οἱ
ἄνεμοι καὶ προσέπεσαν τῇ οἰκίᾳ ἐκείνῃ, καὶ οὐκ ἔπεσεν,
τεθεμελίωτο γὰρ ἐπὶ τὴν πέτραν.

ὁμοιόω (fut pass 3 sg): be like – φρόνιμος: sensible – οἰκοδομέω (aor 3 sg): build – πέτρα: rock – καταβαίνω (aor 3 sg): come down – βροχή: rain – ποταμός: stream – πνέω (aor 3 pl): blow – ἄνεμος: wind – προσπίπτω (aor 3 pl): beat against – πίπτω (aor act ind): fall – θεμελιόω (plpf pass 3 sg): have a foundation

---

Apology IV (II) 119

In the Church there must be the teaching by which the pious may receive the sure hope of salvation. For the adversaries give people bad advice when they tell them to doubt whether they receive forgiveness of sins.

FEBRUARY 28

Leviticus 17:11

כִּי נֶפֶשׁ הַבָּשָׂר בַּדָּם הִוא וַאֲנִי נְתַתִּיו לָכֶם עַל־הַמִּזְבֵּחַ
לְכַפֵּר עַל־נַפְשֹׁתֵיכֶם כִּי־הַדָּם הוּא בַּנֶּפֶשׁ יְכַפֵּר׃

נֶפֶשׁ: life – בָּשָׂר: flesh, creature – דָּם: blood – נָתַן (qal perf 1 sg): give – מִזְבֵּחַ: altar – כָּפַר (pi inf cst/pi impf 3 sg): make atonement

Hebrews 9:12,22

12οὐδὲ δι’ αἵματος τράγων καὶ μόσχων διὰ δὲ τοῦ
ἰδίου αἵματος εἰσῆλθεν ἐφάπαξ εἰς τὰ ἅγια αἰωνίαν
λύτρωσιν εὑράμενος. . . . 22καὶ χωρὶς αἱματεκχυσίας
οὐ γίνεται ἄφεσις.

αἷμα: blood – τράγος: he-goat – μόσχος: calf – εἰσέρχομαι (aor ind 3 sg): enter – ἐφάπαξ: once for all – ἅγιος (pl n): holy = the Most Holy Place – αἰώνιος: eternal – λύτρωσις: redemption – εὑρίσκω (aor dep ptcp): obtain – χωρίς: without – αἱματεκχυσία: shedding of blood – ἄφεσις: forgiveness

Apology XXIV (XII) 22

In fact there has been only one atoning sacrifice in the world, namely, Christ's death, as the Epistle to the Hebrews teaches, "It is impossible for the blood of bulls and goats to take away sins" (10:4).

February 29

Genesis 32:31

וַיִּקְרָא יַעֲקֹב שֵׁם הַמָּקוֹם פְּנִיאֵל כִּי־רָאִיתִי אֱלֹהִים פָּנִים
אֶל־פָּנִים וַתִּנָּצֵל נַפְשִׁי׃

קָרָא (qal v-c impf 3 sg): call – שֵׁם: name – מָקוֹם: place – רָאָה (qal perf 1 sg): see – פָּנִים: face – נָצַל (niph v-c impf 3 sg f): be spared – נֶ֫פֶשׁ: life

---

Luke 19:9-10

9εἶπεν δὲ πρὸς αὐτὸν ὁ Ἰησοῦς ὅτι σήμερον σωτηρία
τῷ οἴκῳ τούτῳ ἐγένετο, καθότι καὶ αὐτὸς υἱὸς Ἀβραάμ
ἐστιν· 10ἦλθεν γὰρ ὁ υἱὸς τοῦ ἀνθρώπου ζητῆσαι καὶ σῶσαι
τὸ ἀπολωλός.

σήμερον: today – σωτηρία: salvation – οἶκος: house – γίνομαι (aor 3 sg): come – καθότι: because – ἔρχομαι (aor 3 sg): come – ζητέω (aor inf): seek – σῴζω (aor inf): save – ἀπόλλυμι (pf act ptcp): the lost

---

Formula of Concord SD III 13

Faith justifies not because it is such a good work or because it is so beautiful a virtue. It justifies because it lays hold of and accepts Christ's merit in the promise of the Holy Gospel.

Psalm 23:3-4

3 נַפְשִׁי יְשׁוֹבֵב יַֽנְחֵנִי בְמַעְגְּלֵי־צֶדֶק לְמַעַן שְׁמֽוֹ׃
4 גַּם כִּֽי־אֵלֵךְ בְּגֵיא צַלְמָוֶת לֹא־אִירָא רָע
כִּי־אַתָּה עִמָּדִי שִׁבְטְךָ וּמִשְׁעַנְתֶּךָ הֵמָּה יְנַֽחֲמֻֽנִי׃

נֶפֶשׁ: soul – שׁוּב (polel impf 3 sg): restore, reclaim – נָחָה (hiph impf 3 sg + 1 sg sf): guide – מַעְגָּל (cst pl): path – הָלַךְ (qal impf 1 sg): walk – גַּיְא (cst sg): valley – צַלְמָוֶת: death-shadow, deep darkness – יָרֵא (qal impf 1 sg): fear – עִם (1 sg sf): with – שֵׁבֶט (2 sg sf): rod – מִשְׁעֶנֶת (2 sg sf): staff – נָחַם (pi impf 3 pl + 1 sg sf): comfort

---

John 14:6

λέγει αὐτῷ [ὁ] Ἰησοῦς· ἐγώ εἰμι ἡ ὁδὸς καὶ ἡ ἀλήθεια καὶ ἡ ζωή· οὐδεὶς ἔρχεται πρὸς τὸν πατέρα εἰ μὴ δι' ἐμοῦ.

ὁδός: way – ἀλήθεια: truth – ζωή: life – ἔρχομαι (pres dep ind 3 sg): come – εἰ μή: if not, except

---

Formula of Concord SD II 17

God's Word testifies that the intellect, heart, and will of the natural, unregenerate person in divine things are not only turned entirely away from God, but also are turned and perverted against God to every evil.

MARCH 2

Genesis 18:16-17

16 וַיָּקֻמוּ מִשָּׁם הָאֲנָשִׁים וַיַּשְׁקִפוּ עַל־פְּנֵי סְדֹם וְאַבְרָהָם
הֹלֵךְ עִמָּם לְשַׁלְּחָם׃ 17 וַיהוָה אָמָר הַמְכַסֶּה אֲנִי
מֵאַבְרָהָם אֲשֶׁר אֲנִי עֹשֶׂה׃

קוּם (qal v-c impf 3 pl): arise – אִישׁ (pl): man – שָׁקַף (hiph v-c impf 3 pl): look down on – הָלַךְ (qal ptcp sg): go – שָׁלַח (pi inf cst + 3 pl sf): send, escort – כָּסָה (pi ptcp sg + interrog הֲ): hide – עָשָׂה (qal ptcp sg): do

Ephesians 2:19-20

19 Ἄρα οὖν οὐκέτι ἐστὲ ξένοι καὶ πάροικοι ἀλλὰ
ἐστὲ συμπολῖται τῶν ἁγίων καὶ οἰκεῖοι τοῦ θεοῦ,
20 ἐποικοδομηθέντες ἐπὶ τῷ θεμελίῳ τῶν ἀποστόλων καὶ
προφητῶν, ὄντος ἀκρογωνιαίου αὐτοῦ Χριστοῦ Ἰησοῦ.

οὐκέτι: no longer – ξένος: foreigner – πάροικος: alien – συμπολίτης: fellow citizen – ἅγιος: saint – οἰκεῖος: member of the household – ἐποικοδομέω (aor pass ptcp pl): build on – θεμέλιον: foundation – ἀκρογωνιαῖος: cornerstone

Apology VII-VIII (IV) 9

No matter how great the multitude of the wicked is, we may know that the Church still exists and Christ provides those gifts He has promised to the Church—to forgive sins, to hear prayer, to give the Holy Spirit.

March 3

Psalm 14:2-3

2יְהוָה מִשָּׁמַיִם הִשְׁקִיף עַל־בְּנֵי־אָדָם
לִרְאוֹת הֲיֵשׁ מַשְׂכִּיל דֹּרֵשׁ אֶת־אֱלֹהִים׃
3הַכֹּל סָר יַחְדָּו נֶאֱלָחוּ
אֵין עֹשֵׂה־טוֹב אֵין גַּם־אֶחָד׃

שָׁקַף (hiph pf 3 sg): look down – יֵשׁ: existence = if there are any who – שָׂכַל (hiph ptcp sg): have insight, understand – דָּרַשׁ (qal ptcp): seek – סוּר (qal pf 3 sg): turn aside – יַחְדָּו (adv): together – אָלַח (niph pf 3 pl): be corrupt – אַיִן (cst): nonexistence = there is no one

1 John 1:8-9

8ἐὰν εἴπωμεν ὅτι ἁμαρτίαν οὐκ ἔχομεν, ἑαυτοὺς πλανῶμεν
καὶ ἡ ἀλήθεια οὐκ ἔστιν ἐν ἡμῖν. 9ἐὰν ὁμολογῶμεν τὰς
ἁμαρτίας ἡμῶν, πιστός ἐστιν καὶ δίκαιος, ἵνα ἀφῇ ἡμῖν
τὰς ἁμαρτίας καὶ καθαρίσῃ ἡμᾶς ἀπὸ πάσης ἀδικίας.

εἴπωμεν (aor act subj of εἶπον): say – ἁμαρτία: sin – πλανάω (pres ind 1 pl): deceive – ἀλήθεια: truth – ὁμολογέω (pres subj 1 pl): confess – πιστός: faithful – δίκαιος: just – ἀφίημι (aor subj 3 sg): forgive – καθαρίζω (aor subj 3 sg): cleanse – ἀδικία: unrighteousness

Apology II (I) 10

Why do we need Christ's grace if we can be justified as a result of our own righteousness? Why do we need the Holy Spirit if we are strong enough on our own to love God above all things and fulfill God's commandments?

March 4

Psalm 51:9-10

9תְּחַטְּאֵנִי בְאֵזוֹב וְאֶטְהָר תְּכַבְּסֵנִי וּמִשֶּׁלֶג אַלְבִּין׃
10תַּשְׁמִיעֵנִי שָׂשׂוֹן וְשִׂמְחָה תָּגֵלְנָה עֲצָמוֹת דִּכִּיתָ׃

חָטָא (pi impf 2 sg + 1 sg sf): purify from sin – אֵזוֹב: hyssop – טָהֵר (qal impf 1 sg): be clean – כָּבַס (pi impf 2 sg + 1 sg sf): wash – שֶׁלֶג: snow – לָבֵן (hiph impf 1 sg): be white – שָׁמַע (hiph impf 2 sg + 1 sg sf): cause to hear – שָׂשׂוֹן: joy – שִׂמְחָה: gladness – גִּיל (qal impf 3 pl): rejoice – עֶצֶם (pl): bone – דָּכָא (pi pf 2 sg): crush

---

1 Corinthians 6:11

ἀλλὰ ἀπελούσασθε, ἀλλὰ ἡγιάσθητε, ἀλλὰ ἐδικαιώθητε ἐν τῷ ὀνόματι τοῦ κυρίου Ἰησοῦ Χριστοῦ καὶ ἐν τῷ πνεύματι τοῦ θεοῦ ἡμῶν.

ἀπολούω (aor mid 2 pl): wash – ἁγιάζω (aor pass 2 pl): sanctify – δικαιόω (aor pass 2 pl): justify – ὄνομα: name – πνεῦμα: Spirit

---

Formula of Concord SD III 31

Furthermore, neither contrition nor love nor any other virtue, but faith alone is the only means and instrument by which, and through which, we can receive and accept God's grace, Christ's merit, and the forgiveness of sins, which are brought to us in the Gospel promise.

Exodus 33:19

וַיֹּאמֶר אֲנִי אַעֲבִיר כָּל־טוּבִי עַל־פָּנֶיךָ וְקָרָאתִי בְשֵׁם
יְהוָה לְפָנֶיךָ וְחַנֹּתִי אֶת־אֲשֶׁר אָחֹן וְרִחַמְתִּי אֶת־אֲשֶׁר
אֲרַחֵם׃

עָבַר (hiph impf 1 sg): cause to pass by – טוּב (1 sg sf): goodness – קָרָא (qal v-c pf 1 sg): proclaim – שֵׁם: name – חָנַן (qal v-c pf 1 sg/qal impf 1 sg): have mercy – רָחַם (pi v-c pf 1 sg/pi impf 1 sg): have compassion

---

John 1:15-18

15'Ιωάννης μαρτυρεῖ περὶ αὐτοῦ καὶ κέκραγεν λέγων·
οὗτος ἦν ὃν εἶπον· ὁ ὀπίσω μου ἐρχόμενος ἔμπροσθέν
μου γέγονεν, ὅτι πρῶτός μου ἦν. 16ὅτι ἐκ τοῦ πληρώματος
αὐτοῦ ἡμεῖς πάντες ἐλάβομεν, καὶ χάριν ἀντὶ χάριτος·
17ὅτι ὁ νόμος διὰ Μωϋσέως ἐδόθη, ἡ χάρις καὶ ἡ ἀλήθεια
διὰ 'Ιησοῦ Χριστοῦ ἐγένετο. 18Θεὸν οὐδεὶς ἑώρακεν
πώποτε· μονογενὴς θεὸς ὁ ὢν εἰς τὸν κόλπον τοῦ
πατρὸς ἐκεῖνος ἐξηγήσατο.

μαρτυρέω (pres ind 3 sg): testify – κράζω (pf ind 3 sg): call out – ὀπίσω: after – ἔμπροσθεν: before, higher than – πρῶτός μου: before me – πλήρωμα: fullness – ἀντί: in place of – μονογενής: only-begotten – κόλπος: bosom – ἐξηγέομαι (aor 3 sg): make known

---

Augsburg Confession V 1

So that we may obtain this faith, the ministry of teaching the Gospel and administering the Sacraments was instituted.

MARCH 6

Psalm 142:2-3

[2]קוֹלִי אֶל־יְהוָה אֶזְעָק קוֹלִי אֶל־יְהוָה אֶתְחַנָּן׃
[3]אֶשְׁפֹּךְ לְפָנָיו שִׂיחִי צָרָתִי לְפָנָיו אַגִּיד׃

קוֹל (1 sg sf): voice – זָעַק (qal impf 1 sg): call out – חָנַן (hithp impf 1 sg): ask for mercy – שָׁפַךְ (qal impf 1 sg): pour out – שִׂיחַ (1 sg sf): complaint – צָרָה (1 sg sf): trouble – נָגַד (hiph impf 1 sg): tell

---

Mark 14:36

καὶ ἔλεγεν· αββα ὁ πατήρ, πάντα δυνατά σοι· παρένεγκε τὸ ποτήριον τοῦτο ἀπ' ἐμοῦ· ἀλλ' οὐ τί ἐγὼ θέλω ἀλλὰ τί σύ.

δυνατός: possible – παραφέρω (aor imv 2 sg): remove – ποτήριον: cup – θέλω (pres ind 1 sg): will, desire

---

Large Catechism III 26

But where there is to be a true prayer, there must be seriousness. People must feel their distress, and such distress presses them and compels them to call and cry out. Then prayer will be made willingly, as it ought to be. People will need no teaching about how to prepare for it and to reach the proper devotion.

Isaiah 53:7

נִגַּשׂ וְהוּא נַעֲנֶה וְלֹא יִפְתַּח־פִּיו
כַּשֶּׂה לַטֶּבַח יוּבָל וּכְרָחֵל לִפְנֵי גֹזְזֶיהָ נֶאֱלָמָה
וְלֹא יִפְתַּח פִּיו׃

נָגַשׂ (niph pf 3 sg): be oppressed – עָנָה (niph ptcp): be afflicted – פָּתַח (qal impf 3 sg): open – פֶּה (3 sg sf): mouth – שֶׂה: sheep – טֶבַח: slaughter – יָבַל (hoph impf 3 sg): be led – רָחֵל: ewe – גָּזַז (qal ptcp pl + 3 sg sf): shear – אָלַם (niph pf 3 sg f): be mute

Romans 5:9-10

9πολλῷ οὖν μᾶλλον δικαιωθέντες νῦν ἐν τῷ αἵματι αὐτοῦ
σωθησόμεθα δι' αὐτοῦ ἀπὸ τῆς ὀργῆς. 10εἰ γὰρ ἐχθροὶ ὄντες
κατηλλάγημεν τῷ θεῷ διὰ τοῦ θανάτου τοῦ υἱοῦ αὐτοῦ,
πολλῷ μᾶλλον καταλλαγέντες σωθησόμεθα ἐν τῇ ζωῇ αὐτοῦ·

δικαιόω (aor pass ptcp pl): justify – αἷμα: blood – σῴζω (fut pass 1 pl): save – ὀργή: wrath – ἐχθρός: enemy – καταλλάσσω (aor pass ind 1 pl/aor pass ptcp pl): reconcile – θάνατος: death – ζωή: life

Formula of Concord Ep V 5

But the Gospel is properly the kind of teaching that shows what a person who has not kept the Law (and therefore is condemned by it) is to believe. It teaches that Christ has paid for and made satisfaction for all sins [Rom 5:9]. Christ has gained and acquired for an individual—without any of his own merit—forgiveness of sins, righteousness that avails before God, and eternal life [Rom 5:10].

Leviticus 16:14-15

14 וְלָקַח מִדַּם הַפָּר וְהִזָּה בְאֶצְבָּעוֹ עַל־פְּנֵי הַכַּפֹּרֶת קֵדְמָה
וְלִפְנֵי הַכַּפֹּרֶת יַזֶּה שֶׁבַע־פְּעָמִים מִן־הַדָּם בְּאֶצְבָּעוֹ׃
15 וְשָׁחַט אֶת־שְׂעִיר הַחַטָּאת אֲשֶׁר לָעָם וְהֵבִיא אֶת־דָּמוֹ
אֶל־מִבֵּית לַפָּרֹכֶת וְעָשָׂה אֶת־דָּמוֹ כַּאֲשֶׁר עָשָׂה לְדַם
הַפָּר וְהִזָּה אֹתוֹ עַל־הַכַּפֹּרֶת וְלִפְנֵי הַכַּפֹּרֶת׃

דָּם: blood – פַּר: bull – נָזָה (hiph v-c pf 3 sg/hiph impf 3 sg): sprinkle – אֶצְבַּע: finger – כַּפֹּרֶת: atonement cover – קֵדְמָה: on the east side – לִפְנֵי: before – שֶׁבַע־פְּעָמִים: seven times – שָׁחַט (qal v-c pf 3 sg): slaughter – שָׂעִיר: goat – חַטָּאת: sin offering – בּוֹא (hiph v-c pf 3 sg): bring – מִבֵּית: behind – פָּרֹכֶת: curtain

---

Romans 3:25

ὃν προέθετο ὁ θεὸς ἱλαστήριον διὰ [τῆς] πίστεως ἐν τῷ αὐτοῦ αἵματι εἰς ἔνδειξιν τῆς δικαιοσύνης αὐτοῦ διὰ τὴν πάρεσιν τῶν προγεγονότων ἁμαρτημάτων.

προτίθημι (aor mid 3 sg): present – ἱλαστήριον: sacrifice of atonement – ἔνδειξις: sign, proof – πάρεσις: passing over, forbearance – προγίνομαι (pf ptcp): committed in former times – ἁμάρτημα: sin

---

Apology XX 87

As the saying goes, at the top of his voice, Paul cries out that sins are freely forgiven for Christ's sake. "It depends on faith," he says, "in order that the promise may rest on grace and be guaranteed" (Rom 4:16; see also Rom 3:24-25).

March 9

Psalm 42:2

כְּאַיָּל תַּעֲרֹג עַל־אֲפִֽיקֵי־מָ֑יִם
כֵּן נַפְשִׁי תַעֲרֹג אֵלֶ֣יךָ אֱלֹהִֽים׃

אַיָּל: deer – עָרַג (qal impf 3 sg f): long for – אָפִיק (cst pl): stream – מַיִם: water – נֶפֶשׁ (1 sg sf): soul

---

Revelation 7:17

ὅτι τὸ ἀρνίον τὸ ἀνὰ μέσον τοῦ θρόνου ποιμανεῖ αὐτοὺς καὶ ὁδηγήσει αὐτοὺς ἐπὶ ζωῆς πηγὰς ὑδάτων, καὶ ἐξαλείψει ὁ θεὸς πᾶν δάκρυον ἐκ τῶν ὀφθαλμῶν αὐτῶν.

ἀρνίον: Lamb – ἀνὰ μέσον: in the center – ποιμαίνω (fut 3 sg): be a shepherd – ὁδηγέω (fut 3 sg): lead – ζωή: life – πηγή: spring – ὕδωρ: water – ἐξαλείφω (fut 3 sg): wipe away – δάκρυον: tear – ὀφθαλμός: eye

---

Large Catechism V 32

When I urge you to go to Confession, I am doing nothing else than urging you to be a Christian. If I have brought you to the point of being a Christian, I have thereby also brought you to Confession. For those who really desire to be true Christians, to be rid of their sins, and to have a cheerful conscience already possess the true hunger and thirst. They reach for the bread, just as Ps 42:1 says of a hunted deer, burning in the heat with thirst.

March 10

Exodus 25:21-22

21 וְנָתַתָּ אֶת־הַכַּפֹּרֶת עַל־הָאָרֹן מִלְמָעְלָה וְאֶל־הָאָרֹן
תִּתֵּן אֶת־הָעֵדֻת אֲשֶׁר אֶתֵּן אֵלֶיךָ׃ 22 וְנוֹעַדְתִּי לְךָ
שָׁם וְדִבַּרְתִּי אִתְּךָ מֵעַל הַכַּפֹּרֶת מִבֵּין שְׁנֵי הַכְּרֻבִים
אֲשֶׁר עַל־אֲרֹן הָעֵדֻת אֵת כָּל־אֲשֶׁר אֲצַוֶּה אוֹתְךָ אֶל־בְּנֵי
יִשְׂרָאֵל׃

נָתַן (qal v-c pf 2 sg): put – כַּפֹּרֶת: atonement cover – אֲרוֹן: ark – מִלְמַעְלָה (adv): from above – עֵדוּת: testimony – יָעַד (niph v-c pf 1 sg): meet with – דָּבַר (pi v-c pf 1 sg): speak – צָוָה (pi impf 1 sg): command

---

Hebrews 10:19-20

19 Ἔχοντες οὖν, ἀδελφοί, παρρησίαν εἰς τὴν εἴσοδον τῶν
ἁγίων ἐν τῷ αἵματι Ἰησοῦ, 20 ἣν ἐνεκαίνισεν ἡμῖν ὁδὸν
πρόσφατον καὶ ζῶσαν διὰ τοῦ καταπετάσματος, τοῦτ᾽ ἔστιν
τῆς σαρκὸς αὐτοῦ.

παρρησία: confidence, boldness – εἴσοδος: entrance – ἅγιος (pl n): holy = the Most Holy Place – αἷμα: blood – ἐγκαινίζω (aor ind 3 sg): open – ὁδός: way – πρόσφατος: new – ζάω (pres ptcp): living – καταπέτασμα: curtain – σάρξ: flesh, body

---

Apology V (III) 135

The Gospel must also be retained, that through Christ we have access to the Father.

MARCH 11

Exodus 12:42

לֵיל שִׁמֻּרִים הוּא לַיהוָה לְהוֹצִיאָם מֵאֶרֶץ מִצְרָיִם
הוּא־הַלַּיְלָה הַזֶּה לַיהוָה שִׁמֻּרִים לְכָל־בְּנֵי יִשְׂרָאֵל
לְדֹרֹתָם׃

לַיְלָה (cst sg): night – שִׁמֻּר (pl): watching, vigil – יָצָא (hiph inf cst + 3 pl sf): lead out – דּוֹר (pl + 3 pl sf): generation

---

1 Corinthians 11:23-25

23 Ἐγὼ γὰρ παρέλαβον ἀπὸ τοῦ κυρίου, ὃ καὶ παρέδωκα ὑμῖν,
ὅτι ὁ κύριος Ἰησοῦς ἐν τῇ νυκτὶ ᾗ παρεδίδετο ἔλαβεν ἄρτον
24 καὶ εὐχαριστήσας ἔκλασεν καὶ εἶπεν· τοῦτό μού ἐστιν τὸ
σῶμα τὸ ὑπὲρ ὑμῶν· τοῦτο ποιεῖτε εἰς τὴν ἐμὴν ἀνάμνησιν.
25 ὡσαύτως καὶ τὸ ποτήριον μετὰ τὸ δειπνῆσαι λέγων· τοῦτο
τὸ ποτήριον ἡ καινὴ διαθήκη ἐστὶν ἐν τῷ ἐμῷ αἵματι· τοῦτο
ποιεῖτε, ὁσάκις ἐὰν πίνητε, εἰς τὴν ἐμὴν ἀνάμνησιν.

παραλαμβάνω (aor ind 1 sg): receive – ἄρτος: bread – εὐχαριστέω (aor ptcp): give thanks – κλάω (aor ind 3 sg): break – ἀνάμνησις: reminder, remembrance – ὡσαύτως: similarly – ποτήριον: cup – δειπνέω (aor inf): eat – διαθήκη: covenant – ὁσάκις: as often as – πίνω (pres subj 2 pl): drink

---

Augsburg Confession X

Our churches teach that the body and blood of Christ are truly present and distributed to those who eat the Lord's Supper [1 Cor 10:16]. They reject those who teach otherwise.

MARCH 12

Exodus 12:13

וְהָיָה הַדָּם לָכֶם לְאֹת עַל הַבָּתִּים אֲשֶׁר אַתֶּם שָׁם
וְרָאִיתִי אֶת־הַדָּם וּפָסַחְתִּי עֲלֵכֶם וְלֹא־יִהְיֶה בָכֶם נֶגֶף
לְמַשְׁחִית בְּהַכֹּתִי בְּאֶרֶץ מִצְרָיִם׃

דָּם: blood – אוֹת: sign – בַּיִת (pl): house – רָאָה (qal v-c pf 1 sg): see – פָּסַח (qal v-c pf 1 sg): pass over – נֶגֶף: plague – מַשְׁחִית: destruction – נָכָה (hiph inf cst + 1 sg sf): strike

---

Romans 8:1-2

1Οὐδὲν ἄρα νῦν κατάκριμα τοῖς ἐν Χριστῷ Ἰησοῦ.
2ὁ γὰρ νόμος τοῦ πνεύματος τῆς ζωῆς ἐν Χριστῷ
Ἰησοῦ ἠλευθέρωσέν σε ἀπὸ τοῦ νόμου τῆς ἁμαρτίας
καὶ τοῦ θανάτου.

κατάκριμα: condemnation – νόμος: law – ζωή: life – ἐλευθερόω (aor ind 3 sg): set free – ἁμαρτία: sin – θάνατος: death

---

Apology II (I) 38-40

They *[the adversaries]* argue that concupiscence is a penalty, but not a sin. Luther maintains that it is a sin. . . . Besides, Paul says in Rom 7:7, “I would not have known what it is to covet [concupiscence] if the law had not said, ‘You shall not covet.’” Likewise, “I see in my members another law waging war against the law of my mind and making me captive to the law of sin that dwells in my members” (Rom 7:23). No amount of sophistry can overthrow these points. They clearly call concupiscence sin, which is not charged against those who are in Christ [Rom 8:1].

March 13

Psalm 22:7-9

7 וְאָנֹכִי תוֹלַעַת וְלֹא־אִישׁ חֶרְפַּת אָדָם וּבְזוּי עָם׃
8 כָּל־רֹאַי יַלְעִגוּ לִי יַפְטִירוּ בְשָׂפָה יָנִיעוּ רֹאשׁ׃
9 גֹּל אֶל־יְהוָה יְפַלְּטֵהוּ יַצִּילֵהוּ כִּי חָפֵץ בּוֹ׃

תּוֹלַעַת: worm – חֶרְפָּה (cst sg): taunt, scorn – בָּזָה (qal pass ptcp cst): despised – לָעַג (hiph impf 3 pl): mock – פָּטַר (hiph impf 3 pl): separate = open the mouth wide insultingly – שָׂפָה: lip – נוּעַ (hiph impf 3 pl): shake – גָּלַל: roll = trusting the Lord; MT: גֹּל (qal imv); LXX: גַּל (qal pf 3 sg) – פָּלַט (pi impf 3 sg + 3 sg sf): rescue – נָצַל (hiph impf 3 sg + 3 sg sf): deliver – חָפֵץ (qal pf 3 sg): delight

---

Matthew 27:41-42

41 ὁμοίως καὶ οἱ ἀρχιερεῖς ἐμπαίζοντες μετὰ τῶν
γραμματέων καὶ πρεσβυτέρων ἔλεγον· 42 ἄλλους
ἔσωσεν, ἑαυτὸν οὐ δύναται σῶσαι· βασιλεὺς Ἰσραήλ
ἐστιν, καταβάτω νῦν ἀπὸ τοῦ σταυροῦ καὶ πιστεύσομεν
ἐπ᾽ αὐτόν.

ἐμπαίζω (pres ptcp pl): ridicule – γραμματεύς: scholar versed in the law – πρεσβύτερος: elder – καταβαίνω (aor imv 3 sg): come down – σταυρός: cross

---

Formula of Concord SD VIII 10

These are properties of the human nature: being a bodily creation or creature, flesh and blood, finite and located in one place; it suffers, dies, ascends, and descends . . .

Isaiah 50:5-6

5 אֲדֹנָי יְהוִה פָּתַח־לִי אֹזֶן
וְאָנֹכִי לֹא מָרִיתִי אָחוֹר לֹא נְסוּגֹתִי׃
6 גֵּוִי נָתַתִּי לְמַכִּים וּלְחָיַי לְמֹרְטִים
פָּנַי לֹא הִסְתַּרְתִּי מִכְּלִמּוֹת וָרֹק׃

פָּתַח (qal pf 3 sg): open – אֹזֶן: ear – מָרָה (qal pf 1 sg): be rebellious – אָחוֹר (adv): back – סוּג (niph pf 1 sg): turn away – גֵּו (1 sg sf): back – נָכָה (hiph ptcp pl): beat – לְחִי (pl + 1 sg sf): cheek – מָרַט (qal ptcp pl): make bare (by pulling out the beard) – פָּנִים (1 sg sf): face – סָתַר (hiph pf 1 sg): hide – כְּלִמָּה: mocking – רֹק: spit

---

Hebrews 2:17

ὅθεν ὤφειλεν κατὰ πάντα τοῖς ἀδελφοῖς ὁμοιωθῆναι, ἵνα ἐλεήμων γένηται καὶ πιστὸς ἀρχιερεὺς τὰ πρὸς τὸν θεὸν εἰς τὸ ἱλάσκεσθαι τὰς ἁμαρτίας τοῦ λαοῦ.

ὅθεν: therefore – ὀφείλω (impf ind): be obligated – ὁμοιόω (aor pass inf): make like – ἐλεήμων: merciful – γίνομαι (aor subj): become – πιστός: faithful – ἀρχιερεύς: high priest – τὰ πρός: in respect to – ἱλάσκομαι (pres inf): make atonement for

---

Formula of Concord SD VIII 50-51

Some have wished to argue that even in the personal union with divinity it *[Christ's human nature]* has nothing else and nothing more than only its natural, essential properties according to which it is in all things like its brethren [Heb 2:17]. . . . This opinion is false and incorrect.

March 15

Psalm 93:2

נָכוֹן כִּסְאֲךָ מֵאָז מֵעוֹלָם אָתָּה׃

כּוּן (niph pf 3 sg): be established – כִּסֵּא (2 sg sf): throne – מֵאָז (adv): of old – עוֹלָם: eternity

---

Revelation 22:13

ἐγὼ τὸ ἄλφα καὶ τὸ ὦ, ὁ πρῶτος καὶ ὁ ἔσχατος, ἡ ἀρχὴ καὶ τὸ τέλος.

ὦ: last letter of Greek alphabet – πρῶτος: first – ἔσχατος: last – ἀρχή: beginning – τέλος: end

---

Formula of Concord SD VIII 7

We believe, teach, and confess that now, in this one undivided person of Christ, there are two distinct natures: the divine, which is from eternity, and the human, which in time was received into the unity of the person of God's Son.

Psalm 25:6-7

6זְכֹר־רַחֲמֶיךָ יְהוָה וַחֲסָדֶיךָ כִּי מֵעוֹלָם הֵמָּה׃
7חַטֹּאות נְעוּרַי וּפְשָׁעַי אַל־תִּזְכֹּר כְּחַסְדְּךָ זְכָר־לִי־אַתָּה
לְמַעַן טוּבְךָ יְהוָה׃

זָכַר (qal imv sg/qal juss 2 sg): remember – רַחֲמִים (2 sg sf): mercy – חֶסֶד (pl + 2 sg sf/sg + 2 sg sf): faithful love – עוֹלָם: eternity – חַטָּאת (cst pl): sin – נְעוּרִים (1 sg sf): youth – טוּב (2 sg sf): goodness

---

Luke 1:70-72

70καθὼς ἐλάλησεν διὰ στόματος τῶν ἁγίων ἀπ' αἰῶνος
προφητῶν αὐτοῦ, 71σωτηρίαν ἐξ ἐχθρῶν ἡμῶν καὶ ἐκ χειρὸς
πάντων τῶν μισούντων ἡμᾶς, 72ποιῆσαι ἔλεος μετὰ τῶν
πατέρων ἡμῶν καὶ μνησθῆναι διαθήκης ἁγίας αὐτοῦ . . .

λαλέω (aor 3 sg): speak – στόμα: mouth – ἅγιος: holy – αἰών: age long past – σωτηρία: salvation – ἐχθρός (pl): enemy – χείρ: hand – μισέω (pres ptcp pl): hate – ποίεω (aor inf): show – ἔλεος: mercy – μιμνῄσκομαι (aor pass inf): remember – διαθήκη: covenant

---

Apology V (III) 208-209

Namely, flesh and righteousness of the flesh cannot endure God's judgment. Jonah 2:8 also says, "Those who pay regard to vain idols forsake their hope of steadfast love," that is, all confidence is empty, except confidence in mercy. Mercy delivers us; our own merits, our own efforts, do not.

March 17

Psalm 91:1-2

[1]יֹשֵׁב בְּסֵתֶר עֶלְיוֹן בְּצֵל שַׁדַּי יִתְלוֹנָן׃
[2]אֹמַר לַיהוָה מַחְסִי וּמְצוּדָתִי אֱלֹהַי אֶבְטַח־בּוֹ׃

יָשַׁב (qal ptcp sg): one who dwells – סֵתֶר: hiding place – עֶלְיוֹן: the Most High – צֵל (cst sg): shadow – שַׁדַּי: the Almighty – לִין (hithpolal impf 3 sg): remain – אָמַר (qal impf 1 sg): say – מַחְסֶה (1 sg sf): refuge – מְצוּדָה (1 sg sf): fortress – בָּטַח (qal impf 1 sg): trust

---

Romans 5:1-2

[1]Δικαιωθέντες οὖν ἐκ πίστεως εἰρήνην ἔχομεν πρὸς
τὸν θεὸν διὰ τοῦ κυρίου ἡμῶν Ἰησοῦ Χριστοῦ [2]δι᾽ οὗ
καὶ τὴν προσαγωγὴν ἐσχήκαμεν [τῇ πίστει] εἰς τὴν
χάριν ταύτην ἐν ᾗ ἑστήκαμεν καὶ καυχώμεθα ἐπ᾽ ἐλπίδι
τῆς δόξης τοῦ θεοῦ.

δικαιόω (aor pass ptcp pl): justify – εἰρήνη: peace – ἔχω: (pres ind 1 pl/pf ind 1 pl): have – προσαγωγή: access – ἵστημι (pf ind 1 pl with pres meaning): stand – καυχάομαι (pres ind 1 pl): boast – ἐλπίς: hope

---

Augsburg Confession XX 15-16

Consciences cannot be set at rest through any works, but only by faith, when they take the sure ground that for Christ's sake they have a gracious God. As Paul teaches, "since we have been justified by faith, we have peace with God" (Rom 5:1).

Exodus 28:12

וְשַׂמְתָּ אֶת־שְׁתֵּי הָאֲבָנִים עַל כִּתְפֹת הָאֵפֹד אַבְנֵי זִכָּרֹן
לִבְנֵי יִשְׂרָאֵל וְנָשָׂא אַהֲרֹן אֶת־שְׁמוֹתָם לִפְנֵי יְהוָה
עַל־שְׁתֵּי כְתֵפָיו לְזִכָּרֹן׃

שִׂים (qal v-c pf 2 sg): place – שְׁתַּיִם (cst): two – אֶבֶן (pl/cst pl): stone – כָּתֵף (cst pl/pl + 3 sg sf): shoulder piece – אֵפֹד: ephod – זִכָּרוֹן: remembrance – נָשָׂא (qal v-c pf 3 sg): bear – שֵׁם (pl + 3 pl sf): name – לִפְנֵי: before

---

Hebrews 7:24-25

24 ὁ δὲ διὰ τὸ μένειν αὐτὸν εἰς τὸν αἰῶνα ἀπαράβατον ἔχει
τὴν ἱερωσύνην· 25 ὅθεν καὶ σῴζειν εἰς τὸ παντελὲς δύναται
τοὺς προσερχομένους δι’ αὐτοῦ τῷ θεῷ, πάντοτε ζῶν εἰς τὸ
ἐντυγχάνειν ὑπὲρ αὐτῶν.

μένω (pres inf): remain – αἰών: eternity – ἀπαράβατος: permanent, unchangeable – ἱερωσύνη: priesthood – ὅθεν: therefore – σῴζω (pres inf): save – παντελής: complete, absolute – δύναμαι (pres ind 3 sg): be able – προσέρχομαι (pres ptcp acc pl): come to – πάντοτε: always – ζάω (pres ptcp): live – ἐντυγχάνω (pres inf): intercede

---

Apology V (III) 212

So prayer relies upon God’s mercy, when we believe that we are heard for Christ’s sake. He is our High Priest, as He Himself says, “Whatever you ask in My name, this I will do, that the Father may be glorified in the Son. If you ask Me anything in My name, I will do it” (John 14:13-14). Without this High Priest we cannot approach the Father.

March 19

Isaiah 53:12

לָכֵן אֲחַלֶּק־לוֹ בָרַבִּים וְאֶת־עֲצוּמִים יְחַלֵּק שָׁלָל
תַּחַת אֲשֶׁר הֶעֱרָה לַמָּוֶת נַפְשׁוֹ וְאֶת־פֹּשְׁעִים נִמְנָה
וְהוּא חֵטְא־רַבִּים נָשָׂא וְלַפֹּשְׁעִים יַפְגִּיעַ׃

חָלַק (pi impf 1 sg/3 sg): divide as one's portion – רַב (pl): the great – עָצוּם (pl): the strong – שָׁלָל: as his spoils – תַּחַת אֲשֶׁר: because – עָרָה (hiph pf 3 sg): pour out – נֶפֶשׁ: life – פָּשַׁע (qal ptcp pl): transgress – מָנָה (niph pf 3 sg): be numbered with – חֵטְא: sin – נָשָׂא (qal pf 3 sg): bear – פָּגַע (hiph impf 3 sg): make intercession for

John 3:36

ὁ πιστεύων εἰς τὸν υἱὸν ἔχει ζωὴν αἰώνιον· ὁ δὲ ἀπειθῶν τῷ υἱῷ οὐκ ὄψεται ζωήν, ἀλλ᾽ ἡ ὀργὴ τοῦ θεοῦ μένει ἐπ᾽ αὐτόν.

πιστεύω (pres ptcp): believe – υἱός: son – ζωή: life – αἰώνιος: eternal – ἀπειθέω (pres act ptcp): be an unbeliever – ὁράω (fut dep ind): see – ὀργή: wrath – μένω: remain

Apology V (III) 235

Here the adversaries reply that eternal life is called a reward and that, therefore, it is merited in a wholly deserving way *(de condigno)* by good works. We reply briefly and plainly. Paul calls eternal life a "gift" (Rom 6:23), because by the righteousness presented for Christ's sake, we are made at the same time sons of God and coheirs of Christ. As John says, "Whoever believes in the Son has eternal life" (John 3:36).

MARCH 20

Exodus 24:8

וַיִּקַּח מֹשֶׁה אֶת־הַדָּם וַיִּזְרֹק עַל־הָעָם וַיֹּאמֶר הִנֵּה דַם־
הַבְּרִית אֲשֶׁר כָּרַת יְהוָה עִמָּכֶם עַל כָּל־הַדְּבָרִים
הָאֵלֶּה׃

לָקַח (qal v-c impf 3 sg): take – דָּם: blood – זָרַק (qal v-c impf 3 sg): sprinkle – בְּרִית: covenant – כָּרַת (qal pf 3 sg): cut = make a covenant

---

John 19:34-35

34 ἀλλ’ εἷς τῶν στρατιωτῶν λόγχῃ αὐτοῦ τὴν πλευρὰν
ἔνυξεν, καὶ ἐξῆλθεν εὐθὺς αἷμα καὶ ὕδωρ. 35 καὶ ὁ ἑωρακὼς
μεμαρτύρηκεν, καὶ ἀληθινὴ αὐτοῦ ἐστιν ἡ μαρτυρία, καὶ
ἐκεῖνος οἶδεν ὅτι ἀληθῆ λέγει, ἵνα καὶ ὑμεῖς πιστεύ[σ]ητε.

εἷς: one – στρατιώτης: soldier – λόγχη: spear – πλευρά: side – νύσσω (aor ind 3 sg): pierce – ἐξέρχομαι (aor ind 3 sg): come out – αἷμα: blood – ὕδωρ: water – ὁράω (pf ptcp): see

---

Formula of Concord SD VII 53

The words of Luke and Paul, “This cup is the new covenant in My blood,” can have no other meaning than what St. Matthew and St. Mark give: “This [namely, what you orally drink out of the cup] is My blood of the covenant,” whereby I establish, seal, and confirm with you this: My testament and new covenant (i.e., the forgiveness of sins).

Isaiah 53:10

וַיהוָה חָפֵץ דַּכְּאוֹ הֶחֱלִי אִם־תָּשִׂים אָשָׁם נַפְשׁוֹ
יִרְאֶה זֶרַע יַאֲרִיךְ יָמִים וְחֵפֶץ יְהוָה בְּיָדוֹ יִצְלָח׃

חָפֵץ (qal pf 3 sg): be pleased – דָּכָא (pi inf cst + 3 sg sf): crush – חָלָה (hiph pf 3 sg): cause to suffer – שִׂים (qal impf 2 sg): though you make – אָשָׁם: guilt offering – נֶפֶשׁ: life – רָאָה (qal impf 3 sg): see – זֶרַע: offspring – אָרַךְ (hiph impf 3 sg): prolong – יוֹם (pl): day – חֵפֶץ: the will – צָלַח (qal impf 3 sg): prosper

Romans 14:9

εἰς τοῦτο γὰρ Χριστὸς ἀπέθανεν καὶ ἔζησεν, ἵνα καὶ νεκρῶν καὶ ζώντων κυριεύσῃ.

ἀποθνῄσκω (aor ind 3 sg): die – ζάω (aor ind 3 sg/pres act ptcp): return to life, live – κυριεύω (aor subj 3 sg): be lord of

Apology XXIV (XII) 23

Isaiah interprets the Law, so that we may know Christ's death is truly a satisfaction for our sins, or remedy, and that the ceremonies of the Law are not. He says, "When his soul makes an offering for sin, he shall see his offspring," and so on (Isa 53:10).

March 22

Isaiah 43:11

אָנֹכִי אָנֹכִי יְהוָה וְאֵין מִבַּלְעָדַי מוֹשִׁיעַ׃

מִבַּלְעֲדֵי: (1 sg sf): apart from – יָשַׁע (hiph ptcp): savior

Acts 4:12

καὶ οὐκ ἔστιν ἐν ἄλλῳ οὐδενὶ ἡ σωτηρία, οὐδὲ γὰρ ὄνομά ἐστιν ἕτερον ὑπὸ τὸν οὐρανὸν τὸ δεδομένον ἐν ἀνθρώποις ἐν ᾧ δεῖ σωθῆναι ἡμᾶς.

ἄλλος: other, another – οὐδείς (dat sg): no one – σωτηρία: salvation – ἕτερος: other – δίδωμι (pf pass ptcp): give – δεῖ: it is necessary – σῴζω (aor pass inf): save

Apology IV (II) 98

Christ's name is received only by faith. Therefore, we are saved by confidence in Christ's name, and not by confidence in our works. For "the name" here means the cause that is mentioned, because of which salvation is gained.

March 23

Psalm 100:3

דְּעוּ כִּֽי־יְהוָה הוּא אֱלֹהִים הֽוּא־עָשָׂנוּ וְלֹא אֲנַחְנוּ
עַמּוֹ וְצֹאן מַרְעִיתֽוֹ׃

יָדַע (qal imv pl): know – עָשָׂה (qal pf 3 sg + 1 pl sf): make – אֲנַחְנוּ: we – עַם (3 sg sf): people – מַרְעִית (3 sg sf): pasture

---

1 Peter 1:18-19

18εἰδότες ὅτι οὐ φθαρτοῖς, ἀργυρίῳ ἢ χρυσίῳ, ἐλυτρώθητε
ἐκ τῆς ματαίας ὑμῶν ἀναστροφῆς πατροπαραδότου, 19ἀλλὰ
τιμίῳ αἵματι ὡς ἀμνοῦ ἀμώμου καὶ ἀσπίλου Χριστοῦ . . .

οἶδα (pf ptcp with pres meaning): know – φθαρτός: perishable – ἀργύριον: silver – χρυσίον: gold – λυτρόω (aor pass 2 pl): redeem – μάταιος: empty – ἀναστροφή: way of life – πατροπαράδοτος: inherited from your ancestors – τίμιος: precious – αἷμα: blood – ἀμνός: lamb – ἄμωμος: unblemished – ἄσπιλος: spotless

---

Large Catechism II 31

He suffered, died, and was buried so that He might make satisfaction for me and pay what I owe [1 Cor 15:3-4], not with silver or gold, but with His own precious blood [1 Pet 1:18-19].

March 24

Psalm 116:3-4

3 אֲפָפ֤וּנִי ׀ חֶבְלֵי־מָ֗וֶת וּמְצָרֵ֣י שְׁא֣וֹל מְצָא֑וּנִי צָרָ֖ה וְיָג֣וֹן
אֶמְצָֽא׃
4 וּבְשֵׁם־יְהוָ֥ה אֶקְרָ֑א אָֽנָּ֥ה יְ֝הוָ֗ה מַלְּטָ֥ה נַפְשִֽׁי׃

אָפַף (qal pf 3 pl + 1 sg sf): surround – חֶבֶל (cst pl): cord – מֵצַר (cst pl): anguish – שְׁאוֹל: the grave – מָצָא (qal pf 3 pl/qal impf 1 sg): find – צָרָה: trouble – יָגוֹן: sorrow – אָנָּה: oh! – מָלַט (pi imv sg): deliver – נֶפֶשׁ (1 sg sf): soul = me

---

Matthew 26:38-39

38 τότε λέγει αὐτοῖς· περίλυπός ἐστιν ἡ ψυχή μου
ἕως θανάτου· μείνατε ὧδε καὶ γρηγορεῖτε μετ' ἐμοῦ.
39 καὶ προελθὼν μικρὸν ἔπεσεν ἐπὶ πρόσωπον αὐτοῦ
προσευχόμενος καὶ λέγων· πάτερ μου, εἰ δυνατόν ἐστιν,
παρελθάτω ἀπ' ἐμοῦ τὸ ποτήριον τοῦτο· πλὴν οὐχ ὡς ἐγὼ
θέλω ἀλλ' ὡς σύ.

περίλυπος: very sad – μένω (aor imv 2 pl): remain – γρηγορέω (pres imv 2 pl): keep watch – προέρχομαι (aor ptcp): go farther – μικρόν (adv): a little – πίπτω (aor ind 3 sg): fall – ἐπὶ πρόσωπον: with his face to the ground – προσεύχομαι (pres ptcp): pray – δυνατός: possible – παρέρχομαι (aor imv 3 sg): pass – ποτήριον: cup – πλήν: nevertheless – θέλω (pres ind 1 sg): desire

---

Apology XXIV (XII) 23

In the Law this *[the sacrifice]* illustrated that a certain Victim was to come to make satisfaction for our sins and reconcile God.

March 25

Leviticus 16:30

כִּי־בַיּוֹם הַזֶּה יְכַפֵּר עֲלֵיכֶם לְטַהֵר אֶתְכֶם מִכֹּל
חַטֹּאתֵיכֶם לִפְנֵי יְהוָה תִּטְהָרוּ׃

כָּפַר (pi impf): one will make atonement = atonement will be made – עַל (2 pl sf): for you – טָהֵר (pi inf cst): cleanse – חַטָּאת (pl + 2 pl sf): sin – טָהֵר (qal impf 2 pl): be clean

---

John 19:30

ὅτε οὖν ἔλαβεν τὸ ὄξος [ὁ] Ἰησοῦς εἶπεν· τετέλεσται, καὶ κλίνας τὴν κεφαλὴν παρέδωκεν τὸ πνεῦμα.

λαμβάνω (aor ind 3 sg): receive – ὄξος: sour wine – τελέω (pf pass ind 3 sg): finish, complete – κλίνω (aor act ptcp): bow – παραδίδωμι (aor ind 3 sg): hand over, give up – πνεῦμα: spirit

---

Apology XXIV (XII) 24

Let this remain the case: Christ's death alone is truly an atoning sacrifice. For the Levitical atoning sacrifices were so called only to illustrate a future remedy.

MARCH 26

Jeremiah 14:7

אִם־עֲוֺנֵינוּ עָנוּ בָנוּ יְהוָה עֲשֵׂה לְמַעַן שְׁמֶךָ
כִּי־רַבּוּ מְשׁוּבֹתֵינוּ לְךָ חָטָאנוּ׃

עָוֺן (pl + 1 pl sf): sin (as guilt) – עָנָה (qal pf 3 pl): testify + בְּ: against – עָשָׂה (qal imv sg): act – לְמַעַן: for the sake of – שֵׁם: name – רָבַב (qal pf 3 pl): be many, great – מְשׁוּבָה (pl + 1 pl sf): backsliding, apostasy

1 John 4:9-10

9ἐν τούτῳ ἐφανερώθη ἡ ἀγάπη τοῦ θεοῦ ἐν ἡμῖν, ὅτι
τὸν υἱὸν αὐτοῦ τὸν μονογενῆ ἀπέσταλκεν ὁ θεὸς εἰς
τὸν κόσμον ἵνα ζήσωμεν δι' αὐτοῦ. 10ἐν τούτῳ ἐστὶν
ἡ ἀγάπη, οὐχ ὅτι ἡμεῖς ἠγαπήκαμεν τὸν θεὸν ἀλλ' ὅτι
αὐτὸς ἠγάπησεν ἡμᾶς καὶ ἀπέστειλεν τὸν υἱὸν αὐτοῦ
ἱλασμὸν περὶ τῶν ἁμαρτιῶν ἡμῶν.

φανερόω (aor pass 3 sg): reveal, make known – μονογενής: only-begotten – ἀποστέλλω (pf ind 3 sg/aor ind 3 sg): send – κόσμος: world – ζάω (aor subj 1 pl): live – ἀγαπάω (pf ind 1 pl/aor ind 3 sg): love – ἱλασμός: atoning sacrifice – ἁμαρτία: sin

Apology V (III) 8

God is not loved until we receive mercy through faith. Not until then does He become someone we can love.

Ezekiel 36:25

וְזָרַקְתִּי עֲלֵיכֶם מַיִם טְהוֹרִים וּטְהַרְתֶּם מִכֹּל טֻמְאוֹתֵיכֶם
וּמִכָּל־גִּלּוּלֵיכֶם אֲטַהֵר אֶתְכֶם׃

זָרַק (qal v-c pf 1 sg): sprinkle – טָהוֹר (pl): clean – טָהֵר (qal v-c pf 2 pl): be clean, (pi impf 1 sg): cleanse – טֻמְאָה (pl + 2 pl sf): uncleanness – גִּלּוּל (pl + 2 pl sf): idol

---

Hebrews 9:13-14

13 εἰ γὰρ τὸ αἷμα τράγων καὶ ταύρων καὶ σποδὸς δαμάλεως
ῥαντίζουσα τοὺς κεκοινωμένους ἁγιάζει πρὸς τὴν τῆς
σαρκὸς καθαρότητα, 14 πόσῳ μᾶλλον τὸ αἷμα τοῦ Χριστοῦ,
ὃς διὰ πνεύματος αἰωνίου ἑαυτὸν προσήνεγκεν ἄμωμον
τῷ θεῷ, καθαριεῖ τὴν συνείδησιν ἡμῶν ἀπὸ νεκρῶν ἔργων
εἰς τὸ λατρεύειν θεῷ ζῶντι.

τράγος: he-goat – ταῦρος: bull – σποδός: ashes – δάμαλις: heifer – ῥαντίζω (pres ptcp sg f): sprinkle – κοινόω (pf pass ptcp): make ceremonially unclean – ἁγιάζω (pres 3 sg): sanctify – σάρξ: flesh – καθαρότης: (ritual) purity – πόσῳ μᾶλλον: how much more – αἰώνιος: eternal – προσφέρω (aor ind 3 sg): offer – ἄμωμος: unblemished – καθαρίζω (fut ind 3 sg): cleanse – συνείδησις: conscience – νεκρός: dead – λατρεύω (pres inf): serve – ζάω (pres ptcp): living

---

Apology XXIV (XII) 38

Faith truly believes that, by Christ's death, God has been reconciled. A drink offering is required, that is, the effect of preaching, in order that, being sprinkled by the Gospel with the blood of Christ, we may be sanctified, as those put to death and made alive.

MARCH 28

Isaiah 55:8-9

8כִּי לֹא מַחְשְׁבוֹתַי מַחְשְׁבוֹתֵיכֶם וְלֹא דַרְכֵיכֶם דְּרָכָי
נְאֻם יְהוָה׃
9כִּי־גָבְהוּ שָׁמַיִם מֵאָרֶץ כֵּן גָּבְהוּ דְרָכַי מִדַּרְכֵיכֶם
וּמַחְשְׁבֹתַי מִמַּחְשְׁבֹתֵיכֶם׃

מַחֲשָׁבָה (pl + 1 sg sf/pl + 2 pl sf): thought – דֶּרֶךְ (pl + 1 sg sf/pl + 2 pl sf): way – גָּבַהּ (qal pf 3 pl): be high – שָׁמַיִם: the heavens

---

Romans 11:32-33

32συνέκλεισεν γὰρ ὁ θεὸς τοὺς πάντας εἰς ἀπείθειαν, ἵνα
τοὺς πάντας ἐλεήσῃ. 33Ὦ βάθος πλούτου καὶ σοφίας καὶ
γνώσεως θεοῦ· ὡς ἀνεξεραύνητα τὰ κρίματα αὐτοῦ καὶ
ἀνεξιχνίαστοι αἱ ὁδοὶ αὐτοῦ.

συγκλείω (aor ind 3 sg): enclose, imprison – ἀπείθεια: disobedience – ἐλεέω (aor subj 3 sg): have mercy – βάθος: depth – πλοῦτος: riches – σοφία: wisdom – γνῶσις: knowledge – ἀνεξεραύνητος: unsearchable, unfathomable – κρίμα (pl): judgment – ἀνεξιχνίαστος: inscrutable, incomprehensible – ὁδός (pl): way

---

Formula of Concord SD XI 28

If we want to think about our eternal election to salvation helpfully, we must in every way hold strongly and firmly to this truth: just as the preaching of repentance is universal, so also the promise of the Gospel is universal, that is, it belongs to all people.

Exodus 3:5-6

5 וַיֹּאמֶר אַל־תִּקְרַב הֲלֹם שַׁל־נְעָלֶיךָ מֵעַל רַגְלֶיךָ כִּי
הַמָּקוֹם אֲשֶׁר אַתָּה עוֹמֵד עָלָיו אַדְמַת־קֹדֶשׁ הֽוּא׃
6 וַיֹּאמֶר אָנֹכִי אֱלֹהֵי אָבִיךָ אֱלֹהֵי אַבְרָהָם אֱלֹהֵי יִצְחָק
וֵאלֹהֵי יַעֲקֹב וַיַּסְתֵּר מֹשֶׁה פָּנָיו כִּי יָרֵא מֵהַבִּיט
אֶל־הָאֱלֹהִים׃

קָרַב (qal juss 2 sg): come near – הֲלֹם: here – נָשַׁל (qal imv sg): take off – נַעַל (pl + 2 sg sf): sandal – רֶגֶל (pl + 2 sg sf): foot – מָקוֹם: place – אֲדָמָה (cst sg): ground – סָתַר (hiph v-c impf 3 sg): hide – יָרֵא (qal pf 3 sg): be afraid – נָבַט (hiph inf cst + prep מִן): look at

Luke 20:37-38

37 ὅτι δὲ ἐγείρονται οἱ νεκροί, καὶ Μωϋσῆς ἐμήνυσεν ἐπὶ
τῆς βάτου, ὡς λέγει κύριον τὸν θεὸν Ἀβραὰμ καὶ θεὸν
Ἰσαὰκ καὶ θεὸν Ἰακώβ. 38 θεὸς δὲ οὐκ ἔστιν νεκρῶν ἀλλὰ
ζώντων, πάντες γὰρ αὐτῷ ζῶσιν.

ὅτι: that – ἐγείρω (pres pass dep 3 pl): rise – νεκρός: dead – μηνύω (aor ind 3 sg): reveal, make known – βάτος: bush – ὡς: because – λέγω: call – ζάω (pres ptcp gen pl/pres ind 3 pl): live

Smalcald Articles III VIII 10-11

God does not want to deal with us in any other way than through the spoken Word and the Sacraments. . . . God wanted to appear even to Moses through the burning bush and spoken Word [Ex 3:2-15].

March 30

Joshua 1:9

הֲלוֹא צִוִּיתִיךָ חֲזַק וֶאֱמָץ אַל־תַּעֲרֹץ וְאַל־תֵּחָת כִּי עִמְּךָ
יְהוָה אֱלֹהֶיךָ בְּכֹל אֲשֶׁר תֵּלֵךְ׃

הֲלוֹא (neg + interrog ה): have I not – צָוָה (pi pf 1 sg + 2 sg sf): command – חָזַק (qal imv sg): be strong – אָמֵץ (qal imv sg): be courageous – עָרַץ (qal juss 2 sg): be terrified – חָתַת (qal juss 2 sg): be dismayed

---

Philippians 2:13; 4:13

2:13θεὸς γάρ ἐστιν ὁ ἐνεργῶν ἐν ὑμῖν καὶ τὸ θέλειν καὶ τὸ
ἐνεργεῖν ὑπὲρ τῆς εὐδοκίας . . . 4:13πάντα ἰσχύω ἐν τῷ
ἐνδυναμοῦντί με.

ἐνεργέω (pres ptcp sg/pres inf): be at work, act – θέλω (pres inf): will – εὐδοκία: good pleasure – ἰσχύω (pres ind 1 sg): have power, be able – ἐνδυναμόω (pres act ptcp): strengthen

---

Formula of Concord SD II 52

All who want to be saved ought to listen to this preaching. For the preaching and hearing of God's Word are the Holy Spirit's instruments. By, with, and through these instruments the Spirit desires to work effectively, to convert people to God, and to work in them both to will and to do [Phil 2:13].

MARCH 31

Psalm 40:9

לַעֲשׂוֹת־רְצוֹנְךָ אֱלֹהַי חָפָצְתִּי וְתוֹרָתְךָ בְּתוֹךְ מֵעָי׃

עָשָׂה (qal inf cst): do – רָצוֹן (2 sg sf): will – חָפֵץ (qal pf 1 sg): delight – תּוֹרָה (2 sg sf): law, teaching – תָּוֶךְ (cst): midst – מֵעֶה (pl + 1 sg sf): inner parts, heart

Matthew 5:19-20

19ὃς ἐὰν οὖν λύσῃ μίαν τῶν ἐντολῶν τούτων τῶν ἐλαχίστων
καὶ διδάξῃ οὕτως τοὺς ἀνθρώπους, ἐλάχιστος κληθήσεται
ἐν τῇ βασιλείᾳ τῶν οὐρανῶν· ὃς δ' ἂν ποιήσῃ καὶ διδάξῃ,
οὗτος μέγας κληθήσεται ἐν τῇ βασιλείᾳ τῶν οὐρανῶν.
20Λέγω γὰρ ὑμῖν ὅτι ἐὰν μὴ περισσεύσῃ ὑμῶν ἡ δικαιοσύνη
πλεῖον τῶν γραμματέων καὶ Φαρισαίων, οὐ μὴ εἰσέλθητε
εἰς τὴν βασιλείαν τῶν οὐρανῶν.

λύω (aor subj 3 sg): break – μία: one – ἐντολή (gen pl): commandment – ἐλάχιστος: least – διδάσκω (aor subj 3 sg): teach – καλέω (fut pass 3 sg): call – βασιλεία: kingdom – ποιέω (aor subj 3 sg): do, keep – μέγας: great – περισσεύω (aor subj) surpass – πλεῖον: more

Large Catechism I 333

From this it again appears how highly these Ten Commandments are to be exalted and extolled above all estates, commandments, and works that are taught and done apart from them. For here we can boast and say, "Let all the wise people and saints step forth and produce, if they can, a single work like these commandments . . . "

Zechariah 9:9-10

9 גִּילִי מְאֹד בַּת־צִיּוֹן הָרִיעִי בַּת יְרוּשָׁלִַם
הִנֵּה מַלְכֵּךְ יָבוֹא לָךְ צַדִּיק וְנוֹשָׁע הוּא
עָנִי וְרֹכֵב עַל־חֲמוֹר וְעַל־עַיִר בֶּן־אֲתֹנוֹת׃
10 וּמָשְׁלוֹ מִיָּם עַד־יָם וּמִנָּהָר עַד־אַפְסֵי־אָרֶץ׃

גִּיל (qal imv sg f): rejoice – רוּעַ (hiph imv sg f): shout – יָשַׁע (niph ptcp): be victorious, bring salvation – עָנִי: lowly – רָכַב (qal ptcp): ride – חֲמוֹר: donkey – עַיִר: male donkey – אָתוֹן (pl): female donkey – מָשַׁל (qal inf cst + 3 sg sf): rule – יָם: sea – נָהָר: river (Euphrates) – אֶפֶס (cst pl): end

Matthew 21:4-5

4τοῦτο δὲ γέγονεν ἵνα πληρωθῇ τὸ ῥηθὲν διὰ τοῦ προφήτου
λέγοντος· 5εἴπατε τῇ θυγατρὶ Σιών· ἰδοὺ ὁ βασιλεύς σου
ἔρχεταί σοι πραῢς καὶ ἐπιβεβηκὼς ἐπὶ ὄνον καὶ ἐπὶ πῶλον
υἱὸν ὑποζυγίου.

ῥηθέν (aor pass ptcp of λέγω/εἶπον): speak – θυγατήρ: daughter – πραΰς: gentle, humble – ἐπιβαίνω (pf ptcp): ride – ὄνος: donkey – πῶλος: colt – ὑποζύγιον: beast of burden

Formula of Concord SD VIII 13

Consider this majesty, to which Christ has been exalted according to His humanity. He did not first receive it when He rose from the dead and ascended into heaven. He received it when He was conceived in His mother's womb and became man, and the divine and human natures were personally united with each other.

April 2

Isaiah 53:4-5

4 אָכֵן חֳלָיֵנוּ הוּא נָשָׂא וּמַכְאֹבֵינוּ סְבָלָם
וַאֲנַחְנוּ חֲשַׁבְנֻהוּ נָגוּעַ מֻכֵּה אֱלֹהִים וּמְעֻנֶּה׃
5 וְהוּא מְחֹלָל מִפְּשָׁעֵנוּ מְדֻכָּא מֵעֲוֺנֹתֵינוּ
מוּסַר שְׁלוֹמֵנוּ עָלָיו וּבַחֲבֻרָתוֹ נִרְפָּא־לָנוּ׃

אָכֵן: surely – חֳלִי (pl + 1 pl sf): infirmity – מַכְאוֹב (pl + 1 pl sf): pain – סָבַל (qal pf 3 sg + 3 pl sf): carry – נָגַע (qal pass ptcp): stricken – נָכָה (hoph ptcp): smitten – עָנָה (pu ptcp): afflicted – חָלַל (polal ptcp): pierced – פֶּשַׁע (1 pl sf): sin (as rebellion) – דָּכָא (pu ptcp): crushed – עָוֺן (1 pl sf): sin (as guilt) – מוּסָר (cst sg): punishment – חֲבֻרָה (3 sg sf): blow, suffering – רָפָא (niph pf 3 sg): be healed

Romans 3:23-24

23πάντες γὰρ ἥμαρτον καὶ ὑστεροῦνται τῆς δόξης τοῦ
θεοῦ 24δικαιούμενοι δωρεὰν τῇ αὐτοῦ χάριτι διὰ τῆς
ἀπολυτρώσεως τῆς ἐν Χριστῷ Ἰησοῦ·

ὑστερέω (pres pass 3 pl): fall short of – δωρεάν (adv acc): as a gift – ἀπολύτρωσις: redemption

Formula of Concord Ep XI 11

Now, let whoever is concerned about God's revealed will act on the order that St. Paul has described in the Epistle to the Romans. Paul first directs people to repentance [Rom 1–2], to knowledge of sins [Rom 3:1-20], to faith in Christ [Rom 3:21–5:21], to divine obedience [Rom 6–8].

Zechariah 13:7

חֶ֫רֶב עוּרִי עַל־רֹעִי וְעַל־גֶּ֫בֶר עֲמִיתִי נְאֻם יְהוָה צְבָאוֹת
הַךְ אֶת־הָרֹעֶה וּתְפוּצֶיןָ הַצֹּאן

חֶ֫רֶב: sword – עוּר (qal imv sg f): awake – רֹעֶה (1 sg sf): shepherd – גֶּ֫בֶר: man – עָמִית (1 sg sf): one close to me – נְאֻם: utterance – נָכָה (hiph imv sg): strike – פּוּץ (qal impf 3 pl f): be scattered

---

Matthew 26:31

Τότε λέγει αὐτοῖς ὁ Ἰησοῦς· πάντες ὑμεῖς σκανδαλισθήσεσθε ἐν ἐμοὶ ἐν τῇ νυκτὶ ταύτῃ, γέγραπται γάρ· πατάξω τὸν ποιμένα, καὶ διασκορπισθήσονται τὰ πρόβατα τῆς ποίμνης.

σκανδαλίζω (fut pass 2 pl): take offense at – νύξ: night – γράφω (pf pass ind 3 sg): write – πατάσσω: (fut ind 1 sg): strike down – ποιμήν: shepherd – διασκορπίζω (fut pass 3 pl): scatter – ποίμνη: flock

---

Apology VII-VIII (IV) 10

Rather, the Church is people scattered throughout the whole world. They agree about the Gospel and have the same Christ, the same Holy Spirit, and the same Sacraments, whether they have the same or different human traditions.

April 4

Isaiah 28:16

לָכֵן כֹּה אָמַר אֲדֹנָי יְהוִה
הִנְנִי יִסַּד בְּצִיּוֹן אָבֶן אֶבֶן בֹּחַן
פִּנַּת יִקְרַת מוּסָד מוּסָּד הַמַּאֲמִין לֹא יָחִישׁ׃

לָכֵן: therefore – יָסַד (LXX reads יֹסֵד: qal act ptcp): establish – אֶבֶן: stone – בֹּחַן: testing = a stone tested and approved – פִּנָּה (cst sg): corner (supply אֶבֶן) – יָקָר (cst f): precious – מוּסָד: foundation – יָסַד (hoph ptcp): be founded – אָמַן (hiph ptcp): trust – חוּשׁ (hiph impf 3 sg): be dismayed

1 Peter 2:6-8

6 ἰδοὺ τίθημι ἐν Σιὼν λίθον ἀκρογωνιαῖον ἐκλεκτὸν
ἔντιμον καὶ ὁ πιστεύων ἐπ᾽ αὐτῷ οὐ μὴ καταισχυνθῇ.
7 ὑμῖν οὖν ἡ τιμὴ τοῖς πιστεύουσιν, ἀπιστοῦσιν δὲ
λίθος ὃν ἀπεδοκίμασαν οἱ οἰκοδομοῦντες, οὗτος
ἐγενήθη εἰς κεφαλὴν γωνίας 8 καὶ λίθος προσκόμματος
καὶ πέτρα σκανδάλου·

ἀκρογωνιαῖον: cornerstone – ἔντιμος: precious – καταισχύνω (aor pass subj 3 sg): put to shame – τιμή: honor – ἀπιστέω (pres ptcp): be an unbeliever – ἀποδοκιμάζω (aor ind 3 pl): reject – γωνία: corner – πρόσκομμα: stumbling – σκάνδαλον: offense

Apology IV (II) 98-99

To call upon Christ's name is to trust in His name as the cause, or price, because of which we are saved. Acts 15:9 says, "cleansed by their hearts of faith." Therefore, the faith that the apostles speak about is not useless knowledge, but a reality. It receives the Holy Spirit and justifies us.

Isaiah 53:8

כִּי נִגְזַר מֵאֶרֶץ חַיִּים מִפֶּשַׁע עַמִּי נֶגַע לָמוֹ׃

נִגְזַר (niph pf 3 sg): be cut off – חַי (pl): living – פֶּשַׁע: sin (as rebellion) – נֶגַע: stroke = divine punishment – לָמוֹ = לוֹ

John 1:29

Τῇ ἐπαύριον βλέπει τὸν Ἰησοῦν ἐρχόμενον πρὸς αὐτὸν καὶ λέγει· ἴδε ὁ ἀμνὸς τοῦ θεοῦ ὁ αἴρων τὴν ἁμαρτίαν τοῦ κόσμου.

ἐπαύριον: the next day – ὁράω (aor imv sg): see – ἀμνός: Lamb – αἴρω (pres ptcp): lift up and carry – ἁμαρτία: sin – κόσμος: world

Apology IV (II) 103

Among the Fathers similar testimonies *[to justification by faith alone]* exist. For Ambrose says in his letter to a certain Irenaeus: . . . "Christ took away the sin of the whole world, as John testified, saying in John 1:29, 'Behold, the Lamb of God, who takes away the sin of the world!'"

April 6

Psalm 22:2

אֵלִי אֵלִי לָמָה עֲזַבְתָּנִי רָחוֹק מִישׁוּעָתִי דִּבְרֵי שַׁאֲגָתִי׃

אֵל (1 sg sf): God – עָזַב (qal pf 2 sg + 1 sg sf): forsake – רָחוֹק: distant, far – יְשׁוּעָה (1 sg sf): deliverance, salvation – שְׁאָגָה (1 sg sf): cry of distress

---

John 19:17-19

17καὶ βαστάζων ἑαυτῷ τὸν σταυρὸν ἐξῆλθεν εἰς τὸν
λεγόμενον Κρανίου Τόπον, ὃ λέγεται Ἑβραϊστὶ Γολγοθα,
18ὅπου αὐτὸν ἐσταύρωσαν, καὶ μετ' αὐτοῦ ἄλλους δύο
ἐντεῦθεν καὶ ἐντεῦθεν, μέσον δὲ τὸν Ἰησοῦν. 19ἔγραψεν
δὲ καὶ τίτλον ὁ Πιλᾶτος καὶ ἔθηκεν ἐπὶ τοῦ σταυροῦ·
ἦν δὲ γεγραμμένον· Ἰησοῦς ὁ Ναζωραῖος ὁ βασιλεὺς
τῶν Ἰουδαίων.

βαστάζω (pres ptcp): carry – σταυρός: cross – ἐξέρχομαι (aor ind 3 sg): go out – λέγω (pres pass ptcp): call – κρανίον: skull – τόπος: place – Ἑβραϊστί: in Aramaic – σταυρόω (aor ind 3 pl): crucify – ἐντεῦθεν καὶ ἐντεῦθεν: one on each side – μέσος: middle – γράφω (aor ind 3 sg/pf pass ptcp): write – τίτλος: notice, inscription – τίθημι (aor ind 3 sg): place – βασιλεύς: king

---

Apology XXIV (XII) 56

Therefore, in the New Testament, no sacrifice is left to be applied for the sins of others, except the one sacrifice of Christ upon the cross.

April 7

Numbers 21:8-9

[8]וַיֹּאמֶר יְהוָה אֶל־מֹשֶׁה עֲשֵׂה לְךָ שָׂרָף וְשִׂים אֹתוֹ עַל־
נֵס וְהָיָה כָּל־הַנָּשׁוּךְ וְרָאָה אֹתוֹ וָחָי׃ [9]וַיַּעַשׂ מֹשֶׁה נְחַשׁ
נְחֹשֶׁת וַיְשִׂמֵהוּ עַל־הַנֵּס וְהָיָה אִם־נָשַׁךְ הַנָּחָשׁ אֶת־אִישׁ
וְהִבִּיט אֶל־נְחַשׁ הַנְּחֹשֶׁת וָחָי׃

עָשָׂה (qal imv sg): make – שָׂרָף: fiery serpent – שִׂים (qal imv sg): put – נֵס: standard, pole – נָשַׁךְ (qal pass ptcp): one who is bitten – חָיָה (qal v-c pf 3 sg): live – נָחָשׁ (cst sg): snake – נְחֹשֶׁת: bronze – שִׂים (qal v-c impf 3 sg + 3 sg sf): put – נָבַט (hiph v-c pf 3 sg): look at

---

John 3:14-15

[14]Καὶ καθὼς Μωϋσῆς ὕψωσεν τὸν ὄφιν ἐν τῇ ἐρήμῳ, οὕτως
ὑψωθῆναι δεῖ τὸν υἱὸν τοῦ ἀνθρώπου, [15]ἵνα πᾶς ὁ πιστεύων
ἐν αὐτῷ ἔχῃ ζωὴν αἰώνιον.

ὑψόω (aor ind 3 sg): lift up – ὄφις: snake – ἔρημος: wild wasteland – ὑψόω (aor pass inf): lift up – πιστεύω (pres ptcp): believe – ζωή: life – αἰώνιος: eternal

---

Apology IV (II) 86

Since we receive forgiveness of sins and the Holy Spirit through faith alone, faith alone justifies. For those reconciled are counted as righteous and as God's children. This is not because of their own purity, but through mercy for Christ's sake, provided only that they receive this mercy through faith.

APRIL 8

Psalm 16:10

כִּי לֹא־תַעֲזֹב נַפְשִׁי לִשְׁאוֹל לֹא־תִתֵּן חֲסִידְךָ לִרְאוֹת
שָׁחַת׃

עָזַב (qal impf 2 sg): abandon – חָסִיד (2 sg sf): Holy One – שַׁחַת: decay

---

Acts 2:29-31

29 Ἄνδρες ἀδελφοί, ἐξὸν εἰπεῖν μετὰ παρρησίας πρὸς ὑμᾶς
περὶ τοῦ πατριάρχου Δαυὶδ ὅτι καὶ ἐτελεύτησεν καὶ ἐτάφη,
καὶ τὸ μνῆμα αὐτοῦ ἔστιν ἐν ἡμῖν ἄχρι τῆς ἡμέρας ταύτης.
30 προφήτης οὖν ὑπάρχων καὶ εἰδὼς ὅτι ὅρκῳ ὤμοσεν αὐτῷ
ὁ θεὸς ἐκ καρποῦ τῆς ὀσφύος αὐτοῦ καθίσαι ἐπὶ τὸν θρόνον
αὐτοῦ, 31 προϊδὼν ἐλάλησεν περὶ τῆς ἀναστάσεως τοῦ
Χριστοῦ ὅτι οὔτε ἐγκατελείφθη εἰς ᾅδην οὔτε ἡ σὰρξ
αὐτοῦ εἶδεν διαφθοράν.

ἐξόν: it is proper – παρρησία: confidence – τελευτάω (aor ind 3 sg): die – θάπτω (aor pass 3 sg): bury – μνῆμα: tomb – ἄχρι: until – ὑπάρχω (pres act ptcp): be – οἶδα (pf ptcp with pres meaning): know – ὅρκος: oath – ὀμνύω (aor ind 3 sg): swear – καρπός: offspring – ὀσφύς: reproductive organs – καθίζω (aor inf): sit – προοράω (aor ptcp): see in advance – ἐγκαταλείπω (aor pass 3 sg): abandon – ᾅδης: grave – σάρξ: body – διαφθορά: decay

---

Formula of Concord SD VIII 9

We believe, teach, and confess that it is the property of the divine nature to be almighty, eternal, infinite, everywhere present at the same time, and all-knowing. These are essential attributes of the divine nature. Never in eternity do they become essential properties of the human nature.

APRIL 9

Daniel 12:2-3

²וְרַבִּים מִיְּשֵׁנֵי אַדְמַת־עָפָר יָקִיצוּ
אֵלֶּה לְחַיֵּי עוֹלָם וְאֵלֶּה לַחֲרָפוֹת לְדִרְאוֹן עוֹלָם׃
³וְהַמַּשְׂכִּלִים יַזְהִרוּ כְּזֹהַר הָרָקִיעַ
וּמַצְדִּיקֵי הָרַבִּים כַּכּוֹכָבִים לְעוֹלָם וָעֶד׃

יָשֵׁן (adj cst pl): sleeping – אֲדָמָה (cst sg): earth – עָפָר: dust – קִיץ (hiph impf 3 pl): awake – אֵלֶּה . . . אֵלֶּה: some . . . others – חַיִּים (cst pl): life – עוֹלָם: eternity – חֶרְפָּה (pl): shame – דֵּרָאוֹן (cst): abhorrence – שָׂכַל (hiph ptcp pl): be wise – זָהַר (hiph impf 3 pl): shine – זֹהַר: brightness – רָקִיעַ: the heavens – צָדֵק (hiph ptcp cst pl): lead to righteousness – כּוֹכָב (pl): star – וָעֶד: and ever

---

Colossians 3:3-4

³ἀπεθάνετε γὰρ καὶ ἡ ζωὴ ὑμῶν κέκρυπται σὺν τῷ Χριστῷ
ἐν τῷ θεῷ· ⁴ὅταν ὁ Χριστὸς φανερωθῇ, ἡ ζωὴ ὑμῶν, τότε
καὶ ὑμεῖς σὺν αὐτῷ φανερωθήσεσθε ἐν δόξῃ.

ἀποθνῄσκω (aor ind 2 pl): die – κρύπτω (pf pass 3 sg): hide – φανερόω (aor pass subj 3 sg/fut pass ind 2 pl): reveal, make known, appear

---

Formula of Concord SD VII 99

[The body of Christ has three modes of being.] First, the circumscribed corporeal mode of presence, as when He walked bodily on earth, when He occupied and yielded space according to His size. He can still employ this mode of presence when He wills to do so, as He did after His resurrection and as He will do on the Last Day . . .

Psalm 16:11

תוֹדִיעֵנִי אֹרַח חַיִּים
שֹׂבַע שְׂמָחוֹת אֶת־פָּנֶיךָ נְעִמוֹת בִּימִינְךָ נֶצַח׃

יָדַע (hiph impf 2 sg + 1 sg sf): make known – אֹרַח (cst sg): path – חַיִּים: life – שֹׂבַע (cst sg): abundance – שִׂמְחָה (pl): joy – אֶת־פָּנֶיךָ (pl + 2 sg sf): in your presence – נָעִים (pl): pleasure, delight – יָמִין (2 sg sf): right hand – נֵצַח: forever

---

Revelation 7:16-17

16οὐ πεινάσουσιν ἔτι οὐδὲ διψήσουσιν ἔτι οὐδὲ μὴ πέσῃ
ἐπ' αὐτοὺς ὁ ἥλιος οὐδὲ πᾶν καῦμα, 17ὅτι τὸ ἀρνίον τὸ ἀνὰ
μέσον τοῦ θρόνου ποιμανεῖ αὐτοὺς καὶ ὁδηγήσει αὐτοὺς ἐπὶ
ζωῆς πηγὰς ὑδάτων, καὶ ἐξαλείψει ὁ θεὸς πᾶν δάκρυον ἐκ
τῶν ὀφθαλμῶν αὐτῶν.

πεινάω (fut 3 pl): hunger – διψάω (fut 3 pl): thirst – πίπτω (aor subj 3 sg): fall – καῦμα: scorching heat – ἀρνίον: Lamb – ἀνὰ μέσον: in the center – ποιμαίνω (fut ind 3 sg): be a shepherd – ὁδηγέω (fut ind 3 sg): lead – ζωή: life – πηγή: spring – ἐξαλείφω (fut ind 3 sg): wipe away – δάκρυον: tear – ὀφθαλμός: eye

---

Large Catechism II 62

Through the same Word and the forgiveness of sins He bestows, increases, and strengthens faith. So when He has done it all, and we abide in this and die to the world and to all evil, He may finally make us perfectly and forever holy. Even now we expect this in faith through the Word.

April 11

Job 19:25-27

25 וַאֲנִי יָדַעְתִּי גֹּאֲלִי חָי וְאַחֲרוֹן עַל־עָפָר יָקוּם׃
26 וְאַחַר עוֹרִי נִקְּפוּ־זֹאת וּמִבְּשָׂרִי אֶחֱזֶה אֱלוֹהַּ׃
27 אֲשֶׁר אֲנִי אֶחֱזֶה־לִּי וְעֵינַי רָאוּ וְלֹא־זָר
כָּלוּ כִלְיֹתַי בְּחֵקִי׃

גָּאַל (qal ptcp + 1 sg sf): kinsman-redeemer – חַי (adj): living – אַחֲרוֹן: at the last – עָפָר: dust – קוּם (qal impf 3 sg): stand – אַחַר: after – עוֹר (1 sg sf): skin – נָקַף (pi pf 3 pl): destroy – בָּשָׂר (1 sg sf): flesh – חָזָה (qal impf 1 sg): see – עַיִן (pl + 1 sg sf): eye – רָאָה (qal pf 3 pl): see – זוּר (qal ptcp): a stranger – כָּלָה (qal pf 3 pl): fail, yearn – כִּלְיָה (pl + 1 sg sf): kidney, seat of the emotions – חֵיק (1 sg sf): lap = within me

1 Corinthians 15:20-22

20 Νυνὶ δὲ Χριστὸς ἐγήγερται ἐκ νεκρῶν ἀπαρχὴ τῶν
κεκοιμημένων. 21 ἐπειδὴ γὰρ δι’ ἀνθρώπου θάνατος,
καὶ δι’ ἀνθρώπου ἀνάστασις νεκρῶν. 22 ὥσπερ γὰρ ἐν τῷ
Ἀδὰμ πάντες ἀποθνῄσκουσιν, οὕτως καὶ ἐν τῷ Χριστῷ
πάντες ζῳοποιηθήσονται.

ἐγείρω (pf pass 3 sg): raise – νεκρός: dead – ἀπαρχή: firstfruits – κοιμάω (pf pass ptcp): sleep – θάνατος: dead – ἀνάστασις: resurrection – ἀποθνῄσκω: die – ζωοποιέω (fut pass 3 pl): make alive

Formula of Concord Ep I 10

At that time *[the resurrection]* our nature, which we now bear, will rise and live eternally without original sin and be separated and divided from it. As it is written in Job 19:26-27 . . .

Isaiah 65:19

וְגַלְתִּי בִירוּשָׁלַ͏ִם וְשַׂשְׂתִּי בְעַמִּ֑י
וְלֹֽא־יִשָּׁמַע בָּהּ עוֹד קוֹל בְּכִי וְקוֹל זְעָקָֽה׃

גִּיל (qal v-c pf 1 sg): rejoice – שִׂישׂ (qal v-c pf 1 sg): take delight in – עַם (1 sg sf): people – שָׁמַע (niph impf 3 sg): be heard – בְּכִי: weeping – זְעָקָה: crying

1 Corinthians 15:53-54

53Δεῖ γὰρ τὸ φθαρτὸν τοῦτο ἐνδύσασθαι ἀφθαρσίαν καὶ τὸ
θνητὸν τοῦτο ἐνδύσασθαι ἀθανασίαν. 54ὅταν δὲ τὸ φθαρτὸν
τοῦτο ἐνδύσηται ἀφθαρσίαν καὶ τὸ θνητὸν τοῦτο ἐνδύσηται
ἀθανασίαν, τότε γενήσεται ὁ λόγος ὁ γεγραμμένος·
κατεπόθη ὁ θάνατος εἰς νῖκος.

δεῖ: it is necessary – φθαρτός: perishable – ἐνδύω (aor mid inf/aor mid subj): clothe oneself – ἀφθαρσία: the imperishable – θνητός: mortal – ἀθανασία: immortality – γίνομαι (fut dep ind 3 sg): come to be – γράφω (pf pass ptcp): write – καταπίνω (aor pass ind 3 sg): swallow up – νῖκος: victory

Large Catechism II 58

He *[the Holy Spirit]* must daily administer forgiveness until we reach the life to come. At that time there will be no more forgiveness, but only perfectly pure and holy people [1 Cor 13:10]. We will be full of godliness and righteousness, removed and free from sin, death, and all evil, in a new, immortal, and glorified body [1 Cor 15:43,53].

Exodus 12:14-15

[14]וְהָיָה הַיּוֹם הַזֶּה לָכֶם לְזִכָּרוֹן וְחַגֹּתֶם אֹתוֹ חַג לַיהוָה
לְדֹרֹתֵיכֶם חֻקַּת עוֹלָם תְּחָגֻּהוּ׃ [15]שִׁבְעַת יָמִים מַצּוֹת
תֹּאכֵלוּ אַךְ בַּיּוֹם הָרִאשׁוֹן תַּשְׁבִּיתוּ שְּׂאֹר מִבָּתֵּיכֶם
כִּי כָּל־אֹכֵל חָמֵץ וְנִכְרְתָה הַנֶּפֶשׁ הַהִוא מִיִּשְׂרָאֵל
מִיּוֹם הָרִאשֹׁן עַד־יוֹם הַשְּׁבִעִי׃

זִכָּרוֹן: memorial day – חָגַג (qal v-c pf 2 pl/qal impf 2 pl + 3 sg sf): celebrate – חַג: festival – שִׁבְעָה: seven – מַצָּה: unleavened bread – שָׁבַת (hiph impf 2 pl): remove – שְׂאֹר: leaven – חָמֵץ: something leavened – כָּרַת (niph v-c pf 3 sg): be cut off

1 Corinthians 5:7-8

[7]ἐκκαθάρατε τὴν παλαιὰν ζύμην, ἵνα ἦτε νέον φύραμα,
καθώς ἐστε ἄζυμοι· καὶ γὰρ τὸ πάσχα ἡμῶν ἐτύθη Χριστός.
[8]ὥστε ἑορτάζωμεν μὴ ἐν ζύμῃ παλαιᾷ μηδὲ ἐν ζύμῃ κακίας
καὶ πονηρίας ἀλλ’ ἐν ἀζύμοις εἰλικρινείας καὶ ἀληθείας.

ἐκκαθαίρω (aor imv 2 pl): clean out, get rid of – παλαιός: old – ζύμη: yeast – φύραμα: batch (of dough) – ἄζυμος: unleavened – πάσχα: Passover lamb – θύω (aor pass): sacrifice – ἑορτάζω (pres subj 1 pl): celebrate the festival – κακία: malice – πονηρία: wickedness – εἰλικρινεία: sincerity, purity

Apology XXIV (XII) 36

The *[ceremonial]* Law had pictures or shadows of future things [Col 2:17]. So Christ and the entire worship of the New Testament are shown in this picture. The burning of the lamb illustrates Christ's death.

APRIL 14

Isaiah 26:19

יִחְיוּ מֵתֶיךָ נְבֵלָתִי יְקוּמוּן הָקִיצוּ וְרַנְּנוּ שֹׁכְנֵי עָפָר
כִּי טַל אוֹרֹת טַלֶּךָ וָאָרֶץ רְפָאִים תַּפִּיל׃

חָיָה (qal impf 3 pl): live – מוּת (qal ptcp pl + 2 sg sf): your dead – נְבֵלָתִי: my corpse; NIV following Syriac and Targum: their bodies – קִיץ (hiph imv pl): awake – רָנַן (pi imv pl): shout for joy – שָׁכַן (qal ptcp cst pl): dwell – עָפָר: dust – טַל (cst sg): dew – אוֹר: dawn – רְפָאִים: the dead – נָפַל (hiph impf 3 sg): give birth to

---

1 Thessalonians 4:16-17

16ὅτι αὐτὸς ὁ κύριος ἐν κελεύσματι, ἐν φωνῇ ἀρχαγγέλου
καὶ ἐν σάλπιγγι θεοῦ, καταβήσεται ἀπ' οὐρανοῦ καὶ οἱ
νεκροὶ ἐν Χριστῷ ἀναστήσονται πρῶτον, 17ἔπειτα ἡμεῖς
οἱ ζῶντες οἱ περιλειπόμενοι ἅμα σὺν αὐτοῖς ἁρπαγησόμεθα
ἐν νεφέλαις εἰς ἀπάντησιν τοῦ κυρίου εἰς ἀέρα· καὶ οὕτως
πάντοτε σὺν κυρίῳ ἐσόμεθα.

κέλευσμα: command – φωνή: voice – σάλπιγξ: trumpet – καταβαίνω (fut dep ind 3 sg): come down – οὐρανός: heaven – νεκρός: dead – ἀνίστημι (fut mid 3 pl): rise – ζάω (pres ptcp pl): live – περιλείπομαι (pres ptcp pl): remain – ἅμα: at the same time – ἁρπάζω (fut pass 1 pl): be caught up – νεφέλη: cloud – ἀπάντησις: meeting – ἀήρ: air – πάντοτε: always

---

Small Catechism Third Article

On the Last Day He will raise up me and all the dead and will give eternal life to me and to all believers in Christ. This is most certainly true.

April 15

Isaiah 25:8

בִּלַּע הַמָּוֶת לָנֶצַח
וּמָחָה אֲדֹנָי יְהוִה דִּמְעָה מֵעַל כָּל־פָּנִים
וְחֶרְפַּת עַמּוֹ יָסִיר מֵעַל כָּל־הָאָרֶץ כִּי יְהוָה דִּבֵּר׃

בִּלַּע (pi pf 3 sg): swallow up – מָוֶת: death – לָנֶצַח: forever – מָחָה (qal v-c pf 3 sg): wipe away – דִּמְעָה: tears – חֶרְפָּה (cst sg): disgrace – סוּר (hiph impf 3 sg): remove

---

Philippians 3:20-21

20ἡμῶν γὰρ τὸ πολίτευμα ἐν οὐρανοῖς ὑπάρχει, ἐξ οὗ
καὶ σωτῆρα ἀπεκδεχόμεθα κύριον Ἰησοῦν Χριστόν,
21ὃς μετασχηματίσει τὸ σῶμα τῆς ταπεινώσεως ἡμῶν
σύμμορφον τῷ σώματι τῆς δόξης αὐτοῦ κατὰ τὴν
ἐνέργειαν τοῦ δύνασθαι αὐτὸν καὶ ὑποτάξαι αὐτῷ
τὰ πάντα.

πολίτευμα: citizenship – ὑπάρχω (pres ind 3 sg): be – σωτήρ: Savior – ἀπεκδέχομαι (pres ind 1 pl): await eagerly – μετασχηματίζω (fut ind 3 sg): change – σῶμα: body – ταπείνωσις: humble station – σύμμορφος: having the same form – δόξα: glory – ἐνέργεια: power – δύναμαι (pres inf): be able – ὑποτάσσω (aor inf): subdue

---

Augsburg Confession XXVIII 12

Therefore, the Church's authority and the State's authority must not be confused. The Church's authority has its own commission to teach the Gospel and to administer the Sacraments [Matt 28:19-20].

Ezekiel 16:8

וָאֶשָּׁבַע לָךְ וָאָבוֹא בִבְרִית אֹתָךְ נְאֻם אֲדֹנָי יְהוִה וַתִּהְיִי לִי׃

שָׁבַע (niph v-c impf 1 sg): give an oath to – בּוֹא (qal v-c impf 1 sg) + בְּ: enter into – בְּרִית: covenant – אֹתָךְ = אִתָּךְ (sg f): with you – נְאֻם: utterance – וַתִּהְיִי לִי: you became mine

Hebrews 6:17

ἐν ᾧ περισσότερον βουλόμενος ὁ θεὸς ἐπιδεῖξαι τοῖς κληρονόμοις τῆς ἐπαγγελίας τὸ ἀμετάθετον τῆς βουλῆς αὐτοῦ ἐμεσίτευσεν ὅρκῳ . . .

περισσότερον (adv): even more clearly – βούλομαι (pres ptcp sg): want – ἐπιδείκνυμι (aor inf): point out – κληρονόμος: heir – ἐπαγγελία: promise – τὸ ἀμετάθετον: unchangeableness – βουλή: purpose – μεσιτεύω (aor ind 3 sg): guarantee – ὅρκος: oath

Formula of Concord SD XI 75

Our election to eternal life is founded not on our godliness or virtue, but on Christ's merit alone and His Father's gracious will. He cannot deny Himself [2 Tim 2:13], because He is unchangeable in will and essence [Heb 6:17-18].

April 17

Hosea 13:14

מִיַּד שְׁאוֹל אֶפְדֵּם מִמָּוֶת אֶגְאָלֵם
אֱהִי דְבָרֶיךָ מָוֶת אֱהִי קָטָבְךָ שְׁאוֹל

יָד: hand, power – שְׁאוֹל: the grave – פָּדָה (qal impf + 3 pl sf): ransom – מָוֶת: death – גָּאַל (qal impf + 3 pl sf): redeem – אֱהִי: where? – דֶּבֶר (pl + 2 sg sf): plague – קֶטֶב (2 sg sf): destruction

---

1 Corinthians 15:55-57

55 ποῦ σου, θάνατε, τὸ νῖκος; ποῦ σου, θάνατε, τὸ κέντρον;
56 τὸ δὲ κέντρον τοῦ θανάτου ἡ ἁμαρτία, ἡ δὲ δύναμις τῆς
ἁμαρτίας ὁ νόμος· 57 τῷ δὲ θεῷ χάρις τῷ διδόντι ἡμῖν τὸ
νῖκος διὰ τοῦ κυρίου ἡμῶν Ἰησοῦ Χριστοῦ.

ποῦ: where? – νῖκος: victory – κέντρον: sting – χάρις: thanks – δίδωμι (pres ptcp): give

---

Apology IV (II) 79

In the forgiveness of sins, the terrors of sin and of eternal death must be overcome in the heart. Paul testifies about this in 1 Cor 15:56-57, "The sting of death is sin, and the power of sin is the law. But thanks be to God, who gives us the victory through our Lord Jesus Christ." In other words, sin terrifies consciences. This happens through the Law, which shows God's wrath against sin. But we gain the victory through Christ. How? Through faith, when we comfort ourselves by confidence in the mercy promised for Christ's sake.

April 18

Malachi 3:20

וְזָרְחָה לָכֶם יִרְאֵי שְׁמִי שֶׁמֶשׁ צְדָקָה וּמַרְפֵּא בִּכְנָפֶיהָ
וִיצָאתֶם וּפִשְׁתֶּם כְּעֶגְלֵי מַרְבֵּק׃

זָרַח (qal v-c pf 3 sg f): rise – יָרֵא (cst pl): fearing – שֶׁמֶשׁ: sun – צְדָקָה: righteousness – מַרְפֵּא: healing – כָּנָף (pl + 3 sg sf): wing – יָצָא (qal v-c pf 2 pl): go out – פּוּשׁ (qal v-c pf 2 pl): leap – עֵגֶל (cst pl): calf – מַרְבֵּק: stall

Romans 8:32

ὅς γε τοῦ ἰδίου υἱοῦ οὐκ ἐφείσατο ἀλλὰ ὑπὲρ ἡμῶν πάντων παρέδωκεν αὐτόν, πῶς οὐχὶ καὶ σὺν αὐτῷ τὰ πάντα ἡμῖν χαρίσεται;

ἴδιος: his own – υἱός: son – φείδομαι (aor ind 3 sg): spare – παραδίδωμι (aor ind 3 sg): give up – χαρίζομαι (fut ind 3 sg): give freely

Large Catechism II 17

He directs all sorts of danger and disaster away from us. We confess that He does all this out of pure love and goodness, without our merit, as a kind Father. He cares for us so that no evil falls upon us.

Psalm 86:15-16

15 וְאַתָּה אֲדֹנָי אֵל־רַחוּם וְחַנּוּן
אֶרֶךְ אַפַּיִם וְרַב־חֶסֶד וֶאֱמֶת׃
16 פְּנֵה אֵלַי וְחָנֵּנִי
תְּנָה־עֻזְּךָ לְעַבְדֶּךָ וְהוֹשִׁיעָה לְבֶן־אֲמָתֶךָ׃

רַחוּם: merciful – חַנּוּן: gracious – אֶרֶךְ (cst): long – אַף (du): anger = slow to anger – רַב: abounding – חֶסֶד: faithful love – אֱמֶת: faithfulness – פָּנָה (qal imv sg): turn – חָנַן (qal imv sg + 1 sg sf): show mercy – נָתַן (qal imv sg): grant – עֹז (2 sg sf): strength – עֶבֶד: servant – יָשַׁע (hiph imv): save – אָמָה: maidservant

---

Hebrews 13:8

Ἰησοῦς Χριστὸς ἐχθὲς καὶ σήμερον ὁ αὐτὸς καὶ εἰς τοὺς αἰῶνας.

ἐχθές: yesterday – σήμερον: today – ὁ αὐτός: the same – αἰών: eternity

---

Formula of Concord SD VIII 7

These two natures in the person of Christ are never either separated from or mingled with each other. Nor are they changed into each other. Each one abides in its nature and essence in the person of Christ to all eternity.

April 20

Isaiah 25:9

וְאָמַר בַּיּוֹם הַהוּא הִנֵּה אֱלֹהֵינוּ זֶה קִוִּינוּ לוֹ וְיוֹשִׁיעֵנוּ
זֶה יְהוָה קִוִּינוּ לוֹ נָגִילָה וְנִשְׂמְחָה בִּישׁוּעָתוֹ׃

קָוָה (pi pf 1 pl): trust – יָשַׁע (hiph impf 3 sg + 1 pl sf): save – גִּיל (qal coh 1 pl): rejoice – שָׂמַח (qal coh 1 pl): be glad – יְשׁוּעָה (3 sg sf): salvation

2 Peter 3:18

αὐξάνετε ἐν χαρίτι καὶ γνώσει τοῦ κυρίου ἡμῶν καὶ σωτῆρος Ἰησοῦ Χριστοῦ. αὐτῷ ἡ δόξα καὶ νῦν καὶ εἰς ἡμέραν αἰῶνος.

αὐξάνω (pres imv pl): grow – χάρις: grace – γνῶσις: knowledge – δόξα: glory – αἰών: eternity

Formula of Concord SD II 49

It is not God's will that anyone should be damned, but that all people should be converted to Him and be saved eternally [2 Pet 3:9].

APRIL 21

Psalm 48:15

כִּי זֶה אֱלֹהִים אֱלֹהֵינוּ עוֹלָם וָעֶד
הוּא יְנַהֲגֵנוּ עַל־מוּת׃

עוֹלָם וָעֶד: forever and ever – נָהַג (pi impf 3 sg + 1 pl sf): lead, guide – מוּת (inf cst): death

---

2 Corinthians 12:9

καὶ εἴρηκέν μοι· ἀρκεῖ σοι ἡ χάρις μου, ἡ γὰρ δύναμις ἐν ἀσθενείᾳ τελεῖται. ἥδιστα οὖν μᾶλλον καυχήσομαι ἐν ταῖς ἀσθενείαις μου, ἵνα ἐπισκηνώσῃ ἐπ' ἐμὲ ἡ δύναμις τοῦ Χριστοῦ.

λέγω (pf ind 3 sg): say – ἀρκέω (pres ind 3 sg): be sufficient – χάρις: grace – δύναμις: power – ἀσθένεια: weakness – τελέω (pres pass ind 3 sg): reach perfection – ἥδιστα: very gladly – καυχάομαι (fut ind 1 sg): boast – ἐπισκηνόω (aor subj 3 sg): spread a tent over, dwell

---

Formula of Concord SD VII 69

Some Christians have a weak faith and are shy, troubled, and heartily terrified because of the great number of their sins. They think that in their great impurity they are not worthy of this precious treasure and Christ's benefits. They feel their weakness of faith and lament it, and from their hearts desire that they may serve God with stronger, more joyful faith and pure obedience. These are the truly worthy guests for whom this highly venerable Sacrament has been especially instituted and appointed.

APRIL 22

Isaiah 40:11

כְּרֹעֶה עֶדְרוֹ יִרְעֶה בִּזְרֹעוֹ יְקַבֵּץ טְלָאִים
וּבְחֵיקוֹ יִשָּׂא עָלוֹת יְנַהֵל׃

רֹעֶה: shepherd – עֵדֶר (3 sg sf): flock – רָעָה (qal impf 3 sg): tend a flock – זְרֹעַ (3 sg sf): arm – קָבַץ (pi impf 3 sg): gather – טְלָאִים: lambs – חֵיק (3 sg sf): lap – עוּל (qal ptcp pl f): nurse – נָהַל (pi impf 3 sg): lead gently

---

Matthew 9:36

Ἰδὼν δὲ τοὺς ὄχλους ἐσπλαγχνίσθη περὶ αὐτῶν, ὅτι ἦσαν ἐσκυλμένοι καὶ ἐρριμμένοι ὡσεὶ πρόβατα μὴ ἔχοντα ποιμένα.

ὁράω (aor ptcp sg): see – ὄχλος: crowd – σπλαγχνίζομαι (aor pass 3 sg): feel sympathy for – σκύλλω (pf pass ptcp pl): harass – ῥίπτω (pf pass ptcp pl): throw down – ὡσεί: like – πρόβατον: sheep – ἔχω (pres ptcp pl): have – ποιμήν: shepherd

---

Smalcald Articles Preface 10

But we see throughout the bishops' jurisdictions so many parishes vacant and desolate that it breaks our heart. Still, neither the bishops nor the Church officials care how the poor people live or die. Christ has died for them, and yet they are not allowed to hear Him speak as the true Shepherd with His sheep [John 10:11-18].

Micah 5:3

וְעָמַד וְרָעָה בְּעֹז יְהוָה בִּגְאוֹן שֵׁם יְהוָה אֱלֹהָיו
וְיָשָׁבוּ כִּי־עַתָּה יִגְדַּל עַד־אַפְסֵי־אָרֶץ׃

עָמַד (qal v-c pf 3 sg): stand – רָעָה (qal v-c pf 3 sg): tend a flock – עֹז (cst sg): strength – גָּאוֹן (cst sg): majesty – יָשַׁב (qal v-c pf 3 pl): dwell (securely) – גָּדַל (qal impf 3 sg): be great – אֶפֶס (cst pl): end

---

John 10:14-15

14Ἐγώ εἰμι ὁ ποιμὴν ὁ καλὸς καὶ γινώσκω τὰ ἐμὰ καὶ
γινώσκουσί με τὰ ἐμά, 15καθὼς γινώσκει με ὁ πατὴρ
κἀγὼ γινώσκω τὸν πατέρα, καὶ τὴν ψυχήν μου τίθημι
ὑπὲρ τῶν προβάτων.

ποιμήν: shepherd – γινώσκω (pres ind 1 sg/3 pl/3 sg): know – ψυχή: life – τίθημι (pres ind 1 sg): lay down – πρόβατον: sheep

---

Formula of Concord SD Summary 14

Faithful shepherds, as Luther says, should do both things: (a) feed or nourish the lambs and (b) resist the wolves.

Ezekiel 34:15

אֲנִי אֶרְעֶה צֹאנִי וַאֲנִי אַרְבִּיצֵם נְאֻם אֲדֹנָי יְהוִה׃

רָעָה (qal impf 1 sg): tend a flock – צֹאן (1 sg sf): flock – רָבַץ (hiph impf 1 sg + 3 pl sf): cause to lie down

Matthew 15:32

Ὁ δὲ Ἰησοῦς προσκαλεσάμενος τοὺς μαθητὰς αὐτοῦ εἶπεν· σπλαγχνίζομαι ἐπὶ τὸν ὄχλον, ὅτι ἤδη ἡμέραι τρεῖς προσμένουσίν μοι καὶ οὐκ ἔχουσιν τί φάγωσιν· καὶ ἀπολῦσαι αὐτοὺς νήστεις οὐ θέλω, μήποτε ἐκλυθῶσιν ἐν τῇ ὁδῷ.

προσκαλέω (aor mid ptcp): call to oneself – μαθητής: disciple – σπλαγχνίζομαι: feel sympathy for – ὄχλος: multitude – ἡμέρα: day – προσμένω (pres 3 pl): remain with – ἐσθίω (aor subj 3 pl): eat – ἀπολύω (aor inf): send away – νῆστις (acc pl): hungry – μήποτε: that . . . not – ἐκλύω (aor pass subj 3 pl): become weary – ὁδός: way

Large Catechism II 30

He *[Jesus Christ]* has delivered us poor, lost people from hell's jaws, has won us, has made us free [Rom 8:1-2], and has brought us again into the Father's favor and grace.

Psalm 149:4

כִּי־רוֹצֶה יְהוָה בְּעַמּוֹ יְפָאֵר עֲנָוִים בִּישׁוּעָה׃

רָצָה (qal ptcp sg): take delight in – עַם (3 sg sf): people – פָּאַר (pi impf 3 sg): glorify, crown – עָנָו (pl): humble – יְשׁוּעָה: salvation

John 10:27-28

27τὰ πρόβατα τὰ ἐμὰ τῆς φωνῆς μου ἀκούουσιν, κἀγὼ
γινώσκω αὐτὰ καὶ ἀκολουθοῦσίν μοι, 28κἀγὼ δίδωμι αὐτοῖς
ζωὴν αἰώνιον καὶ οὐ μὴ ἀπόλωνται εἰς τὸν αἰῶνα καὶ οὐχ
ἁρπάσει τις αὐτὰ ἐκ τῆς χειρός μου.

πρόβατον: sheep – φωνή: voice – ἀκούω (pres ind 3 pl): listen to – γινώσκω (pres ind 1 sg): know – ἀκολουθέω (pres ind 3 pl): follow – ζωή: life – αἰώνιος: eternal – ἀπόλλυμι (aor mid subj 3 pl): perish – ἁρπάζω (fut ind 3 sg): snatch – χείρ: hand

Formula of Concord SD XI 8

God's eternal election does not just foresee and foreknow the salvation of the elect. From God's gracious will and pleasure in Christ Jesus, election is a cause that gains, works, helps, and promotes our salvation and what belongs to it. Our salvation is so founded on it that "the gates of hell shall not prevail against it" (Matt 16:18), as is written in John 10:28, "no one will snatch [My sheep] out of My hand."

April 26

Psalm 119:9-10

9 בַּמֶּה יְזַכֶּה־נַּעַר אֶת־אָרְחוֹ לִשְׁמֹר כִּדְבָרֶךָ׃
10 בְּכָל־לִבִּי דְרַשְׁתִּיךָ אַל־תַּשְׁגֵּנִי מִמִּצְוֺתֶיךָ׃

בַּמֶּה: how? – זָכָה (pi impf 3 sg): keep pure – נַעַר: young man – אֹרַח (3 sg sf): way – שָׁמַר (qal inf cst): obey, live according to – דָּבָר (2 sg sf): word – לֵב (1 sg sf): heart – דָּרַשׁ (qal pf 1 sg + 2 sg sf): seek – שָׁגָה (hiph juss 2 sg + 1 sg sf): cause to stray = do not let me stray – מִצְוָה (pl + 2 sg sf): command

1 Timothy 6:12

ἀγωνίζου τὸν καλὸν ἀγῶνα τῆς πίστεως, ἐπιλαβοῦ τῆς αἰωνίου ζωῆς, εἰς ἣν ἐκλήθης καὶ ὡμολόγησας τὴν καλὴν ὁμολογίαν ἐνώπιον πολλῶν μαρτύρων.

ἀγωνίζομαι (pres imv sg): fight – καλός: good – ἀγών: struggle, fight – ἐπιλαμβάνομαι (aor imv sg): take hold of – αἰώνιος: eternal – ζωή: life – καλέω (aor pass 2 sg): call – ὁμολογέω (aor ind 2 sg): make a confession – ὁμολογία: confession – ἐνώπιον: in the presence of – μάρτυς (gen pl): witness

Large Catechism I 208

For marriage has the highest importance to God so that people are raised up who may serve the world and promote the knowledge of God, godly living, and all virtues, to fight against wickedness and the devil.

April 27

Isaiah 54:7-8

7בְּרֶגַע קָטֹן עֲזַבְתִּיךְ וּבְרַחֲמִים גְּדֹלִים אֲקַבְּצֵךְ׃
8בְּשֶׁצֶף קֶצֶף הִסְתַּרְתִּי פָנַי רֶגַע מִמֵּךְ
וּבְחֶסֶד עוֹלָם רִחַמְתִּיךְ אָמַר גֹּאֲלֵךְ יְהוָה׃

רֶגַע: moment – קָטֹן: brief – עָזַב (qal pf 1 sg + 2 sg sf): abandon – רַחֲמִים: mercies – קָבַץ (pi impf 1 sg + 2 sg sf): gather – שֶׁצֶף: surge – קֶצֶף: anger – סָתַר (hiph pf 1 sg): hide – רָחַם (pi pf 1 sg): have mercy – גָּאַל (qal ptcp + 2 sg sf): Redeemer

---

John 16:20

ἀμὴν ἀμὴν λέγω ὑμῖν ὅτι κλαύσετε καὶ θρηνήσετε ὑμεῖς, ὁ δὲ κόσμος χαρήσεται· ὑμεῖς λυπηθήσεσθε, ἀλλ᾽ ἡ λύπη ὑμῶν εἰς χαρὰν γενήσεται.

ἀμήν: truly – κλαίω (fut ind 2 pl): weep – θρηνέω (fut ind 2 pl): mourn – κόσμος: world – χαίρω (fut mid 3 sg): rejoice – λυπέω (fut pass 2 pl): become sad – λύπη: sorrow – χαρά: joy

---

Apology V (III) 242-243

The justified are due the crown because of the promise. Saints should know this promise, not that they may labor for their own profit, for they ought to labor for God's glory. But saints should know it so they may not despair in troubles.

April 28

Psalm 138:7

אִם־אֵלֵךְ בְּקֶרֶב צָרָה תְּחַיֵּנִי עַל אַף אֹיְבַי
תִּשְׁלַח יָדֶךָ וְתוֹשִׁיעֵנִי יְמִינֶךָ׃

הָלַךְ (qal impf 1 sg): walk – קֶרֶב: midst – צָרָה: trouble – חָיָה (pi impf 2 sg + 1 sg sf): preserve life – עַל: against – אַף: anger – אֹיֵב (pl + 1 sg sf): enemy – שָׁלַח (qal impf 2 sg): stretch out – יָד (2 sg sf): hand – יָשַׁע (hiph impf 2 sg + 1 sg sf): save – יָמִין (2 sg sf): right hand

---

1 Corinthians 1:8-9

8ὃς καὶ βεβαιώσει ὑμᾶς ἕως τέλους ἀνεγκλήτους ἐν
τῇ ἡμέρᾳ τοῦ κυρίου ἡμῶν 'Ιησοῦ [Χριστοῦ]. 9πιστὸς
ὁ θεός, δι' οὗ ἐκλήθητε εἰς κοινωνίαν τοῦ υἱοῦ αὐτοῦ
'Ιησοῦ Χριστοῦ τοῦ κυρίου ἡμῶν.

βεβαιόω (fut ind 3 sg): strengthen – τέλος: end – ἀνέγκλητος: blameless – ἡμέρα: day – πιστός: faithful – καλέω (aor pass 2 pl): call – κοινωνία: fellowship

---

Formula of Concord Ep XI 5

Predestination, or God's eternal election, covers only the godly, beloved children of God. It is a cause of their salvation, which He also provides. He plans what belongs to it as well. Our salvation is founded so firmly on it that the gates of hell cannot overcome it (John 10:28; Matt 16:18).

April 29

1 Chronicles 29:14

וְכִי מִי אֲנִי וּמִי עַמִּי כִּי־נַעְצֹר כֹּחַ לְהִתְנַדֵּב כָּזֹאת
כִּי־מִמְּךָ הַכֹּל וּמִיָּדְךָ נָתַנּוּ לָךְ׃

מִי (interrog pron): who? – עַם (1 sg sf): people – עָצַר (qal impf 1 pl): retain – כֹּחַ: strength = be able – נָדַב (hithp inf cst): give generously – כָּזֹאת: as this – יָד (2 sg sf): hand – נָתַן (qal pf 1 pl): give

Ephesians 2:8-10

8Τῇ γὰρ χάριτί ἐστε σεσῳσμένοι διὰ πίστεως· καὶ
τοῦτο οὐκ ἐξ ὑμῶν, θεοῦ τὸ δῶρον· 9οὐκ ἐξ ἔργων, ἵνα
μή τις καυχήσηται. 10αὐτοῦ γάρ ἐσμεν ποίημα, κτισθέντες
ἐν Χριστῷ Ἰησοῦ ἐπὶ ἔργοις ἀγαθοῖς, οἷς προητοίμασεν
ὁ θεὸς, ἵνα ἐν αὐτοῖς περιπατήσωμεν.

χάρις (dat sg): grace – σῴζω (pf pass ptcp pl): save – πίστις: faith – δῶρον: gift – ἔργον: work – καυχάομαι (aor subj 3 sg): boast – ποίημα: workmanship – κτίζω (aor pass ptcp pl): create – ἀγαθός: good – προετοιμάζω (aor ind 3 sg): prepare beforehand

Formula of Concord Ep IV 7

We believe, teach, and confess that good works should be entirely excluded from the question about salvation, just as they are excluded from the article of justification before God. The apostle testifies with clear words when he writes as follows, "Just as David also speaks of the blessing of the one to whom God counts righteousness apart from works: . . . 'Blessed is the man against whom the Lord will not count his sin'" (Rom 4:6-8).

APRIL 30

Hosea 5:15

אֵלֵךְ אָשׁוּבָה אֶל־מְקוֹמִי
עַד אֲשֶׁר־יֶאְשְׁמוּ וּבִקְשׁוּ פָנָי
בַּצַּר לָהֶם יְשַׁחֲרֻנְנִי׃

הָלַךְ (qal impf 1 sg): go – שׁוּב (qal coh 1 sg): return – מָקוֹם (1 sg sf): place – עַד אֲשֶׁר: until – אָשַׁם (qal impf 3 pl): be guilty = admit their guilt – בָּקַשׁ (pi v-c pf 3 pl): seek – צַר: misery – שָׁחַר (pi impf 3 pl + 1 sg sf): seek earnestly

---

Luke 1:54-55

54ἀντελάβετο Ἰσραὴλ παιδὸς αὐτοῦ, μνησθῆναι ἐλέους,
55καθὼς ἐλάλησεν πρὸς τοὺς πατέρας ἡμῶν, τῷ Ἀβραὰμ
καὶ τῷ σπέρματι αὐτοῦ εἰς τὸν αἰῶνα.

ἀντιλαμβάνω (aor mid 3 sg): come to the help of – παῖς: child, servant – μιμνῄσκομαι (aor inf): remember – ἔλεος: mercy – λαλέω (aor ind 3 sg): speak – σπέρμα: descendants – αἰών: eternity

---

Apology V (III) 21

I mean that faith is conceived in the terrors of conscience, which feels God's wrath against our sins and seeks forgiveness of sins, seeks to be freed from sin. In such terrors and other troubles, this faith ought to grow and be strengthened.

May 1

Isaiah 42:2-3

2 לֹא יִצְעַק וְלֹא יִשָּׂא וְלֹא־יַשְׁמִיעַ בַּחוּץ קוֹלוֹ׃
3 קָנֶה רָצוּץ לֹא יִשְׁבּוֹר וּפִשְׁתָּה כֵהָה לֹא יְכַבֶּנָּה
לֶאֱמֶת יוֹצִיא מִשְׁפָּט׃

צָעַק (qal impf 3 sg): shout – נָשָׂא (qal impf 3 sg): raise (his voice) – שָׁמַע (hiph impf 3 sg): cause to be heard – חוּץ: street – קָנֶה: reed – רָצַץ (qal pass ptcp): bruised – שָׁבַר (qal impf 3 sg): break – פִּשְׁתָּה: wick – כֵּהֶה (f): dim, faint – כָּבָה (pi impf 3 sg + 3 sg sf): extinguish – יָצָא (hiph impf 3 sg): bring forth – מִשְׁפָּט: justice

John 8:10-11

10 ἀνακύψας δὲ ὁ Ἰησοῦς εἶπεν αὐτῇ· γύναι, ποῦ εἰσιν;
οὐδείς σε κατέκρινεν; 11 ἡ δὲ εἶπεν· οὐδείς, κύριε. εἶπεν
δὲ ὁ Ἰησοῦς· οὐδὲ ἐγώ σε κατακρίνω· πορεύου, [καὶ] ἀπὸ
τοῦ νῦν μηκέτι ἁμάρτανε.

ἀνακύπτω (aor ptcp): raise oneself up – κατακρίνω (aor ind 3 sg): condemn – πορεύομαι (pres imv 2 sg): go – ἁμαρτάνω (pres imv 2 sg): sin

Large Catechism II 28-29

So we fell under God's wrath and displeasure and were doomed to eternal damnation, just as we had merited and deserved. There was no counsel, help, or comfort until this only and eternal Son of God—in His immeasurable goodness—had compassion upon our misery and wretchedness.

May 2

Genesis 12:1

וַיֹּאמֶר יְהוָה אֶל־אַבְרָם לֶךְ־לְךָ מֵאַרְצְךָ וּמִמּוֹלַדְתְּךָ
וּמִבֵּית אָבִיךָ אֶל־הָאָרֶץ אֲשֶׁר אַרְאֶךָּ׃

הָלַךְ (qal imv sg): go – אֶרֶץ (2 sg sf): land – מוֹלֶדֶת (2 sg sf): family – רָאָה (hiph impf 1 sg + 2 sg sf): cause to see, show

---

Hebrews 11:8-9

8Πίστει καλούμενος Ἀβραὰμ ὑπήκουσεν ἐξελθεῖν εἰς
τόπον ὃν ἤμελλεν λαμβάνειν εἰς κληρονομίαν, καὶ ἐξῆλθεν
μὴ ἐπιστάμενος ποῦ ἔρχεται. 9Πίστει παρῴκησεν εἰς γῆν
τῆς ἐπαγγελίας ὡς ἀλλοτρίαν ἐν σκηναῖς κατοικήσας μετὰ
Ἰσαὰκ καὶ Ἰακὼβ τῶν συγκληρονόμων τῆς ἐπαγγελίας
τῆς αὐτῆς·

ὑπακούω (aor ind 3 sg): obey – ἐξέρχομαι (aor inf): go out – μέλλω (impf 3 sg + inf = fut): which he would receive – κληρονομία: inheritance – ἐπίσταμαι (pres ptcp): know – παροικέω (aor ind): inhabit (a place) as a stranger – ἔπαγγελία: promise – ἀλλότριος: belonging to another – σκηνή: tent – κατοικέω (aor ptcp): inhabit, live in – συγκληρονόμος: fellow-heir

---

Formula of Concord SD III 32

It is also correct to say that believers who have been justified through faith in Christ first have the righteousness of faith credited to them in this life. Then, they also have the initial righteousness of the new obedience or of good works. But these two types of righteousness must not be mixed with each other or both be injected into the article of justification by faith before God.

Song of Songs 4:7

כֻּלָּךְ יָפָה רַעְיָתִי וּמוּם אֵין בָּךְ׃

כֹּל (2 sg f sf): all – יָפֶה (f): beautiful – רַעְיָה (1 sg sf): darling – מוּם: flaw – אַיִן (cst): nonexistence

Ephesians 5:25-27

25Οἱ ἄνδρες, ἀγαπᾶτε τὰς γυναῖκας, καθὼς καὶ ὁ Χριστὸς
ἠγάπησεν τὴν ἐκκλησίαν καὶ ἑαυτὸν παρέδωκεν ὑπὲρ
αὐτῆς, 26ἵνα αὐτὴν ἁγιάσῃ καθαρίσας τῷ λουτρῷ τοῦ
ὕδατος ἐν ῥήματι, 27ἵνα παραστήσῃ αὐτὸς ἑαυτῷ ἔνδοξον
τὴν ἐκκλησίαν, μὴ ἔχουσαν σπίλον ἢ ῥυτίδα ἤ τι τῶν
τοιούτων, ἀλλ' ἵνα ᾖ ἁγία καὶ ἄμωμος.

ἀγαπάω (pres imv 2 pl): love – ἐκκλησία: church – παραδίδωμι (aor ind 3 sg): give up – ἁγιάζω (aor subj): make holy – καθαρίζω (aor ptcp): cleanse – λουτρός: washing – ῥῆμα: word – παρίστημι (aor subj): present – ἔνδοξος: splendid – σπίλος: moral blemish – ῥυτίς: wrinkle – ἄμωμος: blameless

Large Catechism I 208

Therefore, God has also most richly blessed this estate *[of marriage]* above all others. In addition, He has bestowed on it and wrapped up in it everything in the world, so that this estate might be well and richly provided for. Married life is, therefore, no joke or presumption. It is an excellent thing and a matter of divine seriousness.

May 4

Genesis 18:27-28

27וַיַּעַן אַבְרָהָם וַיֹּאמַר הִנֵּה־נָא הוֹאַלְתִּי לְדַבֵּר אֶל־
אֲדֹנָי וְאָנֹכִי עָפָר וָאֵפֶר׃ 28אוּלַי יַחְסְרוּן חֲמִשִּׁים
הַצַּדִּיקִם חֲמִשָּׁה הֲתַשְׁחִית בַּחֲמִשָּׁה אֶת־כָּל־הָעִיר וַיֹּאמֶר
לֹא אַשְׁחִית אִם־אֶמְצָא שָׁם אַרְבָּעִים וַחֲמִשָּׁה׃

עָנָה (qal v-c impf): answer – יָאַל (hiph pf 1 sg): undertake – עָפָר: dust – אֵפֶר: ashes – אוּלַי: perhaps – חָסֵר (qal impf 3 pl): be lacking – חֲמִשִּׁים: fifty – חֲמִשָּׁה: five – שָׁחַת (hiph impf 2 sg + interrog ה): destroy – אַרְבָּעִים: forty

---

James 5:17-18

17Ἠλίας ἄνθρωπος ἦν ὁμοιοπαθὴς ἡμῖν, καὶ προσευχῇ
προσηύξατο τοῦ μὴ βρέξαι, καὶ οὐκ ἔβρεξεν ἐπὶ τῆς γῆς
ἐνιαυτοὺς τρεῖς καὶ μῆνας ἕξ· 18καὶ πάλιν προσηύξατο,
καὶ ὁ οὐρανὸς ὑετὸν ἔδωκεν καὶ ἡ γῆ ἐβλάστησεν τὸν
καρπὸν αὐτῆς.

ὁμοιοπαθής: with the same nature – προσευχή: prayer – προσεύχομαι (aor ind 3 sg): pray – βρέχω (aor inf/aor ind 3 sg): rain – ἐνιαυτός: year – ὑετός: rain – δίδωμι (aor ind 3 sg): give – βλαστάνω (aor ind): produce – καρπός: fruit

---

Large Catechism III 8

But praying, as the Second Commandment teaches, is to call upon God in every need. He requires this of us and has not left it to our choice. But it is our duty and obligation to pray, if we would be Christians.

May 5

Jeremiah 17:9

עָקֹ֥ב הַלֵּ֛ב מִכֹּ֖ל וְאָנֻ֣שׁ ה֑וּא מִ֖י יֵדָעֶֽנּוּ׃

עָקֹב: deceitful – **לֵב**: heart – **אָנֻשׁ**: incurable – **יָדַע** (qal impf 3 sg + 3 sg sf): understand

Luke 22:61

καὶ στραφεὶς ὁ κύριος ἐνέβλεψεν τῷ Πέτρῳ, καὶ ὑπεμνήσθη ὁ Πέτρος τοῦ ῥήματος τοῦ κυρίου ὡς εἶπεν αὐτῷ ὅτι πρὶν ἀλέκτορα φωνῆσαι σήμερον ἀπαρνήσῃ με τρίς.

> στρέφω (aor pass ptcp): turn around – ἐμβλέπω (aor ind 3 sg): look at – ὑπομιμνήσκω (aor pass 3 sg): remember – ῥῆμα: word – πρίν: before – ἀλέκτωρ: rooster – φωνέω (aor inf): call out, crow – σήμερον: today – ἀπαρνέομαι (fut 2 sg): deny

Large Catechism I 273

Therefore, if you meet an idle tongue that betrays and slanders someone, contradict such a person promptly to his face [Prov 10:31], so he may blush.

May 6

Exodus 16:15

וַיִּרְאוּ בְנֵֽי־יִשְׂרָאֵל וַיֹּאמְרוּ אִישׁ אֶל־אָחִיו מָן הוּא כִּי
לֹא יָדְעוּ מַה־הוּא וַיֹּאמֶר מֹשֶׁה אֲלֵהֶם הוּא הַלֶּחֶם אֲשֶׁר
נָתַן יְהוָה לָכֶם לְאָכְלָה׃

רָאָה (qal v-c impf 3 pl): see – אָח (3 sg sf): brother = one to another – מָן: manna – אָכְלָה: food

John 6:51-53

51ἐγώ εἰμι ὁ ἄρτος ὁ ζῶν ὁ ἐκ τοῦ οὐρανοῦ καταβάς· ἐάν τις
φάγῃ ἐκ τούτου τοῦ ἄρτου ζήσει εἰς τὸν αἰῶνα, καὶ ὁ ἄρτος
δὲ ὃν ἐγὼ δώσω ἡ σάρξ μού ἐστιν ὑπὲρ τῆς τοῦ κόσμου
ζωῆς. 52Ἐμάχοντο οὖν πρὸς ἀλλήλους οἱ Ἰουδαῖοι λέγοντες·
πῶς δύναται οὗτος ἡμῖν δοῦναι τὴν σάρκα [αὐτοῦ] φαγεῖν;
53εἶπεν οὖν αὐτοῖς ὁ Ἰησοῦς· ἀμὴν ἀμὴν λέγω ὑμῖν, ἐὰν μὴ
φάγητε τὴν σάρκα τοῦ υἱοῦ τοῦ ἀνθρώπου καὶ πίητε αὐτοῦ
τὸ αἷμα, οὐκ ἔχετε ζωὴν ἐν ἑαυτοῖς.

ἄρτος: bread – ζάω (pres ptcp/fut ind): live – καταβαίνω (aor ptcp): come down – ἐσθίω (aor subj 3 sg): eat – αἰών: eternity – δίδωμι (fut ind 1 sg): give – σάρξ: flesh – κόσμος: world – μάχομαι (impf 3 pl): argue – δύναμαι (pres ind 3 sg): be able – δίδωμι (aor inf): give – πίνω (aor subj 2 pl): drink – αἷμα: blood – ζωή: life

Apology XXII (X) 10

The Sacrament was instituted to comfort terrified minds. This happens when they believe that Christ's flesh is given as food for the life of the world [John 6:51] and when they believe that, being joined to Christ, they are made alive.

Genesis 3:7

וַתִּפָּקַחְנָה עֵינֵי שְׁנֵיהֶם וַיֵּדְעוּ כִּי עֵירֻמִּם הֵם וַיִּתְפְּרוּ
עֲלֵה תְאֵנָה וַיַּעֲשׂוּ לָהֶם חֲגֹרֹת׃

פָּקַח (niph v-c impf 3 pl f): be opened – עַיִן (cst pl): eye – שְׁנַיִם (3 pl sf): two – יָדַע (qal v-c impf 3 pl): know – עֵירֹם: naked – תָּפַר (qal v-c impf 3 pl): sew together – עָלֶה (cst sg): leaf – תְּאֵנָה: fig tree – חֲגוֹרָה (pl): loincloth

---

2 Corinthians 11:3

φοβοῦμαι δὲ μή πως, ὡς ὁ ὄφις ἐξηπάτησεν Εὕαν ἐν τῇ πανουργίᾳ αὐτοῦ, φθαρῇ τὰ νοήματα ὑμῶν ἀπὸ τῆς ἁπλότητος [καὶ τῆς ἁγνότητος] τῆς εἰς τὸν Χριστόν.

φοβοῦμαι (pres 1 sg): be afraid – πως (enclitic particle): somehow, perhaps – ὄφις: snake – ἐξαπατάω (aor 3 sg): deceive – πανουργία: cunning – φθείρω (aor pass subj): be led astray – νόημα: mind – ἁπλότης: sincerity – ἁγνότης: purity

---

Formula of Concord SD I 9

Because of the disobedience of Adam and Eve, hereditary evil is the guilt by which we are all in God's displeasure and are, by nature, children of wrath, as the apostle shows (Rom 5:12-14 [;Eph 2:3]).

May 8

Psalm 139:23-24

23 חָקְרֵ֣נִי אֵ֭ל וְדַ֣ע לְבָבִ֑י בְּ֝חָנֵ֗נִי וְדַ֣ע שַׂרְעַפָּֽי׃

24 וּרְאֵ֗ה אִם־דֶּֽרֶךְ־עֹ֥צֶב בִּ֑י וּ֝נְחֵ֗נִי בְּדֶ֣רֶךְ עוֹלָֽם׃

חָקַר (qal imv + 1 sg sf): search – יָדַע (qal imv): know – לֵבָב (1 sg sf): heart – בָּחַן (qal imv + 1 sg sf): examine – שַׂרְעַפִּים (1 sg sf): disquieting thoughts – רָאָה (qal imv sg): see – עֹצֶב: pain = hurtful way – נָחָה (qal imv + 1 sg sf): lead

---

Romans 12:1

Παρακαλῶ οὖν ὑμᾶς, ἀδελφοί, διὰ τῶν οἰκτιρμῶν τοῦ θεοῦ παραστῆσαι τὰ σώματα ὑμῶν θυσίαν ζῶσαν ἁγίαν εὐάρεστον τῷ θεῷ, τὴν λογικὴν λατρείαν ὑμῶν·

> παρακαλέω (pres ind): urge, encourage – οἰκτιρμός: mercy – παρίστημι (aor inf): offer – σῶμα (pl): body – θυσία: sacrifice – ζάω (pres ptcp): live – ἅγιος: holy – εὐάρεστος: pleasing – λογικός: spiritual – λατρεία: act of worship

---

Apology XV (VIII) 45

We teach this about the putting to death of the flesh and discipline of the body. Just as the Confession states, a true and not a false putting to death [mortification] happens through the cross and troubles, by which God exercises us. In them we must obey God's will, as Paul says, "Present your bodies as a living sacrifice" (Rom 12:1). They are the spiritual exercises of fear and faith.

MAY 9

Genesis 3:6

וַתֵּרֶא הָאִשָּׁה כִּי טוֹב הָעֵץ לְמַאֲכָל וְכִי תַאֲוָה־הוּא
לָעֵינַיִם וְנֶחְמָד הָעֵץ לְהַשְׂכִּיל וַתִּקַּח מִפִּרְיוֹ וַתֹּאכַל
וַתִּתֵּן גַּם־לְאִישָׁהּ עִמָּהּ וַיֹּאכַל׃

רָאָה (qal v-c impf 3 sg f): see – עֵץ: tree – מַאֲכָל: food – תַּאֲוָה: a thing desirable – עַיִן (du): eye – חָמַד (niph ptcp): desirable – שָׂכַל (hiph inf cst): gain wisdom – לָקַח (qal v-c impf): take – פְּרִי (3 sg sf): fruit – אָכַל (qal v-c impf 3 sg f/3 sg m): eat

---

Matthew 4:3-4

3καὶ προσελθὼν ὁ πειράζων εἶπεν αὐτῷ· εἰ υἱὸς εἶ τοῦ θεοῦ,
εἰπὲ ἵνα οἱ λίθοι οὗτοι ἄρτοι γένωνται. 4ὁ δὲ ἀποκριθεὶς
εἶπεν· γέγραπται· οὐκ ἐπ' ἄρτῳ μόνῳ ζήσεται ὁ ἄνθρωπος,
ἀλλ' ἐπὶ παντὶ ῥήματι ἐκπορευομένῳ διὰ στόματος θεοῦ.

προσέρχομαι (aor ptcp): come to – πειράζω (pres ptcp): tempt – υἱός: son – εἶπον (aor imv): tell – λίθος: stone – ἄρτος: bread – γίνομαι (aor subj): become – ἀποκρίνομαι (aor pass ptcp): answer – γράφω (pf pass): write – ζάω (fut ind 3 sg): live – ῥῆμα: word – ἐκπορεύομαι (pres ptcp): come out of – στόμα: mouth

---

Apology XX 85

The consciences of the pious will not have sure enough comfort against the terrors of sin and of death, and against the devil tempting with despair, if they do not know that their confidence lies in the forgiveness of sins freely for Christ's sake.

MAY 10

Deuteronomy 8:2

וְזָכַרְתָּ אֶת־כָּל־הַדֶּרֶךְ אֲשֶׁר הֹלִיכֲךָ יְהוָה אֱלֹהֶיךָ
זֶה אַרְבָּעִים שָׁנָה בַּמִּדְבָּר לְמַעַן עַנֹּתְךָ לְנַסֹּתְךָ לָדַעַת
אֶת־אֲשֶׁר בִּלְבָבְךָ הֲתִשְׁמֹר מִצְוֹתָו [מִצְוֹתָיו] אִם־לֹא׃

זָכַר (qal v-c pf 2 sg): remember – הָלַךְ (hiph pf 3 sg + 2 sg sf): lead – אַרְבָּעִים: forty – מִדְבָּר: wild wasteland – עָנָה (pi inf cst + 2 sg sf): humble – נָסָה (pi inf cst + 2 sg sf): test – יָדַע (qal inf cst): know – לֵבָב (2 sg sf): heart

---

John 13:6-8

6ἔρχεται οὖν πρὸς Σίμωνα Πέτρον· λέγει αὐτῷ· κύριε, σύ
μου νίπτεις τοὺς πόδας; 7ἀπεκρίθη Ἰησοῦς καὶ εἶπεν αὐτῷ·
ὃ ἐγὼ ποιῶ σὺ οὐκ οἶδας ἄρτι, γνώσῃ δὲ μετὰ ταῦτα. 8λέγει
αὐτῷ Πέτρος· οὐ μὴ νίψῃς μου τοὺς πόδας εἰς τὸν αἰῶνα.
ἀπεκρίθη Ἰησοῦς αὐτῷ· ἐὰν μὴ νίψω σε, οὐκ ἔχεις μέρος
μετ᾽ ἐμοῦ.

νίπτω (pres ind 2 sg/aor subj 2 sg/aor subj 1 sg): wash – ποῦς (acc pl): foot – ἀποκρίνομαι (aor ind 3 sg): answer – οἶδα (pf 2 sg with pres meaning): know – ἄρτι: now – γινώσκω (fut ind 2 sg): know – αἰών: eternity – μέρος: part

---

Small Catechism Table of Duties

Likewise, husbands, live with your wives in an understanding way, showing honor to the woman as the weaker vessel, since they are heirs with you of the grace of life, so that your prayers may not be hindered. (1 Pet 3:7).

MAY 11

Psalm 37:30-31

30פִּֽי־צַ֭דִּיק יֶהְגֶּ֣ה חָכְמָ֑ה וּ֝לְשׁוֹנ֗וֹ תְּדַבֵּ֥ר מִשְׁפָּֽט׃
31תּוֹרַ֣ת אֱלֹהָ֣יו בְּלִבּ֑וֹ לֹ֖א תִמְעַ֣ד אֲשֻׁרָֽיו׃

פֶּה (cst sg): mouth – צַדִּיק: righteous – הָגָה (qal impf 3 sg): speak – חָכְמָה: wisdom – לָשׁוֹן (3 sg sf): tongue – מִשְׁפָּט: what is just – תּוֹרָה (cst sg): law, teaching – לֵב (3 sg sf): heart – מָעַד (qal impf 3 sg f): slip – אָשֻׁר (pl f + 3 sg sf): step

---

Acts 4:18-20

18Καὶ καλέσαντες αὐτοὺς παρήγγειλαν τὸ καθόλου μὴ
φθέγγεσθαι μηδὲ διδάσκειν ἐπὶ τῷ ὀνόματι τοῦ Ἰησοῦ.
19ὁ δὲ Πέτρος καὶ Ἰωάννης ἀποκριθέντες εἶπον πρὸς
αὐτούς· εἰ δίκαιόν ἐστιν ἐνώπιον τοῦ θεοῦ ὑμῶν ἀκούειν
μᾶλλον ἢ τοῦ θεοῦ, κρίνατε· 20οὐ δυνάμεθα γὰρ ἡμεῖς ἃ
εἴδαμεν καὶ ἠκούσαμεν μὴ λαλεῖν.

καλέω (aor ptcp pl): call – παραγγέλλω (aor ind 3 pl): command – καθόλου: at all – φθέγγομαι (pres inf): speak – διδάσκω (pres inf): teach – δίκαιος: right – ἀκούω (pres inf): listen, obey – κρίνω (aor imv 2 pl): judge – δύναμαι (pres 1 pl): be able – ὁράω (aor ind 1 pl): see – λαλέω (pres inf): speak

---

Large Catechism I 70

On the other hand, children should be constantly urged and moved to honor God's name and to have it always upon their lips for everything that may happen to them or come to their notice [Ps 8:2; 34:1; Matt 21:16; Heb 13:15].

May 12

Psalm 25:18

רְאֵה עָנְיִי וַעֲמָלִי וְשָׂא לְכָל־חַטֹּאותָי׃

רָאָה (qal imv sg): look upon – עֳנִי (1 sg sf): affliction – עָמָל (1 sg sf): trouble – נָשָׂא (qal imv sg): forgive – חַטָּאת (pl + 1 sg sf): sin

---

Matthew 9:5-7

5τί γάρ ἐστιν εὐκοπώτερον, εἰπεῖν· ἀφίενταί σου αἱ
ἁμαρτίαι, ἢ εἰπεῖν· ἔγειρε καὶ περιπάτει; 6ἵνα δὲ εἰδῆτε
ὅτι ἐξουσίαν ἔχει ὁ υἱὸς τοῦ ἀνθρώπου ἐπὶ τῆς γῆς ἀφιέναι
ἁμαρτίας—τότε λέγει τῷ παραλυτικῷ—ἐγερθεὶς ἆρόν σου
τὴν κλίνην καὶ ὕπαγε εἰς τὸν οἶκον σου 7καὶ ἐγερθεὶς
ἀπῆλθεν εἰς τὸν οἶκον αὐτοῦ.

εὐκοπώτερον: easier – εἶπον (inf): say – ἀφίημι (pres pass 3 pl/pres act inf): pardon – ἁμαρτία: sin – ἐγείρω (pres imv 2 sg): get up – περιπατέω (pres imv 2 sg): walk – οἶδα (subj 2 pl): know – ἐξουσία: authority – παραλυτικός: paralyzed man – αἴρω (aor imv 2 sg): lift up – κλίνη: mat – ὑπάγω (pres imv): go – οἶκος: house

---

Large Catechism III 88

There is here again great need for us to call upon God and to pray, "Dear Father, forgive us our trespasses." It is not as though He did not forgive sin without and even before our prayer. (He has given us the Gospel, in which is pure forgiveness before we prayed or ever thought about it [Rom 5:8].) But the purpose of this prayer is that we may recognize and receive such forgiveness.

MAY 13

1 Samuel 12:22

כִּי לֹא־יִטֹּשׁ יְהוָה אֶת־עַמּוֹ בַּעֲבוּר שְׁמוֹ הַגָּדוֹל
כִּי הוֹאִיל יְהוָה לַעֲשׂוֹת אֶתְכֶם לוֹ לְעָם׃

נָטַשׁ (qal impf 3 sg): forsake – עַם (3 sg sf): people – בַּעֲבוּר: for the sake of – שֵׁם (3 sg sf): name – גָּדוֹל: great – יָאַל (hiph pf 3 sg): be pleased – עָשָׂה (qal inf cst): make

---

2 Corinthians 6:2

λέγει γάρ· καιρῷ δεκτῷ ἐπήκουσά σου καὶ ἐν ἡμέρᾳ σωτηρίας ἐβοήθησά σοι. ἰδοὺ νῦν καιρὸς εὐπρόσδεκτος, ἰδοὺ νῦν ἡμέρα σωτηρίας.

καιρός: time – δεκτός: favorable (God's favor) – ἐπακούω (aor ind 1 sg): listen to – βοηθέω (aor ind 1 sg): help – εὐπρόσδεκτος: favorable

---

Apology IV (II) 40-41

But the promise of forgiveness of sins and of justification has been given us for Christ's sake, who was given for us in order that He might make satisfaction for the sins of the world. He has been appointed as the Mediator and Atoning Sacrifice. This promise does not depend on our merits, but freely offers forgiveness of sins and justification.

May 14

Proverbs 3:13,17

13 אַשְׁרֵי אָדָם מָצָא חָכְמָה וְאָדָם יָפִיק תְּבוּנָה׃

17 דְּרָכֶיהָ דַרְכֵי־נֹעַם וְכָל־נְתִיבוֹתֶיהָ שָׁלוֹם׃

אֶשֶׁר (cst pl): blessedness – מָצָא (qal pf 3 sg): find – חָכְמָה: wisdom – פּוּק (hiph impf 3 sg): obtain – תְּבוּנָה: understanding – דֶּרֶךְ (pl + 3 sg sf/cst pl): way – נֹעַם: pleasantness – נְתִיבָה (pl + 3 sg sf): path – שָׁלוֹם: peace

---

John 14:21

ὁ ἔχων τὰς ἐντολάς μου καὶ τηρῶν αὐτὰς ἐκεῖνός ἐστιν ὁ ἀγαπῶν με· ὁ δὲ ἀγαπῶν με ἀγαπηθήσεται ὑπὸ τοῦ πατρός μου, κἀγὼ ἀγαπήσω αὐτὸν καὶ ἐμφανίσω αὐτῷ ἐμαυτόν.

ἐντολή (acc pl): command – τηρέω (pres ptcp): obey – ἀγαπάω (pres ptcp/fut pass 3 sg/fut ind 1 sg): love – ἐμφανίζω (fut ind 1 sg): reveal

---

Apology V (III) 67

Therefore, we tell godly minds to consider the promises, and we teach about free forgiveness of sins and about reconciliation, which happens through faith in Christ. Afterward, we add also the teaching of the Law. It is necessary to distinguish these things aright, as Paul says in 2 Tim 2:15. We must see what Scripture says about the Law and what it says about the promises. For it praises works in such a way that it does not remove the free promise.

MAY 15

Psalm 19:2

הַשָּׁמַיִם מְסַפְּרִים כְּבוֹד־אֵל וּמַעֲשֵׂה יָדָיו מַגִּיד הָרָקִיעַ׃

הַשָּׁמַיִם: the heavens – סָפַר (pi ptcp pl): declare – כָּבוֹד (cst sg): glory – מַעֲשֶׂה (cst sg): work – נָגַד (hiph ptcp): tell – רָקִיעַ: firmament, skies

---

Romans 1:19-20

19διότι τὸ γνωστὸν τοῦ θεοῦ φανερόν ἐστιν ἐν αὐτοῖς· ὁ
θεὸς γὰρ αὐτοῖς ἐφανέρωσεν. 20τὰ γὰρ ἀόρατα αὐτοῦ ἀπὸ
κτίσεως κόσμου τοῖς ποιήμασιν νοούμενα καθορᾶται, ἥ τε
ἀΐδιος αὐτοῦ δύναμις καὶ θειότης, εἰς τὸ εἶναι αὐτοὺς
ἀναπολογήτους . . .

γνωστός: known, capable of being known – φανερός: plain, evident – φανερόω (aor ind 3 sg): make known – ἀόρατος: unseen, invisible – κτίσις: creation – ποίημα: what is made – νοέω (pres pass ptcp): understand – καθοράω (pres pass 3 sg): perceive – ἀΐδιος: eternal – θειότης: deity – ἀναπολόγητος: without excuse

---

Apology II (I) 11

Scripture everywhere warns us, as the Prophets constantly complain, about putting our confidence in our human abilities, contempt for God, hating God, and similar faults with which we are born.

MAY 16

Ecclesiastes 12:7

וְיָשֹׁב הֶעָפָר עַל־הָאָרֶץ כְּשֶׁהָיָה
וְהָרוּחַ תָּשׁוּב אֶל־הָאֱלֹהִים אֲשֶׁר נְתָנָהּ׃

שׁוּב (qal impf 3 sg m/3 sg f): return – עָפָר: dust – שֶׁהָיָה (שֶׁ = אֲשֶׁר): as it was – רוּחַ: spirit – נָתַן (qal pf 3 sg + 3 sg f sf): give

---

1 Corinthians 15:47, 49

47ὁ πρῶτος ἄνθρωπος ἐκ γῆς χοϊκός, ὁ δεύτερος ἄνθρωπος ἐξ οὐρανοῦ . . . 49καὶ καθὼς ἐφορέσαμεν τὴν εἰκόνα τοῦ χοϊκοῦ, φορέσομεν καὶ τὴν εἰκόνα τοῦ ἐπουρανίου.

πρῶτος: first – γῆ: earth – χοϊκός: made of earth – δεύτερος: second – φορέω (aor ind 1 pl/fut ind 1 pl): bear, wear – εἰκών: likeness – ἐπουράνιος: heavenly

---

Formula of Concord SD I 33

But a distinction must also be maintained between our nature as created and preserved by God (in which sin is indwelling) and original sin (which dwells in the nature). These two things can, and must, be considered, taught, and believed separately according to Holy Scripture.

MAY 17

Isaiah 55:10-11

10 כִּי כַּאֲשֶׁר יֵרֵד הַגֶּשֶׁם וְהַשֶּׁלֶג מִן־הַשָּׁמַיִם
וְשָׁמָּה לֹא יָשׁוּב כִּי אִם־הִרְוָה אֶת־הָאָרֶץ
וְהוֹלִידָהּ וְהִצְמִיחָהּ וְנָתַן זֶרַע לַזֹּרֵעַ וְלֶחֶם לָאֹכֵל׃
11 כֵּן יִהְיֶה דְבָרִי אֲשֶׁר יֵצֵא מִפִּי לֹא־יָשׁוּב אֵלַי רֵיקָם
כִּי אִם־עָשָׂה אֶת־אֲשֶׁר חָפַצְתִּי וְהִצְלִיחַ אֲשֶׁר שְׁלַחְתִּיו׃

גֶּשֶׁם: rain – שֶׁלֶג: snow – שָׁמָּה: there – רָוָה (hiph pf 3 sg): water – יָלַד (hiph pf 3 sg + 3 sg f sf): cause to bear – צָמַח (hiph pf 3 sg + 3 sg f sf): cause to bud – זָרַע (qal ptcp): sower – אָכַל (qal ptcp): eater – רֵיקָם: empty – חָפֵץ (qal pf 1 sg): delight in, desire – צָלַח (hiph pf 3 sg): prosper – שָׁלַח (qal pf 1 sg + 3 sg sf): send

1 John 1:3

ὃ ἑωράκαμεν καὶ ἀκηκόαμεν, ἀπαγγέλλομεν καὶ ὑμῖν, ἵνα καὶ ὑμεῖς κοινωνίαν ἔχητε μεθ’ ἡμῶν. καὶ ἡ κοινωνία δὲ ἡ ἡμετέρα μετὰ τοῦ πατρὸς καὶ μετὰ τοῦ υἱοῦ αὐτοῦ Ἰησοῦ Χριστοῦ.

ὁράω (pf ind 1 pl): see – ἀκούω (pf ind 1 pl): hear – ἀπαγγέλλω (pres ind 1 pl): proclaim – κοινωνία: fellowship

Large Catechism IV 17

Therefore, Baptism is not only natural water, but a divine, heavenly, holy, and blessed water, and whatever other terms we can find to praise it. This is all because of the Word, which is a heavenly, holy Word, which no one can praise enough. For it has, and is able to do, all that God is and can do [Isa 55:10-11].

May 18

Psalm 47:6-8

6 עָלָה אֱלֹהִים בִּתְרוּעָה יְהוָה בְּקוֹל שׁוֹפָר׃
7 זַמְּרוּ אֱלֹהִים זַמֵּרוּ זַמְּרוּ לְמַלְכֵּנוּ זַמֵּרוּ׃
8 כִּי מֶלֶךְ כָּל־הָאָרֶץ אֱלֹהִים זַמְּרוּ מַשְׂכִּיל׃

עָלָה (qal pf 3 sg): go up – תְּרוּעָה: shout of joy – קוֹל: sound – שׁוֹפָר: trumpet – זָמַר (pi imv pl): sing praises – מֶלֶךְ (1 pl sf): king – מַשְׂכִּיל: song of praise

---

Ephesians 1:20-22

20 Ἣν ἐνήργησεν ἐν τῷ Χριστῷ ἐγείρας αὐτὸν ἐκ νεκρῶν
καὶ καθίσας ἐν δεξιᾷ αὐτοῦ ἐν τοῖς ἐπουρανίοις 21 ὑπεράνω
πάσης ἀρχῆς καὶ ἐξουσίας καὶ δυνάμεως καὶ κυριότητος
καὶ παντὸς ὀνόματος ὀνομαζομένου, οὐ μόνον ἐν τῷ αἰῶνι
τούτῳ ἀλλὰ καὶ ἐν τῷ μέλλοντι· 22 καὶ πάντα ὑπέταξεν ὑπὸ
τοὺς πόδας αὐτοῦ καὶ αὐτὸν ἔδωκεν κεφαλὴν ὑπὲρ πάντα
τῇ ἐκκλησίᾳ . . .

ἐνεργέω (aor ind 3 sg): be at work, produce – ἐγείρω (aor ptcp): raise – νεκρός: dead – καθίζω (aor ptcp): seat, set – δεξιά (χείρ): the right hand – ἐπουράνιος: heavenly (place) – ὑπεράνω: far above – ἀρχή: rule – ἐξουσία: authority – κυριότης: dominion – ὀνομάζω (pres pass ptcp): give a name, call – αἰών: age – μέλλω (pres ptcp): be about to, coming – ὑποτάσσω (aor ind 3 sg): subordinate

---

Formula of Concord SD VIII 12

Christ's human nature has been exalted to the right hand of majesty, power, and might, over everything that can be named, not only in this world, but also in that which is to come [Eph 1:21].

Genesis 28:15

וְהִנֵּה אָנֹכִי עִמָּךְ וּשְׁמַרְתִּיךָ בְּכֹל אֲשֶׁר־תֵּלֵךְ וַהֲשִׁבֹתִיךָ
אֶל־הָאֲדָמָה הַזֹּאת כִּי לֹא אֶעֱזָבְךָ עַד אֲשֶׁר אִם־עָשִׂיתִי
אֵת אֲשֶׁר־דִּבַּרְתִּי לָךְ׃

שָׁמַר (qal v-c pf 1 sg + 2 sg sf): watch over – שׁוּב (hiph v-c pf 1 sg + 2 sg sf): bring back – אֲדָמָה: land – עָזַב (qal impf 1 sg + 2 sg sf): leave, forsake

---

John 14:18

Οὐκ ἀφήσω ὑμᾶς ὀρφανούς, ἔρχομαι πρὸς ὑμᾶς.

ἀφίημι (fut ind 1 sg): leave – ὀρφανός (acc pl): orphan – ἔρχομαι (pres ind 1 sg): come

---

Apology XVII

The adversaries accept Article XVII without qualification. In it we confess that Christ will appear at the consummation of the world. He will raise up all the dead and will give eternal life and eternal joys to the godly [2 Tim 4:8], but He will condemn the ungodly to endless punishment with the devil [Matt 25:46].

May 20

Isaiah 41:10

אַל־תִּירָא כִּי עִמְּךָ־אָנִי אַל־תִּשְׁתָּע כִּי־אֲנִי אֱלֹהֶיךָ
אִמַּצְתִּיךָ אַף־עֲזַרְתִּיךָ אַף־תְּמַכְתִּיךָ בִּימִין צִדְקִי׃

יָרֵא (qal juss 2 sg): fear – שָׁעָה (hithp juss 2 sg): be anxious – אָמֵץ (pi pf 1 sg + 2 sg sf): strengthen – עָזַר (qal pf 1 sg + 2 sg sf): help – תָּמַךְ (qal pf 1 sg + 2 sg sf): support – יָמִין: right hand – צֶדֶק: righteousness

---

Hebrews 2:17

ὅθεν ὤφειλεν κατὰ πάντα τοῖς ἀδελφοῖς ὁμοιωθῆναι, ἵνα ἐλεήμων γένηται καὶ πιστὸς ἀρχιερεὺς τὰ πρὸς τὸν θεὸν εἰς τὸ ἱλάσκεσθαι τὰς ἁμαρτίας τοῦ λαοῦ.

ὅθεν: therefore – ὀφείλω (impf ind): be obligated – ὁμοιόω (aor pass inf): make like – ἐλεήμων: merciful – γίνομαι (aor subj): become – πιστός: faithful – ἀρχιερεύς: high priest – τὰ πρός: in respect to – ἱλάσκομαι (pres inf): make atonement for

---

Formula of Concord SD I 43

Second, in the article of Redemption the Scriptures testify forcefully that God's Son received our human nature without sin. So He was in all ways—sin excluded—made like us, His brethren (Heb 2:14-17).

May 21

Isaiah 53:4

אָכֵן חֳלָיֵנוּ הוּא נָשָׂא וּמַכְאֹבֵינוּ סְבָלָם
וַאֲנַחְנוּ חֲשַׁבְנֻהוּ נָגוּעַ מֻכֵּה אֱלֹהִים וּמְעֻנֶּה׃

אָכֵן: surely – חֳלִי (pl + 1 pl sf): infirmity – מַכְאֹב (pl + 1 pl sf): pain – סָבַל (qal pf 3 sg + 3 pl sf): carry – חָשַׁב (qal pf 1 pl + 3 sg sf): consider – נָגַע (qal pass ptcp): stricken – נָכָה (hoph ptcp cst): smitten – עָנָה (pu ptcp): afflicted

Matthew 8:16-17

16 Ὀψίας δὲ γενομένης προσήνεγκαν αὐτῷ δαιμονιζομένους
πολλούς· καὶ ἐξέβαλεν τὰ πνεύματα λόγῳ καὶ πάντας τοὺς
κακῶς ἔχοντας ἐθεράπευσεν, 17 ὅπως πληρωθῇ τὸ ῥηθὲν διὰ
Ἠσαΐου τοῦ προφήτου λέγοντος· Αὐτὸς τὰς ἀσθενείας
ἡμῶν ἔλαβεν καὶ τὰς νόσους ἐβάστασεν.

ὀψία: evening – προσφέρω (aor ind 3 pl): bring – δαιμονίζομαι (pres ptcp): be possessed – κακῶς ἔχοντες: those who were sick – πληρόω (aor pass subj 3 sg): fulfill – ῥηθέν (aor pass ptcp of λέγω/εἶπον): speak – ἀσθένεια: infirmity – νόσος: disease – βαστάζω (aor ind 3 sg): carry

Large Catechism II 30

He *[Jesus Christ]* has taken us as His own property under His shelter and protection [Ps 61:3-4] so that He may govern us by His righteousness, wisdom, power, life, and blessedness.

May 22

Psalm 106:1

הַלְלוּיָהּ
הוֹדוּ לַיהוָה כִּי־טוֹב כִּי לְעוֹלָם חַסְדּוֹ׃

הָלַל (pi imv pl): praise – יָהּ (proper name contracted from יְהוָה): the LORD – יָדָה (hiph imv pl): give thanks – לְעוֹלָם: forever – חֶסֶד (3 sg sf): faithful love

---

Ephesians 4:7-8

7 Ἑνὶ δὲ ἑκάστῳ ἡμῶν ἐδόθη ἡ χάρις κατὰ τὸ μέτρον
τῆς δωρεᾶς τοῦ Χριστοῦ. 8 διὸ λέγει· ἀναβὰς εἰς
ὕψος ᾐχμαλώτευσεν αἰχμαλωσίαν, ἔδωκεν δόματα
τοῖς ἀνθρώποις.

> ἕκαστος: each – δίδωμι (aor pass 3 sg): give – μέτρον: measure – δωρεά: gift – ἀναβαίνω (aor ptcp): ascend – ὕψος: high place, heaven – αἰχμαλωτεύω (aor ind 3 sg): take captive – αἰχμαλωσία: captivity – δίδωμι (aor ind 3 sg): give – δόμα (pl): gift

---

Power and Primacy 67

Wherever the Church is, there is the authority to administer the Gospel. Therefore, it is necessary for the Church to retain the authority to call, elect, and ordain ministers. This authority is a gift that in reality is given to the Church. No human power can take this gift away from the Church. As Paul testifies to the Ephesians, when "He ascended . . . He gave gifts to men" (Eph 4:8).

May 23

Psalm 103:19

יְהוָה בַּשָּׁמַיִם הֵכִין כִּסְאוֹ וּמַלְכוּתוֹ בַּכֹּל מָשָׁלָה׃

שָׁמַיִם: heaven – כּוּן (hiph pf 3 sg): establish – כִּסֵּא: throne – מַלְכוּת: kingdom – מָשַׁל (qal pf 3 sg f): rule

1 Corinthians 15:24-25

24εἶτα τὸ τέλος, ὅταν παραδιδῷ τὴν βασιλείαν τῷ θεῷ καὶ
πατρί, ὅταν καταργήσῃ πᾶσαν ἀρχὴν καὶ πᾶσαν ἐξουσίαν
καὶ δύναμιν. 25δεῖ γὰρ αὐτὸν βασιλεύειν ἄχρι οὗ θῇ πάντας
τοὺς ἐχθροὺς ὑπὸ τοὺς πόδας αὐτοῦ.

εἶτα: then – τέλος: end – παραδίδωμι (pres subj 3 sg): hand over – βασιλεία: kingdom – καταργέω (aor subj 3 sg): destroy – ἀρχή: dominion – ἐξουσία: authority – δύναμις: power – βασιλεύω (pres inf): reign – ἄχρι οὗ: until – τίθημι (aor act subj 3 sg): put – ἐχθρός: enemy

Formula of Concord Ep VIII 16

Christ always had this majesty according to the personal union. Yet He abstained from using it in the state of His humiliation, and because of this He truly increased in all wisdom and favor with God and men. Therefore, He did not always use this majesty, but only when it pleased Him. Then, after His resurrection, He entirely laid aside the form of a servant, but not the human nature, and was established in the full use, manifestation, and declaration of the divine majesty.

May 24

Genesis 3:15

וְאֵיבָה אָשִׁית בֵּינְךָ וּבֵין הָאִשָּׁה וּבֵין זַרְעֲךָ וּבֵין זַרְעָהּ
הוּא יְשׁוּפְךָ רֹאשׁ וְאַתָּה תְּשׁוּפֶנּוּ עָקֵב׃

אֵיבָה: enmity – שִׁית (qal impf 1 sg): put, set – זֶרַע (2 sg m sf/3 sg f sf): seed – שׁוּף: (qal impf 3 sg m + 2 sg m sf/2 sg m + 3 sg m sf): strike at – עָקֵב: heel

Romans 16:20

ὁ δὲ θεὸς τῆς εἰρήνης συντρίψει τὸν σαταναν̂ ὑπὸ τοὺς πόδας ὑμῶν ἐν τάχει. Ἡ χάρις τοῦ κυρίου ἡμῶν Ἰησοῦ μεθ' ὑμῶν.

εἰρήνη: peace – συντρίβω (fut ind 3 sg): crush – τάχος: speed, quickness

Formula of Concord SD V 23

They *[the patriarchs]* encouraged and comforted themselves again by the preaching about the woman's seed, who would bruise the Serpent's head (Gen 3:15); Abraham's seed, in whom "all the nations of the earth [will] be blessed" (Gen 22:18); David's Son, who should "bring back the preserved of Israel" and be "a light for the nations" (Is 49:6; see also Ps 110:1; Luke 2:32), and who "was wounded for our transgressions; He was crushed for our iniquities . . . and with His stripes we are healed" (Is 53:5).

May 25

Psalm 86:4-5

4שַׂמֵּחַ נֶפֶשׁ עַבְדֶּךָ כִּי אֵלֶיךָ אֲדֹנָי נַפְשִׁי אֶשָּׂא׃
5כִּי־אַתָּה אֲדֹנָי טוֹב וְסַלָּח וְרַב־חֶסֶד לְכָל־קֹרְאֶיךָ׃

שָׂמַח (pi imv sg): bring joy to – נֶ֫פֶשׁ: soul – עֶ֫בֶד (2 sg sf): servant – נָשָׂא: (qal impf 1 sg): lift up – טוֹב: good, kind – סַלָּח: forgiving – רַב: abounding in – חֶ֫סֶד: faithful love – קָרָא (qal ptcp + 2 sg sf): call upon

John 14:13-14

13καὶ ὅ τι ἂν αἰτήσητε ἐν τῷ ὀνόματί μου τοῦτο ποιήσω,
ἵνα δοξασθῇ ὁ πατὴρ ἐν τῷ υἱῷ. 14ἐάν τι αἰτήσητέ με ἐν
τῷ ὀνόματί μου ἐγὼ ποιήσω.

αἰτέω (aor subj 2 pl): ask – ὄνομα: name – ποιέω (fut ind 1 sg): do – δοξάζω (aor pass subj 3 sg): be glorified

Augsburg Confession XXI 2-3

Scripture sets before us the one Christ as the Mediator, Atoning Sacrifice, High Priest, and Intercessor [1 Tim 2:5-6]. He is to be prayed to. He has promised that He will hear our prayer [John 14:13]. This is the worship that He approves above all other worship, that He be called upon in all afflictions.

May 26

Psalm 143:10

לַמְּדֵנִי לַעֲשׂוֹת רְצוֹנֶךָ כִּי־אַתָּה אֱלוֹהָי
רוּחֲךָ טוֹבָה תַּנְחֵנִי בְּאֶרֶץ מִישׁוֹר׃

לָמַד (pi imv sg + 1 sg sf): teach – עָשָׂה (qal inf cst): do – רָצוֹן (2 sg sf): pleasure = what pleases you – רוּחַ (2 sg sf): Spirit – נָחָה (hiph juss 3 sg + 1 sg sf): lead – מִישׁוֹר: plain = on level ground

1 John 4:13

ἐν τούτῳ γινώσκομεν ὅτι ἐν αὐτῷ μένομεν καὶ αὐτὸς ἐν ἡμῖν, ὅτι ἐκ τοῦ πνεύματος αὐτοῦ δέδωκεν ἡμῖν.

γινώσκω (pres ind 1 pl): know – μένω (pres ind 1 pl): remain – πνεῦμα: Spirit – δίδωμι (perf ind 3 sg): give

Apology IV (II) 64

We speak of the kind of faith that is not an idle thought, but that liberates from death and produces new life in hearts. This is the work of the Holy Spirit.

May 27

Jeremiah 31:18

הֲשִׁבֵ֫נִי וְאָשׁ֫וּבָה כִּי אַתָּה יְהוָה אֱלֹהָֽי׃

שׁוּב (hiph imv sg + 1 sg sf): restore – שׁוּב (qal coh 1 sg): return

---

Acts 11:21

καὶ ἦν χεὶρ κυρίου μετ' αὐτῶν, πολύς τε ἀριθμὸς ὁ πιστεύσας ἐπέστρεψεν ἐπὶ τὸν κύριον.

> χείρ: hand – πολύς: large – ἀριθμός: number – πιστεύω (aor ptcp): believe – ἐπιστρέφω (aor ind 3 sg): turn to

---

Formula of Concord Ep II 5

With this Word the Holy Spirit is present and opens hearts, so that people (like Lydia in Acts 16:14) pay attention to it and are converted only through the Holy Spirit's grace and power, who alone does the work of converting a person.

MAY 28

Ezekiel 36:27

וְאֶת־רוּחִי אֶתֵּן בְּקִרְבְּכֶם וְעָשִׂיתִי אֵת אֲשֶׁר־בְּחֻקַּי תֵּלֵכוּ וּמִשְׁפָּטַי תִּשְׁמְרוּ וַעֲשִׂיתֶם׃

רוּחַ: Spirit – נָתַן (qal impf 1 sg): put – קֶרֶב (2 pl sf): inward part – חֹק: (pl + 1 sg sf): decree – מִשְׁפָּט (pl + 1 sg sf): law – שָׁמַר (qal impf 2 pl): observe

---

John 16:13

ὅταν δὲ ἔλθῃ ἐκεῖνος, τὸ πνεῦμα τῆς ἀληθείας, ὁδηγήσει ὑμᾶς ἐν τῇ ἀληθείᾳ πάσῃ· οὐ γὰρ λαλήσει ἀφ’ ἑαυτοῦ, ἀλλ’ ὅσα ἀκούσει λαλήσει καὶ τὰ ἐρχόμενα ἀναγγελεῖ ὑμῖν.

ἔρχομαι (aor subj 3 sg): come – πνεῦμα: Spirit – ἀλήθεια: truth – ὁδηγέω (fut ind 3 sg): lead – λαλέω (fut ind 3 sg): speak – ἀκούω: hear – ἔρχομαι (pres ptcp): come – ἀναγγέλλω (fut ind 3 sg): announce, tell

---

Large Catechism II 38

So that this treasure *[of redemption]* might not stay buried, but be received and enjoyed, God has caused the Word to go forth and be proclaimed. In the Word He has the Holy Spirit bring this treasure home and make it our own.

Joel 3:1-2

1 וְהָיָה אַחֲרֵי־כֵן
אֶשְׁפּוֹךְ אֶת־רוּחִי עַל־כָּל־בָּשָׂר וְנִבְּאוּ בְּנֵיכֶם וּבְנוֹתֵיכֶם
זִקְנֵיכֶם חֲלֹמוֹת יַחֲלֹמוּן בַּחוּרֵיכֶם חֶזְיֹנוֹת יִרְאוּ׃
2 וְגַם עַל־הָעֲבָדִים וְעַל־הַשְּׁפָחוֹת בַּיָּמִים הָהֵמָּה אֶשְׁפּוֹךְ
אֶת־רוּחִי׃

אַחֲרֵי־כֵן: afterwards – שָׁפַךְ (qal impf 1 sg): pour out – בָּשָׂר: flesh, people – נָבָא (niph v-c pf 3 pl): prophesy – זָקֵן (pl): old man – חֲלוֹם (pl): dream – חָלַם (qal impf 3 pl): dream – בָּחוּר (pl + 2 pl sf): young man – חִזָּיוֹן (pl): vision – עֶבֶד (pl): servant – שִׁפְחָה (pl): maidservant

---

Acts 2:38-39

38 Πέτρος δὲ πρὸς αὐτούς· μετανοήσατε, [φησίν,] καὶ βαπτισθήτω ἕκαστος ὑμῶν ἐπὶ τῷ ὀνόματι Ἰησοῦ Χριστοῦ εἰς ἄφεσιν τῶν ἁμαρτιῶν ὑμῶν καὶ λήμψεσθε τὴν δωρεὰν τοῦ ἁγίου πνεύματος.
39 ὑμῖν γάρ ἐστιν ἡ ἐπαγγελία καὶ τοῖς τέκνοις ὑμῶν καὶ πᾶσιν τοῖς εἰς μακράν, ὅσους ἂν προσκαλέσηται κύριος ὁ θεὸς ἡμῶν.

ἄφεσις: forgiveness – λαμβάνω (fut mid 2 pl): receive – δωρεά: gift – ἐπαγγελία: promise – τέκνον (pl): child – εἰς μακράν: far away – προσκαλέω (aor mid subj): call

---

Smalcald Articles III V 4

Of the Baptism of children, we hold that children should be baptized, for they belong to the promised redemption made through Christ [Acts 2:39]. Therefore, the Church should administer Baptism to them.

MAY 30

Zecheriah 4:6

וַיַּ֜עַן וַיֹּ֤אמֶר אֵלַי֙ לֵאמֹ֔ר זֶ֚ה דְּבַר־יְהוָ֔ה אֶל־זְרֻבָּבֶ֖ל לֵאמֹ֑ר
לֹ֤א בְחַ֙יִל֙ וְלֹ֣א בְכֹ֔חַ כִּ֣י אִם־בְּרוּחִ֔י אָמַ֖ר יְהוָ֥ה צְבָאֽוֹת׃

עָנָה (qal v-c impf 3 sg): answer – חַ֫יִל: might – כֹּחַ: power – רוּחַ (1 sg sf): Spirit – צָבָא (pl): army, host

John 3:6-8

6τὸ γεγεννημένον ἐκ τῆς σαρκὸς σάρξ ἐστιν, καὶ τὸ γεγεννημένον ἐκ τοῦ πνεύματος πνεῦμα ἐστιν. 7μὴ θαυμάσῃς ὅτι εἶπόν σοι· δεῖ ὑμᾶς γεννηθῆναι ἄνωθεν.
8τὸ πνεῦμα ὅπου θέλει πνεῖ καὶ τὴν φωνὴν αὐτοῦ ἀκούεις, ἀλλ' οὐκ οἶδας πόθεν ἔρχεται καὶ ποῦ ὑπάγει· οὕτως ἐστὶν πᾶς ὁ γεγεννημένος ἐκ τοῦ πνεύματος.

γεννάω (perf pass ptcp/aor pass inf): become, be born – σάρξ (gen sg): sinful nature – πνεῦμα: Spirit, spirit – θαυμάζω (aor subj 2 sg): be surprised – δεῖ: it is necessary – ἄνωθεν: again – πνεῦμα: wind – θέλω (pres ind 3 sg): want – πνέω (pres ind 3 sg): blow – φωνή: sound – ἀκούω: hear – ὑπάγω: go

Augsburg Confession V 2-3

Through the Word and Sacraments, as through instruments, the Holy Spirit is given [John 20:22]. He works faith, when and where it pleases God [John 3:8], in those who hear the good news that God justifies those who believe that they are received into grace for Christ's sake.

1 Kings 19:11-12

11וַיֹּאמֶר צֵא וְעָמַדְתָּ בָהָר לִפְנֵי יְהוָה וְהִנֵּה יְהוָה
עֹבֵר וְרוּחַ גְּדוֹלָה וְחָזָק מְפָרֵק הָרִים וּמְשַׁבֵּר סְלָעִים
לִפְנֵי יְהוָה לֹא בָרוּחַ יְהוָה וְאַחַר הָרוּחַ רַעַשׁ
לֹא בָרַעַשׁ יְהוָה׃ 12וְאַחַר הָרַעַשׁ אֵשׁ לֹא בָאֵשׁ
יְהוָה וְאַחַר הָאֵשׁ קוֹל דְּמָמָה דַקָּה׃

יָצָא (qal imv sg): go out – עָמַד (qal v-c pf 2 sg): stand – הַר: mountain – עָבַר (qal ptcp): pass by – רוּחַ: wind – חָזָק: powerful – פָּרַק (pi ptcp): tear apart – שָׁבַר (pi ptcp): shatter – סֶלַע (pl): rock – רַעַשׁ: earthquake – אֵשׁ: fire – קוֹל: voice – דְּמָמָה: whisper – דַּק: small

1 Corinthians 1:22-23

22ἐπειδὴ καὶ Ἰουδαῖοι σημεῖα αἰτοῦσιν καὶ Ἕλληνες σοφίαν
ζητοῦσιν, 23ἡμεῖς δὲ κηρύσσομεν Χριστὸν ἐσταυρωμένον,
Ἰουδαίοις μὲν σκάνδαλον, ἔθνεσιν δὲ μωρίαν . . .

ἐπειδή: since – σημεῖον: sign – αἰτέω (pres ind 3 pl): demand – σοφία: wisdom – ζητέω (pres ind 3 pl): look for – κηρύσσω (pres ind 1 pl): preach – σταυρόω (pf pass ptcp): crucify – σκάνδαλον: stumbling block – ἔθνη: (dat pl): Gentiles – μωρία: foolishness

Formula of Concord SD II 50

By this means, and in no other way (i.e., through His holy Word, when people hear it preached or read it, and through the holy Sacraments when they are used according to His Word), God desires to call people to eternal salvation.

June 1

Deuteronomy 32:45-47

45 וַיְכַל מֹשֶׁה לְדַבֵּר אֶת־כָּל־הַדְּבָרִים הָאֵלֶּה אֶל־כָּל־
יִשְׂרָאֵל׃ 46 וַיֹּאמֶר אֲלֵהֶם שִׂימוּ לְבַבְכֶם לְכָל־הַדְּבָרִים
אֲשֶׁר אָנֹכִי מֵעִיד בָּכֶם הַיּוֹם אֲשֶׁר תְּצַוֻּם אֶת־בְּנֵיכֶם
לִשְׁמֹר לַעֲשׂוֹת אֶת־כָּל־דִּבְרֵי הַתּוֹרָה הַזֹּאת׃ 47 כִּי לֹא־
דָבָר רֵק הוּא מִכֶּם כִּי־הוּא חַיֵּיכֶם

כָּלָה (pi v-c impf 3 sg): finish – דָּבַר (pi inf cst): speak – דָּבָר (pl): word – שִׂים (qal imv pl): put + לֵבָב: heart = take to heart – עוּד (hiph ptcp sg): affirm solemnly – צָוָה (pi impf 2 pl + 3 pl sf): command – בֵּן (pl): children – שָׁמַר (qal inf cst): obey – עָשָׂה (qal inf cst): do – תּוֹרָה: law, teaching – רֵק: empty, worthless – חַיִּים (2 pl sf): life

---

Romans 10:8-9

8 ἀλλὰ τί λέγει; ἐγγύς σου τὸ ῥῆμά ἐστιν ἐν τῷ στόματί
σου καὶ ἐν τῇ καρδίᾳ σου, τοῦτ᾽ ἔστιν τὸ ῥῆμα τῆς πίστεως
ὃ κηρύσσομεν. 9 ὅτι ἐὰν ὁμολογήσῃς ἐν τῷ στόματί σου
κύριον Ἰησοῦν καὶ πιστεύσῃς ἐν τῇ καρδίᾳ σου ὅτι ὁ θεὸς
αὐτὸν ἤγειρεν ἐκ νεκρῶν, σωθήσῃ . . .

ἐγγύς: near – ῥῆμα: word – στόμα: mouth – κηρύσσω (pres ind 1 pl): proclaim – ὁμολογέω (aor subj 2 sg): confess – κύριος: Lord – ἐγείρω (aor ind 3 sg): raise – σῴζω (fut pass 2 sg): save

---

Large Catechism IV 33

Since these blessings are presented here *[in Baptism]* and promised through the words in and with the water, they cannot be received in any other way than by believing them with the heart [Rom 10:9].

June 2

Exodus 20:24

בְּכָל־הַמָּקוֹם אֲשֶׁר אַזְכִּיר אֶת־שְׁמִי אָבוֹא אֵלֶיךָ וּבֵרַכְתִּיךָ׃

מָקוֹם: place – **זָכַר** (hiph impf 1 sg): remind, cause to be remembered – **שֵׁם** (1 sg sf): name – **בּוֹא** (qal impf 1 sg): come – **בָּרַךְ** (pi v-c pf 1 sg + 2 sg m sf): bless

---

Romans 10:13

πᾶς γὰρ ὃς ἂν ἐπικαλέσηται τὸ ὄνομα κυρίου σωθήσεται.

ἐπικαλέω (aor mid subj 3 sg): call upon (someone for aid) – ὄνομα: name – σῴζω (fut pass 3 sg): save

---

Augsburg Confession XX 24

The person who knows that he has a Father who is gracious to him through Christ truly knows God [John 14:7]. He also knows that God cares for him [1 Pet 5:7], and he calls upon God [Rom 10:13].

Lamentations 3:22-23

22 חַסְדֵי יְהוָה כִּי לֹא־תָמְנוּ כִּי לֹא־כָלוּ רַחֲמָיו׃
23 חֲדָשִׁים לַבְּקָרִים רַבָּה אֱמוּנָתֶךָ׃

חֶסֶד (cst pl): faithful love – תָּמַם (qal pf 1 pl): be consumed – כָּלָה (qal pf 3 pl): fail – רַחֲמִים (3 sg sf): mercy – חָדָשׁ: new – בֹּקֶר (pl): morning – רַב (sg f): great – אֱמוּנָה (2 sg sf): faithfulness

---

Romans 3:28

λογιζόμεθα γὰρ δικαιοῦσθαι πίστει ἄνθρωπον χωρὶς ἔργων νόμου.

λογίζομαι (pres ind 1 pl): believe, be of the opinion – δικαιόω (pres pass inf): declare righteous, justify – πίστις: faith – χωρίς: without

---

Apology IV (II) 87

In the Epistle to the Romans, Paul discusses this topic *[of justification]* specifically. He declares that when we believe, God (for Christ's sake) is reconciled to us, we are justified freely through faith.

June 4

Ezekiel 11:19

וְנָתַתִּי לָהֶם לֵב אֶחָד וְרוּחַ חֲדָשָׁה אֶתֵּן בְּקִרְבְּכֶם
וַהֲסִרֹתִי לֵב הָאֶבֶן מִבְּשָׂרָם וְנָתַתִּי לָהֶם לֵב בָּשָׂר׃

נָתַן (qal v-c pf 1 sg/qal impf 1 sg): give – לֵב אֶחָד: an undivided heart – רוּחַ: spirit – חָדָשׁ: new – קֶרֶב (2 pl sf): inward part – סוּר (hiph v-c pf 1 sg): remove – אֶבֶן: stone – בָּשָׂר (3 pl sf): flesh = from them

---

2 Corinthians 5:17

ὥστε εἴ τις ἐν Χριστῷ, καινὴ κτίσις· τὰ ἀρχαῖα παρῆλθεν, ἰδοὺ γέγονεν καινά·

> ὥστε: so that – καινός: new – κτίσις: creation, creature – ἀρχαῖος: old – παρέρχομαι (aor ind 3 sg): pass – γίνομαι (pf ind 3 sg): become

---

Large Catechism II 13

But what is the force of this, or what do you mean by these words, "I believe in God the Father Almighty, maker of heaven and earth?" Answer: "This is what I mean and believe, that I am God's creature" [2 Cor 5:17].

JUNE 5

Psalm 145:8-9

8חַנּוּן וְרַחוּם יְהוָה אֶרֶךְ אַפַּיִם וּגְדָל־חָסֶד׃
9טוֹב־יְהוָה לַכֹּל וְרַחֲמָיו עַל־כָּל־מַעֲשָׂיו׃

חַנּוּן: gracious – רַחוּם: merciful – אֶרֶךְ (adj cst): long, slow – גָּדוֹל (adj cst): great – חֶסֶד: faithful love – רַחֲמִים (3 sg sf): mercy – מַעֲשֶׂה (pl + 3 sg sf): work

---

Titus 3:4-6

4ὅτε δὲ ἡ χρηστότης καὶ ἡ φιλανθρωπία ἐπεφάνη τοῦ
σωτῆρος ἡμῶν θεοῦ, 5οὐκ ἐξ ἔργων τῶν ἐν δικαιοσύνῃ
ἃ ἐποιήσαμεν ἡμεῖς ἀλλὰ κατὰ τὸ αὐτοῦ ἔλεος ἔσωσεν
ἡμᾶς διὰ λουτροῦ παλιγγενεσίας καὶ ἀνακαινώσεως
πνεύματος ἁγίου, 6οὗ ἐξέχεεν ἐφ᾽ ἡμᾶς πλουσίως διὰ
Ἰησοῦ Χριστοῦ τοῦ σωτῆρος ἡμῶν . . .

χρηστότης: goodness – φιλανθρωπία: loving kindness – ἐπιφαίνω (aor pass 3 sg): appear – σωτήρ: Savior – δικαιοσύνη: righteousness – λουτρόν: washing – παλιγγενεσία: rebirth – ἀνακαίνωσις: renewal – ἐκχέω (aor ind 3 sg): pour out – πλουσίως: abundantly

---

Large Catechism IV 27

Where God's name is, there must also be life and salvation [Ps 54:1]. So Baptism may certainly be called a divine, blessed, fruitful, and gracious water. Such power is given to Baptism by the Word that it is a washing of new birth, as St. Paul also calls it in Titus 3:5.

June 6

Deuteronomy 13:5; 14:2

13:5 אַחֲרֵי יְהוָה אֱלֹהֵיכֶם תֵּלֵכוּ וְאֹתוֹ תִירָאוּ וְאֶת־מִצְוֺתָיו
תִּשְׁמֹרוּ וּבְקֹלוֹ תִשְׁמָעוּ וְאֹתוֹ תַעֲבֹדוּ וּבוֹ תִדְבָּקוּן׃
14:2 כִּי עַם קָדוֹשׁ אַתָּה לַיהוָה אֱלֹהֶיךָ וּבְךָ בָּחַר יְהוָה
לִהְיוֹת לוֹ לְעַם סְגֻלָּה מִכֹּל הָעַמִּים אֲשֶׁר עַל־פְּנֵי
הָאֲדָמָה׃

הָלַךְ (qal impf 2 pl) + אַחֲרֵי: follow – יָרֵא (qal impf 2 pl): revere – מִצְוָה (pl + 3 sg sf) commandment – שָׁמַר (qal impf 2 pl): obey – קוֹל (3 sg sf): voice – עָבַד (qal impf 2 pl): serve – דָּבַק (qal impf 2 pl): cling – בָּחַר (qal pf 3 sg) + בְּ: choose – הָיָה (qal inf cst): be – סְגֻלָּה: treasured possession – אֲדָמָה: earth

Galatians 4:6-7

6 Ὅτι δέ ἐστε υἱοί, ἐξαπέστειλεν ὁ θεὸς τὸ πνεῦμα τοῦ υἱοῦ αὐτοῦ εἰς τὰς καρδίας ἡμῶν κρᾶζον· ἀββα ὁ πατήρ. 7 ὥστε οὐκέτι εἶ δοῦλος ἀλλὰ υἱός· εἰ δὲ υἱός, καὶ κληρονόμος διὰ θεοῦ.

υἱός: son – ἐξαποστέλλω (aor ind 3 sg): send out – πνεῦμα: Spirit – καρδία: heart – κράζω (pres ptcp): call out – δοῦλος: slave – κληρονόμος: heir

Formula of Concord SD II 54

Through the preaching of, and reflection on, the Holy Gospel about the gracious forgiveness of sins in Christ, a spark of faith is kindled in him. This faith accepts the forgiveness of sins for Christ's sake and comforts itself with the Gospel promise. So the Holy Spirit (who does all this) is sent into the heart [Gal 4:6].

June 7

2 Chronicles 7:14

וְיִכָּנְעוּ עַמִּי אֲשֶׁר נִקְרָא־שְׁמִי עֲלֵיהֶם וְיִתְפַּלְלוּ וִיבַקְשׁוּ
פָנַי וְיָשֻׁבוּ מִדַּרְכֵיהֶם הָרָעִים וַאֲנִי אֶשְׁמַע מִן־הַשָּׁמַיִם
וְאֶסְלַח לְחַטָּאתָם וְאֶרְפָּא אֶת־אַרְצָם׃

כָּנַע (niph impf 3 pl): humble oneself – קָרָא (niph ptcp): be called – שֵׁם: name – פָּלַל (hithp impf 3 pl): pray – בָּקַשׁ (pi impf 3 pl): seek – פָּנִים (1 sg sf): face – שׁוּב (qal impf 3 pl): turn, return – דֶּרֶךְ (pl + 3 pl sf): way – רַע: evil – שָׁמַע (qal impf 1 sg): hear – שָׁמַיִם: heaven – סָלַח (qal impf 1 sg): forgive – חַטָּאת (3 pl sf): sin – רָפָא (qal impf 1 sg): heal – אֶרֶץ (3 pl sf): land

John 17:14

ἐγὼ δέδωκα αὐτοῖς τὸν λόγον σου καὶ ὁ κόσμος ἐμίσησεν αὐτούς, ὅτι οὐκ εἰσὶν ἐκ τοῦ κόσμου καθὼς ἐγὼ οὐκ εἰμὶ ἐκ τοῦ κόσμου.

δίδωμι (pf ind 1 sg): give – κόσμος: world – μισέω (aor ind 3 sg): hate

Apology XX 83

Our consciences understand that the adversaries condemn the clear truth, whose defense is necessary for the Church and increases Christ's glory. Therefore, we easily look down on the terrors of the world, and we will bear with a strong spirit all suffering for Christ's glory and the Church's benefits.

Genesis 3:4-5

4וַיֹּאמֶר הַנָּחָשׁ אֶל־הָאִשָּׁה לֹא־מוֹת תְּמֻתוּן׃ 5כִּי יֹדֵעַ
אֱלֹהִים כִּי בְּיוֹם אֲכָלְכֶם מִמֶּנּוּ וְנִפְקְחוּ עֵינֵיכֶם וִהְיִיתֶם
כֵּאלֹהִים יֹדְעֵי טוֹב וָרָע׃

נָחָשׁ: serpent – אָכַל (qal inf cst + 2 pl sf): eat – פָּקַח (niph v-c pf 3 pl): open – עַיִן (pl + 2 pl sf): eye – הָיָה (qal v-c pf 2 pl): be – רַע: evil

---

Ephesians 6:12-13

12ὅτι οὐκ ἔστιν ἡμῖν ἡ πάλη πρὸς αἷμα καὶ σάρκα ἀλλὰ πρὸς
τὰς ἀρχάς, πρὸς τὰς ἐξουσίας, πρὸς τοὺς κοσμοκράτορας
τοῦ σκότους τούτου, πρὸς τὰ πνευματικὰ τῆς πονηρίας ἐν
τοῖς ἐπουρανίοις. 13διὰ τοῦτο ἀναλάβετε τὴν πανοπλίαν τοῦ
θεοῦ, ἵνα δυνηθῆτε ἀντιστῆναι ἐν τῇ ἡμέρᾳ τῇ πονηρᾷ καὶ
ἅπαντα κατεργασάμενοι στῆναι.

πάλη: struggle – ἀρχή: ruler – ἐξουσία: authority – κοσμοκράτωρ: world ruler – σκότος: darkness – πνευματικός: spiritual force – πονηρία: wickedness – ἐπουράνιος: heavenly realm – ἀναλαμβάνω (aor imv 2 pl): put on – πανοπλία: full armor – δύναμαι (aor subj 2 pl): be able – ἀνθίστημι (aor inf): withstand, set oneself against – πονηρός: evil – κατεργάζομαι (aor ptcp pl): accomplish – ἵστημι (aor inf): stand

---

Large Catechism III 104

Despair, denial of God, blasphemy . . . These are snares and nets [2 Tim 2:26], indeed, real fiery darts that are shot like poison into the heart, not by flesh and blood, but by the devil [Eph 6:12,16].

June 9

Genesis 50:20

וְאַתֶּם חֲשַׁבְתֶּם עָלַי רָעָה אֱלֹהִים חֲשָׁבָהּ לְטֹבָה לְמַעַן
עֲשֹׂה כַּיּוֹם הַזֶּה לְהַחֲיֹת עַם־רָב׃

חָשַׁב (qal pf 2 pl/qal pf 3 sg + 3 sg sf): intend, plan – רָעָה: evil – טוֹבָה: good – עָשָׂה (qal inf cst): do – חָיָה (hiph inf cst): preserve alive – עַם: people

---

Romans 5:3-5

3 οὐ μόνον δέ, ἀλλὰ καὶ καυχώμεθα ἐν ταῖς θλίψεσιν, εἰδότες ὅτι ἡ θλῖψις ὑπομονὴν κατεργάζεται,
4 ἡ δὲ ὑπομονὴ δοκιμήν, ἡ δὲ δοκιμὴ ἐλπίδα.
5 ἡ δὲ ἐλπὶς οὐ καταισχύνει, ὅτι ἡ ἀγάπη τοῦ θεοῦ ἐκκέχυται ἐν ταῖς καρδίαις ἡμῶν διὰ πνεύματος ἁγίου τοῦ δοθέντος ἡμῖν.

καυχάομαι (pres ind 1 pl): boast – θλῖψις (dat pl): suffering – οἶδα (ptcp pl): know – ὑπομονή: perseverance – κατεργάζομαι (pres 3 sg): produce – δοκιμή: character – ἐλπίς: hope – καταισχύνω (pres ind 3 sg): disgrace, disappoint – ἐκχέω (pf pass 3 sg): pour out – δίδωμι (aor pass ptcp): give

---

Formula of Concord SD XI 4

First, the distinction between God's eternal foreknowledge and the eternal election of His children to eternal salvation is to be made carefully. Foreknowledge or prevision means that God sees and knows everything before it happens. This is called God's foreknowledge, which extends over all creatures, good and bad.

June 10

Psalm 124:8

עֶ֭זְרֵנוּ בְּשֵׁ֣ם יְהוָ֑ה עֹ֝שֵׂ֗ה שָׁמַ֥יִם וָאָֽרֶץ׃

עֵ֫זֶר (1 pl sf): help – שֵׁם: name – עָשָׂה (qal ptcp cst sg): Maker

---

Luke 18:26-27

26εἶπαν δὲ οἱ ἀκούσαντες· καὶ τίς δύναται σωθῆναι;
27ὁ δὲ εἶπεν· τὰ ἀδύνατα παρὰ ἀνθρώποις δυνατὰ παρὰ
τῷ θεῷ ἐστιν.

εἶπον (aor ind 3 pl): say – ἀκούω (aor ptcp pl): hear – δύναμαι (pres ind 3 sg): be able – σῴζω (aor pass inf): save – ἀδύνατος: impossible – δυνατός: possible

---

Formula of Concord Ep VIII 16

So now not just as God, but also as man He knows all things and can do all things. He is present with all creatures, and has under His feet and in His hands everything that is in heaven and on earth and under the earth, as He Himself testifies [in Matt 28:18], "All authority in heaven and on earth has been given to Me" [see also John 13:3]. And St. Paul says in Eph 4:10, "He . . . ascended far above all the heavens, that He might fill all things." Because He is present, He can exercise His power everywhere. To Him everything is possible and everything is known.

June 11

Psalm 142:3-4

3אֶשְׁפֹּךְ לְפָנָיו שִׂיחִי צָרָתִי לְפָנָיו אַגִּיד׃
4בְּהִתְעַטֵּף עָלַי רוּחִי וְאַתָּה יָדַעְתָּ נְתִיבָתִי
בְּאֹרַח־זוּ אֲהַלֵּךְ טָמְנוּ פַח לִי׃

שָׁפַךְ (qal impf 1 sg): pour out – לִפְנֵי (3 sg sf): before – שִׂיחַ (1 sg sf): complaint – צָרָה (1 sg sf): trouble – נָגַד (hiph impf 1 sg): tell – עָטַף (hithp inf cst): grow faint – רוּחַ (1 sg sf): spirit – נְתִיבָה (1 sg sf): path – אֹרַח: way – זוּ: where – הָלַךְ (pi impf 1 sg): walk – טָמַן (qal pf 3 pl): hide – פַּח: snare

Acts 18:9-10

9Εἶπεν δὲ ὁ κύριος ἐν νυκτὶ δι' ὁράματος τῷ Παύλῳ· μὴ
φοβοῦ, ἀλλὰ λάλει καὶ μὴ σιωπήσῃς, 10διότι ἐγώ εἰμι μετὰ
σοῦ καὶ οὐδεὶς ἐπιθήσεταί σοι τοῦ κακῶσαί σε, διότι λαός
ἐστί μοι πολὺς ἐν τῇ πόλει ταύτῃ.

εἶπον (aor ind 3 sg): say – νύξ: night – ὅραμα: vision – φοβέομαι (pres imv 2 sg): be afraid – λαλέω (pres imv 2 sg): speak – σιωπάω (aor subj): be silent – διότι: because – ἐπιτίθημι (fut mid 3 sg): attack – κακόω (aor inf): harm

Large Catechism I 39

For those who cling to God alone should be sure that He will show them mercy. In other words, He will show them pure goodness and blessing, not only for themselves, but also to their children and their children's children, even to the thousandth generation and beyond that.

Psalm 27:11

הוֹרֵנִי יְהוָה דַּרְכֶּךָ
וּנְחֵנִי בְּאֹרַח מִישׁוֹר לְמַעַן שׁוֹרְרָי׃

יָרָה (hiph imv + 1 sg sf): teach – דֶּרֶךְ (2 sg sf): way – נָחָה (qal imv + 1 sg sf): lead – אֹרַח: way – מִישׁוֹר: level place, uprightness – לְמַעַן: because of – שׁוֹרֵר (pl + 1 sg sf): oppressor

---

John 10:9

ἐγώ εἰμι ἡ θύρα· δι' ἐμοῦ ἐάν τις εἰσέλθῃ σωθήσεται καὶ εἰσελεύσεται καὶ ἐξελεύσεται καὶ νομὴν εὑρήσει.

θύρα: door – εἰσέρχομαι (aor subj 3 sg/fut ind 3 sg): enter – σῴζω (fut pass 3 sg): save – ἐξέρχομαι (fut ind 3 sg): go out – νομή: pasture – εὑρίσκω (fut ind 3 sg): find

---

Apology IV (II) 69

To believe is to trust in Christ's merits, that for His sake God certainly wishes to be reconciled with us.

Isaiah 59:2

כִּי אִם־עֲוֹנֹתֵיכֶם הָיוּ מַבְדִּלִים בֵּינֵכֶם לְבֵין אֱלֹהֵיכֶם
וְחַטֹּאותֵיכֶם הִסְתִּירוּ פָנִים מִכֶּם מִשְּׁמוֹעַ׃

כִּי אִם: but – עָוֹן (pl + 2 pl sf): sin (as guilt) – בָּדַל (hiph ptcp pl): separate – חַטָּאת (pl + 2 pl sf): sin (as missing the mark) – סָתַר (hiph pf 3 pl): hide – פָּנִים: face; LXX reads פָּנָיו: his face – שָׁמַע (qal inf cst): hear + מִן: so as not to hear

---

Matthew 7:14

ὅτι στενὴ ἡ πύλη καὶ τεθλιμμένη ἡ ὁδὸς ἡ ἀπάγουσα εἰς τὴν ζωὴν καὶ ὀλίγοι εἰσὶν οἱ εὑρίσκοντες αὐτήν.

στενός: narrow – πύλη: gate – θλίβω (pf pass ptcp): compress = make narrow – ὁδός: road – ἀπάγω (pres ptcp sg f): lead – ζωή: life – ὀλίγος (pl): few – εὑρίσκω (pres ptcp pl): find

---

Apology II (I) 3

We teach that those who are born according to the fleshly nature have concupiscence. This means people not only lack fear and trust in God, but also do not even have the power or gifts to produce fear and trust in God.

Isaiah 57:21

אֵין שָׁלוֹם אָמַר אֱלֹהַי לָרְשָׁעִים׃

אַיִן (cst): nonexistence – שָׁלוֹם: peace – אָמַר (qal pf 3 sg): say – רָשָׁע: wicked

Romans 8:6-8

6τὸ γὰρ φρόνημα τῆς σαρκὸς θάνατος, τὸ δὲ φρόνημα
τοῦ πνεύματος ζωὴ καὶ εἰρήνη· 7διότι τὸ φρόνημα
τῆς σαρκὸς ἔχθρα εἰς θεόν, τῷ γὰρ νόμῳ τοῦ θεοῦ
οὐχ ὑποτάσσεται, οὐδὲ γὰρ δύναται· 8οἱ δὲ ἐν σαρκὶ
ὄντες θεῷ ἀρέσαι οὐ δύνανται.

φρόνημα: way of thinking – θάνατος: death – πνεῦμα: Spirit – ζωή: life – εἰρήνη: peace – διότι: because – σάρξ: corrupt nature – ἔχθρα: enmity – ὑποτάσσω (pres mid 3 sg): subject itself – δύναμαι (pres 3 sg): be able – ἀρέσκω (aor inf): please

Formula of Concord SD II 12-13

"The natural person does not accept [or, as the Greek word properly signifies, grasps not, comprehends not, accepts not] the things of the Spirit of God" (1 Cor 2:14). This means he is not capable of spiritual things. For they are foolishness to him; neither can he know them. Much less will he truly believe the Gospel or agree with it and regard it as truth. For the mind that is set on the flesh [or the mind of the natural man] is hostile to God, for it does not submit to God's law; indeed, it cannot (Rom 8:7).

JUNE 15

Isaiah 43:21; 60:21

עַם־זוּ יָצַרְתִּי לִי תְּהִלָּתִי יְסַפֵּרוּ׃ 43:21

נֵצֶר מַטָּעוֹ [מַטָּעַי] מַעֲשֵׂה יָדַי לְהִתְפָּאֵר׃ 60:21

עַם: people – זוּ = אֲשֶׁר – יָצַר (qal pf 1 sg): form – לִי: for myself – תְּהִלָּה (1 sg sf): praise – סָפַר (pi impf 3 pl): proclaim – נֵצֶר (cst): shoot – מַטָּע (qere: pl + 1 sg sf): planting = the shoot I have planted – מַעֲשֶׂה (cst): work – יָד (1 sg sf): hand – פָּאַר (hithp inf cst): be glorified = for the display of my splendor

Romans 6:19

Ἀνθρώπινον λέγω διὰ τὴν ἀσθένειαν τῆς σαρκὸς ὑμῶν. ὥσπερ γὰρ παρεστήσατε τὰ μέλη ὑμῶν δοῦλα τῇ ἀκαθαρσίᾳ καὶ τῇ ἀνομίᾳ εἰς τὴν ἀνομίαν, οὕτως νῦν παραστήσατε τὰ μέλη ὑμῶν δοῦλα τῇ δικαιοσύνῃ εἰς ἁγιασμόν.

ἀνθρώπινος: in human terms – ἀσθένεια: weakness – σάρξ: human nature – παρίστημι (aor ind 2 pl/aor imv 2 pl): put at someone's disposal – μέλος (pl): member – δοῦλος (adj): in slavery – ἀκαθαρσία: impurity – ἀνομία: wickedness – ἁγιασμός: holiness

Apology XIIB (VI) 34

True terrors, true griefs of mind, do not allow the body to satisfy itself in sensual pleasures, and true faith is not ungrateful to God. Neither does true faith hate God's commandments. In a word, there is no inner repentance unless it also produces the outward putting to death of the flesh.

June 16

Psalm 3:6-7

6אֲנִי שָׁכַבְתִּי וָאִישָׁנָה הֱקִיצוֹתִי כִּי יְהוָה יִסְמְכֵנִי׃
7לֹא־אִירָא מֵרִבְבוֹת עָם אֲשֶׁר סָבִיב שָׁתוּ עָלָי׃

שָׁכַב (qal pf 1 sg): lie down – יָשֵׁן (qal v-c impf 1 sg): sleep – קוּץ (hiph pf 1 sg): wake up – סָמַךְ (qal impf 3 sg + 1 sg sf): sustain – יָרֵא (qal impf 1 sg): fear – מִן: introduces the object of fear – רְבָבָה (cst pl): ten thousand – סָבִיב: on every side – שִׁית (qal pf 3 pl): set, position oneself – עַל: against

John 17:15-16

15οὐκ ἐρωτῶ ἵνα ἄρῃς αὐτοὺς ἐκ τοῦ κόσμου, ἀλλ' ἵνα
τηρήσῃς αὐτοὺς ἐκ τοῦ πονηροῦ. 16ἐκ τοῦ κόσμου οὐκ
εἰσὶν καθὼς ἐγὼ οὐκ εἰμὶ ἐκ τοῦ κόσμου.

ἐρωτάω (pres ind 1 sg): ask – αἴρω (aor subj 2 sg): remove – κόσμος: world – τηρέω (aor subj 2 sg): protect – πονηρός: evil, the evil one

Large Catechism I 128

We all forget God, and no one considers how God nourishes, protects, and defends us, and how He bestows so much good on body and soul [Ps 23]. This is especially true when an evil time comes.

June 17

Jonah 4:2

וַיִּתְפַּלֵּל אֶל־יְהוָה וַיֹּאמַר אָנָּה יְהוָה הֲלוֹא־זֶה דְבָרִי
עַד־הֱיוֹתִי עַל־אַדְמָתִי עַל־כֵּן קִדַּמְתִּי לִבְרֹחַ תַּרְשִׁישָׁה
כִּי יָדַעְתִּי כִּי אַתָּה אֵל־חַנּוּן וְרַחוּם אֶרֶךְ אַפַּיִם וְרַב־
חֶסֶד וְנִחָם עַל־הָרָעָה׃

פלל (hithp v-c impf 3 sg): pray – אָנָּה (interj): oh! – הָיָה (qal inf cst + 1 sg sf): be – אֲדָמָה (1 sg sf): country – קָדַם (pi pf 1 sg): do before, be quick to – בָּרַח (qal inf cst): flee – יָדַע (qal pf 1 sg): know – חַנּוּן: gracious – רַחוּם: merciful – אֶרֶךְ אַפַּיִם:slow to anger – חֶסֶד: faithful love – נָחַם (niph ptcp sg): relent – רָעָה: evil

---

John 1:14

Καὶ ὁ λόγος σὰρξ ἐγένετο καὶ ἐσκήνωσεν ἐν ἡμῖν, καὶ ἐθεασάμεθα τὴν δόξαν αὐτοῦ, δόξαν ὡς μονογενοῦς παρὰ πατρός, πλήρης χάριτος καὶ ἀληθείας.

λόγος: word – σάρξ: flesh – γίνομαι (aor ind 3 sg): become – σκηνόω (aor ind 3 sg): live temporarily – θεάομαι (aor ind 1 pl): see – δόξα: glory – μονογενής (gen sg) only, only begotten

---

Formula of Concord SD VIII 11

So now, since the incarnation, there belongs to the entire person of Christ personally not only His divine nature, but also His received human nature. So without His divinity, and also without His humanity, the person of Christ or the incarnate Son of God is not complete. We mean the Son of God who has received flesh and become man [John 1:14].

June 18

Psalm 81:11

אָנֹכִי יְהוָה אֱלֹהֶיךָ הַמַּעַלְךָ מֵאֶרֶץ מִצְרָיִם
הַרְחֶב־פִּיךָ וַאֲמַלְאֵהוּ׃

עָלָה (hiph ptcp + 2 sg sf): bring up – רָחַב (hiph imv): open – פֶּה (2 sg sf): mouth – מָלֵא (pi impf 1 sg + 3 sg sf): fill

---

Matthew 5:6

μακάριοι οἱ πεινῶντες καὶ διψῶντες τὴν δικαιοσύνην, ὅτι αὐτοὶ χορτασθήσονται.

μακάριος: blessed – πεινάω (pres ptcp pl): hunger – διψάω (pres ptcp pl): thirst – δικαιοσύνη: righteousness – χορτάζω (fut pass 3 pl): eat one's fill, be satisfied

---

Formula of Concord SD XI 30

For this reason the elect are described as follows: "My sheep hear My voice, and I know them, and they follow Me. I give them eternal life" (John 10:27-28). "In Him we have obtained an inheritance, having been predestined according to the purpose of Him who works all things according to the counsel of His will" (Eph 1:11). They hear the Gospel, believe in Christ, pray and give thanks, are sanctified in love, have hope, patience, and comfort under the cross. (See Eph 1:13; Rom 8:25.) Although all this is very weak in them, they hunger and thirst for righteousness (Matt 5:6).

Ecclesiastes 4:6

טוֹב מְלֹא כַף נָחַת מִמְּלֹא חָפְנַיִם עָמָל וּרְעוּת רוּחַ׃

טוֹב: good + מִן of comparison: better – מְלֹא כַף: handful – נַחַת: tranquility – חֹפֶן (du): two fistfuls – עָמָל: (with) toil – רְעוּת: striving, chasing – רוּחַ: wind

---

1 Timothy 6:9-10

9 οἱ δὲ βουλόμενοι πλουτεῖν ἐμπίπτουσιν εἰς πειρασμὸν
καὶ παγίδα καὶ ἐπιθυμίας πολλὰς ἀνοήτους καὶ βλαβεράς,
αἵτινες βυθίζουσιν τοὺς ἀνθρώπους εἰς ὄλεθρον καὶ
ἀπώλειαν. 10 ῥίζα γὰρ πάντων τῶν κακῶν ἐστιν ἡ φιλαργυρία,
ἧς τινες ὀρεγόμενοι ἀπεπλανήθησαν ἀπὸ τῆς πίστεως καὶ
ἑαυτοὺς περιέπειραν ὀδύναις πολλαῖς.

βούλομαι (pres ptcp): wish – πλουτέω (pres inf): be rich – ἐμπίπτω: fall into – πειρασμός: temptation – παγίς: snare, trap – ἐπιθυμία: desire – ἀνόητος: foolish – βλαβερός: hurtful – βυθίζω (3 pl): drown – ὄλεθρος: ruin – ἀπώλεια: destruction – ῥίζα: root – φιλαργυρία: love of money – ὀρέγω (pres mid ptcp): desire – ἀποπλανάω (aor pass): wander away from – περιπείρω (aor ind 3 pl): pierce through – ὀδύνη: grief, pain

---

Smalcald Articles III I 3

This hereditary sin is such a deep corruption of nature that no reason can understand it. Rather, it must be believed from the revelation of Scripture.

Psalm 36:6-7

6 יְהוָה בְּהַשָּׁמַיִם חַסְדֶּךָ אֱמוּנָתְךָ עַד־שְׁחָקִים׃
7 צִדְקָתְךָ כְּהַרְרֵי־אֵל מִשְׁפָּטֶךָ תְּהוֹם רַבָּה
אָדָם־וּבְהֵמָה תוֹשִׁיעַ יְהוָה׃

אֱמוּנָה (2 sg sf): faithfulness – שַׁחַק (pl): the skies – צְדָקָה (2 sg sf): righteousness – הַר (cst pl): mountain – מִשְׁפָּט: justice – תְּהוֹם: the deep – אָדָם: man – בְּהֵמָה: beast – יָשַׁע (hiph impf 2 sg): save, preserve

John 7:37-39

37 Ἐν δὲ τῇ ἐσχάτῃ ἡμέρᾳ τῇ μεγάλῃ τῆς ἑορτῆς εἱστήκει
ὁ Ιησοῦς καὶ ἔκραξεν λέγων· ἐάν τις διψᾷ ἐρχέσθω πρός
με καὶ πινέτω. 38 ὁ πιστεύων εἰς ἐμέ, καθὼς εἶπεν ἡ γραφή,
ποταμοὶ ἐκ τῆς κοιλίας αὐτοῦ ῥεύσουσιν ὕδατος ζῶντος.
39 τοῦτο δὲ εἶπεν περὶ τοῦ πνεύματος ὃ ἔμελλον λαμβάνειν
οἱ πιστεύσαντες εἰς αὐτόν· οὔπω γὰρ ἦν πνεῦμα, ὅτι
Ἰησοῦς οὐδέπω ἐδοξάσθη.

ἑορτή: festival (of tabernacles) – ἵστημι (plpf 3 sg with impf meaning): stand – κράζω (aor 3 sg): call out – διψάω (pres subj 3 sg): be thirsty – πίνω (pres imv 3 sg): drink – ποταμός: stream – κοιλία: innermost recesses of the human body – ῥέω (fut ind 3 pl): flow

Apology IV (II) 31

In John 3:5, it is written, "Unless one is born of water and the Spirit, he cannot enter the kingdom of God." But if it is necessary to be born again of the Holy Spirit, the righteousness of reason does not justify us before God and does not fulfill the Law.

JUNE 21

Proverbs 11:2

בָּא־זָדוֹן וַיָּבֹא קָלוֹן וְאֶת־צְנוּעִים חָכְמָה׃

בּוֹא (qal pf 3 sg/qal v-c impf 3 sg): come – זָדוֹן: pride – קָלוֹן: disgrace, dishonor – אֵת: with – צְנוּעִים: humility – חָכְמָה: wisdom

---

Matthew 18:3-4

[3]καὶ εἶπεν· ἀμὴν λέγω ὑμῖν, ἐὰν μὴ στραφῆτε καὶ γένησθε
ὡς τὰ παιδία, οὐ μὴ εἰσέλθητε εἰς τὴν βασιλείαν τῶν
οὐρανῶν. [4]ὅστις οὖν ταπεινώσει ἑαυτὸν ὡς τὸ παιδίον
τοῦτο, οὗτός ἐστιν ὁ μείζων ἐν τῇ βασιλείᾳ τῶν οὐρανῶν.

στρέφω (aor pass subj 2 pl): change – γίνομαι (aor mid subj 2 pl): become – παιδίον: child – εἰσέρχομαι (aor subj 2 pl): enter – ταπεινόω (fut ind 3 sg): humble – μείζων: greater

---

Apology XXVII (XIII) 4-5

It is clear how much hypocrisy, ambition, and greed there are in the monasteries, how much ignorance and cruelty exists among all the unlearned, what pride there is in their sermons. . . . Monasteries were schools for Christian instruction; now they have deteriorated, as though from a golden to an iron age.

1 Samuel 3:10,21

10 וַיָּבֹא יְהוָה וַיִּתְיַצַּב וַיִּקְרָא כְפַעַם־בְּפַעַם שְׁמוּאֵל
שְׁמוּאֵל וַיֹּאמֶר שְׁמוּאֵל דַּבֵּר כִּי שֹׁמֵעַ עַבְדֶּךָ׃
21 וַיֹּסֶף יְהוָה לְהֵרָאֹה בְשִׁלֹה כִּי־נִגְלָה יְהוָה אֶל־
שְׁמוּאֵל בְּשִׁלוֹ בִּדְבַר יְהוָה׃

בּוֹא (qal v-c impf 3 sg): come – יָצַב (hithp v-c impf 3 sg): stand – קָרָא (qal v-c impf 3 sg): call – פַּעַם: time = as the other times – דָּבַר (pi imv): speak – שָׁמַע (qal ptcp): listen – עֶבֶד (2 sg sf): servant – יָסַף (hiph v-c impf 3 sg): continue – רָאָה (niph inf cst): appear – גָּלָה (niph pf 3 sg): reveal oneself – בִּדְבַר: through the word

---

Hebrews 1:1-2

1Πολυμερῶς καὶ πολυτρόπως πάλαι ὁ θεὸς λαλήσας τοῖς πατράσιν ἐν τοῖς προφήταις 2ἐπ' ἐσχάτου τῶν ἡμερῶν τούτων ἐλάλησεν ἡμῖν ἐν υἱῷ, ὃν ἔθηκεν κληρονόμον πάντων, δι' οὗ καὶ ἐποίησεν τοὺς αἰῶνας·

πολυμερῶς: in many portions, piecemeal – πολυτρόπως: in various ways – πάλαι: long ago – λαλέω (aor ptcp): speak – πατήρ (dat pl): ancestor – ἔσχατος: last – υἱός: Son – τίθημι (aor ind): appoint – κληρονόμος: heir

---

Formula of Concord SD XI 13

We should think or speak about how God's counsel, purpose, and ordination in Christ Jesus—who is the true Book of Life—is revealed to us through the Word.

June 23

1 Kings 19:19,21

19 וַיֵּלֶךְ מִשָּׁם וַיִּמְצָא אֶת־אֱלִישָׁע בֶּן־שָׁפָט וְהוּא חֹרֵשׁ
שְׁנֵים־עָשָׂר צְמָדִים לְפָנָיו וְהוּא בִּשְׁנֵים הֶעָשָׂר וַיַּעֲבֹר
אֵלִיָּהוּ אֵלָיו וַיַּשְׁלֵךְ אַדַּרְתּוֹ אֵלָיו׃
21 וַיָּשָׁב מֵאַחֲרָיו וַיִּקַּח אֶת־צֶמֶד הַבָּקָר וַיִּזְבָּחֵהוּ וּבִכְלִי
הַבָּקָר בִּשְּׁלָם הַבָּשָׂר וַיִּתֵּן לָעָם וַיֹּאכֵלוּ וַיָּקָם וַיֵּלֶךְ
אַחֲרֵי אֵלִיָּהוּ וַיְשָׁרְתֵהוּ׃

חָרַשׁ (qal ptcp): plow – צֶמֶד (pl): yoke – עָבַר (qal v-c impf): go over to – שָׁלַךְ (hiph v-c impf): throw – אַדֶּרֶת (3 sg sf): cloak – שׁוּב (qal v-c impf): turn – בָּקָר: cattle – זָבַח (qal v-c impf + 3 sg sf): slaughter – כְּלִי: equipment – בָּשַׁל (pi pf + 3 pl sf): cook – שָׁרַת (pi v-c impf): serve

Luke 14:19

καὶ ἕτερος εἶπεν· ζεύγη βοῶν ἠγόρασα πέντε καὶ πορεύομαι δοκιμάσαι αὐτά· ἐρωτῶ σε, ἔχε με παρῃτημένον.

ἕτερος: another – ζεῦγος (pl): yoke – βοῦς: ox – ἀγοράζω (aor 1 sg): buy – πορεύομαι: go – δοκιμάζω (aor inf): try out – ἐρωτάω: ask – ἔχω (pres imv): have – παραιτέομαι (pf pass ptcp): excuse

Large Catechism I 15

It is as though He *[God]* would say, "Whatever you have previously sought from the saints, or for whatever things you have trusted in money or anything else, expect it all from Me. Think of Me as the one who will help you and pour out upon you richly all good things."

JUNE 24

Exodus 20:11

כִּי שֵׁשֶׁת־יָמִים עָשָׂה יְהוָה אֶת־הַשָּׁמַיִם וְאֶת־הָאָרֶץ אֶת־
הַיָּם וְאֶת־כָּל־אֲשֶׁר־בָּם וַיָּנַח בַּיּוֹם הַשְּׁבִיעִי עַל־כֵּן בֵּרַךְ
יְהוָה אֶת־יוֹם הַשַּׁבָּת וַיְקַדְּשֵׁהוּ׃

שֵׁשׁ (cst): six – נוּחַ (qal v-c impf 3 sg): rest – שְׁבִיעִי: seventh – בָּרַךְ (pi pf 3 sg): bless – שַׁבָּת: Sabbath – קָדַשׁ (pi v-c impf 3 sg + 3 sg sf): make holy

---

Hebrews 11:3

πίστει νοοῦμεν κατηρτίσθαι τοὺς αἰῶνας ῥήματι θεοῦ, εἰς τὸ μὴ ἐκ φαινομένων τὸ βλεπόμενον γεγονέναι.

πίστις: faith – νοέω (pres ind 1 pl): understand – καταρτίζω (pf pass inf): form – αἰών (pl): universe – ῥῆμα: word – φαίνομαι (pres ptcp): appear – βλέπω (pres pass ptcp): see – γίνομαι (pf act inf): be made, created

---

Large Catechism II 16

We learn from this *[first]* article that none of us owns for himself, nor can preserve, his life nor anything that is here listed or can be listed. This is true no matter how small and unimportant a thing might be. For it is all included in the word *Creator*.

JUNE 25

Isaiah 44:21-22

21זְכָר־אֵלֶּה יַעֲקֹב וְיִשְׂרָאֵל כִּי עַבְדִּי־אָתָּה
יְצַרְתִּיךָ עֶבֶד־לִי אַתָּה יִשְׂרָאֵל לֹא תִנָּשֵׁנִי׃
22מָחִיתִי כָעָב פְּשָׁעֶיךָ וְכֶעָנָן חַטֹּאותֶיךָ
שׁוּבָה אֵלַי כִּי גְאַלְתִּיךָ׃

זָכַר (qal imv): remember – עֶבֶד (1 sg sf): servant – יָצַר (qal pf 1 sg + 2 sg sf): form, make – נָשָׁה (niph impf 2 sg + 1 sg sf): be forgotten by me – מָחָה (qal pf 1 sg): wipe out, sweep away – עָב: cloud – פֶּשַׁע (pl + 2 sg sf): sin (as rebellion) – עָנָן: morning mist – שׁוּב (qal imv): return – גָּאַל (qal pf 1 sg + 2 sg sf): redeem

---

John 11:4-5

4ἀκούσας δὲ ὁ Ἰησοῦς εἶπεν· αὕτη ἡ ἀσθένεια οὐκ ἔστιν
πρὸς θάνατον ἀλλ᾽ ὑπὲρ τῆς δόξης τοῦ θεοῦ, ἵνα δοξασθῇ
ὁ υἱὸς τοῦ θεοῦ δι᾽ αὐτῆς. 5ἠγάπα δὲ ὁ Ἰησοῦς τὴν Μάρθαν
καὶ τὴν ἀδελφὴν αὐτῆς καὶ τὸν Λάζαρον.

ἀκούω (aor ptcp): hear – εἶπον (3 sg): say – ἀσθένεια: sickness – θάνατος: death – δόξα: glory – δοξάζω (aor pass subj 3 sg): glorify – ἀγαπάω (impf 3 sg): love – ἀδελφή: sister

---

Large Catechism II 26

As we have said, we may learn from this *[second]* article how we have been redeemed. We shall base this on these words, "In Jesus Christ, our Lord."

Job 23:10

כִּי־יָדַע דֶּ֣רֶךְ עִמָּדִ֑י בְּחָנַ֗נִי כַּזָּהָב אֵצֵֽא׃

יָדַע (qal pf 3 sg): know – דֶּ֫רֶךְ: way – עִם (prep + 1 sg sf): with – בָּחַן (qal pf 3 sg + 1 sg sf): examine, test – זָהָב: gold – יָצָא (qal impf 1 sg): come forth

1 Peter 4:19

ὥστε καὶ οἱ πάσχοντες κατὰ τὸ θέλημα τοῦ θεοῦ πιστῷ κτίστῃ παρατιθέσθωσαν τὰς ψυχὰς αὐτῶν ἐν ἀγαθοποιΐᾳ.

πάσχω (pres ptcp pl): suffer – θέλημα: will – πιστός: faithful – κτίστης: Creator – παρατίθημι (pres imv 3 pl): entrust – ψυχή: soul, life, self – ἀγαθοποιΐα: doing good

Large Catechism III 65-66

And let no one think that he shall have peace [Matt 10:34]. He must risk whatever he has upon earth—possessions, honor, house and estate, wife and children, body and life. Now, this hurts our flesh and the old Adam [Eph 4:22]. The test is to be steadfast and to suffer with patience [Jas 5:7-8] in whatever way we are assaulted, and to let go whatever is taken from us [1 Pet 2:20-21].

Genesis 6:11-14

11 וַתִּשָּׁחֵת הָאָרֶץ לִפְנֵי הָאֱלֹהִים וַתִּמָּלֵא הָאָרֶץ חָמָס׃
12 וַיַּרְא אֱלֹהִים אֶת־הָאָרֶץ וְהִנֵּה נִשְׁחָתָה כִּי־הִשְׁחִית
כָּל־בָּשָׂר אֶת־דַּרְכּוֹ עַל־הָאָרֶץ׃ 13 וַיֹּאמֶר אֱלֹהִים
לְנֹחַ קֵץ כָּל־בָּשָׂר בָּא לְפָנַי כִּי־מָלְאָה הָאָרֶץ חָמָס
מִפְּנֵיהֶם וְהִנְנִי מַשְׁחִיתָם אֶת־הָאָרֶץ׃ 14 עֲשֵׂה לְךָ תֵּבַת
עֲצֵי־גֹפֶר קִנִּים תַּעֲשֶׂה אֶת־הַתֵּבָה

שָׁחַת (niph v-c impf 3 sg/niph pf 3 sg f): be corrupt – מָלֵא (niph v-c impf): be filled – חָמָס: violence – שָׁחַת (hiph pf 3 sg): corrupt – קֵץ: end – מִפְּנֵי: because of – שָׁחַת (hiph ptcp + 3 pl sf): destroy – תֵּבָה (cst sg): ark – עֵץ (cst pl): wood – גֹּפֶר: cypress (?) – קֵן (pl): nest, room

---

Hebrews 11:7

Πίστει χρηματισθεὶς Νῶε περὶ τῶν μηδέπω βλεπομένων, εὐλαβηθεὶς κατεσκεύασεν κιβωτὸν εἰς σωτηρίαν τοῦ οἴκου αὐτοῦ δι’ ἧς κατέκρινεν τὸν κόσμον, καὶ τῆς κατὰ πίστιν δικαιοσύνης ἐγένετο κληρονόμος.

χρηματίζω (aor pass ptcp): warn – μηδέπω: not yet – εὐλαβέομαι (aor ptcp): be afraid, respect – κατασκευάζω (aor ind 3 sg): prepare, build – κιβωτός: ark – κατακρίνω (aor ind 3 sg): condemn – κληρονόμος: heir

---

Apology V (III) 4

Faith brings the Holy Spirit and produces a new life in hearts. It must also produce spiritual movements in hearts.

Genesis 19:24-25

24 וַיהוָה הִמְטִיר עַל־סְדֹם וְעַל־עֲמֹרָה גָּפְרִית וָאֵשׁ מֵאֵת
יְהוָה מִן־הַשָּׁמָיִם׃ 25 וַיַּהֲפֹךְ אֶת־הֶעָרִים הָאֵל וְאֵת
כָּל־הַכִּכָּר וְאֵת כָּל־יֹשְׁבֵי הֶעָרִים וְצֶמַח הָאֲדָמָה׃

מָטַר (hiph pf 3 sg): rain down – סְדֹם: Sodom – עֲמֹרָה: Gomorrah – גָּפְרִית: brimstone – אֵשׁ: fire – הָפַךְ (qal v-c impf 3 sg): overthrow – עִיר (pl): city – הָאֵל = הָאֵלֶּה: these – כִּכָּר: round district, plain – יָשַׁב (qal ptcp cst pl): inhabitant – צֶמַח: growth, vegetation

---

Romans 1:18

Ἀποκαλύπτεται γὰρ ὀργὴ θεοῦ ἀπ' οὐρανοῦ ἐπὶ πᾶσαν ἀσέβειαν καὶ ἀδικίαν ἀνθρώπων τῶν τὴν ἀλήθειαν ἐν ἀδικίᾳ κατεχόντων . . .

> ἀποκαλύπτω (pres pass 3 sg): reveal – ὀργή: wrath – οὐρανός: heaven – ἀσέβεια: godlessness – ἀδικία: wickedness – ἀλήθεια: truth – κατέχω (pres ptcp pl): suppress

---

Formula of Concord Ep V 8

Therefore, Christ takes the Law into His hands and explains it spiritually (Matt 5:21-48; Rom 7:14). In this way God's wrath is revealed from heaven against all sinners [Rom 1:18], so that they see how great it is. In this way they are directed back to the Law, and then they first learn from it to know their sins correctly—a knowledge that Moses never could have forced out of them.

JUNE 29

Psalm 100:1-2

[1]הָרִיעוּ לַיהוָה כָּל־הָאָרֶץ׃
[2]עִבְדוּ אֶת־יְהוָה בְּשִׂמְחָה בֹּאוּ לְפָנָיו בִּרְנָנָה׃

רוּעַ (hiph imv pl): shout for joy – עָבַד (qal imv pl): serve – שִׂמְחָה: gladness – בּוֹא (qal imv pl): come – לְפָנָיו: before him – רְנָנָה: joy

Romans 15:13

Ὁ δὲ θεὸς τῆς ἐλπίδος πληρώσαι ὑμᾶς πάσης χαρᾶς καὶ εἰρήνης ἐν τῷ πιστεύειν, εἰς τὸ περισσεύειν ὑμᾶς ἐν τῇ ἐλπίδι ἐν δυνάμει πνεύματος ἁγίου.

ἐλπίς: hope – πληρόω (aor opt 3 sg): fill – χαρά: joy – εἰρήνη: peace – πιστεύω (pres inf): believe – περισσεύω (pres inf): overflow – δύναμις: power

Apology IV (II) 100

Hab 2:4 says, "The righteous shall live by his faith." Here he says, first, that people are just by faith. By faith they believe that God is favorable, and he adds that the same faith gives life because this faith produces peace and joy in the heart and eternal life.

June 30

Jeremiah 9:22-23

22אַל־יִתְהַלֵּל חָכָם בְּחָכְמָתוֹ וְאַל־יִתְהַלֵּל הַגִּבּוֹר בִּגְבוּרָתוֹ
אַל־יִתְהַלֵּל עָשִׁיר בְּעָשְׁרוֹ׃ 23כִּי אִם־בְּזֹאת יִתְהַלֵּל
הַמִּתְהַלֵּל הַשְׂכֵּל וְיָדֹעַ אוֹתִי כִּי אֲנִי יְהוָה עֹשֶׂה חֶסֶד
מִשְׁפָּט וּצְדָקָה בָּאָרֶץ כִּי־בְאֵלֶּה חָפַצְתִּי נְאֻם־יְהוָה׃

הָלַל (hithp juss 3 sg/hithp ptcp sg): boast – חָכָם: wise man – חָכְמָה: wisdom – גִּבּוֹר: strong man – גְּבוּרָה: strength – עָשִׁיר: rich man – עֹשֶׁר: riches – כִּי אִם: but – שָׂכַל (hiph inf abs): have understanding – יָדַע (qal inf abs): know – חֶסֶד: faithful love – מִשְׁפָּט: justice – צְדָקָה: righteousness – חָפֵץ (qal perf 1 sg): delight – נְאֻם: utterance

---

1 Corinthians 2:1-2

1Κἀγὼ ἐλθὼν πρὸς ὑμᾶς, ἀδελφοί, ἦλθον οὐ καθ' ὑπεροχὴν
λόγου ἢ σοφίας καταγγέλλων ὑμῖν τὸ μυστήριον τοῦ θεοῦ.
2οὐ γὰρ ἔκρινά τι εἰδέναι ἐν ὑμῖν εἰ μὴ 'Ιησοῦν Χριστὸν
καὶ τοῦτον ἐσταυρωμένον.

ὑπεροχή: superiority – καταγγέλλω (pres ptcp sg): proclaim – κρίνω (aor ind 1 sg): resolve – οἶδα (inf): know – εἰ μή: if not, except – σταυρόω (pf pass ptcp): crucify

---

Large Catechism II 63

See, here *[in the three articles of the Creed]* you have the entire divine essence, will, and work shown most completely in quite short and yet rich words. In these words all our wisdom stands, which surpasses and exceeds the wisdom, mind, and reason of all people.

Exodus 15:11

מִי־כָמֹכָה בָּאֵלִם יְהוָה מִי כָּמֹכָה נֶאְדָּר בַּקֹּדֶשׁ
נוֹרָא תְהִלֹּת עֹשֵׂה פֶלֶא׃

מִי: who? – כָּמוֹ (prep + 2 sg sf): like you – אֵל (pl): god – אדר (niph ptcp): majestic – קֹדֶשׁ: holiness – יָרֵא (niph ptcp): awesome – תְּהִלָּה (pl): praise – עָשָׂה (qal ptcp): do – פֶּלֶא: wonder, miracle

Galatians 3:13

Χριστὸς ἡμᾶς ἐξηγόρασεν ἐκ τῆς κατάρας τοῦ νόμου γενόμενος ὑπὲρ ἡμῶν κατάρα, ὅτι γέγραπται· ἐπικατάρατος πᾶς ὁ κρεμάμενος ἐπὶ ξύλου . . .

ἐξαγοράζω (aor ind 3 sg): redeem – κατάρα: curse – νόμος: law – γίνομαι (aor ptcp): become – γράφω (pf pass 3 sg): write – ἐπικατάρατος: cursed – κρεμάννυμι (pres ptcp): hang – ξύλον: wood, tree

Apology V (III) 57-58

We have a gracious God because of Christ's satisfaction and not because of our fulfilling the Law. Paul teaches this in Gal 3:13, when he says, "Christ redeemed us from the curse of the law by becoming a curse for us." This means that the Law condemns all people. But Christ—without sin—has borne the punishment of sin.

Numbers 6:24-27

24 יְבָרֶכְךָ יְהוָה וְיִשְׁמְרֶךָ׃
25 יָאֵר יְהוָה פָּנָיו אֵלֶיךָ וִיחֻנֶּךָּ׃
26 יִשָּׂא יְהוָה פָּנָיו אֵלֶיךָ וְיָשֵׂם לְךָ שָׁלוֹם׃
27 וְשָׂמוּ אֶת־שְׁמִי עַל־בְּנֵי יִשְׂרָאֵל וַאֲנִי אֲבָרְכֵם׃

בָּרַךְ (pi juss 3 sg + 2 sg sf): bless – שָׁמַר (qal juss 3 sg + 2 sg sf): keep – אוֹר (hiph juss 3 sg): cause to shine – פָּנִים (3 sg sf): face – חָנַן (qal juss 3 sg + 2 sg sf): be gracious to – נָשָׂא (qal juss 3 sg): lift up – שִׂים (qal juss 3 sg/qal v-c pf 3 pl): place, give – שָׁלוֹם: peace – בָּרַךְ (pi impf 1 sg + 3 pl sf): bless

---

2 Corinthians 13:14

ἡ χάρις τοῦ κυρίου Ἰησοῦ Χριστοῦ καὶ ἡ ἀγάπη τοῦ θεοῦ καὶ ἡ κοινωνία τοῦ ἁγίου πνεύματος μετὰ πάντων ὑμῶν.

χάρις: grace – ἀγάπη: love – κοινωνία: fellowship

Formula of Concord SD III 25

Not everything that belongs to conversion also belongs to the article of justification. Only God's grace, Christ's merit, and faith belong and are necessary to the article of justification. Faith receives these blessings in the promise of the Gospel, by which Christ's righteousness is credited to us. From this we receive and have forgiveness of sins, reconciliation with God, sonship, and are made heirs of eternal life.

July 3

Psalm 143:2

וְאַל־תָּבוֹא בְמִשְׁפָּט אֶת־עַבְדֶּךָ כִּי לֹא־יִצְדַּק לְפָנֶיךָ
כָל־חָי׃

בּוֹא (qal juss 2 sg): enter – מִשְׁפָּט: judgment – עֶבֶד (2 sg sf): servant – צָדֵק (qal impf 3 sg): be righteous – לְפָנֶיךָ: in your sight – חַי: living

Galatians 2:16

εἰδότες [δὲ] ὅτι οὐ δικαιοῦται ἄνθρωπος ἐξ ἔργων νόμου ἐὰν μὴ διὰ πίστεως Ἰησοῦ Χριστοῦ, καὶ ἡμεῖς εἰς Χριστὸν Ἰησοῦν ἐπιστεύσαμεν, ἵνα δικαιωθῶμεν ἐκ πίστεως Χριστοῦ καὶ οὐκ ἐξ ἔργων νόμου, ὅτι ἐξ ἔργων νόμου οὐ δικαιωθήσεται πᾶσα σάρξ.

οἶδα (pf ptcp pl with pres meaning): know – δικαιόω (pres pass 3 sg/aor pass subj 1 pl/fut pass 3 sg): justify – ἔργον (pl): work – νόμος: law – πίστις: faith – πιστεύω (aor ind 1 pl): believe – σάρξ: flesh

Apology IV (II) 89

Faith is that thing God declares to be righteousness. Paul adds that righteousness is credited freely. He says that it could not be credited freely if it were due because of works. Therefore, he excludes also the merit of moral works. For if justification before God were due to these moral works, faith would not be credited for righteousness without works.

July 4

Jeremiah 23:31

הִנְנִי עַל־הַנְּבִיאִם נְאֻם־יְהוָה הַלֹּקְחִים לְשׁוֹנָם וַיִּנְאֲמוּ נְאֻם׃

עַל: against – נָבִיא (pl): prophet – נְאֻם: declaration, utterance (of the Lord) – לָקַח (qal ptcp pl): take, use – לָשׁוֹן (3 pl sf): tongue – נָאַם (qal v-c impf 3 pl): speak as a prophet

---

2 Peter 2:1

Ἐγένοντο δὲ καὶ ψευδοπροφῆται ἐν τῷ λαῷ, ὡς καὶ ἐν ὑμῖν ἔσονται ψευδοδιδάσκαλοι, οἵτινες παρεισάξουσιν αἱρέσεις ἀπωλείας καὶ τὸν ἀγοράσαντα αὐτοὺς δεσπότην ἀρνούμενοι, ἐπάγοντες ἑαυτοῖς ταχινὴν ἀπώλειαν . . .

γίνομαι (aor 3 pl): be – ψευδοπροφήτης (pl): false prophet – λαός: people – ψευδοδιδάσκαλος (pl): false teacher – παρεισάγω (fut ind 3 pl): bring in, introduce – αἵρεσις (pl): heresy – ἀπώλεια: destruction – ἀγοράζω (aor ptcp): buy – δεσπότης: Lord – ἀρνέομαι (pres ptcp): deny – ἐπάγω (pres ptcp pl): bring on – ταχινός: swift

---

Power and Primacy 57

Even if the bishop of Rome did have the primacy by divine right, since he defends godless services and doctrine conflicting with the Gospel, obedience is not due him. Indeed, it is necessary to resist him as Antichrist.

July 5

Habakkuk 3:18

וַאֲנִי בַּיהוָה אֶעְלֽוֹזָה אָגִילָה בֵּאלֹהֵי יִשְׁעִי׃

עָלַז (qal coh 1 sg): rejoice – גִּיל (qal coh 1 sg): be joyful – יֵשַׁע (1 sg sf): salvation

---

Acts 5:41-42

41Οἱ μὲν οὖν ἐπορεύοντο χαίροντες ἀπὸ προσώπου
τοῦ συνεδρίου, ὅτι κατηξιώθησαν ὑπὲρ τοῦ ὀνόματος
ἀτιμασθῆναι, 42πᾶσάν τε ἡμέραν ἐν τῷ ἱερῷ καὶ κατ'
οἶκον οὐκ ἐπαύοντο διδάσκοντες καὶ εὐαγγελιζόμενοι
τὸν χριστόν 'Ιησοῦν.

πορεύομαι (impf ind 3 pl): depart – χαίρω (pres ptcp pl): rejoice – πρόσωπον: presence – συνέδριον: Sanhedrin – καταξιόω (aor pass 3 pl): consider worthy – ὄνομα: name – ἀτιμάζω (aor pass inf): dishonor – ἡμέρα: day – παύω (impf mid 3 pl): stop – διδάσκω (pres ptcp pl): teach – εὐαγγελίζω (pres mid ptcp pl): announce good news

---

Large Catechism III 100

Although we have received forgiveness and a good conscience and are entirely acquitted, yet our life is of such a nature that we stand today, and tomorrow we fall [Is 40:6-8]. Therefore, even though we are godly now and stand before God with a good conscience, we must pray again *[the Sixth Petition]* that He would not allow us to fall again and yield to trials and temptations.

JULY 6

Jeremiah 10:12

עֹשֵׂה אֶרֶץ בְּכֹחוֹ מֵכִין תֵּבֵל בְּחָכְמָתוֹ וּבִתְבוּנָתוֹ נָטָה שָׁמָיִם׃

עָשָׂה (qal ptcp sg): make – כֹּחַ (3 sg sf): strength – כּוּן (hiph ptcp): establish – תֵּבֵל: world – חָכְמָה (3 sg sf): wisdom – תְּבוּנָה (3 sg sf): understanding – נָטָה (qal pf): stretch out – שָׁמַיִם: the heavens

---

Colossians 1:16

ὅτι ἐν αὐτῷ ἐκτίσθη τὰ πάντα ἐν τοῖς οὐρανοῖς καὶ ἐπὶ τῆς γῆς, τὰ ὁρατὰ καὶ τὰ ἀόρατα, εἴτε θρόνοι εἴτε κυριότητες εἴτε ἀρχαὶ εἴτε ἐξουσίαι· τὰ πάντα δι᾽ αὐτοῦ καὶ εἰς αὐτὸν ἔκτισται·

κτίζω (aor pass 3 sg/pf pass 3 sg): create – ὁρατός: visible – ἀόρατος: invisible – θρόνος (pl): throne – κυριότης: ruling power – ἀρχή: ruler – ἐξουσία: authority

---

Formula of Concord SD VIII 61

This divine power, life, might, majesty, and glory was given to the received human nature in Christ. This did not happen the way the Father from eternity has communicated to the Son (according to the divine nature) His essence and all divine attributes, by which He is of one essence with the Father and is equal to God. (For Christ is equal to the Father only according to the divine nature. According to the received human nature, He is beneath God. From this it is clear that we make no confusion, equalization, or abolition of natures in Christ.) So the power to give life is not the same in Christ's flesh as it is in His divine nature, where it is an essential property.

JULY 7

Isaiah 49:14-16

14 וַתֹּאמֶר צִיּוֹן עֲזָבַנִי יְהוָה וַאדֹנָי שְׁכֵחָנִי׃
15 הֲתִשְׁכַּח אִשָּׁה עוּלָהּ מֵרַחֵם בֶּן־בִּטְנָהּ
גַּם־אֵלֶּה תִשְׁכַּחְנָה וְאָנֹכִי לֹא אֶשְׁכָּחֵךְ׃
16 הֵן עַל־כַּפַּיִם חַקֹּתִיךְ

עָזַב (qal pf 3 sg + 1 sg sf): forsake – שָׁכַח (qal pf 3 sg + 1 sg sf/qal impf 3 sg f/qal impf 3 pl f/qal impf 1 sg + 2 sg sf): forget – אִשָּׁה: mother – עוּל (3 sg f sf): nursing child – רָחַם (pi inf cst + מִן): have no compassion – בֶּטֶן (3 sg f sf): womb = the child she has borne – כַּף (du): palm of the hand – חָקַק (qal pf 1 sg + 2 sg sf): engrave

---

John 17:24

Πάτερ, ὃ δέδωκάς μοι, θέλω ἵνα ὅπου εἰμὶ ἐγὼ κἀκεῖνοι ὦσιν μετ᾽ ἐμοῦ, ἵνα θεωρῶσιν τὴν δόξαν τὴν ἐμήν, ἣν δέδωκάς μοι, ὅτι ἠγάπησάς με πρὸ καταβολῆς κόσμου.

δίδωμι (pf ind 2 sg): give – θέλω: want – εἰμί (pres ind 1 sg/pres subj 3 pl): be – θεωρέω (pres subj 3 pl): see – δόξα: glory – ἀγαπάω (aor ind 2 sg): love – καταβολή: beginning – κόσμος: world

---

Formula of Concord SD VIII 65

This power was concealed and withheld at the time of the humiliation. But now, after the form of a servant has been laid aside, it is fully, powerfully, and publicly exercised before all saints, in heaven and on earth. In the life to come we shall also behold His glory face-to-face (John 17:24).

JULY 8

Genesis 11:4

וַיֹּאמְרוּ הָבָה נִבְנֶה־לָּנוּ עִיר וּמִגְדָּל וְרֹאשׁוֹ בַשָּׁמַיִם
וְנַעֲשֶׂה־לָּנוּ שֵׁם פֶּן־נָפוּץ עַל־פְּנֵי כָל־הָאָרֶץ׃

הָבָה (imv of יָהַב): come now! – בָּנָה (qal coh 1 pl): build – עִיר: city – מִגְדָּל: tower – רֹאשׁ: top – פֶּן: lest – פוּץ (qal impf 1 pl): be scattered

---

1 Corinthians 3:9-11

9θεοῦ γάρ ἐσμεν συνεργοί, θεοῦ γεώργιον, θεοῦ οἰκοδομή
ἐστε. 10Κατὰ τὴν χάριν τοῦ θεοῦ τὴν δοθεῖσάν μοι ὡς
σοφὸς ἀρχιτέκτων θεμέλιον ἔθηκα, ἄλλος δὲ ἐποικοδομεῖ.
ἕκαστος δὲ βλεπέτω πῶς ἐποικοδομεῖ. 11θεμέλιον γὰρ
ἄλλον οὐδεὶς δύναται θεῖναι παρὰ τὸν κείμενον, ὅς
ἐστιν Ιησοῦς Χριστός.

συνεργός: fellow worker – γεώργιον: field – οἰκοδομή: building – χάρις: grace – δίδωμι (aor pass ptcp): give – σοφός: wise – ἀρχιτέκτων: builder – θεμέλιον: foundation – τίθημι (aor ind 1 sg/aor inf): lay – ἐποικοδομέω (pres 3 sg): build on – βλέπω (pres imv 3 sg): take care – κεῖμαι (pres ptcp): be laid

---

Apology VII-VIII (IV) 20

This Church is properly the pillar of the truth (1 Tim 3:15). For it keeps the pure Gospel as Paul says in 1 Cor 3:11. The "foundation" is the true knowledge of Christ and faith. There are also many weak persons, who build upon the foundation stubble that will perish (v. 12), holding certain harmful opinions.

July 9

Proverbs 14:12

יֵשׁ דֶּרֶךְ יָשָׁר לִפְנֵי־אִישׁ וְאַחֲרִיתָהּ דַּרְכֵי־מָוֶת׃

יֵשׁ: there is – דֶּרֶךְ (abs sg/cst pl): way – יָשָׁר: right – אַחֲרִית (3 sg sf): end – מָוֶת: death

Luke 12:19-20

19καὶ ἐρῶ τῇ ψυχῇ μου· ψυχή, ἔχεις πολλὰ ἀγαθὰ κείμενα
εἰς ἔτη πολλά· ἀναπαύου, φάγε, πίε, εὐφραίνου. 20εἶπεν
δὲ αὐτῷ ὁ θεός· ἄφρων, ταύτῃ τῇ νυκτὶ τὴν ψυχήν σου
ἀπαιτοῦσιν ἀπὸ σοῦ· ἃ δὲ ἡτοίμασας, τίνι ἔσται;

ἐρῶ (fut 1 sg of λέγω/εἶπον): say – ψυχή: soul, self – ἀγαθός: good – κεῖμαι (pres ptcp): be stored up – ἔτος (pl): year – ἀναπαύω (pres mid imv): take one's rest – φάγε (aor imv sg of ἐσθίω): eat – πίνω (aor imv sg): drink – εὐφραίνω (pres pass imv): be glad, enjoy oneself – ἄφρων: foolish, ignorant – νύξ: night – ἀπαιτέω (pres ind 3 pl): demand (impersonal = passive) – ἑτοιμάζω (aor ind): prepare

Large Catechism I 241-242

We will indeed look on and let these people skin, pinch, and hoard. But we will trust in God, who will do the following: after you have been skinning and scraping for a long time, He will pronounce such a blessing on your gains that your grain in the silo, your beer in the cellar, and your cattle in the stalls shall perish [Luke 12:16-21].

Ecclesiastes 7:20

כִּי אָדָם אֵין צַדִּיק בָּאָרֶץ אֲשֶׁר יַעֲשֶׂה־טּוֹב וְלֹא יֶחֱטָא׃

אָדָם: man – אַיִן (cst): nonexistence – עָשָׂה (qal impf 3 sg): do – טוֹב: good – חָטָא (qal impf 3 sg): sin

---

Galatians 6:7-8

7Μὴ πλανᾶσθε, θεὸς οὐ μυκτηρίζεται. ὃ γὰρ ἐὰν σπείρῃ
ἄνθρωπος, τοῦτο καὶ θερίσει· 8ὅτι ὁ σπείρων εἰς τὴν
σάρκα ἑαυτοῦ ἐκ τῆς σαρκὸς θερίσει φθοράν, ὁ δὲ σπείρων
εἰς τὸ πνεῦμα ἐκ τοῦ πνεύματος θερίσει ζωὴν αἰώνιον.

πλανάω (pres pass imv 2 pl): be misled – μυκτηρίζω (pres pass 3 sg): mock – ὃ . . . ἐάν: whatever – σπείρω (pres subj 3 sg/pres ptcp): sow – θερίζω (fut ind): reap – σάρξ: flesh, sinful nature – φθορά: destruction – ζωή: life – αἰώνιος: eternal

---

Apology V (III) 246

But whenever merit is mentioned, the adversaries immediately transfer the matter from other rewards to justification. Yet the Gospel freely offers justification because of Christ's merits and not of our own. His merits are delivered to us through faith. Works and troubles do not merit justification, but other payments, as the reward is offered for the works in these passages: "Whoever sows sparingly will also reap sparingly, and whoever sows bountifully will also reap bountifully" (2 Cor 9:6).

July 11

Isaiah 53:6

כֻּלָּנוּ כַּצֹּאן תָּעִינוּ אִישׁ לְדַרְכּוֹ פָּנִינוּ
וַֽיהוָה הִפְגִּיעַ בּוֹ אֵת עֲוֺן כֻּלָּנוּ׃

כֹּל (1 pl sf): all – צֹאן: sheep – תָּעָה (qal pf 1 pl): stray – דֶּרֶךְ (3 sg sf): way – פָּנָה (qal pf 1 pl): turn – פָּגַע (hiph pf 3 sg): lay, burden – עָוֺן: sin (as guilt)

1 Peter 2:24-25

24ὃς τὰς ἁμαρτίας ἡμῶν αὐτὸς ἀνήνεγκεν ἐν τῷ σώματι
αὐτοῦ ἐπὶ τὸ ξύλον, ἵνα ταῖς ἁμαρτίαις ἀπογενόμενοι τῇ
δικαιοσύνῃ ζήσωμεν, οὗ τῷ μώλωπι ἰάθητε. 25ἦτε γὰρ ὡς
πρόβατα πλανώμενοι, ἀλλὰ ἐπεστράφητε νῦν ἐπὶ τὸν
ποιμένα καὶ ἐπίσκοπον τῶν ψυχῶν ὑμῶν.

ἁμαρτία: sin – ἀναφέρω (aor ind 3 sg): bear – σῶμα: body – ξύλον: wood, cross – ἀπογίνομαι (aor ptcp): die – δικαιοσύνη: righteousness – ζάω (aor subj 1 pl): live – μώλωψ: wound, bruise – ἰάομαι (aor pass 2 pl): heal – πρόβατον (pl): sheep – πλανάω (pass ptcp): go astray – ἐπιστρέφω (aor pass 2 pl): turn back – ποιμήν: shepherd – ἐπίσκοπος: overseer – ψυχή: soul

Smalcald Articles II I 2

He alone is the Lamb of God who takes away the sins of the world (John 1:29), and God has laid upon Him the iniquities of us all (Isa 53:6).

July 12

Proverbs 15:15-16

15 כָּל־יְמֵי עָנִי רָעִים וְטוֹב־לֵב מִשְׁתֶּה תָמִיד׃
16 טוֹב־מְעַט בְּיִרְאַת יְהוָה מֵאוֹצָר רָב וּמְהוּמָה בוֹ׃

יוֹם (cst pl): day – עָנִי: the oppressed – רַע (pl): wretched – טוֹב: good, cheerful – לֵב: heart – מִשְׁתֶּה: feast – תָּמִיד: perpetual – טוֹב + מִן of comparison: better – מְעַט: little – יִרְאָה (cst sg): fear – אוֹצָר: wealth – רַב: great – מְהוּמָה: turmoil

---

1 Timothy 6:6-8

6 Ἔστιν δὲ πορισμὸς μέγας ἡ εὐσέβεια μετὰ αὐταρκείας·
7 οὐδὲν γὰρ εἰσηνέγκαμεν εἰς τὸν κόσμον, ὅτι οὐδὲ
ἐξενεγκεῖν τι δυνάμεθα· 8 ἔχοντες δὲ διατροφὰς καὶ
σκεπάσματα, τούτοις ἀρκεσθησόμεθα.

> πορισμός: means of gain – μέγας: great – εὐσέβεια: godliness – αὐταρκεία: contentment – εἰσφέρω (aor 1 pl): bring into – ἐκφέρω (aor inf): take out – δύναμαι (pres 1 pl): be able – διατροφή: food – σκέπασμα: clothing – ἀρκέω (fut pass 1 pl): be content

---

Large Catechism I 296-297

But here *[in the Ninth and Tenth Commandments]* it is also forbidden for you to alienate anything from your neighbor, even though you could do so with honor in the eyes of the world, so that no one could accuse or blame you as though you had gotten it wrongfully. For our natural instinct is that no one wants to see someone else have as much as himself. Each one acquires as much as he can.

July 13

Psalm 73:25-26

25מִי־לִי בַשָּׁמָיִם וְעִמְּךָ לֹא־חָפַצְתִּי בָאָרֶץ׃
26כָּלָה שְׁאֵרִי וּלְבָבִי צוּר־לְבָבִי וְחֶלְקִי אֱלֹהִים
לְעוֹלָם׃

שָׁמַיִם: heaven – עִם (2 sg sf): with = being with you – חָפֵץ (qal pf 1 sg): desire – כָּלָה (qal pf 3 sg): fail – שְׁאֵר (1 sg sf): flesh – לֵבָב (1 sg sf): heart – צוּר: rock, strength – חֵלֶק (1 sg sf): portion – לְעוֹלָם: forever

Matthew 13:16-17

16ὑμῶν δὲ μακάριοι οἱ ὀφθαλμοὶ ὅτι βλέπουσιν καὶ
τὰ ὦτα ὑμῶν ὅτι ἀκούουσιν. 17ἀμὴν γὰρ λέγω ὑμῖν ὅτι
πολλοὶ προφῆται καὶ δίκαιοι ἐπεθύμησαν ἰδεῖν ἃ βλέπετε
καὶ οὐκ εἶδαν, καὶ ἀκοῦσαι ἃ ἀκούετε καὶ οὐκ ἤκουσαν.

μακάριος: blessed – ὀφθαλμός: eye – βλέπω (pres ind 3 pl): see – οὖς: ear – ἀκούω (pres ind 3 pl): hear – δίκαιος: righteous – ἐπιθυμέω (aor ind 3 pl): desire, long for – ὁράω (aor inf/aor ind 3 pl): see

Formula of Concord SD II 9

They *[natural men]* want to understand these spiritual things with their reason. But the more diligently and seriously they try, the less they understand or believe. Before they become enlightened and are taught by the Holy Spirit, they regard all this only as foolishness or fictions.

JULY 14

Jeremiah 23:26,28

26עַד־מָתַי הֲיֵשׁ בְּלֵב הַנְּבִאִים נִבְּאֵי הַשָּׁקֶר וּנְבִיאֵי
תַּרְמִת לִבָּם׃
28הַנָּבִיא אֲשֶׁר־אִתּוֹ חֲלוֹם יְסַפֵּר חֲלוֹם וַאֲשֶׁר דְּבָרִי
אִתּוֹ יְדַבֵּר דְּבָרִי אֱמֶת מַה־לַתֶּבֶן אֶת־הַבָּר נְאֻם־יְהוָה׃

עַד־מָתַי: how long? – יֵשׁ: existence + interrog ה: will it be? – לֵב: heart – נָבִיא (pl/cst pl): prophet – נָבָא (niph ptcp pl): prophesy – שֶׁקֶר: falsehood – תַּרְמִית (cst): deceitfulness – חֲלוֹם: dream – סָפַר (pi juss 3 sg): tell – אֱמֶת: truthfully – תֶּבֶן: straw – בַּר: grain

Matthew 7:15-16

15Προσέχετε ἀπὸ τῶν ψευδοπροφητῶν, οἵτινες ἔρχονται
πρὸς ὑμᾶς ἐν ἐνδύμασιν προβάτων, ἔσωθεν δέ εἰσιν
λύκοι ἅρπαγες. 16ἀπὸ τῶν καρπῶν αὐτῶν ἐπιγνώσεσθε
αὐτούς. μήτι συλλέγουσιν ἀπὸ ἀκανθῶν σταφυλὰς ἢ ἀπὸ
τριβόλων σῦκα;

προσέχω (pres imv 2 pl): be on one's guard – ἔνδυμα: clothing – πρόβατον: sheep – ἔσωθεν: inside – λύκος: wolf – ἅρπαξ: ravenous – καρπός: fruit – ἐπιγινώσκω (fut dep 2 pl): recognize – συλλέγω (pres ind 3 pl): gather in, pick – ἄκανθα: thornbush – σταφυλή: (bunch of) grapes – τρίβολος: thistle – σῦκον: fig

Formula of Concord SD X 25

[Adiaphora should be handled in such a way that] God may not be angered, love may not be injured, the enemies of God's Word may not be strengthened, nor the weak in faith offended.

July 15

Psalm 50:10-11

10 כִּי־לִי כָל־חַיְתוֹ־יָעַר בְּהֵמוֹת בְּהַרְרֵי־אָלֶף׃
11 יָדַעְתִּי כָּל־עוֹף הָרִים וְזִיז שָׂדַי עִמָּדִי׃

חַיָּה (cst): animal – יַעַר: forest – בְּהֵמָה (pl): cattle – הַר (cst pl): mountain – אֶלֶף: thousand – עוֹף: bird – זִיז: creatures – שָׂדַי: field – עִם (1 sg sf): mine

---

Matthew 10:29-31

29οὐχὶ δύο στρουθία ἀσσαρίου πωλεῖται; καὶ ἓν ἐξ αὐτῶν οὐ
πεσεῖται ἐπὶ τὴν γῆν ἄνευ τοῦ πατρὸς ὑμῶν. 30ὑμῶν δὲ καὶ
αἱ τρίχες τῆς κεφαλῆς πᾶσαι ἠριθμημέναι εἰσίν. 31μὴ οὖν
φοβεῖσθε· πολλῶν στρουθίων διαφέρετε ὑμεῖς.

στρουθίον: sparrow – ἀσσάριον: penny – πωλέω (pres pass): sell – πίπτω (fut dep ind): fall – ἄνευ: without – θρίξ (pl): hair – ἀριθμέω (pf pass ptcp pl): count – φοβέομαι (pres imv 2 pl): fear – διαφέρω (pres ind 2 pl): be superior to, be worth more than

---

Large Catechism II 14

He causes all created things to serve for the uses and necessities of life. These include the sun, moon, and stars in the heavens, day and night, air, fire, water, earth, and whatever it bears and produces. They include birds and fish, beasts, grain, and all kinds of produce [Ps 104].

JULY 16

Deuteronomy 30:19

הַעִידֹ֨תִי בָכֶ֣ם הַיּוֹם֮ אֶת־הַשָּׁמַ֣יִם וְאֶת־הָאָ֒רֶץ֒ הַחַיִּ֣ים
וְהַמָּ֗וֶת נָתַ֣תִּי לְפָנֶ֔יךָ הַבְּרָכָ֖ה וְהַקְּלָלָ֑ה וּבָחַרְתָּ֙ בַּחַיִּ֔ים
לְמַ֥עַן תִּחְיֶ֖ה אַתָּ֥ה וְזַרְעֶֽךָ׃

עוד (hiph pf 1 sg): call as a witness – הַיּוֹם: today – שָׁמַיִם: heaven – חַיִּים: life – מָוֶת: death – נָתַן (qal pf 1 sg): give, set – לִפְנֵי (2 sg sf): before – בְּרָכָה: blessing – קְלָלָה: curse – בָּחַר (qal v-c pf 2 sg): choose – לְמַעַן: so that – חָיָה (qal impf 2 sg): live – זֶרַע (2 sg sf): seed, offspring

Romans 6:23

τὰ γὰρ ὀψώνια τῆς ἁμαρτίας θάνατος, τὸ δὲ χάρισμα τοῦ θεοῦ ζωὴ αἰώνιος ἐν Χριστῷ Ἰησοῦ τῷ κυρίῳ ἡμῶν.

ὀψώνιον (pl): compensation – ἁμαρτία: sin – θάνατος: death – χάρισμα: gift – ζωή: life – αἰώνιος: eternal

Formula of Concord SD XI 81

All preparation for condemnation is by the devil and a person, through sin. In no way does it come from God, who does not want any person to be damned. How, then, should He Himself prepare any person for condemnation? God is not a cause of sins. He is also not the cause of punishment or damnation. The only cause of damnation is sin. "For the wages of sin is death" [Rom 6:23].

Psalm 42:12

מַה־תִּשְׁתּוֹחֲחִי נַפְשִׁי וּמַה־תֶּהֱמִי עָלָי
הוֹחִילִי לֵאלֹהִים כִּי־עוֹד אוֹדֶנּוּ יְשׁוּעֹת פָּנַי וֵאלֹהָי׃

מָה: why – שָׁחַח (hithpoel impf 2 sg f): be downcast – נֶפֶשׁ (1 sg sf): soul – הָמָה (qal impf 2 sg f): be disturbed – יָחַל (hiph imv): hope – יָדָה (hiph impf 1 sg + 3 sg sf): praise – יְשׁוּעָה: deliverance, salvation – פָּנַי: my face = my

---

Mark 6:50-51

50πάντες γὰρ αὐτὸν εἶδον καὶ ἐταράχθησαν. ὁ δὲ
εὐθὺς ἐλάλησεν μετ’ αὐτῶν, καὶ λέγει αὐτοῖς· θαρσεῖτε,
ἐγώ εἰμι· μὴ φοβεῖσθε. 51καὶ ἀνέβη πρὸς αὐτοὺς εἰς τὸ
πλοῖον καὶ ἐκόπασεν ὁ ἄνεμος, καὶ λίαν [ἐκ περισσοῦ]
ἐν ἑαυτοῖς ἐξίσταντο·

ὁράω (aor ind 3 pl): see – ταράσσω (aor pass 3 pl): be terrified – εὐθύς: immediately – λαλέω (aor ind 3 sg): speak – θαρσέω (pres imv 2 pl): be courageous – φοβέομαι (pres imv 2 pl): be afraid – ἀναβαίνω (aor ind 3 sg): go up – κοπάζω (aor ind 3 sg): abate – ἄνεμος: wind – λίαν ἐκ περισσοῦ: exceedingly – ἐξίστημι (impf mid 3 pl): be amazed

---

Apology IV (II) 48

But the faith that justifies is not merely a knowledge of history. It is to believe in God's promise.

July 18

Job 42:1-2

1 וַיַּ֣עַן אִיּ֣וֹב אֶת־יְהוָ֗ה וַיֹּאמַֽר׃
2 יָ֭דַעְתִּי כִּי־כֹ֣ל תּוּכָ֑ל וְלֹא־יִבָּצֵ֖ר מִמְּךָ֣ מְזִמָּֽה׃

עָנָה (qal v-c impf 3 sg): answer – יָדַע (qal pf 1 sg): know – יָכֹל (qal impf 2 sg): be able – בָּצַר (niph impf 3 sg): be thwarted – מְזִמָּה: plan, purpose

Matthew 8:2-3

2 καὶ ἰδοὺ λεπρὸς προσελθὼν προσεκύνει αὐτῷ λέγων·
κύριε, ἐὰν θέλῃς δύνασαί με καθαρίσαι. 3 καὶ ἐκτείνας
τὴν χεῖρα ἥψατο αὐτοῦ λέγων· θέλω, καθαρίσθητι· καὶ
εὐθέως ἐκαθαρίσθη αὐτοῦ ἡ λέπρα.

ἰδού: like הִנֵּה, behold! – προσέρχομαι (aor ptcp): come – προσκυνέω (impf 3 sg): prostrate oneself before – θέλω (pres subj 2 sg): desire – δύναμαι (pres 2 sg): be able – καθαρίζω (aor inf): make clean – ἐκτείνω (aor ptcp): hold out (one's hand) – ἅπτω (aor mid 3 sg): touch, take hold of – καθαρίζω (aor pass imv 2 sg/aor pass ind 3 sg): be made clean

Large Catechism III 30

We need to know this: all our shelter and protection rest in prayer alone. For we are far too weak to deal with the devil and all his power and followers who set themselves against us.

JULY 19

Jeremiah 17:14

רְפָאֵנִי יְהוָה וְאֵרָפֵא הוֹשִׁיעֵנִי וְאִוָּשֵׁעָה כִּי תְהִלָּתִי אָתָּה׃

רָפָא (qal imv + 1 sg sf/niph coh 1 sg): heal – יָשַׁע (hiph imv + 1 sg sf/niph coh 1 sg): save – תְּהִלָּה (1 sg sf): the object of praise

---

Luke 17:15-17

15εἷς δὲ ἐξ αὐτῶν, ἰδὼν ὅτι ἰάθη, ὑπέστρεψεν μετὰ φωνῆς
μεγάλης δοξάζων τὸν θεόν, 16καὶ ἔπεσεν ἐπὶ πρόσωπον
παρὰ τοὺς πόδας αὐτοῦ εὐχαριστῶν αὐτῷ· καὶ αὐτὸς ἦν
Σαμαρίτης. 17ἀποκριθεὶς δὲ ὁ Ἰησοῦς εἶπεν· οὐχὶ οἱ δέκα
ἐκαθαρίσθησαν; οἱ δὲ ἐννέα ποῦ;

εἷς: one – ὁράω (aor ptcp sg): see – ἰάομαι (aor pass 3 sg): heal – ὑποστρέφω (aor ind 3 sg): turn back – φωνή: voice – δοξάζω (pres ptcp): praise – πίπτω (aor ind 3 sg): fall – πρόσωπον: face – πούς (pl): foot – εὐχαριστέω (pres ptcp): give thanks – καθαρίζω (aor pass 3 pl): cleanse – ἐννέα: nine – ποῦ: where?

Formula of Concord SD I 14

Furthermore, human nature, which is perverted and corrupted by original sin, must and can be healed only by the regeneration and renewal of the Holy Spirit [Titus 3:5].

July 20

Psalm 37:25

נַ֣עַר הָ֭יִיתִי גַּם־זָ֑קַנְתִּי וְֽלֹא־רָ֭אִיתִי צַדִּ֣יק נֶעֱזָ֑ב וְ֝זַרְע֗וֹ מְבַקֶּשׁ־לָֽחֶם׃

נַ֫עַר: youth – זָקֵן (qal pf 1 sg): grow old – רָאָה (qal pf 1 sg): see – צַדִּיק: righteous – עָזַב (niph ptcp): be forsaken – זֶ֫רַע (3 sg sf): offspring – בָּקַשׁ (pi ptcp): seek, beg – לֶ֫חֶם: bread

---

John 6:32

εἶπεν οὖν αὐτοῖς ὁ Ἰησοῦς· ἀμὴν ἀμὴν λέγω ὑμῖν, οὐ Μωϋσῆς δέδωκεν ὑμῖν τὸν ἄρτον ἐκ τοῦ οὐρανοῦ, ἀλλ' ὁ πατήρ μου δίδωσιν ὑμῖν τὸν ἄρτον ἐκ τοῦ οὐρανοῦ τὸν ἀληθινόν·

εἶπον (aor 3 sg): say – δίδωμι (pf ind 3 sg/pres ind 3 sg): give – ἄρτος: bread – οὐρανός: heaven – ἀληθινός: true

---

Smalcald Articles III VI 1

Of the Sacrament of the Altar, we hold that the bread and wine in the Supper are Christ's true body and blood. These are given and received not only by the godly but also by wicked Christians [1 Cor 11:29-30].

July 21

Isaiah 54:10

כִּי הֶהָרִים יָמוּשׁוּ וְהַגְּבָעוֹת תְּמוּטֶנָה
וְחַסְדִּי מֵאִתֵּךְ לֹא־יָמוּשׁ וּבְרִית שְׁלוֹמִי לֹא תָמוּט
אָמַר מְרַחֲמֵךְ יְהוָה׃

הַר (pl): mountain – מוּשׁ (qal impf 3 pl): depart, be removed – גִּבְעָה (pl): hill – מוּט (qal impf 3 pl f): totter, be shaken – חֶסֶד (1 sg sf): faithful love – בְּרִית: covenant – שָׁלוֹם (1 sg sf): peace – רָחַם (pi ptcp + 2 sg sf): have mercy

---

Romans 8:38-39

38πέπεισμαι γὰρ ὅτι οὔτε θάνατος οὔτε ζωὴ οὔτε ἄγγελοι
οὔτε ἀρχαὶ οὔτε ἐνεστῶτα οὔτε μέλλοντα οὔτε δυνάμεις
39οὔτε ὕψωμα οὔτε βάθος οὔτε τις κτίσις ἑτέρα δυνήσεται
ἡμᾶς χωρίσαι ἀπὸ τῆς ἀγάπης τοῦ θεοῦ τῆς ἐν Χριστῷ
Ἰησοῦ τῷ κυρίῳ ἡμῶν.

πείθω (pf pass 1 sg): be convinced – ἀρχή: demonic power – ἐνεστῶτα (pf ptcp of ἐνίστημι): the present – μέλλοντα (pres ptcp of μέλλω): the future – ὕψωμα: height – βάθος: depth – κτίσις: creature – δύναμαι (fut ind 3 sg): be able – χωρίζω (aor inf): separate

---

Formula of Concord SD XI 46-47

He *[God]* placed salvation for safekeeping in the almighty hand of our Savior, Jesus Christ, from which no one can snatch us (John 10:28). Therefore, Paul asks in Romans, because we "are called according to His purpose" (8:28), who "will be able to separate us from the love of God in Christ Jesus our Lord?" (8:39).

Deuteronomy 32:4

הַצּוּר תָּמִים פָּעֳלוֹ כִּי כָל־דְּרָכָיו מִשְׁפָּט
אֵל אֱמוּנָה וְאֵין עָוֶל צַדִּיק וְיָשָׁר הוּא׃

צוּר: Rock – תָּמִים: sound, having integrity – פֹּעַל (3 sg sf): work, deeds – דֶּרֶךְ (pl + 3 sg sf): way – מִשְׁפָּט: justice, right – אֱמוּנָה: faithfulness – אַיִן (cst): nonexistence – עָוֶל: injustice – צַדִּיק: righteous, just – יָשָׁר: upright

---

2 Corinthians 5:10

τοὺς γὰρ πάντας ἡμᾶς φανερωθῆναι δεῖ ἔμπροσθεν τοῦ βήματος τοῦ Χριστοῦ, ἵνα κομίσηται ἕκαστος τὰ διὰ τοῦ σώματος πρὸς ἃ ἔπραξεν, εἴτε ἀγαθὸν εἴτε φαῦλον.

φανερόω (aor pass inf): be revealed, appear – δεῖ: it is necessary – βῆμα: judgment seat – κομίζω (aor mid subj 3 sg): get for oneself, receive – σῶμα: body – πράσσω (aor ind 3 sg): do – ἀγαθός: good – φαῦλος: bad

---

Smalcald Articles Preface 9

Imagine those whose writings have instilled such crude lies into the king and other countries, presenting them as the pure truth. How will they face us when we are brought before the judgment seat of Christ [2 Cor 5:10]? . . . May God convert to repentance those who can be converted! To the rest will be said, “Woe and alas!” for eternity.

Genesis 1:26-27

26וַיֹּאמֶר אֱלֹהִים נַעֲשֶׂה אָדָם בְּצַלְמֵנוּ כִּדְמוּתֵנוּ וְיִרְדּוּ
בִדְגַת הַיָּם וּבְעוֹף הַשָּׁמַיִם וּבַבְּהֵמָה וּבְכָל־הָאָרֶץ וּבְכָל־
הָרֶמֶשׂ הָרֹמֵשׂ עַל־הָאָרֶץ׃ 27וַיִּבְרָא אֱלֹהִים אֶת־הָאָדָם
בְּצַלְמוֹ בְּצֶלֶם אֱלֹהִים בָּרָא אֹתוֹ זָכָר וּנְקֵבָה בָּרָא
אֹתָם׃

עָשָׂה (qal coh): make – צֶלֶם (1 pl sf): image – דְּמוּת (1 pl sf): likeness – רָדָה (qal juss 3 pl): have dominion – דָּגָה (cst): fish – עוֹף: bird – בְּהֵמָה: cattle – רֶמֶשׂ: creeping things – רָמַשׂ (qal ptcp): creep – בָּרָא (qal v-c impf 3 sg/ qal pf 3 sg): create – זָכָר: male – נְקֵבָה: female

---

Acts 17:28-29

28ἐν αὐτῷ γὰρ ζῶμεν καὶ κινούμεθα καὶ ἐσμέν, ὡς καί τινες
τῶν καθ' ὑμᾶς ποιητῶν εἰρήκασιν· τοῦ γὰρ καὶ γένος ἐσμέν.
29γένος οὖν ὑπάρχοντες τοῦ θεοῦ οὐκ ὀφείλομεν νομίζειν
χρυσῷ ἢ ἀργύρῳ ἢ λίθῳ, χαράγματι τέχνης καὶ ἐνθυμήσεως
ἀνθρώπου, τὸ θεῖον εἶναι ὅμοιον.

κινέω (pres pass 1 pl): move – ποιητής (gen pl): poet – εἰρήκασιν (pf ind 3 pl of λέγω/εἶπον): say – γένος: offspring – λίθος: stone – χάραγμα: image – τέχνη: skill – ἐνθύμησις: thought – τὸ θεῖον: the deity – εἶναι: obj of νομίζειν – ὅμοιος: like

---

Smalcald Articles III III 34

And God now "commands all people everywhere to repent" (Acts 17:30). "All people," He says. No one is an exception who is a human being.

July 24

Genesis 5:3-5

³וַיְחִי אָדָם שְׁלֹשִׁים וּמְאַת שָׁנָה וַיּוֹלֶד בִּדְמוּתוֹ כְּצַלְמוֹ
וַיִּקְרָא אֶת־שְׁמוֹ שֵׁת׃ ⁴וַיִּהְיוּ יְמֵי־אָדָם אַחֲרֵי הוֹלִידוֹ
אֶת־שֵׁת שְׁמֹנֶה מֵאֹת שָׁנָה וַיּוֹלֶד בָּנִים וּבָנוֹת׃ ⁵וַיִּהְיוּ
כָּל־יְמֵי אָדָם אֲשֶׁר־חַי תְּשַׁע מֵאוֹת שָׁנָה וּשְׁלֹשִׁים שָׁנָה
וַיָּמֹת׃

חָיָה (qal v-c impf 3 sg): live – שְׁלֹשִׁים וּמְאַת: 130 – יָלַד (hiph v-c impf 3 sg/hiph inf cst): father (a child) – דְּמוּת (3 sg sf): likeness – צֶלֶם (3 sg sf): image – קָרָא (qal v-c impf 3 sg): call – שְׁמֹנֶה מֵאֹת: 800 – בֵּן (pl): son – בַּת (pl):daughter – תְּשַׁע מֵאוֹת וּשְׁלֹשִׁים: 930 – מוּת (qal v-c impf 3 sg): die

---

Romans 7:18-19

18Οἶδα γὰρ ὅτι οὐκ οἰκεῖ ἐν ἐμοί, τοῦτ᾽ ἔστιν ἐν τῇ
σαρκί μου, ἀγαθόν· τὸ γὰρ θέλειν παράκειταί μοι, τὸ
δὲ κατεργάζεσθαι τὸ καλὸν οὔ· 19οὐ γὰρ ὃ θέλω ποιῶ
ἀγαθόν, ἀλλὰ ὃ οὐ θέλω κακὸν τοῦτο πράσσω.

οἰκέω (pres ind 3 sg): live – σάρξ: flesh, sinful nature – παράκειμαι: be present – κατεργάζομαι (pres inf): carry out – οὔ: no – κακός: evil – πράσσω: do

---

Smalcald Articles III XIII 1

God will and does account us entirely righteous and holy for the sake of Christ, our Mediator [1 Tim 2:5]. Although sin in the flesh has not yet been completely removed or become dead [Rom 7:18], yet He will not punish or remember it.

July 25

Micah 7:18-19

18מִי־אֵל כָּמוֹךָ נֹשֵׂא עָוֹן וְעֹבֵר עַל־פֶּשַׁע לִשְׁאֵרִית נַחֲלָתוֹ
לֹא־הֶחֱזִיק לָעַד אַפּוֹ כִּי־חָפֵץ חֶסֶד הוּא׃ 19יָשׁוּב יְרַחֲמֵנוּ
יִכְבֹּשׁ עֲוֺנֹתֵינוּ וְתַשְׁלִיךְ בִּמְצֻלוֹת יָם כָּל־חַטֹּאותָם׃

כָּמוֹךָ: like you – נָשָׂא (qal ptcp): forgive – עָוֹן: sin (as guilt) – עָבַר (qal ptcp): pass by, pardon – פֶּשַׁע: sin (as rebellion) – שְׁאֵרִית: remnant – נַחֲלָה: inheritance – חָזַק (hiph pf 3 sg): retain – לָעַד: forever – אַף (3 sg sf): anger – חָפֵץ (qal pf 3 sg): delight – יָשׁוּב (adv): again – רָחַם (pi impf): have compassion – כָּבַשׁ (qal impf 3 sg): subdue – שָׁלַךְ (hiph impf 2 sg): cast – מְצוּלָה (pl): depth – חַטָּאת (pl + 3 pl sf): sin (as missing the mark)

John 1:35-36

35Τῇ ἐπαύριον πάλιν εἱστήκει ὁ Ἰωάννης καὶ ἐκ τῶν μαθητῶν
αὐτοῦ δύο 36καὶ ἐμβλέψας τῷ Ἰησοῦ περιπατοῦντι λέγει· ἴδε
ὁ ἀμνὸς τοῦ θεοῦ.

τῇ ἐπαύριον: the following day – ἵστημι (plpf ind with impf meaning): stand – ἐμβλέπω (aor ptcp): look at – περιπατέω (pres ptcp): walk – ὁράω (aor imv): see – ἀμνός: Lamb

Smalcald Articles II II 1

For this sacrifice or work of the Mass is thought to free people from sins, both in this life and also in purgatory. It does so even when offered by a wicked scoundrel. Yet only the Lamb of God can and will do this.

July 26

2 Chronicles 1:7

בַּלַּיְלָה הַהוּא נִרְאָה אֱלֹהִים לִשְׁלֹמֹה וַיֹּאמֶר לוֹ שְׁאַל
מָה אֶתֶּן־לָךְ׃

לַיְלָה: night – רָאָה (niph pf 3 sg): appear – שָׁאַל (qal imv sg): ask – מָה: what – נָתַן (qal impf 1 sg): give

---

2 Corinthians 6:16

εἶπεν ὁ θεὸς ὅτι ἐνοικήσω ἐν αὐτοῖς καὶ ἐμπεριπατήσω καὶ ἔσομαι αὐτῶν θεὸς καὶ αὐτοὶ ἔσονταί μου λαός.

εἶπον (aor 3 sg): say – ἐνοικέω (fut ind 1 sg): live with – ἐμπεριπατέω (fut ind 1 sg): walk among – εἰμί (fut ind): be – λαός: people

---

Formula of Concord SD II 65

From this evidence the following is certain: as soon as the Holy Spirit has begun His work of regeneration and renewal in us through the Word and holy Sacraments, we can and should cooperate through His power, although still in great weakness. This cooperation does not come from our fleshly natural powers, but from the new powers and gifts that the Holy Spirit has begun in us in conversion.

Job 14:1-2

1 אָדָם יְלוּד אִשָּׁה קְצַר יָמִים וּשְׂבַע־רֹגֶז׃
2 כְּצִיץ יָצָא וַיִּמָּל וַיִּבְרַח כַּצֵּל וְלֹא יַעֲמוֹד׃

אָדָם: man – יָלַד (qal pass ptcp cst): be born of – קָצֵר (cst): short-lived – שָׂבֵעַ (adj cst): full – רֹגֶז: turmoil – צִיץ: flower – יָצָא (qal pf 3 sg): come out – מָלַל (qal v-c impf 3 sg): wither – בָּרַח (qal v-c impf 3 sg): flee – צֵל: shadow – עָמַד (qal impf 3 sg): stand, continue

Romans 14:7-8

7 οὐδεὶς γὰρ ἡμῶν ἑαυτῷ ζῇ καὶ οὐδεὶς ἑαυτῷ ἀποθνῄσκει·
8 ἐάν τε γὰρ ζῶμεν, τῷ κυρίῳ ζῶμεν, ἐάν τε ἀποθνῄσκωμεν,
τῷ κυρίῳ ἀποθνῄσκομεν. ἐάν τε οὖν ζῶμεν ἐάν τε
ἀποθνῄσκωμεν τοῦ κυρίου ἐσμέν.

ἑαυτῷ: to himself alone – ζάω (pres ind 3 sg/pres subj 1 pl/pres ind 1 pl): live – ἀποθνῄσκω (pres ind 3 sg/pres subj 1 pl/pres ind 1 pl): die – κύριος: Lord

Apology XX 84

Who would not joyfully die in the confession of these articles, that we receive the forgiveness of sins through faith freely for Christ's sake, and that we do not merit the forgiveness of sins by our works?

Genesis 28:16-17

16 וַיִּיקַץ יַעֲקֹב מִשְּׁנָתוֹ וַיֹּאמֶר אָכֵן יֵשׁ יְהוָה בַּמָּקוֹם הַזֶּה
וְאָנֹכִי לֹא יָדָעְתִּי׃ 17 וַיִּירָא וַיֹּאמַר מַה־נּוֹרָא הַמָּקוֹם
הַזֶּה אֵין זֶה כִּי אִם־בֵּית אֱלֹהִים וְזֶה שַׁעַר הַשָּׁמָיִם׃

יָקַץ (qal v-c impf 3 sg): awake – שֵׁנָה (3 sg sf + prep מִן): sleep – אָכֵן: surely – יֵשׁ: existence = is – מָקוֹם: place – יָדַע (qal pf 1 sg): know – יָרֵא (qal v-c impf 3 sg): be afraid; (niph ptcp): awesome – אֵין כִּי אִם: none other than – שַׁעַר: gate

---

John 14:23

ἀπεκρίθη Ἰησοῦς καὶ εἶπεν αὐτῷ· ἐάν τις ἀγαπᾷ με τὸν λόγον μου τηρήσει, καὶ ὁ πατήρ μου ἀγαπήσει αὐτὸν καὶ πρὸς αὐτὸν ἐλευσόμεθα καὶ μονὴν παρ’ αὐτῷ ποιησόμεθα.

ἀγαπάω (pres ind 3 sg/fut ind 3 sg): love – τηρέω (fut ind 3 sg): keep – ἔρχομαι (fut ind 1 pl): come – μονή: dwelling place – ποιέω (fut mid 1 pl): make

---

Formula of Concord SD II 57

For Christ, in whom we are chosen, offers to all people His grace in the Word and holy Sacraments. He sincerely wants it to be heard. He has promised that where two or three are gathered together in His name and have His holy Word, He will be in their midst [Matt 18:20].

Jeremiah 2:13

כִּֽי־שְׁתַּ֥יִם רָע֖וֹת עָשָׂ֣ה עַמִּ֑י אֹתִ֨י עָזְב֜וּ
מְק֣וֹר ׀ מַ֣יִם חַיִּ֗ים לַחְצֹ֤ב לָהֶם֙ בֹּאר֔וֹת
בֹּארֹת֙ נִשְׁבָּרִ֔ים אֲשֶׁ֥ר לֹא־יָכִ֖לוּ הַמָּֽיִם׃

שְׁתַּ֥יִם: two – רַע (pl f): evil, sin – עָזַב (qal pf 3 pl): forsake – מָקוֹר: spring – חַי (pl): living – חָצַב (qal inf cst): hew out – בְּאֵר (pl): cistern – שָׁבַר (niph ptcp pl): broken – כּוּל (hiph impf 3 pl): contain

---

1 Corinthians 10:1-4

1Οὐ θέλω γὰρ ὑμᾶς ἀγνοεῖν, ἀδελφοί, ὅτι οἱ πατέρες
ἡμῶν πάντες ὑπὸ τὴν νεφέλην ἦσαν καὶ πάντες διὰ
τῆς θαλάσσης διῆλθον 2καὶ πάντες εἰς τὸν Μωϋσῆν
ἐβαπτίσθησαν ἐν τῇ νεφέλῃ καὶ ἐν τῇ θαλάσσῃ 3καὶ
πάντες τὸ αὐτὸ πνευματικὸν βρῶμα ἔφαγον 4καὶ πάντες τὸ
αὐτὸ πνευματικὸν ἔπιον πόμα· ἔπινον γὰρ ἐκ πνευματικῆς
ἀκολουθούσης πέτρας, ἡ πέτρα δὲ ἦν ὁ Χριστός.

ἀγνοέω (pres inf): be ignorant – νεφέλη: cloud – θάλασσα: sea – πνευματικός: spiritual – βρῶμα: bread – ἔφαγον (aor ind 3 pl of ἐσθίω): eat – πίνω (aor ind/impf ind): drink – πόμα: drink – ἀκολουθέω (pres ptcp): follow

---

Augsburg Confession IX 1-2

Concerning Baptism, our churches teach that Baptism is necessary for salvation [Mark 16:16] and that God's grace is offered through Baptism [Titus 3:4-7]. They teach that children are to be baptized [Acts 2:38-39]. Being offered to God through Baptism, they are received into God's grace.

July 30

Psalm 119:34-35

34 הֲבִינֵנִי וְאֶצְּרָה תוֹרָתֶךָ וְאֶשְׁמְרֶנָּה בְכָל־לֵב׃

35 הַדְרִיכֵנִי בִּנְתִיב מִצְוֺתֶיךָ כִּי־בוֹ חָפָצְתִּי׃

בִּין (hiph imv sg + 1 sg sf): give understanding – נָצַר (qal coh 1 sg): keep – תּוֹרָה: law, teaching – שָׁמַר (qal impf 1 sg + 3 sg sf): obey – לֵב: heart – דָּרַךְ (hiph imv + 1 sg sf): lead – נָתִיב (cst sg): path – מִצְוָה (pl + 2 sg sf): command – חָפֵץ (qal pf 1 sg): find delight

---

John 8:34-36

34 ἀπεκρίθη αὐτοῖς ὁ Ἰησοῦς· ἀμὴν ἀμὴν λέγω ὑμῖν ὅτι πᾶς
ὁ ποιῶν τὴν ἁμαρτίαν δοῦλός ἐστιν τῆς ἁμαρτίας. 35 ὁ δὲ
δοῦλος οὐ μένει ἐν τῇ οἰκίᾳ εἰς τὸν αἰῶνα, ὁ υἱὸς μένει
εἰς τὸν αἰῶνα. 36 ἐὰν οὖν ὁ υἱὸς ὑμᾶς ἐλευθερώσῃ, ὄντως
ἐλεύθεροι ἔσεσθε.

ἀποκρίνομαι (aor ind 3 sg): answer – ποιέω (pres ptcp): commit – ἁμαρτία: sin – δοῦλος: slave – μένω (pres ind 3 sg): have a place – οἰκία: family – αἰών: eternity – ἐλευθερόω (aor subj 3 sg): make free – ὄντως: really

---

Formula of Concord SD VI 17

When a person is born anew by God's Spirit, liberated from the Law (i.e., freed from this driver), and led by Christ's Spirit, he lives according to God's unchangeable will revealed in the Law. Since he is born anew, he does everything from a free, cheerful spirit.

July 31

Psalm 103:7

יוֹדִ֣יעַ דְּרָכָ֣יו לְמֹשֶׁ֑ה לִבְנֵ֥י יִ֝שְׂרָאֵ֗ל עֲלִילוֹתָֽיו׃

יָדַע (hiph impf 3 sg): make known – דֶּרֶךְ (pl + 3 sg sf): way – עֲלִילָה (pl + 3 sg sf): deed

2 Peter 1:19-21

[19]καὶ ἔχομεν βεβαιότερον τὸν προφητικὸν λόγον, ᾧ καλῶς
ποιεῖτε προσέχοντες ὡς λύχνῳ φαίνοντι ἐν αὐχμηρῷ τόπῳ,
ἕως οὗ ἡμέρα διαυγάσῃ καὶ φωσφόρος ἀνατείλῃ ἐν ταῖς
καρδίαις ὑμῶν, [20]τοῦτο πρῶτον γινώσκοντες ὅτι πᾶσα
προφητεία γραφῆς ἰδίας ἐπιλύσεως οὐ γίνεται· [21]οὐ γὰρ
θελήματι ἀνθρώπου ἠνέχθη προφητεία ποτέ, ἀλλὰ ὑπὸ
πνεύματος ἁγίου φερόμενοι ἐλάλησαν ἀπὸ θεοῦ ἄνθρωποι.

βέβαιος (comparative adj): more firm – ποιέω (pres ind 2 pl): do – προσέχω (pres ptcp pl): pay attention to – λύχνος: lamp – φαίνω (pres ptcp): shine – αὐχμηρός: dark – τόπος: place – διαυγάζω (aor subj 3 sg): shine through – φωσφόρος: morning star – ἀνατέλλω (aor subj 3 sg): rise – προφητεία: prophetic word – γραφή (gen sg): Scripture – ἴδιος: one's own – ἐπίλυσις: interpretation – θέλημα: will – φέρω (aor pass 3 sg): bring, utter (of a divine proclamation) – ποτέ: ever – φέρω (pres pass ptcp): carry along

Smalcald Articles III VIII 10

Therefore, we must constantly maintain this point: God does not want to deal with us in any other way than through the spoken Word and the Sacraments. Whatever is praised as from the Spirit—without the Word and Sacraments—is the devil himself.

August 1

Genesis 21:17

וַיִּשְׁמַע אֱלֹהִים אֶת־קוֹל הַנַּעַר וַיִּקְרָא מַלְאַךְ אֱלֹהִים
אֶל־הָגָר מִן־הַשָּׁמַיִם וַיֹּאמֶר לָהּ מַה־לָּךְ הָגָר אַל־תִּירְאִי
כִּי־שָׁמַע אֱלֹהִים אֶל־קוֹל הַנַּעַר בַּאֲשֶׁר הוּא־שָׁם׃

שָׁמַע (qal v-c impf 3 sg): hear – קוֹל: voice – נַעַר: boy (Ishmael) – קָרָא (qal v-c impf 3 sg): call – מַלְאָךְ: angel – מַה־לָּךְ: what is the matter? – יָרֵא (qal juss 2 sg): fear – בַּאֲשֶׁר הוּא־שָׁם: where he is

---

Matthew 6:31-32

31μὴ οὖν μεριμνήσητε λέγοντες· τί φάγωμεν; ἤ· τί πίωμεν; ἤ· τί περιβαλώμεθα; 32πάντα γὰρ ταῦτα τὰ ἔθνη ἐπιζητοῦσιν· οἶδεν γὰρ ὁ πατὴρ ὑμῶν ὁ οὐράνιος ὅτι χρῄζετε τούτων ἁπάντων.

μεριμνάω (aor subj 2 pl): worry – φάγωμεν (aor subj 1 pl of ἐσθίω): eat – πίνω (aor subj 1 pl): drink – περιβάλλω (aor mid subj 1 pl): clothe oneself – ἔθνη: pagans – ἐπιζητέω (pres ind 3 pl): strive for – οὐράνιος: heavenly – χρῄζω (pres ind 2 pl): have need of

---

Small Catechism Fourth Petition

Give us this day our daily bread.

What does this mean?

Answer: God gives daily bread, even without our prayer, to all wicked people; but we pray in this petition that He would lead us to realize this and to receive our daily bread with thanksgiving.

August 2

2 Samuel 7:18-19

18 וַיָּבֹא הַמֶּלֶךְ דָּוִד וַיֵּשֶׁב לִפְנֵי יְהוָה וַיֹּאמֶר מִי אָנֹכִי
אֲדֹנָי יְהוִה וּמִי בֵיתִי כִּי הֲבִיאֹתַנִי עַד־הֲלֹם׃ 19 וַתִּקְטַן
עוֹד זֹאת בְּעֵינֶיךָ אֲדֹנָי יְהוִה וַתְּדַבֵּר גַּם אֶל־בֵּית־עַבְדְּךָ
לְמֵרָחוֹק וְזֹאת תּוֹרַת הָאָדָם אֲדֹנָי יְהוִה׃

בּוֹא (qal v-c impf 3 sg): go; (hiph pf 2 sg + 1 sg sf): bring – יָשַׁב (qal v-c impf 3 sg): sit – עַד־הֲלֹם: this far – קָטֹן (qal v-c impf 3 sg f): be small, insignificant – עַיִן (pl + 2 sg sf): eye – דָּבַר (pi v-c impf 2 sg): speak – עֶבֶד: servant – רָחוֹק: distant future – תּוֹרָה: manner

---

1 Corinthians 1:31

ἵνα καθὼς γέγραπται· ὁ καυχώμενος ἐν κυρίῳ καυχάσθω.

γράφω (pf pass 3 sg): write – καυχάομαι (pres ptcp sg/pres imv 3 sg): boast

---

Smalcald Articles III XIII 3

Therefore, we cannot boast of many merits and works, if they are viewed apart from grace and mercy. As it is written, "Let the one who boasts, boast in the Lord" (1 Cor 1:31); namely, that he has a gracious God. For with that, all is well.

August 3

Psalm 55:23

הַשְׁלֵךְ עַל־יְהוָה יְהָבְךָ וְהוּא יְכַלְכְּלֶךָ
לֹא־יִתֵּן לְעוֹלָם מוֹט לַצַּדִּיק׃

שָׁלַךְ (hiph imv sg): cast – יְהָב (2 sg sf): lot, anxiety – כּוּל (pilpel impf + 2 sg sf): support – מוֹט: shaking, tottering (and falling) – צַדִּיק: the righteous

Luke 12:22-23

22Εἶπεν δὲ πρὸς τοὺς μαθητὰς [αὐτοῦ]· διὰ τοῦτο λέγω
ὑμῖν· μὴ μεριμνᾶτε τῇ ψυχῇ τί φάγητε, μηδὲ τῷ σώματι
τί ἐνδύσησθε. 23ἡ γὰρ ψυχὴ πλεῖόν ἐστιν τῆς τροφῆς καὶ
τὸ σῶμα τοῦ ἐνδύματος.

μαθητής: disciple – μεριμνάω (pres imv 2 pl): worry – ψυχή: life – φάγητε (aor subj 2 pl of ἐσθίω): eat – σῶμα: body – ἐνδύω (aor mid subj 2 pl): clothe oneself – πλεῖον: more – τροφή: food – ἔνδυμα: clothes

Small Catechism Grace at the Table

The children and servants shall go to the table with folded hands, reverently, and say:

The eyes of all look to You, and You give them their food in due season. You open Your hand; You satisfy the desire of every living thing. [Ps 145:15-16]

(Note: "To satisfy the desire" means that all animals receive so much to eat that they are made joyful and of good cheer. For worry and greed hinder such satisfaction.)

August 4

Nahum 1:7

טוֹב יְהוָה לְמָעוֹז בְּיוֹם צָרָה
וְיֹדֵעַ חֹסֵי בוֹ׃

טוֹב: good – **מָעוֹז**: refuge – **יוֹם** (cst sg): day – **צָרָה**: trouble – **יָדַע** (qal ptcp sg): take notice of, care of – **חָסָה** (qal ptcp cst pl): trust

2 Timothy 2:19

ὁ μέντοι στερεὸς θεμέλιος τοῦ θεοῦ ἕστηκεν, ἔχων τὴν σφραγῖδα ταύτην· Ἔγνω κύριος τοὺς ὄντας αὐτοῦ . . .

μέντοι: but – στερεός: firm – θεμέλιος: foundation – ἵστημι (pf ind 3 sg with pres meaning): stand – ἔχω (pres ptcp): have – σφραγίς: seal – γινώσκω (aor ind 3 sg): know, acknowledge

Large Catechism II 17

Further, we also confess that God the Father has not only given us all that we have and see before our eyes, but He daily preserves and defends us against all evil and misfortune [Ps 5:11].

AUGUST 5

Genesis 39:2-3

2וַיְהִי יְהוָה אֶת־יוֹסֵף וַיְהִי אִישׁ מַצְלִיחַ וַיְהִי בְּבֵית
אֲדֹנָיו הַמִּצְרִי׃ 3וַיַּרְא אֲדֹנָיו כִּי יְהוָה אִתּוֹ וְכֹל אֲשֶׁר־
הוּא עֹשֶׂה יְהוָה מַצְלִיחַ בְּיָדוֹ׃

אֵת (prep): with – צָלַח (hiph ptcp): prosper, cause to prosper – אָדוֹן (pl of rank + 3 sg sf): master – מִצְרִי: Egyptian – רָאָה (qal v-c impf 3 sg): see – עָשָׂה (qal ptcp): do – יָד (3 sg sf): hand

---

Luke 11:9-10

9Κἀγὼ ὑμῖν λέγω, αἰτεῖτε καὶ δοθήσεται ὑμῖν, ζητεῖτε
καὶ εὑρήσετε, κρούετε καὶ ἀνοιγήσεται ὑμῖν· 10πᾶς γὰρ
ὁ αἰτῶν λαμβάνει καὶ ὁ ζητῶν εὑρίσκει καὶ τῷ κρούοντι
ἀνοιγ[ήσ]εται.

αἰτέω (pres imv 2 pl/pres ptcp sg): ask – δίδωμι (fut pass 3 sg): give – ζητέω (pres imv 2 pl/pres ptcp sg): seek – εὑρίσκω (fut ind 2 pl): find – κρούω (pres imv 2 pl/pres ptcp dat sg): knock – ἀνοίγω (fut pass 3 sg): open

---

Large Catechism I 63

Besides this you must also know how to use God's name rightly. For when He says, "You shall not take the name of the LORD, your God, in vain," He wants us to understand at the same time that His name is to be used properly. For His name has been revealed and given to us so that it may be of constant use and profit.

AUGUST 6

Zephaniah 3:17

יְהוָה אֱלֹהַיִךְ בְּקִרְבֵּךְ גִּבּוֹר יוֹשִׁיעַ
יָשִׂישׂ עָלַיִךְ בְּשִׂמְחָה יַחֲרִישׁ בְּאַהֲבָתוֹ
יָגִיל עָלַיִךְ בְּרִנָּה׃

קֶרֶב (2 sg f sf): midst – גִּבּוֹר: mighty one – יָשַׁע (hiph impf 3 sg): save – שִׂישׂ (qal impf 3 sg): delight in – שִׂמְחָה: joy – חָרַשׁ (hiph impf 3 sg): quiet – אַהֲבָה (3 sg sf): love – גִּיל (qal impf 3 sg): rejoice – רִנָּה: singing

---

Luke 8:24

προσελθόντες δὲ διήγειραν αὐτὸν λέγοντες· ἐπιστάτα ἐπιστάτα, ἀπολλύμεθα. ὁ δὲ διεγερθεὶς ἐπετίμησεν τῷ ἀνέμῳ καὶ τῷ κλύδωνι τοῦ ὕδατος· καὶ ἐπαύσαντο καὶ ἐγένετο γαλήνη.

προσέρχομαι (aor ptcp pl): approach – διεγείρω (aor ind 3 pl/aor pass ptcp): awaken – ἐπιστάτης: master – ἀπόλλυμι (pres mid 1 pl): perish – ἐπιτιμάω (aor ind 3 sg): rebuke – ἄνεμος: wind – κλύδων: raging water – παύω (aor mid 3 pl): stop – γαλήνη: calm

---

Large Catechism I 39

But as terrible as these threatenings *[of the Law]* are, so much more powerful is the consolation in the promise. For those who cling to God alone should be sure that He will show them mercy. In other words, He will show them pure goodness and blessing, not only for themselves, but also to their children and their children's children, even to the thousandth generation and beyond that.

AUGUST 7

Genesis 49:18

לִֽישׁוּעָתְךָ֖ קִוִּ֥יתִי יְהוָֽה׃

יְשׁוּעָה (2 sg m sf): deliverance, salvation – קָוָה (pi pf 1 sg): wait for

---

Romans 5:2,5

[2]δι' οὗ καὶ τὴν προσαγωγὴν ἐσχήκαμεν [τῇ πίστει] εἰς τὴν χάριν ταύτην ἐν ᾗ ἑστήκαμεν καὶ καυχώμεθα ἐπ' ἐλπίδι τῆς δόξης τοῦ θεοῦ. . . . [5]ἡ δὲ ἐλπὶς οὐ καταισχύνει, ὅτι ἡ ἀγάπη τοῦ θεοῦ ἐκκέχυται ἐν ταῖς καρδίαις ἡμῶν διὰ πνεύματος ἁγίου τοῦ δοθέντος ἡμῖν.

προσαγωγή: access – ἔχω (pf ind 1 pl): have, hold – χάρις: grace – ἵστημι (pf 1 pl with pres meaning): stand – καυχάομαι (pres ind 1 pl): boast – ἐλπίς: hope – δόξα: glory – καταισχύνω (pres 3 sg): disappoint – ἀγάπη: love – ἐκχέω (pf pass 3 sg): pour out – καρδία: heart – πνεῦμα: Spirit – δίδωμι (aor pass ptcp gen sg): give

---

Apology IV (II) 80-81

Therefore, by faith alone we receive forgiveness of sins when we comfort our hearts with confidence in the mercy promised for Christ's sake. Likewise, Paul says in Rom 5:2, "Through Him we have also obtained access" and adds, "by faith." Therefore, we are reconciled to the Father and receive forgiveness of sins when we are comforted with confidence in the mercy promised for Christ's sake.

August 8

Genesis 9:12-13

12וַיֹּ֣אמֶר אֱלֹהִ֗ים זֹ֤את אֽוֹת־הַבְּרִית֙ אֲשֶׁר־אֲנִ֣י נֹתֵ֗ן בֵּינִי֙
וּבֵ֣ינֵיכֶ֔ם וּבֵ֛ין כָּל־נֶ֥פֶשׁ חַיָּ֖ה אֲשֶׁ֣ר אִתְּכֶ֑ם לְדֹרֹ֖ת עוֹלָֽם׃
13אֶת־קַשְׁתִּ֕י נָתַ֖תִּי בֶּֽעָנָ֑ן וְהָֽיְתָה֙ לְא֣וֹת בְּרִ֔ית בֵּינִ֖י וּבֵ֥ין
הָאָֽרֶץ׃

זֹאת: this – אוֹת: sign – בְּרִית: covenant – נָתַן (qal ptcp sg): give, make – בַּיִן (1 sg sf/2 pl sf): between – נֶ֫פֶשׁ חַיָּה: living creature – אֵת (prep + 2 pl sf): with – דּוֹר (pl): generation – קֶ֫שֶׁת (1 sg sf): bow – נָתַן (qal pf 1 sg): put – עָנָן: cloud

Acts 13:32-33

32Καὶ ἡμεῖς ὑμᾶς εὐαγγελιζόμεθα τὴν πρὸς τοὺς πατέρας
ἐπαγγελίαν γενομένην, 33ὅτι ταύτην ὁ θεὸς ἐκπεπλήρωκεν
τοῖς τέκνοις [αὐτῶν] ἡμῖν ἀναστήσας Ἰησοῦν ὡς καὶ ἐν τῷ
ψαλμῷ γέγραπται τῷ δευτέρῳ· υἱός μου εἶ σύ, ἐγὼ σήμερον
γεγέννηκά σε.

εὐαγγελίζω (pres mid 1 pl): announce good news – ἐπαγγελία: promise – γίνομαι (aor ptcp): be given – ἐκπληρόω (pf ind 3 sg): fulfill – τέκνον: child – ἀνίστημι (aor ptcp): raise – γράφω (pf pass ind 3 sg): write – δεύτερος: second – υἱός: son – σήμερον: today – γεννάω (pf act ind 1 sg): beget

Apology XIIA (V) 94

As God swears *[in Ezek 33:11]* that He does not want the death of a sinner, He shows that faith is required, in order that we may believe the one swearing and be firmly confident that He forgives us. In our estimation, the authority of the divine promises should be great by itself.

August 9

Psalm 67:2-3

[2]אֱלֹהִים יְחָנֵּנוּ וִיבָרְכֵנוּ יָאֵר פָּנָיו אִתָּנוּ סֶלָה׃
[3]לָדַעַת בָּאָרֶץ דַּרְכֶּךָ בְּכָל־גּוֹיִם יְשׁוּעָתֶךָ׃

חָנַן (qal juss 3 sg + 1 pl sf): be gracious – בָּרַךְ (pi juss 3 sg + 1 pl sf): bless – אוֹר (hiph juss 3 sg): cause to shine – סֶלָה: unknown musical term – יָדַע (qal inf cst): know – דֶּרֶךְ (2 sg sf): way – גּוֹי (pl): nation – יְשׁוּעָה (2 sg sf): salvation

1 Corinthians 2:3-5

[3]κἀγὼ ἐν ἀσθενείᾳ καὶ ἐν φόβῳ καὶ ἐν τρόμῳ πολλῷ
ἐγενόμην πρὸς ὑμᾶς, [4]καὶ ὁ λόγος μου καὶ τὸ κήρυγμά
μου οὐκ ἐν πειθοῖ[ς] σοφίας [λόγοις] ἀλλ' ἐν ἀποδείξει
πνεύματος καὶ δυνάμεως, [5]ἵνα ἡ πίστις ὑμῶν μὴ ᾖ ἐν
σοφίᾳ ἀνθρώπων ἀλλ' ἐν δυνάμει θεοῦ.

ἀσθένεια: weakness – φόβος: fear – τρόμος: trembling – γίνομαι (aor ind 1 sg): came to – κήρυγμα: message – πειθός: persuasive – σοφία: wisdom – ἀπόδειξις: demonstration – πνεῦμα: Spirit – δύναμις: power

Formula of Concord Ep XI 7

God's Word leads us to Christ, who is the Book of Life, in whom all are written and elected who are to be saved in eternity.

AUGUST 10

Isaiah 8:19-20

[19]וְכִֽי־יֹאמְר֣וּ אֲלֵיכֶ֗ם דִּרְשׁ֤וּ אֶל־הָאֹבוֹת֙ וְאֶל־הַיִּדְּעֹנִ֔ים
הַֽמְצַפְצְפִ֖ים וְהַמַּהְגִּ֑ים הֲלוֹא־עַם֙ אֶל־אֱלֹהָ֣יו יִדְרֹ֔שׁ בְּעַ֥ד
הַחַיִּ֖ים אֶל־הַמֵּתִֽים׃ [20]לְתוֹרָ֖ה וְלִתְעוּדָ֑ה אִם־לֹ֤א יֹֽאמְרוּ֙
כַּדָּבָ֣ר הַזֶּ֔ה אֲשֶׁ֥ר אֵֽין־ל֖וֹ שָֽׁחַר׃

כִּי: when – דָּרַשׁ (qal imv pl/qal impf 3 sg): consult – אוֹב (pl): sorcerer, medium – יִדְּעֹנִי (pl): spiritist – צָפַף (pilpel ptcp pl): chirp, whisper – הָגָה (hiph ptcp pl): mutter – בְּעַד: on behalf of – חַיִּים: the living – מֵתִים: the dead – תְּעוּדָה: testimony – אַיִן: not – שַׁחַר: light of dawn

---

Luke 16:27-28,31

[27]εἶπεν δέ· ἐρωτῶ σε οὖν, πάτερ, ἵνα πέμψῃς αὐτὸν εἰς
τὸν οἶκον τοῦ πατρός μου, [28]ἔχω γὰρ πέντε ἀδελφούς,
ὅπως διαμαρτύρηται αὐτοῖς, ἵνα μὴ καὶ αὐτοὶ ἔλθωσιν
εἰς τὸν τόπον τοῦτον τῆς βασάνου. . . . [31]εἶπεν δὲ αὐτῷ·
εἰ Μωϋσέως καὶ τῶν προφητῶν οὐκ ἀκούουσιν, οὐδ' ἐάν
τις ἐκ νεκρῶν ἀναστῇ πεισθήσονται.

πέντε: five – ἀδελφός: brother – διαμαρτύρομαι (pres subj 3 sg): warn – τόπος: place – βάσανος: torment — νεκρός: dead – ἀνίστημι (aor subj 3 sg): rise – πείθω (fut pass): persuade

---

Formula of Concord Ep XI 12

But the reason some are not saved is as follows: They do not listen to God's Word at all, but willfully despise it, plug their ears, and harden their hearts. In this way they block the ordinary way [Luke 16:29-31] for the Holy Spirit so He cannot perform His work in them.

August 11

Proverbs 4:23

מִכָּל־מִשְׁמָר נְצֹר לִבֶּךָ כִּי־מִמֶּנּוּ תּוֹצְאוֹת חַיִּים׃

מִשְׁמָר: guarding – נָצַר (qal imv sg): guard – לֵב (2 sg sf): heart – מִן (prep + 3 sg sf): from – תּוֹצָאָה (cst pl): source, wellspring – חַיִּים: life

Matthew 6:21

ὅπου γάρ ἐστιν ὁ θησαυρός σου, ἐκεῖ ἔσται καὶ ἡ καρδία σου.

ὅπου: where – θησαυρός: treasure – καρδία: heart

Large Catechism I 6-8

Such a person has a god by the name of "Mammon" (i.e., money and possessions; [Matt 6:24]), on which he sets all his heart. This is the most common idol on earth. He who has money and possessions feels secure [Luke 12:16-21] and is joyful and undismayed as though he were sitting in the midst of Paradise. On the other hand, he who has no money doubts and is despondent, as though he knew of no God.

AUGUST 12

Jeremiah 17:7-8

7בָּר֣וּךְ הַגֶּ֔בֶר אֲשֶׁ֥ר יִבְטַ֖ח בַּיהוָ֑ה וְהָיָ֥ה יְהוָ֖ה מִבְטַחֽוֹ׃
8וְהָיָ֞ה כְּעֵ֣ץ ׀ שָׁת֣וּל עַל־מַ֗יִם וְעַל־יוּבַל֙ יְשַׁלַּ֣ח שָׁרָשָׁ֔יו
וְלֹ֤א יִרְא֙ [יִרְאֶה] כִּֽי־יָ֣בֹא חֹ֔ם וְהָיָ֥ה עָלֵ֖הוּ רַֽעֲנָ֑ן
וּבִשְׁנַ֤ת בַּצֹּ֙רֶת֙ לֹ֣א יִדְאָ֔ג וְלֹ֥א יָמִ֖ישׁ מֵעֲשׂ֥וֹת פֶּֽרִי׃

גֶּ֫בֶר: man – בָּטַח (qal impf 3 sg): trust – מִבְטָח (3 sg sf): confidence – עֵץ: tree – שָׁתַל (qal pass ptcp): planted – יוּבַל: stream – שָׁלַח (pi impf 3 sg): send out – שֹׁ֫רֶשׁ (pl + 3 sg sf): root – יָרֵא: (ketiv: qal impf 3 sg): fear – חֹם: heat – עָלֶה (3 sg sf): leaf – רַעֲנָן: green – שָׁנָה (cst sg): year – בַּצֹּ֫רֶת: drought – דָּאַג (qal impf 3 sg): worry – מוּשׁ (hiph impf 3 sg): cease from

John 15:4-5

4μείνατε ἐν ἐμοί, κἀγὼ ἐν ὑμῖν. καθὼς τὸ κλῆμα οὐ
δύναται καρπὸν φέρειν ἀφ᾽ ἑαυτοῦ ἐὰν μὴ μένῃ ἐν τῇ
ἀμπέλῳ, οὕτως οὐδὲ ὑμεῖς ἐὰν μὴ ἐν ἐμοὶ μένητε. 5ἐγώ
εἰμι ἡ ἄμπελος, ὑμεῖς τὰ κλήματα. ὁ μένων ἐν ἐμοὶ κἀγὼ
ἐν αὐτῷ οὗτος φέρει καρπὸν πολύν, ὅτι χωρὶς ἐμοῦ οὐ
δύνασθε ποιεῖν οὐδέν.

κλῆμα: branch – καρπός: fruit – φέρω (pres inf): bear – ἄμπελος: vine – πολύς: much – χωρίς: apart from

Augsburg Confession XX 30-31

Ambrose says: "Faith is the mother of a good will and doing what is right." Without the Holy Spirit people are full of ungodly desires. They are too weak to do works that are good in God's sight [John 15:5].

August 13

Job 28:12

וְהַֽחָכְמָה מֵאַ֣יִן תִּמָּצֵ֑א וְאֵ֥י זֶ֝֗ה מְק֣וֹם בִּינָֽה׃

חָכְמָה: wisdom – מֵאַיִן: where? – מָצָא (niph impf 3 sg): be found – אֵי: where? – מָקוֹם: place – בִּינָה: understanding

---

1 Corinthians 2:7-10

7ἀλλὰ λαλοῦμεν θεοῦ σοφίαν ἐν μυστηρίῳ τὴν
ἀποκεκρυμμένην, ἣν προώρισεν ὁ θεὸς πρὸ τῶν αἰώνων
εἰς δόξαν ἡμῶν, 8ἣν οὐδεὶς τῶν ἀρχόντων τοῦ αἰῶνος
τούτου ἔγνωκεν· εἰ γὰρ ἔγνωσαν, οὐκ ἂν τὸν κύριον τῆς
δόξης ἐσταύρωσαν. 9ἀλλὰ καθὼς γέγραπται· ἃ ὀφθαλμὸς
οὐκ εἶδεν καὶ οὖς οὐκ ἤκουσεν καὶ ἐπὶ καρδίαν ἀνθρώπου
οὐκ ἀνέβη, ἃ ἡτοίμασεν ὁ θεὸς τοῖς ἀγαπῶσιν αὐτόν.
10ἡμῖν δὲ ἀπεκάλυψεν ὁ θεὸς διὰ τοῦ πνεύματος . . .

μυστήριον: secret – ἀποκρύπτω (pf pass ptcp): hidden – προορίζω (aor ind 3 sg): decide upon beforehand – αἰών: age – δόξα: glory – ἄρχων: ruler – γινώσκω (pf ind 3 sg/aor ind 3 pl): know – σταυρόω (aor ind 3 pl): crucify – γράφω (pf pass ind 3 sg): write – ὀφθαλμός: eye – εἶδεν (aor of ὁράω): see – οὖς: ear – ἀκούω (aor ind 3 sg): hear – καρδία: heart – ἀναβαίνω (aor ind 3 sg): enter – ἑτοιμάζω (aor ind 3 sg): prepare – ἀγαπάω (pres act ptcp dat pl): love – ἀποκαλύπτω (aor ind 3 sg): reveal

---

Large Catechism II 61

The Holy Spirit carries on His work without ceasing to the Last Day. For that purpose He has appointed a congregation upon earth by which He speaks and does everything.

Genesis 8:21

לֹא־אֹסִף לְקַלֵּל עוֹד אֶת־הָאֲדָמָה בַּעֲבוּר הָאָדָם כִּי יֵצֶר לֵב הָאָדָם רַע מִנְּעֻרָיו

יָסַף (hiph impf 1 sg) + inf: do again – קָלַל (pi inf cst): curse – עוֹד: again – אֲדָמָה: ground – בַּעֲבוּר: for the sake of – יֵצֶר: imagination – לֵב: heart – נְעוּרִים (3 sg sf): youth

---

Romans 5:12

διὰ τοῦτο ὥσπερ δι' ἑνὸς ἀνθρώπου ἡ ἁμαρτία εἰς τὸν κόσμον εἰσῆλθεν καὶ διὰ τῆς ἁμαρτίας ὁ θάνατος, καὶ οὕτως εἰς πάντας ἀνθρώπους ὁ θάνατος διῆλθεν, ἐφ' ᾧ πάντες ἥμαρτον·

ἁμαρτία: sin – κόσμος: world – εἰσέρχομαι (aor ind 3 sg): enter – θάνατος: death – διέρχομαι (aor ind 3 sg): come – ἐφ' ᾧ: because – ἁμαρτάνω (aor ind 3 pl): sin

---

Augsburg Confession II 1

Our churches teach that since the fall of Adam [Rom 5:12], all who are naturally born are born with sin [Ps 51:5], that is, without the fear of God, without trust in God, and with the inclination to sin, called concupiscence.

Isaiah 43:24-25

24 אַךְ הֶעֱבַדְתַּנִי בְּחַטֹּאותֶיךָ הוֹגַעְתַּנִי בַּעֲוֺנֹתֶיךָ׃
25 אָנֹכִי אָנֹכִי הוּא מֹחֶה פְשָׁעֶיךָ לְמַעֲנִי וְחַטֹּאתֶיךָ לֹא
אֶזְכֹּר׃

עָבַד (hiph pf 2 sg + 1 sg sf): burden – חַטָּאת (pl + 2 sg sf): sin (as missing the mark) – יָגַע (hiph pf 2 sg + 1 sg sf): weary – עָוֺן (pl + 2 sg sf): sin (as guilt) – מָחָה (qal ptcp): blot out – פֶּשַׁע (pl + 2 sg sf): sin (as rebellion) – לְמַעַן (1 sg sf): for my sake – זָכַר (qal impf 1 sg): remember

John 3:16

οὕτως γὰρ ἠγάπησεν ὁ θεὸς τὸν κόσμον, ὥστε τὸν υἱὸν τὸν μονογενῆ ἔδωκεν, ἵνα πᾶς ὁ πιστεύων εἰς αὐτὸν μὴ ἀπόληται ἀλλ' ἔχῃ ζωὴν αἰώνιον.

ἀγαπάω (aor 3 sg): love – κόσμος: world – μονογενής: only-begotten – δίδωμι (aor ind 3 sg): give – πιστεύω (pres ptcp): believe – ἀπόλλυμι (aor mid subj 3 sg): be lost, destroyed – ἔχω (pres subj 3 sg): have – ζωή: life – αἰώνιος: eternal

Formula of Concord SD II 51

The eternal Father calls down from heaven about His dear Son and about all who preach repentance and forgiveness of sins in His name, "Listen to Him" (Matt 17:5).

Isaiah 50:4

אֲדֹנָ֣י יְהוִ֗ה נָ֤תַן לִי֙ לְשׁ֣וֹן לִמּוּדִ֔ים
לָדַ֛עַת לָע֥וּת אֶת־יָעֵ֖ף דָּבָ֑ר

נָתַן (qal pf 3 sg): give – לְשׁוֹן (cst sg): tongue – לִמּוּד (pl): learned person – יָדַע (qal inf cst): know how to – עוּת (qal inf cst): sustain, give rest – יָעֵף: the weary – דָּבָר (adverbial acc): with a word

Matthew 11:28-30

28Δεῦτε πρός με πάντες οἱ κοπιῶντες καὶ πεφορτισμένοι,
κἀγὼ ἀναπαύσω ὑμᾶς. 29ἄρατε τὸν ζυγόν μου ἐφ' ὑμᾶς καὶ
μάθετε ἀπ' ἐμοῦ, ὅτι πραΰς εἰμι καὶ ταπεινὸς τῇ καρδίᾳ,
καὶ εὑρήσετε ἀνάπαυσιν ταῖς ψυχαῖς ὑμῶν· 30ὁ γὰρ ζυγός
μου χρηστὸς καὶ τὸ φορτίον μου ἐλαφρόν ἐστιν.

δεῦτε: come! – κοπιάω (pres ptcp pl): become weary – φορτίζω (pf pass ptcp): burden – ἀναπαύω (fut ind 1 sg): give rest – αἴρω (aor imv 2 pl): take – ζυγός: yoke – μανθάνω (aor imv 2 pl): learn – πραΰς: gentle – ταπεινός: humble – ψυχή: soul – χρηστός: easy (to wear) – φορτίον: burden – ἐλαφρός: light

Formula of Concord SD VII 71

Worthiness does not depend on the greatness or smallness, the weakness or strength of faith. Instead, it depends on Christ's merit, which the distressed father of little faith [Mk 9:24] enjoyed as well as Abraham, Paul, and others who have a joyful and strong faith.

August 17

Proverbs 3:5-6

5 בְּטַח אֶל־יְהוָה בְּכָל־לִבֶּךָ וְאֶל־בִּינָתְךָ אַל־תִּשָּׁעֵן׃
6 בְּכָל־דְּרָכֶיךָ דָעֵהוּ וְהוּא יְיַשֵּׁר אֹרְחֹתֶיךָ׃

בָּטַח (qal imv sg): trust – לֵב (2 sg sf): heart – בִּינָה (2 sg sf): understanding – שָׁעַן (niph juss 2 sg): lean on – דֶּרֶךְ (pl + 2 sg sf): way – יָדַע (qal imv + 3 sg sf): acknowledge – יָשַׁר (pi impf 3 sg): make straight – אֹרַח (pl + 2 sg sf): path

---

Colossians 2:8

Βλέπετε μή τις ὑμᾶς ἔσται ὁ συλαγωγῶν διὰ τῆς φιλοσοφίας καὶ κενῆς ἀπάτης κατὰ τὴν παράδοσιν τῶν ἀνθρώπων, κατὰ τὰ στοιχεῖα τοῦ κόσμου καὶ οὐ κατὰ Χριστόν·

βλέπω (pres imv 2 sg): see to it – συλαγωγέω (pres ptcp): carry off as a captive – κενός: empty – ἀπάτη: deception – παράδοσις: tradition – στοιχεῖον: basic principle

---

Apology V (III) 272

Scripture, furthermore, has predicted that the righteousness of faith would be clouded over by human traditions and the teaching of works in this way. Paul often complains about this (See Gal 4:9; 5:7; Col 2:8,16-19; 1 Tim 4:2-5; etc.).

AUGUST 18

Joel 2:13

וְקִרְעוּ לְבַבְכֶם וְאַל־בִּגְדֵיכֶם
וְשׁוּבוּ אֶל־יְהוָה אֱלֹהֵיכֶם כִּי־חַנּוּן וְרַחוּם הוּא
אֶרֶךְ אַפַּיִם וְרַב־חֶסֶד וְנִחָם עַל־הָרָעָה׃

קָרַע (qal imv pl): rend – לֵבָב (2 pl sf): heart – בֶּגֶד (pl + 2 pl sf): garment – שׁוּב (qal imv pl): return – חַנּוּן: gracious – רַחוּם: merciful – אֶרֶךְ אַפַּיִם: slow to anger – רַב: abounding in – חֶסֶד: faithful love – נָחַם (niph ptcp): relent

---

2 Peter 3:14

Διό, ἀγαπητοί, ταῦτα προσδοκῶντες σπουδάσατε ἄσπιλοι καὶ ἀμώμητοι αὐτῷ εὑρεθῆναι ἐν εἰρήνῃ·

προσδοκάω (pres ptcp pl): look forward to – σπουδάζω (aor imv 2 pl): make every effort – ἄσπιλος: spotless – ἀμώμητος: blameless – εὑρίσκω (aor pass inf): be found – εἰρήνη: peace

---

Large Catechism II 70

Let this be enough about the Creed to lay a foundation for the simple, so that they may not be burdened. Then, if they understand the substance of it, they themselves may afterward strive to gain more, refer to these parts whatever they learn in the Scriptures, and may ever grow and increase in richer understanding [Eph 4:14-15; 2 Pet 3:14]. For as long as we live here, we shall daily have enough to do to preach and to learn this.

AUGUST 19

Psalm 51:19

זִבְחֵי אֱלֹהִים רוּחַ נִשְׁבָּרָה לֵב־נִשְׁבָּר וְנִדְכֶּה אֱלֹהִים לֹא תִבְזֶה׃

זֶבַח (cst pl): sacrifice – רוּחַ: spirit – שָׁבַר (niph ptcp): broken – לֵב: heart – דָּכָה (niph ptcp): crushed – בָּזָה (qal impf 2 sg): despise

James 4:6-7

6ὁ θεὸς ὑπερηφάνοις ἀντιτάσσεται, ταπεινοῖς δὲ δίδωσιν
χάριν. 7ὑποτάγητε οὖν τῷ θεῷ, ἀντίστητε δὲ τῷ διαβόλῳ καὶ
φεύξεται ἀφ' ὑμῶν . . .

ὑπερήφανος: proud – ἀντιτάσσω (pres mid 3 sg): oppose – ταπεινός: humble – δίδωμι (pres ind 3 sg): give – χάρις: grace – ὑποτάσσω (aor pass imv): submit, subordinate oneself – ἀνθίστημι (aor act imv 2 pl): resist – διάβολος: devil – φεύγω (fut dep 3 sg): flee

Large Catechism I 101-102

For these words are not lazy or dead, but are creative, living words [Heb 4:12]. And even though no other interest or necessity moves us, this truth ought to urge everyone to the Word, because thereby the devil is put to flight and driven away [Jas 4:7].

AUGUST 20

Psalm 18:2-3

2 וַיֹּאמַר אֶרְחָמְךָ יְהוָה חִזְקִי׃
3 יְהוָה סַלְעִי וּמְצוּדָתִי וּמְפַלְטִי אֵלִי צוּרִי אֶחֱסֶה־בּוֹ
מָגִנִּי וְקֶרֶן־יִשְׁעִי מִשְׂגַּבִּי׃

רָחַם (qal impf 1 sg + 2 sg sf): love – חֵזֶק (1 sg sf): strength – סֶלַע (1 sg sf): rock – מְצוּדָה (1 sg sf): fortress – פָּלַט (pi ptcp + 1 sg sf): deliverer – צוּר (1 sg sf): rock – חָסָה (qal impf 1 sg): seek refuge – מָגֵן (1 sg sf): shield – קֶרֶן (cst): horn – יֵשַׁע (1 sg sf): salvation – מִשְׂגָּב (1 sg sf): stronghold

---

2 Timothy 1:12

οἶδα γὰρ ᾧ πεπίστευκα καὶ πέπεισμαι ὅτι δυνατός ἐστιν τὴν παραθήκην μου φυλάξαι εἰς ἐκείνην τὴν ἡμέραν.

οἶδα: know – πιστεύω (pf ind 1 sg): believe – πείθω (pf pass 1 sg): convince – δυνατός: able – παραθήκη: what has been entrusted – φυλάσσω (aor inf): guard – ἡμέρα: day

---

Large Catechism I 16

It *[the heart]* must not allow itself to be torn from Him *[God]*. But, for Him, it must risk and disregard everything upon earth.

August 21

Isaiah 45:22-23

22 פְּנוּ־אֵלַי וְהִוָּשְׁעוּ כָּל־אַפְסֵי־אָרֶץ כִּי אֲנִי־אֵל וְאֵין עוֹד׃
23 בִּי נִשְׁבַּעְתִּי יָצָא מִפִּי צְדָקָה דָּבָר וְלֹא יָשׁוּב כִּי־לִי
תִּכְרַע כָּל־בֶּרֶךְ תִּשָּׁבַע כָּל־לָשׁוֹן׃

פָּנָה (qal imv pl): turn – יָשַׁע (niph imv pl): be saved – אֶפֶס (cst pl): end – אַיִן עוֹד: there is no other – שָׁבַע (niph pf 1 sg/niph impf 3 sg f): swear – יָצָא (qal pf 3 sg): go out – פֶּה (1 sg sf): mouth – צְדָקָה: righteousness = in integrity – שׁוּב (qal impf 3 sg): turn back – כָּרַע (qal impf 3 sg f): bow down – בֶּרֶךְ: knee – לָשׁוֹן: tongue

Philippians 2:9-11

9 διὸ καὶ ὁ θεὸς αὐτὸν ὑπερύψωσεν καὶ ἐχαρίσατο αὐτῷ τὸ
ὄνομα τὸ ὑπὲρ πᾶν ὄνομα, 10 ἵνα ἐν τῷ ὀνόματι Ἰησοῦ πᾶν
γόνυ κάμψῃ ἐπουρανίων καὶ ἐπιγείων καὶ καταχθονίων 11 καὶ
πᾶσα γλῶσσα ἐξομολογήσηται ὅτι κύριος Ἰησοῦς Χριστὸς
εἰς δόξαν θεοῦ πατρός.

ὑπερυψόω (aor ind 3 sg): exalt – χαρίζομαι (aor ind 3 sg): give graciously – ὄνομα: name – γόνυ: knee – κάμπτω (aor subj 3 sg): bend – ἐπουράνιος: heavenly – ἐπίγειος: earthly – καταχθόνιος: under the earth – γλῶσσα: tongue – ἐξομολογέω (aor mid subj 3 sg): confess – δόξα: glory

Formula of Concord SD VIII 26

The human nature, after the resurrection from the dead, is exalted above all creatures in heaven and on earth. This is nothing other than that He entirely laid aside the form of a servant [Phil 2:7-11].

AUGUST 22

Psalm 121:7-8

7 יְהוָה יִשְׁמָרְךָ מִכָּל־רָע יִשְׁמֹר אֶת־נַפְשֶׁךָ׃
8 יְהוָה יִשְׁמָר־צֵאתְךָ וּבוֹאֶךָ מֵעַתָּה וְעַד־עוֹלָם׃

שָׁמַר (qal impf 3 sg + 2 sg sf): keep – רַע: evil, harm – נֶפֶשׁ (2 sg sf): soul, life – יָצָא (qal inf cst + 2 sg sf): go out = your going – בּוֹא (qal inf cst + 2 sg sf): come = your coming – עַתָּה: now – עוֹלָם: eternity

---

2 Timothy 4:18

ῥύσεταί με ὁ κύριος ἀπὸ παντὸς ἔργου πονηροῦ καὶ σώσει εἰς τὴν βασιλείαν αὐτοῦ τὴν ἐπουράνιον· ᾧ ἡ δόξα εἰς τοὺς αἰῶνας τῶν αἰώνων, ἀμήν.

ῥύομαι (fut ind 3 sg): rescue – ἔργον: work – πονηρός: evil – σῴζω (fut 3 sg): preserve, save, deliver

---

Large Catechism I 24

And if any evil befall us, He delivers and rescues us. So it is God alone (as has been said well enough) from whom we receive all good and by whom we are delivered from all evil.

Psalm 56:4-5

4יוֹם אִירָא אֲנִי אֵלֶיךָ אֶבְטָח׃
5בֵּאלֹהִים אֲהַלֵּל דְּבָרוֹ בֵּאלֹהִים בָּטַחְתִּי לֹא אִירָא
מַה־יַּעֲשֶׂה בָשָׂר לִי׃

יוֹם: day = when – יָרֵא (qal impf 1 sg): be afraid – בָּטַח (qal impf 1 sg): trust – הָלַל (pi impf 1 sg): praise – דָּבָר (3 sg sf): whose word – עָשָׂה (qal impf 3 sg): do – בָּשָׂר: mortal man

---

1 Peter 5:10-11

10Ὁ δὲ θεὸς πάσης χάριτος, ὁ καλέσας ὑμᾶς εἰς τὴν αἰώνιον αὐτοῦ δόξαν ἐν Χριστῷ [Ἰησοῦ], ὀλίγον παθόντας αὐτὸς καταρτίσει, στηρίξει, σθενώσει, θεμελιώσει. 11αὐτῷ τὸ κράτος εἰς τοὺς αἰῶνας, ἀμήν.

χάρις: grace – καλέω (aor ptcp): call – αἰώνιος: eternal – δόξα: glory – ὀλίγον: a little while – πάσχω (aor ptcp acc pl): suffer – καταρτίζω (fut ind 3 sg): restore – στηρίζω (fut ind 3 sg): establish – σθενόω (fut ind 3 sg): strengthen – θεμελιόω (fut ind 3 sg): establish, make steadfast – κράτος: power

---

Formula of Concord SD XI 32

Holy Scripture also testifies that God, who has called us, is faithful. So when He has begun the good work in us, He will also preserve it to the end and perfect it, if we ourselves do not turn from Him, but firmly hold on to the work begun to the end. He has promised His grace for this very purpose.

August 24

Jeremiah 31:3

מֵרָחוֹק יְהוָה נִרְאָה לִי וְאַהֲבַת עוֹלָם אֲהַבְתִּיךְ עַל־כֵּן
מְשַׁכְתִּיךְ חָסֶד׃

מֵרָחוֹק: from afar, in the past – רָאָה (niph pf 3 sg): appear – אַהֲבָה (cst sg): love – מָשַׁךְ (qal pf 1 sg + 2 sg sf): draw – חֶסֶד: in faithful love

---

Ephesians 2:4-5

4ὁ δὲ θεὸς πλούσιος ὢν ἐν ἐλέει, διὰ τὴν πολλὴν ἀγάπην
αὐτοῦ ἣν ἠγάπησεν ἡμᾶς, 5καὶ ὄντας ἡμᾶς νεκροὺς τοῖς
παραπτώμασιν συνεζωοποίησεν τῷ Χριστῷ, – χάριτί ἐστε
σεσῳσμένοι . . .

πλούσιος: rich – ἔλεος: mercy – ἀγαπάω (aor ind 3 sg): love – νεκρός: dead – παράπτωμα: transgression – συζωοποιέω: make alive together with – χάρις: grace – σῴζω (pf pass ptcp pl): save

---

Formula of Concord SD II 7

So in mankind's nature since the fall, before regeneration, there is not the least spark of spiritual power remaining or present. No person can prepare himself for God's grace or accept the grace God offers. A person is not capable of grace for and of himself. He cannot apply or accommodate himself to it. By his own powers he is not able to aid, do, work, or agree in working anything toward his conversion. He cannot do this fully, halfway, or even in part even in the smallest or most trivial part.

Genesis 3:1

וְהַנָּחָשׁ הָיָה עָרוּם מִכֹּל חַיַּת הַשָּׂדֶה אֲשֶׁר עָשָׂה יְהוָה אֱלֹהִים וַיֹּאמֶר אֶל־הָאִשָּׁה אַף כִּי־אָמַר אֱלֹהִים לֹא תֹאכְלוּ מִכֹּל עֵץ הַגָּן׃

נָחָשׁ: serpent – עָרוּם: crafty, clever – חַיָּה (cst sg): living creature – שָׂדֶה: field – עָשָׂה (qal pf 3 sg): make – אַף כִּי־אָמַר אֱלֹהִים: Did God really say? – אָכַל (qal impf 2 pl): eat – עֵץ: tree – גַּן: garden

Galatians 1:8

ἀλλὰ καὶ ἐὰν ἡμεῖς ἢ ἄγγελος ἐξ οὐρανοῦ εὐαγγελίζηται [ὑμῖν] παρ' ὃ εὐηγγελισάμεθα ὑμῖν, ἀνάθεμα ἔστω.

οὐρανός: heaven – εὐαγγελίζω (pres mid subj 3 sg/aor mid ind 1 pl): proclaim – παρά (prep + acc): contrary to that which – ἀνάθεμα: object of a curse – ἔστω (pres imv 3 sg of εἰμί): be

Power and Primacy 38

In the third place, this must be added: Even if the bishop of Rome did have the primacy and superiority by divine right, nevertheless, obedience would not be due those pontiffs who defend godless services, idolatry, and doctrine conflicting with the Gospel. No, such pontiffs and such a government should be held accursed, as Paul clearly teaches, "If we or an angel from heaven should preach to you a gospel contrary to the one we preached to you, let him be accursed" [Gal 1:8].

2 Samuel 7:25

וְעַתָּה יְהוָה אֱלֹהִים הַדָּבָר אֲשֶׁר דִּבַּרְתָּ עַל־עַבְדְּךָ וְעַל־
בֵּיתוֹ הָקֵם עַד־עוֹלָם וַעֲשֵׂה כַּאֲשֶׁר דִּבַּרְתָּ׃

עַתָּה: now – דָּבָר: the promise – דָּבַר (pi pf 2 sg): speak – עֶבֶד (2 sg sf): servant – בַּיִת (3 sg sf): house – קוּם (hiph imv sg): keep – עוֹלָם: forever – עָשָׂה (qal imv sg): do – כַּאֲשֶׁר: as

2 Peter 1:4

δι' ὧν τὰ τίμια καὶ μέγιστα ἡμῖν ἐπαγγέλματα δεδώρηται, ἵνα διὰ τούτων γένησθε θείας κοινωνοὶ φύσεως ἀποφυγόντες τῆς ἐν τῷ κόσμῳ ἐν ἐπιθυμίᾳ φθορᾶς.

τίμιος: precious – μέγιστος: very great – ἐπάγγελμα (pl): promise – δωρέομαι (pf ind 3 sg): give – γίνομαι (aor subj 2 pl): be – θεῖος: divine – κοινωνός (pl): sharer – φύσις: nature – ἀποφεύγω (aor ptcp pl): escape – ἐπιθυμία: evil desire – φθορά: corruption

Apology V (III) 213

Here Christ's declaration also applies, "So you also, when you have done all that you were commanded say, 'We are unworthy servants; we have only done what was our duty'" (Luke 17:10). These words clearly declare that God saves by mercy and because of His promise, not that it is due because of the value of our works.

AUGUST 27

Isaiah 35:10

וּפְדוּיֵ֨ יְהוָ֜ה יְשֻׁב֗וּן וּבָ֤אוּ צִיּוֹן֙ בְּרִנָּ֔ה וְשִׂמְחַ֥ת עוֹלָ֖ם עַל־
רֹאשָׁ֑ם שָׂשׂ֤וֹן וְשִׂמְחָה֙ יַשִּׂ֔יגוּ וְנָ֖סוּ יָג֥וֹן וַאֲנָחָֽה׃

פָּדָה (qal pass ptcp cst pl): redeem – שׁוּב (qal impf 3 pl): return – בּוֹא (qal v-c pf 3 pl): come – רִנָּה: singing – שִׂמְחָה (cst sg): joy – עוֹלָם: indefinite futurity = everlasting – רֹאשׁ (3 pl sf): head – שָׂשׂוֹן: gladness – נָשַׂג (hiph impf 3 pl): overtake – נוּס (qal v-c pf 3 pl): flee away – יָגוֹן: grief – אֲנָחָה: sighing

---

2 Corinthians 5:6-9

6Θαρροῦντες οὖν πάντοτε καὶ εἰδότες ὅτι ἐνδημοῦντες ἐν
τῷ σώματι ἐκδημοῦμεν ἀπὸ τοῦ κυρίου· 7διὰ πίστεως γὰρ
περιπατοῦμεν, οὐ διὰ εἴδους· 8θαρροῦμεν δὲ καὶ εὐδοκοῦμεν
μᾶλλον ἐκδημῆσαι ἐκ τοῦ σώματος καὶ ἐνδημῆσαι πρὸς
τὸν κύριον. 9διὸ καὶ φιλοτιμούμεθα, εἴτε ἐνδημοῦντες εἴτε
ἐκδημοῦντες, εὐάρεστοι αὐτῷ εἶναι.

θαρρέω (pres ptcp pl): be confident – οἶδα (ptcp pl): know – ἐνδημέω (pres ptcp pl): be at home – σῶμα: body – ἐκδημέω (pres ind 1 pl): be away – πίστις: faith – περιπατέω (pres ind 1 pl): live – εἶδος: sight – εὐδοκέω (pres ind 1 pl): prefer – φιλοτιμέομαι (pres ind 1 pl): have as one's ambition – εὐάρεστος: pleasing

---

Preface to the Book of Concord 16

By God's help, we will retain this *[Augsburg]* Confession to our last breath, when we shall go forth from this life to the heavenly fatherland, to appear with a joyful, undaunted mind and a pure conscience before the court of our Lord Jesus Christ [2 Cor 5:9-10].

August 28

Haggai 2:4

וְעַתָּה חֲזַק זְרֻבָּבֶל נְאֻם־יְהוָה
וַחֲזַק יְהוֹשֻׁעַ בֶּן־יְהוֹצָדָק הַכֹּהֵן הַגָּדוֹל
וַחֲזַק כָּל־עַם הָאָרֶץ נְאֻם־יְהוָה
וַעֲשׂוּ כִּי־אֲנִי אִתְּכֶם נְאֻם יְהוָה צְבָאוֹת׃

עַתָּה: now – חָזַק (qal imv sg): be strong – נְאֻם (cst): utterance – עָשָׂה (qal imv pl): work – אֵת (prep + 2 pl sf): with

---

Galatians 6:9

τὸ δὲ καλὸν ποιοῦντες μὴ ἐγκακῶμεν, καιρῷ γὰρ ἰδίῳ θερίσομεν μὴ ἐκλυόμενοι.

καλός: good – ποιέω (pres ptcp pl): do – ἐγκακέω (pres subj 1 pl): become weary – καιρός: time – ἴδιος: proper – θερίζω (fut ind 1 pl): reap a harvest – ἐκλύομαι (ptcp): give up

---

Large Catechism V 23-24

There are so many hindrances and temptations of the devil and of the world that we often become weary and faint, and sometimes we also stumble [Heb 12:3]. Therefore, the Sacrament *[of the Altar]* is given as a daily pasture and sustenance, that faith may refresh and strengthen itself [Ps 23:1-3] so that it will not fall back in such a battle, but become ever stronger and stronger.

August 29

Psalm 119:124

עֲשֵׂה עִם־עַבְדְּךָ כְחַסְדֶּךָ וְחֻקֶּיךָ לַמְּדֵנִי׃

עָשָׂה (qal imv sg): deal with – עֶבֶד (2 sg sf): servant – חֶסֶד (2 sg sf): faithful love – חֹק (pl + 2 sg sf): decree – לָמַד (pi imv + 1 sg sf): teach

---

John 14:26

ὁ δὲ παράκλητος, τὸ πνεῦμα τὸ ἅγιον, ὃ πέμψει ὁ πατὴρ ἐν τῷ ὀνόματί μου, ἐκεῖνος ὑμᾶς διδάξει πάντα καὶ ὑπομνήσει ὑμᾶς πάντα ἃ εἶπον ὑμῖν [ἐγώ].

παράκλητος: Counselor – πέμπω (fut ind 3 sg): send – ὄνομα: name – ἐκεῖνος: he – διδάσκω (fut ind 3 sg): teach – ὑπομιμνῄσκω (fut ind 3 sg): remind (+ double acc) – εἶπον: told

---

Large Catechism II 38

Neither you nor I could ever know anything about Christ, or believe on Him, and have Him for our Lord, unless it were offered to us and granted to our hearts by the Holy Spirit through the preaching of the Gospel [1 Cor 12:3; Gal 4:6].

August 30

Deuteronomy 6:4-5

4שְׁמַע יִשְׂרָאֵל יְהוָה אֱלֹהֵינוּ יְהוָה אֶחָד׃ 5וְאָהַבְתָּ
אֵת יְהוָה אֱלֹהֶיךָ בְּכָל־לְבָבְךָ וּבְכָל־נַפְשְׁךָ וּבְכָל־
מְאֹדֶךָ׃

שָׁמַע (qal imv sg): hear – אֶחָד: one – אָהֵב (qal v-c pf 2 sg): love – לֵבָב (2 sg sf): heart – נֶפֶשׁ (2 sg sf): soul – מְאֹד (2 sg sf): strength

---

John 14:8-9

8Λέγει αὐτῷ Φίλιππος· κύριε, δεῖξον ἡμῖν τὸν πατέρα, καὶ ἀρκεῖ ἡμῖν.
9λέγει αὐτῷ ὁ Ἰησοῦς· τοσούτῳ χρόνῳ μεθ᾽ ὑμῶν εἰμι καὶ οὐκ ἔγνωκάς με, Φίλιππε; ὁ ἑωρακὼς ἐμὲ ἑώρακεν τὸν πατέρα· πῶς σὺ λέγεις· δεῖξον ἡμῖν τὸν πατέρα;

κύριος (voc): Lord – δείκνυμι (aor imv 2 sg): show – ἀρκέω (pres ind 3 sg): be enough – τοσοῦτος: so great, so long – χρόνος: time – γινώσκω (pf ind 2 sg): know – ὁράω (pf ptcp/pf ind 3 sg): see

---

Formula of Concord Ep VIII 9

[In the union of the two natures of Christ] is described the highest communion that God truly has with the man. From this personal union, the highest and indescribable communion results. There flows everything human that is said and believed about God, and everything divine that is said and believed about the man Christ. The ancient teachers of the Church explained this union and communion of the natures by the illustration of iron glowing with fire, and also by the union of body and soul in man.

AUGUST 31

Micah 6:8

הִגִּיד לְךָ אָדָם מַה־טּוֹב וּמָה־יְהוָה דּוֹרֵשׁ מִמְּךָ
כִּי אִם־עֲשׂוֹת מִשְׁפָּט וְאַהֲבַת חֶסֶד וְהַצְנֵעַ לֶכֶת עִם־
אֱלֹהֶיךָ׃

נָגַד (hiph pf 3 sg): tell – דָּרַשׁ (qal ptcp sg): seek, require – מִן (2 sg sf): from – כִּי אִם: except, but – עָשָׂה (qal inf cst): do – מִשְׁפָּט: justice – אַהֲבָה (cst sg): love – חֶסֶד: faithful love, covenant love – צָנַע (hiph inf abs): be humble – הָלַךְ (qal inf cst): walk

---

Mark 10:43-45

43οὐχ οὕτως δέ ἐστιν ἐν ὑμῖν, ἀλλ' ὃς ἂν θέλῃ μέγας
γενέσθαι ἐν ὑμῖν ἔσται ὑμῶν διάκονος, 44καὶ ὃς ἂν θέλῃ ἐν
ὑμῖν εἶναι πρῶτος ἔσται πάντων δοῦλος· 45καὶ γὰρ ὁ υἱὸς
τοῦ ἀνθρώπου οὐκ ἦλθεν διακονηθῆναι ἀλλὰ διακονῆσαι καὶ
δοῦναι τὴν ψυχὴν αὐτοῦ λύτρον ἀντὶ πολλῶν.

θέλω (pres subj 3 sg): want – μέγας: great – γίνομαι (aor mid inf): become – διάκονος: servant – πρῶτος: first – δοῦλος: slave – ἔρχομαι (aor ind 3 sg): come – διακονέω (aor pass inf/aor act inf): serve – δίδωμι (aor inf): give – λύτρον: ransom

---

Large Catechism I 105-106

He does not simply command us to love our parents, but to honor them. . . . For it is a far higher thing to honor someone than to love someone, because honor includes not only love, but also modesty, humility, and submission to a majesty hidden in them.

September 1

Psalm 4:9

בְּשָׁל֨וֹם יַחְדָּו֮ אֶשְׁכְּבָ֪ה וְאִ֫ישָׁ֥ן כִּֽי־אַתָּ֣ה יְהוָ֣ה לְבָדָ֑ד
לָ֝בֶ֗טַח תּוֹשִׁיבֵֽנִי׃

שָׁלוֹם: peace – יַחְדָּו: together = at once – שָׁכַב (qal coh 1 sg): lie down – יָשֵׁן (qal impf 1 sg): sleep – לְבָדָד: alone – בֶּטַח: safety – יָשַׁב (hiph impf 2 sg + 1 sg sf): make to dwell

John 14:27

Εἰρήνην ἀφίημι ὑμῖν, εἰρήνην τὴν ἐμὴν δίδωμι ὑμῖν· οὐ καθὼς ὁ κόσμος δίδωσιν ἐγὼ δίδωμι ὑμῖν. μὴ ταρασσέσθω ὑμῶν ἡ καρδία μηδὲ δειλιάτω.

εἰρήνη: peace – ἀφίημι (pres ind 1 sg): leave – δίδωμι (pres ind 1 sg): give – κόσμος: world – ταράσσω (pres pass imv 3 sg): be troubled – δειλιάω (pres imv 3 sg): be timid

Formula of Concord SD XI 95

From our explanation, friends and enemies and, therefore, everyone, may clearly see that we have no intention of yielding any part of God's eternal, immutable truth for the sake of temporal peace, tranquility, and unity (which is not in our power to do anyway). Such peace and unity would have no permanence, since it is devised against the truth and for its suppression.

September 2

Joshua 22:5

רַק שִׁמְרוּ מְאֹד לַעֲשׂוֹת אֶת־הַמִּצְוָה וְאֶת־הַתּוֹרָה אֲשֶׁר
צִוָּה אֶתְכֶם מֹשֶׁה עֶבֶד־יְהוָה לְאַהֲבָה אֶת־יְהוָה אֱלֹהֵיכֶם
וְלָלֶכֶת בְּכָל־דְּרָכָיו וְלִשְׁמֹר מִצְוֹתָיו וּלְדָבְקָה־בוֹ
וּלְעָבְדוֹ בְּכָל־לְבַבְכֶם וּבְכָל־נַפְשְׁכֶם׃

רַק: only – שָׁמַר (qal imv pl): be careful, diligent – עָשָׂה (qal inf cst): keep – מִצְוָה: commandment – תּוֹרָה: law, teaching – צָוָה (pi pf 3 sg): command – אָהֵב (qal inf cst): love – הָלַךְ (qal inf cst): walk – דֶּרֶךְ (pl + 3 sg sf): way – דָּבַק (qal inf cst): hold fast – עָבַד (qal inf cst): serve – לֵבָב (2 pl sf): heart – נֶפֶשׁ (2 pl sf): soul

---

Ephesians 5:15-17

[15]Βλέπετε οὖν ἀκριβῶς πῶς περιπατεῖτε μὴ ὡς ἄσοφοι
ἀλλ' ὡς σοφοί, [16]ἐξαγοραζόμενοι τὸν καιρόν, ὅτι αἱ
ἡμέραι πονηραί εἰσιν. [17]διὰ τοῦτο μὴ γίνεσθε ἄφρονες,
ἀλλὰ συνίετε τί τὸ θέλημα τοῦ κυρίου.

βλέπω (pres imv 2 pl): see, consider – ἀκριβῶς: carefully – περιπατέω (pres ind 2 pl): walk, live – ἄσοφος: unwise – ἐξαγοράζω (pres mid ptcp): redeem – καιρός: time, opportunity – ἡμέρα: day – πονηρός: evil – γίνομαι (pres imv 2 pl): be – ἄφρων: foolish – συνίημι (pres imv 2 pl): understand – θέλημα: will

---

Large Catechism I 311

So apart from the Ten Commandments no work or thing can be good or pleasing to God, no matter how great or precious it is in the world's eyes.

Leviticus 26:11-12

11 וְנָתַתִּי מִשְׁכָּנִי בְּתוֹכְכֶם וְלֹא־תִגְעַל נַפְשִׁי אֶתְכֶם׃
12 וְהִתְהַלַּכְתִּי בְּתוֹכְכֶם וְהָיִיתִי לָכֶם לֵאלֹהִים וְאַתֶּם
תִּהְיוּ־לִי לְעָם׃

נָתַן (qal v-c pf 1 sg): give, put – מִשְׁכָּן (1 sg sf): dwelling place – תָּוֶךְ (2 pl sf): midst – גָּעַל (qal impf 3 sg f): abhor – נֶפֶשׁ (1 sg sf): soul, self – הָלַךְ (hithp v-c pf 1 sg): walk about – הָיָה (qal v-c pf 1 sg/qal impf 2 pl): be – עַם: people

---

Ephesians 3:17-19

17 κατοικῆσαι τὸν Χριστὸν διὰ τῆς πίστεως ἐν ταῖς καρδίαις
ὑμῶν, ἐν ἀγάπῃ ἐρριζωμένοι καὶ τεθεμελιωμένοι, 18 ἵνα
ἐξισχύσητε καταλαβέσθαι σὺν πᾶσιν τοῖς ἁγίοις τί τὸ
πλάτος καὶ μῆκος καὶ ὕψος καὶ βάθος, 19 γνῶναί τε τὴν
ὑπερβάλλουσαν τῆς γνώσεως ἀγάπην τοῦ Χριστοῦ, ἵνα
πληρωθῆτε εἰς πᾶν τὸ πλήρωμα τοῦ θεοῦ.

κατοικέω (aor inf): dwell – καρδία: heart – ἀγάπη: love – ῥιζόω (pf pass ptcp pl): rooted – θεμελιόω (pf pass ptcp pl): established – ἐξισχύω (aor subj 2 pl): have power, be strong enough – καταλαμβάνω (aor mid inf): grasp – ἅγιος: saint – πλάτος: width – μῆκος: length – ὕψος: height – βάθος: depth – γινώσκω (aor inf): know – ὑπερβάλλω (pres ptcp): surpass – πληρόω (aor pass subj 2 pl): be filled – πλήρωμα: fullness

---

Large Catechism II 64

For here in all three articles *[of the Creed]* God has revealed Himself and opened the deepest abyss of His fatherly heart and His pure, inexpressible love [Eph 3:18-19].

SEPTEMBER 4

Malachi 3:10

הָבִ֨יאוּ אֶת־כָּל־הַמַּעֲשֵׂ֜ר אֶל־בֵּ֣ית הָאוֹצָ֗ר וִיהִ֥י טֶ֙רֶף֙
בְּבֵיתִ֔י וּבְחָנ֤וּנִי נָא֙ בָּזֹ֔את אָמַ֖ר יְהוָ֣ה צְבָא֑וֹת אִם־לֹ֧א
אֶפְתַּ֣ח לָכֶ֗ם אֵ֚ת אֲרֻבּ֣וֹת הַשָּׁמַ֔יִם וַהֲרִיקֹתִ֥י לָכֶ֛ם בְּרָכָ֖ה
עַד־בְּלִי־דָֽי׃

בוא (hiph imv pl): bring – מַעֲשֵׂר: tithe – אוֹצָר: treasury – טֶ֫רֶף: food – בָּחַן (qal imv pl + 1 sg sf): test – פָּתַח (qal impf 1 sg): open – אֲרֻבָּה (cst pl): floodgate – ריק (hiph v-c pf 1 sg): pour out – בְּרָכָה: blessing – בְּלִי: not – דַּי: sufficiency = room enough

---

2 Corinthians 9:6

Τοῦτο δέ, ὁ σπείρων φειδομένως φειδομένως καὶ θερίσει, καὶ ὁ σπείρων ἐπ᾽ εὐλογίαις ἐπ᾽ εὐλογίαις καὶ θερίσει.

σπείρω (pres ptcp): sow – φειδομένως: sparingly – θερίζω (fut 3 sg): reap – εὐλογία: blessing, bounty

---

Apology V (III) 246

Works and troubles do not merit justification, but other payments, as the reward is offered for the works in these passages: "Whoever sows sparingly will also reap sparingly, and whoever sows bountifully will also reap bountifully" (2 Cor 9:6). Here clearly the measure of the reward is connected with the measure of the work.

Psalm 27:1

יְהוָה אוֹרִי וְיִשְׁעִי מִמִּי אִירָא
יְהוָה מָעוֹז־חַיַּי מִמִּי אֶפְחָד׃

אוֹר (1 sg sf): light – יֵשַׁע (1 sg sf): salvation – יָרֵא (qal impf 1 sg): fear – מָעוֹז: stronghold – חַיִּים (1 sg sf): life – פָּחַד (qal impf 1 sg): be afraid

---

Jude 24-25

[24]Τῷ δὲ δυναμένῳ φυλάξαι ὑμᾶς ἀπταίστους καὶ στῆσαι
κατενώπιον τῆς δόξης αὐτοῦ ἀμώμους ἐν ἀγαλλιάσει,
[25]μόνῳ θεῷ σωτῆρι ἡμῶν διὰ Ἰησοῦ Χριστοῦ τοῦ κυρίου
ἡμῶν δόξα μεγαλωσύνη κράτος καὶ ἐξουσία πρὸ παντὸς
τοῦ αἰῶνος καὶ νῦν καὶ εἰς πάντας τοὺς αἰῶνας, ἀμήν.

δύναμαι (pres ptcp): be able – φυλάσσω (aor inf): guard, keep – ἄπταιστος: without stumbling – ἵστημι (aor inf): present – κατενώπιον: before – δόξα: glory – ἄμωμος: blameless – ἀγαλλίασις: great joy – μεγαλωσύνη: majesty – κράτος: power – ἐξουσία: authority – αἰών: age = eternity past/future

---

Small Catechism Sixth Petition

And lead us not into temptation.

What does this mean?

Answer: God indeed tempts no one. But we pray in this petition that God would guard and keep us, so that the devil, the world, and our flesh may not deceive us nor seduce us into false belief, despair, and other great shame and vice. Though we are attacked by these things, we pray that still we may finally overcome them and gain the victory.

September 6

Psalm 50:14-15

14 זְבַח לֵאלֹהִים תּוֹדָה וְשַׁלֵּם לְעֶלְיוֹן נְדָרֶיךָ׃
15 וּקְרָאֵנִי בְּיוֹם צָרָה אֲחַלֶּצְךָ וּתְכַבְּדֵנִי׃

זָבַח (qal imv): offer – תּוֹדָה: thanksgiving – שָׁלֵם (pi imv): fulfill – עֶלְיוֹן: the Most High – נֶדֶר (pl +2 sg sf): vow – קָרָא (qal imv + 1 sg sf): call upon – צָרָה: trouble – חָלַץ (pi impf 1 sg + 2 sg sf): deliver – כָּבֵד (pi impf 2 sg + 1 sg sf): honor

---

Matthew 6:6

σὺ δὲ ὅταν προσεύχῃ, εἴσελθε εἰς τὸ ταμεῖόν σου καὶ κλείσας τὴν θύραν σου πρόσευξαι τῷ πατρί σου τῷ ἐν τῷ κρυπτῷ· καὶ ὁ πατήρ σου ὁ βλέπων ἐν τῷ κρυπτῷ ἀποδώσει σοι.

προσεύχομαι (pres subj 2 sg/aor imv): pray – εἰσέρχομαι (aor imv): go into – ταμεῖον: inner room – κλείω (aor ptcp): shut – θύρα: door – τὸ κρυπτόν: hidden place – βλέπω (pres ptcp): see – ἀποδίδωμι (fut ind 3 sg): reward

---

Large Catechism I 64

This *[second]* commandment also applies to right teaching and to calling on His name in trouble or praising and thanking Him in prosperity, and so on. All of this is summed up and commanded in Ps 50:15, "Call upon Me in the day of trouble; I will deliver you, and you shall glorify Me." For all this is bringing God's name into the service of truth and using it in a blessed way.

Psalm 28:6-7

6 בָּרוּךְ יְהוָה כִּי־שָׁמַע קוֹל תַּחֲנוּנָי׃
7 יְהוָה עֻזִּי וּמָגִנִּי בּוֹ בָטַח לִבִּי
וְנֶעֱזָרְתִּי וַיַּעֲלֹז לִבִּי וּמִשִּׁירִי אֲהוֹדֶנּוּ׃

קוֹל: voice, cry – תַּחֲנוּן (pl + 1 sg sf): prayer for mercy – עֹז (1 sg sf): strength – מָגֵן (1 sg sf): shield – בָּטַח (qal pf): trust – עָזַר (niph pf 1 sg): be helped – עָלַז (qal v-c impf 3 sg): leap for joy – שִׁיר (1 sg sf): song + prep מִן = with my song – יָדָה (hiph impf 1 sg + 3 sg sf): give thanks

---

Mark 11:23-24

23 ἀμὴν λέγω ὑμῖν ὅτι ὃς ἂν εἴπῃ τῷ ὄρει τούτῳ· ἄρθητι καὶ
βλήθητι εἰς τὴν θάλασσαν, καὶ μὴ διακριθῇ ἐν τῇ καρδίᾳ
αὐτοῦ ἀλλὰ πιστεύῃ ὅτι ὃ λαλεῖ γίνεται, ἔσται αὐτῷ. 24 διὰ
τοῦτο λέγω ὑμῖν, πάντα ὅσα προσεύχεσθε καὶ αἰτεῖσθε,
πιστεύετε ὅτι ἐλάβετε, καὶ ἔσται ὑμῖν.

ὄρος: mountain – αἴρω (aor pass imv): lift up – βάλλω (aor pass imv): throw – θάλασσα: sea – διακρίνω (aor pass subj 3 sg): doubt – αἰτέω (pres mid 2 pl): ask for

---

Large Catechism III 18

We must know that God will not have our prayer treated as a joke. But He will be angry and punish all who do not pray, just as surely as He punishes all other disobedience. Furthermore, He will not allow our prayers to be in vain or lost. For if He did not intend to answer your prayer, He would not ask you to pray and add such a severe commandment to it.

SEPTEMBER 8

Isaiah 30:9-10

9 כִּי עַם מְרִי הוּא בָּנִים כֶּחָשִׁים בָּנִים לֹא־אָבוּ שְׁמוֹעַ
תּוֹרַת יְהוָה׃ 10אֲשֶׁר אָמְרוּ לָרֹאִים לֹא תִרְאוּ וְלַחֹזִים לֹא
תֶחֱזוּ־לָנוּ נְכֹחוֹת דַּבְּרוּ־לָנוּ חֲלָקוֹת חֲזוּ מַהֲתַלּוֹת׃

מְרִי: rebellion – בֵּן (pl): child – כֶּחָשׁ (pl): deceitful – אָבָה (qal pf 3 pl) + לֹא: be unwilling – שְׁמַע (qal inf cst): listen to – תּוֹרָה: teaching – רֹאֶה (pl): seer – חֹזֶה (pl): prophet – חָזָה (qal impf 2 pl/qal imv pl): see – נָכֹחַ (pl f): what is right – דָּבַר (pi imv pl): speak – חָלָק (pl f): smooth, pleasant things – מַהֲתַלּוֹת: deceptions, illusions

2 Timothy 4:3-4

3 Ἔσται γὰρ καιρὸς ὅτε τῆς ὑγιαινούσης διδασκαλίας
οὐκ ἀνέξονται ἀλλὰ κατὰ τὰς ἰδίας ἐπιθυμίας ἑαυτοῖς
ἐπισωρεύσουσιν διδασκάλους κνηθόμενοι τὴν ἀκοὴν 4 καὶ
ἀπὸ μὲν τῆς ἀληθείας τὴν ἀκοὴν ἀποστρέψουσιν, ἐπὶ δὲ
τοὺς μύθους ἐκτραπήσονται.

καιρός: time – ὑγιαίνω (pres ptcp sg): be sound – ἀνέχομαι (fut ind 3 pl): endure – ἴδιος: one's own – ἐπιθυμία: desire – ἐπισωρεύω (fut ind 3 pl): heap up, accumulate – διδάσκαλος: teacher – κνήθομαι (pres pass ptcp): itch – ἀκοή: ear – ἀποστρέφω: turn away from – μύθος (pl): myth – ἐκτρέπω (fut dep 3 pl): turn aside

Large Catechism III 47

Here, now, learn what great need there is for such prayer *[as the First Petition]*. Because we see how full the world is of sects and false teachers, who all wear the holy name as a cover and sham for their doctrines of devils [1 Tim 4:1], we should by all means pray without ceasing [1 Thess 5:17] and cry out and call upon God against all people who preach and believe falsely.

September 9

Joshua 23:14

וְהִנֵּה אָנֹכִי הוֹלֵךְ הַיּוֹם בְּדֶרֶךְ כָּל־הָאָרֶץ וִידַעְתֶּם בְּכָל־
לְבַבְכֶם וּבְכָל־נַפְשְׁכֶם כִּי לֹא־נָפַל דָּבָר אֶחָד מִכֹּל
הַדְּבָרִים הַטּוֹבִים אֲשֶׁר דִּבֶּר יְהוָה אֱלֹהֵיכֶם עֲלֵיכֶם
הַכֹּל בָּאוּ לָכֶם לֹא־נָפַל מִמֶּנּוּ דָּבָר אֶחָד׃

יָדַע (qal v-c pf 2 pl): know – לֵבָב (2 pl sf): heart – נֶפֶשׁ (2 pl sf): soul – נָפַל (qal pf 3 sg): fail – בּוֹא (qal pf 3 pl): have come true

---

John 11:25-26

25εἶπεν αὐτῇ ὁ Ἰησοῦς· ἐγώ εἰμι ἡ ἀνάστασις καὶ ἡ ζωή·
ὁ πιστεύων εἰς ἐμὲ κἂν ἀποθάνῃ ζήσεται, 26καὶ πᾶς ὁ ζῶν
καὶ πιστεύων εἰς ἐμὲ οὐ μὴ ἀποθάνῃ εἰς τὸν αἰῶνα.

εἶπον (aor 3 sg): say – ἀνάστασις: resurrection – ζωή: life – πιστεύω (pres ptcp): believe – ἀποθνῄσκω (aor subj 3 sg): die – ζάω (fut 3 sg/pres ptcp): live – αἰών: eternity

---

Apology XXIV (XII) 69

Those who define Sacraments in the New Testament as signs of grace are correct. There are two things in a Sacrament: a sign and the Word. In the New Testament, the Word is the promise of grace added. The promise of the New Testament is the promise of the forgiveness of sins.

SEPTEMBER 10

Psalm 107:1-2

1 הֹדוּ לַיהוָה כִּי־טוֹב כִּי לְעוֹלָם חַסְדּוֹ׃
2 יֹאמְרוּ גְּאוּלֵי יְהוָה אֲשֶׁר גְּאָלָם מִיַּד־צָר׃

יָדָה (hiph imv pl): give thanks – עוֹלָם: eternity – חֶסֶד (3 sg sf): faithful love – אָמַר (qal juss 3 pl): say – גָּאַל (qal pass ptcp cst pl): the redeemed – צַר: enemy

Matthew 18:32-33

32 τότε προσκαλεσάμενος αὐτὸν ὁ κύριος αὐτοῦ λέγει αὐτῷ· δοῦλε πονηρέ, πᾶσαν τὴν ὀφειλὴν ἐκείνην ἀφῆκά σοι, ἐπεὶ παρεκάλεσάς με· 33 οὐκ ἔδει καὶ σὲ ἐλεῆσαι τὸν σύνδουλόν σου, ὡς κἀγὼ σὲ ἠλέησα;

προσκαλέω (aor mid ptcp sg): summon – κύριος: master – δοῦλος: servant – πονηρός: wicked – ὀφειλή: debt – ἀφίημι (aor ind 1 sg): cancel – παρακαλέω (aor ind 2 sg): beg – δεῖ (impf ind): be necessary, ought, should – ἐλεέω (aor inf/aor ind 1 sg): have mercy – σύνδουλος: fellow servant

Large Catechism I 187

Now, this urge dwells in everyone by nature. It is common practice that no one is willing to suffer at the hands of another person. Therefore, God wants to remove the root and source by which the heart is embittered against our neighbor. He wants to make us used to keeping this *[fifth]* commandment ever in view, always to contemplate ourselves in it as in a mirror [Jas 1:23-25], to regard the will of God, and to turn over to Him the wrong that we suffer with hearty confidence and by calling on His name.

Isaiah 58:7

הֲלוֹא פָרֹס לָרָעֵב לַחְמֶךָ וַעֲנִיִּים מְרוּדִים תָּבִיא בָיִת
כִּי־תִרְאֶה עָרֹם וְכִסִּיתוֹ וּמִבְּשָׂרְךָ לֹא תִתְעַלָּם׃

פָּרַס (qal inf abs): to share – רָעֵב: the hungry – לֶחֶם (2 sg sf): bread – עֲנִיִּים מְרוּדִים: the poor wanderers – בּוֹא (hiph impf 2 sg): bring in – עָרֹם: naked – כָּסָה (pi v-c pf 2 sg + 3 sg sf): clothe – בָּשָׂר (2 sg sf): flesh – עָלַם (hithp impf 2 sg): hide oneself, turn away from

Romans 12:20

ἀλλὰ ἐὰν πεινᾷ ὁ ἐχθρός σου, ψώμιζε αὐτόν· ἐὰν διψᾷ, πότιζε αὐτόν· τοῦτο γὰρ ποιῶν ἄνθρακας πυρὸς σωρεύσεις ἐπὶ τὴν κεφαλὴν αὐτοῦ.

πεινάω (pres subj 3 sg): be hungry – ἐχθρός: enemy – ψωμίζω (pres imv 2 sg): feed – διψάω (pres subj 3 sg): be thirsty – ποτίζω (pres imv 2 sg): give to drink – ἄνθραξ πυρός: burning coal – σωρεύω (fut ind 2 sg): heap up – κεφαλή: head

Large Catechism I 195

Here again *[in the Fifth Commandment]* we have God's Word, by which He would encourage and teach us to do true, noble, and grand works such as gentleness, patience, and, in short, love and kindness to our enemies [Gal 5:22-23].

SEPTEMBER 12

Psalm 24:1-2

1 לַֽיהוָה הָאָרֶץ וּמְלוֹאָהּ תֵּבֵל וְיֹשְׁבֵי בָהּ׃
2 כִּי־הוּא עַל־יַמִּים יְסָדָהּ וְעַל־נְהָרוֹת יְכוֹנְנֶהָ׃

לַיהוָה: dat of possession – מְלוֹא (3 sg sf): fullness, that which fills – תֵּבֵל: world (poetic) – יָשַׁב: (qal ptcp cst pl): dwell – יָם (pl): sea – יָסַד (qal pf + 3 sg sf): set – נָהָר (pl): river, the waters – כּוּן (polel impf 3 sg + 3 sg sf): establish

---

1 Timothy 4:4-5

4ὅτι πᾶν κτίσμα θεοῦ καλὸν καὶ οὐδὲν ἀπόβλητον μετὰ εὐχαριστίας λαμβανόμενον· 5ἁγιάζεται γὰρ διὰ λόγου θεοῦ καὶ ἐντεύξεως.

κτίσμα: that which is created – καλός: good – ἀπόβλητος: to be rejected – εὐχαριστία: thanksgiving – λαμβάνω (pres pass ptcp): received – ἁγιάζω (pres pass 3 sg): consecrate – ἔντευξις: prayer

---

Large Catechism I 211

In general and in all conditions it is solemnly commanded by God that men and women, who were created for marriage, shall be found in this estate.

SEPTEMBER 13

Psalm 103:15-16

15 אֱנוֹשׁ כֶּחָצִיר יָמָיו כְּצִיץ הַשָּׂדֶה כֵּן יָצִיץ׃
16 כִּי רוּחַ עָבְרָה־בּוֹ וְאֵינֶנּוּ וְלֹא־יַכִּירֶנּוּ עוֹד מְקוֹמוֹ׃

אֱנוֹשׁ: man, mankind – חָצִיר: grass – יוֹם (pl + 3 sg sf): day – צִיץ: flower – שָׂדֶה: field – צִיץ (qal impf 3 sg): blossom, flourish – רוּחַ: wind – עָבַר (qal pf 3 sg): pass over – אַיִן (3 sg sf): nonexistence – נָכַר (hiph impf 3 sg + 3 sg sf): recognize – מָקוֹם (3 sg sf): place

---

Mark 8:36-37

36 τί γὰρ ὠφελεῖ ἄνθρωπον κερδῆσαι τὸν κόσμον ὅλον καὶ ζημιωθῆναι τὴν ψυχὴν αὐτοῦ; 37 τί γὰρ δοῖ ἄνθρωπος ἀντάλλαγμα τῆς ψυχῆς αὐτοῦ;

ὠφελέω (pres ind 3 sg): benefit – κερδαίνω (aor inf): gain – κόσμος: world – ὅλος: whole – ζημιόω (aor pass inf): suffer loss – ψυχή: soul – δίδωμι (aor subj 3 sg): give – ἀντάλλαγμα: something given in exchange

---

Smalcald Articles II IV 14

Therefore, just as we cannot worship the devil himself as Lord and God, so we cannot endure his apostle—the pope or Antichrist—in his rule as head or lord. For what his papal government really consists of (as I have very clearly shown in many books) is to lie and kill and destroy body and soul eternally.

September 14

Hosea 14:2-3

2 שׁוּבָה יִשְׂרָאֵל עַד יְהוָה אֱלֹהֶיךָ כִּי כָשַׁלְתָּ בַּעֲוֺנֶךָ׃
3 קְחוּ עִמָּכֶם דְּבָרִים וְשׁוּבוּ אֶל־יְהוָה אִמְרוּ אֵלָיו
כָּל־תִּשָּׂא עָוֺן וְקַח־טוֹב וּנְשַׁלְּמָה פָרִים שְׂפָתֵינוּ׃

שׁוּב (qal imv sg): return – כָּשַׁל (qal pf 2 sg): stumble – עָוֺן (2 sg sf): sin (as guilt) – לָקַח (qal imv pl): take – דָּבָר (pl): word – אָמַר (qal imv pl): say – נָשָׂא (qal impf 2 sg = imv): forgive – טוֹב (adv): graciously – שָׁלֵם (pi coh 1 pl): to offer – פַּר (pl): bull; LXX and NIV translate פְּרִי: fruit – שָׂפָה (pl + 1 pl sf): lip

---

Luke 18:13

ὁ δὲ τελώνης μακρόθεν ἑστὼς οὐκ ἤθελεν οὐδὲ τοὺς ὀφθαλμοὺς ἐπᾶραι εἰς τὸν οὐρανόν, ἀλλʼ ἔτυπτεν τὸ στῆθος αὐτοῦ λέγων· ὁ θεός, ἱλάσθητί μοι τῷ ἁμαρτωλῷ.

> τελώνης: tax collector – μακρόθεν: at a distance – ἵστημι (pf ptcp with pres meaning): stand – θέλω (impf 3 sg): wish, want – ὀφθαλμός: eye – ἐπαίρω (aor inf): lift up – οὐρανός: heaven – τύπτω (impf 3 sg): beat – στῆθος: breast – ἱλάσκομαι (aor pass imv 2 sg): have mercy – ἁμαρτωλός: sinner

---

Apology XIIA (V) 29

We say that contrition is the true terror of conscience, which feels that God is angry with sin and grieves that it has sinned. This contrition takes place when sins are condemned by God's Word.

SEPTEMBER 15

Genesis 8:22

עֹד כָּל־יְמֵי הָאָרֶץ זֶרַע וְקָצִיר וְקֹר וָחֹם
וְקַיִץ וָחֹרֶף וְיוֹם וָלַיְלָה לֹא יִשְׁבֹּתוּ׃

עֹד: continuance – זֶרַע: sowing – קָצִיר: harvest – קֹר: cold – חֹם: heat – קַיִץ: summer – חֹרֶף: autumn rain (beginning of winter) – שָׁבַת (qal impf 3 pl): cease

---

Matthew 5:45

ὅτι τὸν ἥλιον αὐτοῦ ἀνατέλλει ἐπὶ πονηροὺς καὶ ἀγαθοὺς καὶ βρέχει ἐπὶ δικαίους καὶ ἀδίκους.

ἥλιος: sun – ἀνατέλλω (pres 3 sg): cause to rise – πονηρός: wicked – ἀγαθός: good – βρέχω (pres 3 sg): send rain – δίκαιος: just – ἄδικος: unjust

---

Large Catechism III 82-83

You see, in this way *[in the Fourth Petition],* God wishes to show us how He cares for us in all our need and faithfully provides also for our earthly support. He abundantly grants and preserves these things, even for the wicked and rogues [Matt 5:45]. Yet, He wishes that we pray for these goods in order that we may recognize that we receive them from His hand and may feel His fatherly goodness toward us in them [Ps 104:28; 145:16].

September 16

Genesis 39:6-7,9

6 וַיְהִי יוֹסֵף יְפֵה־תֹאַר וִיפֵה מַרְאֶה׃ 7 וַיְהִי אַחַר
הַדְּבָרִים הָאֵלֶּה וַתִּשָּׂא אֵשֶׁת־אֲדֹנָיו אֶת־עֵינֶיהָ אֶל־יוֹסֵף
וַתֹּאמֶר שִׁכְבָה עִמִּי׃
9 וְאֵיךְ אֶעֱשֶׂה הָרָעָה הַגְּדֹלָה הַזֹּאת וְחָטָאתִי לֵאלֹהִים׃

יָפֶה (adj cst): beautiful – תֹּאַר: form – מַרְאֶה: appearance – נָשָׂא (qal v-c impf 3 sg f): lift up – אִשָּׁה (cst sg): wife – שָׁכַב (qal imv sg): lie down – אֵיךְ: how? – רָעָה: evil – חָטָא (qal v-c pf 1 sg): sin

1 Corinthians 10:13

πειρασμὸς ὑμᾶς οὐκ εἴληφεν εἰ μὴ ἀνθρώπινος· πιστὸς δὲ ὁ θεός, ὃς οὐκ ἐάσει ὑμᾶς πειρασθῆναι ὑπὲρ ὃ δύνασθε ἀλλὰ ποιήσει σὺν τῷ πειρασμῷ καὶ τὴν ἔκβασιν τοῦ δύνασθαι ὑπενεγκεῖν.

πειρασμός: temptation – λαμβάνω (pf ind 3 sg): take hold of – εἰ μή: if not, except – ἀνθρώπινος: human, common to us all – πιστός: faithful – ἐάω (fut ind 3 sg): allow – πειράζω (aor pass inf): be tempted – δύναμαι (pres 2 pl): be able – ἔκβασις: a way out – ὑποφέρω (aor inf): stand up under, endure

Large Catechism III 106

This, then, is what "lead us not into temptation" means. It refers to times when God gives us power and strength to resist the temptation [1 Cor 10:13]. However, the temptation is not taken away or removed. While we live in the flesh and have the devil around us, no one can escape his temptation and lures.

September 17

Psalm 86:12-13

12 אוֹדְךָ אֲדֹנָי אֱלֹהַי בְּכָל־לְבָבִי וַאֲכַבְּדָה שִׁמְךָ לְעוֹלָם׃
13 כִּי־חַסְדְּךָ גָּדוֹל עָלָי וְהִצַּלְתָּ נַפְשִׁי מִשְּׁאוֹל תַּחְתִּיָּה׃

יָדָה (hiph impf 1 sg + 2 sg sf): praise – לֵבָב (1 sg sf): heart – כָּבַד (pi coh 1 sg): glorify – שֵׁם (2 sg sf): name – גָּדוֹל: great – נָצַל (hiph pf 2 sg): deliver – נֶפֶשׁ (1 sg sf): soul – שְׁאוֹל: the grave – תַּחְתִּיָּה: depths

---

Ephesians 5:19-20

19 λαλοῦντες ἑαυτοῖς [ἐν] ψαλμοῖς καὶ ὕμνοις καὶ ᾠδαῖς
πνευματικαῖς, ᾄδοντες καὶ ψάλλοντες τῇ καρδίᾳ ὑμῶν τῷ
κυρίῳ, 20 εὐχαριστοῦντες πάντοτε ὑπὲρ πάντων ἐν ὀνόματι
τοῦ κυρίου ἡμῶν Ἰησοῦ Χριστοῦ τῷ θεῷ καὶ πατρί.

ὕμνος: hymn – ᾠδή: song – πνευματικός: spiritual – ψάλλω (pres ptcp pl): sing praise – καρδία: heart – εὐχαριστέω (pres ptcp pl): give thanks – πάντοτε: always

---

Large Catechism Short Preface 24-25

Then we would have all together five whole parts of Christian doctrine *[in the Catechism]*. These should be taught constantly and be required learning for children. You should hear them recited word for word. For you must not rely on the idea that the young people will learn and retain these things from the sermon alone. When these parts have been well learned, you may supplement and strengthen them by also setting before them some psalms or hymns, which have been composed on these parts of the catechism. Lead the young into the Scriptures this way, and make progress in them daily.

September 18

Psalm 32:8

אַשְׂכִּילְךָ֨ ׀ וְֽאוֹרְךָ֗ בְּדֶֽרֶךְ־ז֥וּ תֵלֵ֑ךְ אִֽיעֲצָ֖ה עָלֶ֣יךָ עֵינִֽי׃

שָׂכַל (hiph impf 1 sg + 2 sg sf): instruct – יָרָה (hiph impf 1 sg + 2 sg sf): teach – דֶּ֫רֶךְ: way – זוּ: in which – הָלַךְ (qal impf 2 sg): go – יָעַץ (qal coh 1 sg): counsel – עַ֫יִן (1 sg sf): eye

2 Timothy 3:15-17

15καὶ ὅτι ἀπὸ βρέφους [τὰ] ἱερὰ γράμματα οἶδας, τὰ
δυνάμενά σε σοφίσαι εἰς σωτηρίαν διὰ πίστεως τῆς ἐν
Χριστῷ Ἰησοῦ. 16πᾶσα γραφὴ θεόπνευστος καὶ ὠφέλιμος
πρὸς διδασκαλίαν, πρὸς ἐλεγμόν, πρὸς ἐπανόρθωσιν, πρὸς
παιδείαν τὴν ἐν δικαιοσύνῃ, 17ἵνα ἄρτιος ᾖ ὁ τοῦ θεοῦ
ἄνθρωπος, πρὸς πᾶν ἔργον ἀγαθὸν ἐξηρτισμένος.

βρέφος: infancy – ἱερός: holy – γράμματα: Scriptures – δύναμαι (pres ptcp pl): be able – σοφίζω (aor inf): make wise – σωτηρία: salvation – γραφή: Scripture – θεόπνευστος: inspired by God – ὠφέλιμος: useful – διδασκαλία: teaching – ἐλεγμός: reproof – ἐπανόρθωσις: correcting – παιδεία: training – δικαιοσύνη: righteousness – ἄρτιος: proficient – ἐξαρτίζω (pf pass ptcp): equipped

Formula of Concord SD XI 12

Against this false delusion and thought we should set up the following clear argument, which is sure and cannot fail: All Scripture is inspired by God. It is not for self-confidence and lack of repentance, but "for reproof, for correction, and for training in righteousness" (2 Tim 3:16).

SEPTEMBER 19

Jeremiah 1:19

וְנִלְחֲמוּ אֵלֶיךָ וְלֹא־יוּכְלוּ לָךְ כִּי־אִתְּךָ אֲנִי נְאֻם־יְהוָה לְהַצִּילֶךָ׃

לָחַם (niph v-c pf 3 pl): fight – יָכֹל (qal impf 3 pl): prevail, overcome – אֵת (prep + 2 sg sf): with – נָצַל (hiph inf cst + 2 sg sf): rescue

---

Acts 26:16

ἀλλὰ ἀνάστηθι καὶ στῆθι ἐπὶ τοὺς πόδας σου· εἰς τοῦτο γὰρ ὤφθην σοι, προχειρίσασθαί σε ὑπηρέτην καὶ μάρτυρα ὧν τε εἶδές [με] ὧν τε ὀφθήσομαί σοι . . .

ἀνίστημι (aor imv 2 sg): stand up – πούς (acc pl): foot – ὤφθην (aor pass 1 sg of ὁράω): appear – προχειρίζομαι (aor inf): appoint – ὑπηρέτης: servant – μάρτυς: witness – εἶδες (aor ind 2 sg of ὁράω): see – ὀφθήσομαι (fut pass 1 sg of ὁράω): appear, show

---

Apology XIIA (V) 60

We attribute justification and regeneration to this faith, since it frees from terrors and produces not only peace and joy, but also a new life in the heart. ‹With God's help,› we shall defend ‹to eternity and against all the gates of hell› that this faith is truly necessary for the forgiveness of sins, and so place it among the parts of repentance. Nor does Christ's Church believe otherwise . . .

September 20

2 Chronicles 33:12-13

12וּכְהָצֵר לוֹ חִלָּה אֶת־פְּנֵי יְהוָה אֱלֹהָיו וַיִּכָּנַע מְאֹד
מִלִּפְנֵי אֱלֹהֵי אֲבֹתָיו׃ 13וַיִּתְפַּלֵּל אֵלָיו וַיֵּעָתֶר לוֹ וַיִּשְׁמַע
תְּחִנָּתוֹ וַיְשִׁיבֵהוּ יְרוּשָׁלִַם לְמַלְכוּתוֹ וַיֵּדַע מְנַשֶּׁה
כִּי יְהוָה הוּא הָאֱלֹהִים׃

צָרַר (hiph inf cst): cause distress + לוֹ: in his distress (Manasseh) – חָלָה (pi pf 3 sg): seek the favor of – כָּנַע (niph v-c impf 3 sg): humble oneself – מִלִּפְנֵי (prep): before – פָּלַל (hithp v-c impf 3 sg): pray – עָתַר (niph v-c impf 3 sg): be moved by entreaty – תְּחִנָּה (3 sg sf): plea – שׁוּב (hiph v-c impf 3 sg + 3 sg sf): bring back – מַלְכוּת (3 sg sf): kingdom – יָדַע (qal v-c impf 3 sg): know

---

Acts 2:21

καὶ ἔσται πᾶς ὃς ἂν ἐπικαλέσηται τὸ ὄνομα κυρίου σωθήσεται.

ἐπικαλέω (aor mid subj 3 sg): call on – ὄνομα: name – σῴζω (fut pass 3 sg): be saved

---

Augsburg Confession XII 1

Our churches teach that there is forgiveness of sins for those who have fallen after Baptism whenever they are converted.

Job 5:17-18

17הִנֵּה אַשְׁרֵי אֱנוֹשׁ יוֹכִחֶנּוּ אֱלוֹהַּ וּמוּסַר שַׁדַּי אַל־
תִּמְאָֽס׃
18כִּי הוּא יַכְאִיב וְיֶחְבָּשׁ יִמְחַץ וְיָדוֹ [וְיָדָיו] תִּרְפֶּֽינָה׃

אֶשֶׁר (cst pl): blessedness – אֱנוֹשׁ: man – יָכַח (hiph impf 3 sg + 3 sg sf): correct – מוּסָר: discipline – שַׁדַּי: the Almighty – מָאַס (qal juss 2 sg): despise – כָּאַב (hiph impf 3 sg): wound – חָבַשׁ (qal impf 3 sg): bind up – מָחַץ (qal impf 3 sg): smite, injure – יָד (qere: pl + 3 sg sf): hand – רָפָא (qal impf 3 pl f): heal

---

Hebrews 12:9-10

9εἶτα τοὺς μὲν τῆς σαρκὸς ἡμῶν πατέρας εἴχομεν παιδευτὰς
καὶ ἐνετρεπόμεθα· οὐ πολὺ [δὲ] μᾶλλον ὑποταγησόμεθα τῷ
πατρὶ τῶν πνευμάτων καὶ ζήσομεν; 10οἱ μὲν γὰρ πρὸς ὀλίγας
ἡμέρας κατὰ τὸ δοκοῦν αὐτοῖς ἐπαίδευον, ὁ δὲ ἐπὶ τὸ
συμφέρον εἰς τὸ μεταλαβεῖν τῆς ἁγιότητος αὐτοῦ.

εἶτα: then – παιδευτής: one who disciplines – ἐντρέπω (impf pass dep 1 pl): respect – ὑποτάσσω (fut pass 1 pl): be subjected, obey – ὀλίγος: few – ἡμέρα: day – δοκέω (pres ptcp n): seem good – συμφέρω (pres ptcp n): be helpful, for our good – μεταλαμβάνω (aor inf): share – ἁγιότης: holiness

---

Large Catechism III 66

The test is to be steadfast and to suffer with patience [Jas 5:7-8] in whatever way we are assaulted, and to let go whatever is taken from us [1 Pet 2:20-21].

SEPTEMBER 22

Psalm 40:18

וַאֲנִי עָנִי וְאֶבְיוֹן אֲדֹנָי יַחֲשָׁב לִי
עֶזְרָתִי וּמְפַלְטִי אַתָּה אֱלֹהַי אַל־תְּאַחַר׃

אֲנִי: I – עָנִי: poor – אֶבְיוֹן: needy – חָשַׁב (qal impf 3 sg): think – עֶזְרָה (1 sg sf): help – פָּלַט (pi ptcp + 1 sg sf): deliverer – אָחַר (pi juss 2 sg): delay

---

Mark 2:17

καὶ ἀκούσας ὁ Ἰησοῦς λέγει αὐτοῖς [ὅτι] οὐ χρείαν ἔχουσιν οἱ ἰσχύοντες ἰατροῦ ἀλλ' οἱ κακῶς ἔχοντες· οὐκ ἦλθον καλέσαι δικαίους ἀλλὰ ἁμαρτωλούς.

ἀκούω (aor ptcp): hear – χρεία: need – ἰσχύω (pres ptcp): be in good health – ἰατρός: doctor – κακῶς ἔχειν: be sick – ἔρχομαι (aor ind 1 sg): come – καλέω (aor inf): call – δίκαιος: righteous – ἁμαρτωλός: sinner

---

Formula of Concord SD I 5

First, it is true that Christians should regard and recognize the actual transgression of God's commandments as sin; but sin is also that horrible, dreadful hereditary sickness by which the entire human nature is corrupted.

SEPTEMBER 23

2 Chronicles 6:18

כִּי הַאֻמְנָם יֵשֵׁב אֱלֹהִים אֶת־הָאָדָם עַל־הָאָרֶץ הִנֵּה שָׁמַיִם וּשְׁמֵי הַשָּׁמַיִם לֹא יְכַלְכְּלוּךָ אַף כִּי־הַבַּיִת הַזֶּה אֲשֶׁר בָּנִיתִי׃

אֻמְנָם (adv + interrog ה): truly – יָשַׁב (qal impf 3 sg): dwell — שָׁמַיִם (pl/cst pl): heaven = highest heaven – כּוּל (pilpel impf 3 pl + 2 sg sf): contain – אַף כִּי: how much less – בָּנָה (qal pf 1 sg): build

---

Ephesians 2:19-22

19 Ἄρα οὖν οὐκέτι ἐστὲ ξένοι καὶ πάροικοι ἀλλὰ
ἐστὲ συμπολῖται τῶν ἁγίων καὶ οἰκεῖοι τοῦ θεοῦ,
20 ἐποικοδομηθέντες ἐπὶ τῷ θεμελίῳ τῶν ἀποστόλων
καὶ προφητῶν, ὄντος ἀκρογωνιαίου αὐτοῦ Χριστοῦ
Ἰησοῦ, 21 ἐν ᾧ πᾶσα οἰκοδομὴ συναρμολογουμένη
αὔξει εἰς ναὸν ἅγιον ἐν κυρίῳ, 22 ἐν ᾧ καὶ ὑμεῖς
συνοικοδομεῖσθε εἰς κατοικητήριον τοῦ θεοῦ ἐν πνεύματι.

οὐκέτι: no longer – ξένος: foreigner – πάροικος: alien – συμπολίτης: fellow citizen – ἅγιος (pl): saint – οἰκεῖος: member of the household – ἐποικοδομέω (aor pass ptcp): built upon – θεμέλιον: foundation – ἀκρογωνιαῖος (λίθος): cornerstone – συναρμολογέομαι (pres ptcp): fit together – αὔξω: grow – συνοικοδομέω (pres pass 2 pl): build together – κατοικητήριον: dwelling place

---

Large Catechism II 42

The Spirit has His own congregation in the world, which is the mother that conceives and bears every Christian through God's Word [Gal 4:26]. Through the Word He reveals and preaches, He illumines and enkindles hearts, so that they understand, accept, cling to, and persevere in the Word" [1 Cor 2:12].

SEPTEMBER 24

Proverbs 16:18-19

18לִפְנֵי־שֶׁבֶר גָּאוֹן וְלִפְנֵי כִשָּׁלוֹן גֹּבַהּ רוּחַ׃
19טוֹב שְׁפַל־רוּחַ אֶת־עֲנִיִּים [עֲנָוִים] מֵחַלֵּק שָׁלָל
אֶת־גֵּאִים׃

לִפְנֵי: before – שֶׁבֶר: destruction – גָּאוֹן: pride – כִּשָּׁלוֹן: stumbling – גֹּבַהּ: haughtiness – רוּחַ: spirit – טוֹב: good + מִן of comparison: better – שָׁפָל: lowly – אֵת: with – עָנָו (qere: pl): afflicted, oppressed – חָלַק (pi inf cst): divide, share – שָׁלָל: plunder – גֵּאֶה (pl): the proud

Matthew 5:3-5

3μακάριοι οἱ πτωχοὶ τῷ πνεύματι, ὅτι αὐτῶν ἐστιν ἡ
βασιλεία τῶν οὐρανῶν. 4μακάριοι οἱ πενθοῦντες, ὅτι
αὐτοὶ παρακληθήσονται. 5μακάριοι οἱ πραεῖς, ὅτι αὐτοὶ
κληρονομήσουσιν τὴν γῆν.

μακάριος (pl): blessed – πτωχός (pl): poor – πνεῦμα: spirit – βασιλεία: kingdom – πενθέω (pres ptcp pl): mourn – παρακαλέω (fut pass 3 pl): comfort – πραΰς: meek – κληρονομέω (fut ind 3 pl): inherit – γῆ: earth

Large Catechism III 90

But this *[the Fifth Petition]* should serve God's purpose of breaking our pride and keeping us humble. God has reserved this right for Himself: if anyone wants to boast of his godliness and despise others, that person is to think about himself and place this prayer before his eyes.

SEPTEMBER 25

Psalm 140:7

אָמַ֣רְתִּי לַ֭יהוָה אֵ֣לִי אָ֑תָּה הַאֲזִ֥ינָה יְ֝הוָ֗ה ק֣וֹל תַּחֲנוּנָֽי׃

אָמַר (qal pf 1 sg): say – אָזַן (hiph imv): hear – תַּחֲנוּן (pl + 1 sg sf): plea for mercy

---

1 John 4:16

καὶ ἡμεῖς ἐγνώκαμεν καὶ πεπιστεύκαμεν τὴν ἀγάπην ἣν ἔχει ὁ θεὸς ἐν ἡμῖν. ὁ θεὸς ἀγάπη ἐστίν, καὶ ὁ μένων ἐν τῇ ἀγάπῃ ἐν τῷ θεῷ μένει καὶ ὁ θεὸς ἐν αὐτῷ μένει.

γινώσκω (pf ind 1 pl): know – πιστεύω (pf ind 1 pl): believe – ἀγάπη: love – μένω (pres ptcp/pres ind 3 sg): remain

---

Apology V (III) 20

Our love for God, even though it is small, cannot possibly be separated from faith. For we come to the Father through Christ. When forgiveness of sins has been received, then we are truly certain that we have a God [Ex 20:3], that is, that God cares for us. We call upon Him, we give Him thanks, we fear Him, we love Him as 1 John 4:19 teaches, "We love because He first loved us." In other words, we love Him because He gave His Son for us and forgave us our sins.

SEPTEMBER 26

Psalm 35:28

וּלְשׁוֹנִי תֶּהְגֶּה צִדְקֶךָ כָּל־הַיּוֹם תְּהִלָּתֶךָ׃

לָשׁוֹן (1 sg sf): tongue – הָגָה (qal impf 3 sg f): speak – צֶדֶק (2 sg sf): righteousness – כָּל־הַיּוֹם: all day long – תְּהִלָּה (2 sg sf): praise

2 Corinthians 4:13

Ἔχοντες δὲ τὸ αὐτὸ πνεῦμα τῆς πίστεως κατὰ τὸ γεγραμμένον· ἐπίστευσα, διὸ ἐλάλησα, καὶ ἡμεῖς πιστεύομεν, διὸ καὶ λαλοῦμεν . . .

αὐτός: the same – πνεῦμα: spirit – γράφω (pf pass ptcp): write – πιστεύω (aor ind 1 sg/pres ind 1 pl): believe – διό: therefore – λαλέω (aor ind 1 sg/pres ind 1 pl): speak

Large Catechism I 49-50

The First Commandment has instructed the heart and taught the faith. This *[second]* commandment now leads us forward and directs the mouth and tongue to God. For the first things that spring from the heart and show themselves are words [Matt 12:34].

SEPTEMBER 27

Psalm 103:20-22

20 בָּרֲכוּ יְהוָה מַלְאָכָיו גִּבֹּרֵי כֹחַ עֹשֵׂי דְבָרוֹ לִשְׁמֹעַ
בְּקוֹל דְּבָרוֹ׃
21 בָּרֲכוּ יְהוָה כָּל־צְבָאָיו מְשָׁרְתָיו עֹשֵׂי רְצוֹנוֹ׃
22 בָּרֲכוּ יְהוָה כָּל־מַעֲשָׂיו בְּכָל־מְקֹמוֹת מֶמְשַׁלְתּוֹ
בָּרֲכִי נַפְשִׁי אֶת־יְהוָה׃

בָּרַךְ (pi imv pl): praise – מַלְאָךְ (pl + 3 sg sf): angel – גִּבּוֹר (cst pl): mighty – כֹּחַ: power – עָשָׂה (qal ptcp cst pl): do – דָּבָר (3 sg sf): word = what he says – שָׁמַע (qal inf cst): hear, obey – צָבָא (3 sg sf): (heavenly) host – שָׁרַת (pi ptcp pl + 3 sg sf): serve = you his servants – רָצוֹן (3 sg sf): will, pleasure – מַעֲשֶׂה (pl + 3 sg sf): works – מָקוֹם (cst pl): place – מֶמְשֶׁלֶת (3 sg sf): dominion

Matthew 6:9-10

9 Οὕτως οὖν προσεύχεσθε ὑμεῖς· Πάτερ ἡμῶν ὁ ἐν τοῖς
οὐρανοῖς· ἁγιασθήτω τὸ ὄνομά σου· 10 ἐλθάτω ἡ βασιλεία
σου· γενηθήτω τὸ θέλημά σου, ὡς ἐν οὐρανῷ καὶ ἐπὶ γῆς·

οὕτως: thus – προσεύχομαι (pres ind or imv 2 pl): pray – οὐρανός: heaven – ἁγιάζω (aor pass imv 3 sg): make holy – ἔρχομαι (aor imv 3 sg): come – βασιλεία: kingdom – γίνομαι (aor imv 3 sg): come to be – θέλημα: will

Large Catechism III 2

We must pray that He would give, preserve, and increase faith in us and the fulfillment of the Ten Commandments [2 Thess 1:3].

SEPTEMBER 28

Isaiah 44:23

רָנּוּ שָׁמַיִם כִּי־עָשָׂה יְהוָה הָרִיעוּ תַּחְתִּיּוֹת אָרֶץ
פִּצְחוּ הָרִים רִנָּה יַעַר וְכָל־עֵץ בּוֹ
כִּי־גָאַל יְהוָה יַעֲקֹב וּבְיִשְׂרָאֵל יִתְפָּאָר׃

רָנַן (qal imv pl): sing for joy – שָׁמַיִם: heavens – רוּעַ (hiph imv): shout aloud – תַּחְתִּי (pl): low place = the earth beneath – פָּצַח (qal imv): burst into – הַר (pl): mountain – רִנָּה: song – יַעַר: forest – עֵץ: tree – גָּאַל (qal pf 3 sg): redeem – פָּאַר (hithp impf 3 sg): glorify himself, display his glory

John 13:1

Πρὸ δὲ τῆς ἑορτῆς τοῦ πάσχα εἰδὼς ὁ Ἰησοῦς ὅτι ἦλθεν αὐτοῦ ἡ ὥρα ἵνα μεταβῇ ἐκ τοῦ κόσμου τούτου πρὸς τὸν πατέρα, ἀγαπήσας τοὺς ἰδίους τοὺς ἐν τῷ κόσμῳ εἰς τέλος ἠγάπησεν αὐτούς.

ἑορτή: festival – πάσχα: Passover – οἶδα (pf ptcp with pres meaning): know – ἔρχομαι (aor 3 sg): come – μεταβαίνω (aor subj 3 sg): go from one place to another – κόσμος: world – ἀγαπάω (aor ptcp/aor ind 3 sg): love – ἴδιος: one's own – τέλος: end

Large Catechism II 33

Yes, the entire Gospel that we preach is based on this point, that we properly understand this *[second]* article as that upon which our salvation and all our happiness rests. It is so rich and complete that we can never learn it fully.

September 29

Psalm 119:71-72

71 טוֹב־לִי כִי־עֻנֵּיתִי לְמַעַן אֶלְמַד חֻקֶּיךָ׃
72 טוֹב־לִי תוֹרַת־פִּיךָ מֵאַלְפֵי זָהָב וָכָסֶף׃

טוֹב: good + מִן of comparison: better – עָנָה (pu pf 1 sg): be afflicted – לְמַעַן: so that – לָמַד (qal impf 1 sg): learn – חֹק (pl + 2 sg sf): decree – פֶּה (2 sg sf): mouth – אֶלֶף (cst pl): thousand – זָהָב: gold – כֶּסֶף: silver

---

Romans 8:18

Λογίζομαι γὰρ ὅτι οὐκ ἄξια τὰ παθήματα τοῦ νῦν καιροῦ πρὸς τὴν μέλλουσαν δόξαν ἀποκαλυφθῆναι εἰς ἡμᾶς.

> λογίζομαι (pres 1 sg): estimate – ἄξιος: worthy – πάθημα (pl): suffering – νῦν (adv): now – καιρός: time – πρός: in comparison with – μέλλω (pres ptcp sg + inf): be about to – ἀποκαλύπτω (aor pass inf): reveal

---

Large Catechism III 61

For there will be strange events if we are to abide in God's will. We shall have to suffer many thrusts and blows on that account from everything that seeks to oppose and prevent the fulfillment of the first two petitions.

Ezekiel 33:11

אֱמֹר אֲלֵיהֶם חַי־אָ֫נִי נְאֻם אֲדֹנָי יְהוִה אִם־אֶחְפֹּץ בְּמוֹת
הָרָשָׁע כִּי אִם־בְּשׁוּב רָשָׁע מִדַּרְכּוֹ וְחָיָה שׁ֫וּבוּ שׁ֫וּבוּ
מִדַּרְכֵיכֶם הָרָעִים וְלָ֫מָּה תָמ֫וּתוּ בֵּית יִשְׂרָאֵל׃

חַי־אָנִי (oath formula): as I live – נְאֻם (cst sg): utterance – אִם (after an oath): an emphatic negative – חָפֵץ (qal impf 1 sg): have pleasure in – מָ֫וֶת (cst): death – רָשָׁע: wicked – כִּי אִם: but – שׁוּב (qal inf cst/qal imv pl): turn – דֶּ֫רֶךְ (sg + 3 sg sf/pl + 2 pl sf): way – חָיָה (qal v-c pf 3 sg): live – רַע: evil – לָ֫מָּה: why? – מוּת (qal impf 2 pl): die

---

Matthew 23:37-38

37 Ἰερουσαλὴμ Ἰερουσαλήμ, ἡ ἀποκτείνουσα τοὺς προφήτας
καὶ λιθοβολοῦσα τοὺς ἀπεσταλμένους πρὸς αὐτήν, ποσάκις
ἠθέλησα ἐπισυναγαγεῖν τὰ τέκνα σου, ὃν τρόπον ὄρνις
ἐπισυνάγει τὰ νοσσία αὐτῆς ὑπὸ τὰς πτέρυγας, καὶ οὐκ
ἠθελήσατε. 38 ἰδοὺ ἀφίεται ὑμῖν ὁ οἶκος ὑμῶν ἔρημος.

ἀποκτείνω (pres ptcp sg f): kill – λιθοβολέω (pres ptcp sg f): stone to death – ἀποστέλλω (pf pass ptcp): send – ποσάκις: how often – θέλω: wish – ἐπισυνάγω (aor inf): gather together – τέκνον (pl): child – τρόπος: manner – ὄρνις: bird – νοσσίον: the young – πτέρυξ (pl): wing – ἀφίημι (pres pass): leave – ἔρημος: desolate

---

Formula of Concord SD XI 81

Just as God does not will sin and has no pleasure in sin, so He does not desire "the death of the wicked" [Ezek 33:11], nor has He pleasure in his condemnation.

OCTOBER 1

Hosea 14:10

מִי חָכָם וְיָבֵן אֵלֶּה נָבוֹן וְיֵדָעֵם
כִּי־יְשָׁרִים דַּרְכֵי יְהוָה וְצַדִּקִים יֵלְכוּ בָם
וּפֹשְׁעִים יִכָּשְׁלוּ בָם׃

חָכָם: wise – בִּין (qal juss 3 sg): understand – נָבוֹן: discerning – יָדַע (qal juss 3 sg + 3 pl sf): know – יָשָׁר (pl): right – דֶּרֶךְ (cst pl): way – צַדִּיק: the righteous – הָלַךְ (qal impf 3 pl): walk – פָּשַׁע (qal ptcp pl): the rebellious – כָּשַׁל (niph impf 3 pl): stumble

---

John 7:16-17

16ἀπεκρίθη οὖν αὐτοῖς [ὁ] Ἰησοῦς καὶ εἶπεν· ἡ ἐμὴ διδαχὴ
οὐκ ἔστιν ἐμὴ ἀλλὰ τοῦ πέμψαντός με· 17ἐάν τις θέλῃ τὸ
θέλημα αὐτοῦ ποιεῖν, γνώσεται περὶ τῆς διδαχῆς πότερον
ἐκ τοῦ θεοῦ ἐστιν ἢ ἐγὼ ἀπ' ἐμαυτοῦ λαλῶ.

διδαχή: teaching – πέμπω (aor act ptcp): send – θέλω (pres act subj 3 sg): desire, want, wish – γινώσκω (fut 3 sg): learn – πότερον: whether

---

Formula of Concord Ep XI 14

We should act with the greatest diligence, to live according to God's will. As St. Peter encourages in 2 Pet 1:10, "make your calling and election sure." We should especially cling to ‹not recede a hair's width from› the revealed Word, which cannot and will not fail us.

October 2

Isaiah 5:4

מַה־לַּעֲשׂוֹת עוֹד לְכַרְמִי וְלֹא עָשִׂיתִי בּוֹ
מַדּוּעַ קִוֵּיתִי לַעֲשׂוֹת עֲנָבִים וַיַּעַשׂ בְּאֻשִׁים׃

עָשָׂה (qal inf cst/qal pf 1 sg): do – עוֹד (adv): more – כֶּרֶם (1 sg sf): vineyard – מַדּוּעַ: why? – קָוָה (pi pf 1 sg): wait for – עֵנָב (pl): grape – בְּאֻשִׁים: bad fruit

---

Matthew 7:19-21

19πᾶν δένδρον μὴ ποιοῦν καρπὸν καλὸν ἐκκόπτεται καὶ εἰς
πῦρ βάλλεται. 20ἄρα γε ἀπὸ τῶν καρπῶν αὐτῶν ἐπιγνώσεσθε
αὐτούς. 21Οὐ πᾶς ὁ λέγων μοι· κύριε κύριε, εἰσελεύσεται
εἰς τὴν βασιλείαν τῶν οὐρανῶν, ἀλλʼ ὁ ποιῶν τὸ θέλημα τοῦ
πατρός μου τοῦ ἐν τοῖς οὐρανοῖς.

δένδρον: tree – ποιέω (pres ptcp n sg/pres ptcp masc sg): bear – καρπός: fruit – ἐκκόπτω (pres pass 3 sg): cut down – πῦρ: fire – βάλλω (pres pass 3 sg): throw – ἄρα γε consequently – ἐπιγινώσκω (fut dep 2 pl): recognize – ἐισέρχομαι (fut ind 3 sg): enter – βασιλεία: kingdom – θέλημα: will

---

Augsburg Confession VI 1

Our churches teach that this faith is bound to bring forth good fruit [Gal 5:22-23]. It is necessary to do good works commanded by God [Eph 2:10], because of God's will.

OCTOBER 3

Psalm 72:18

בָּר֥וּךְ ׀ יְהוָ֣ה אֱ֭לֹהִים אֱלֹהֵ֣י יִשְׂרָאֵ֑ל עֹשֵׂ֖ה נִפְלָא֣וֹת לְבַדּֽוֹ׃

בָּרַךְ (qal pass ptcp): blessed – עָשָׂה (qal ptcp cst sg): do – פָּלָא (niph ptcp pl): be extraordinary – לְבַד (3 sg sf): alone

Hebrews 11:17-19

17Πίστει προσενήνοχεν Ἀβραὰμ τὸν Ἰσαὰκ πειραζόμενος
καὶ τὸν μονογενῆ προσέφερεν, ὁ τὰς ἐπαγγελίας
ἀναδεξάμενος, 18πρὸς ὃν ἐλαλήθη ὅτι ἐν Ἰσαὰκ
κληθήσεταί σοι σπέρμα, 19λογισάμενος ὅτι καὶ ἐκ
νεκρῶν ἐγείρειν δυνατὸς ὁ θεός, ὅθεν αὐτὸν καὶ ἐν
παραβολῇ ἐκομίσατο.

πίστις: faith – προσφέρω (pf ind 3 sg/impf ind 3 sg): offer – πειράζω (pres pass ptcp): test – μονογενής: only son – ἐπαγγελία: promise – ἀναδέχομαι (aor ptcp): receive – λαλέω (aor pass 3 sg): say – καλέω (fut pass 3 sg): call – σπέρμα: offspring – λογίζομαι (aor mid ptcp): consider – νεκρός: dead – ἐγείρω (pres inf): raise – δυνατός: able – ὅθεν: from where – παραβολή: type, figure – κομίζω (aor mid 3 sg): receive back

Large Catechism III 56

Because He is God, He also claims the honor of giving much more and more abundantly than anyone can understand [Eph 3:20]. He is like an eternal, unfailing fountain. The more it pours forth and overflows, the more it continues to give. God desires nothing more seriously from us than that we ask Him for much and great things.

October 4

Psalm 39:5-6

5 הוֹדִיעֵנִי יְהוָה קִצִּי וּמִדַּת יָמַי מַה־הִיא
אֵדְעָה מֶה־חָדֵל אָנִי׃
6 הִנֵּה טְפָחוֹת נָתַתָּה יָמַי וְחֶלְדִּי כְאַיִן נֶגְדֶּךָ
אַךְ כָּל־הֶבֶל כָּל־אָדָם נִצָּב סֶלָה׃

יָדַע (hiph imv): cause to know – קֵץ (1 sg sf): end – מִדָּה (cst sg): measure, number – חָדֵל (adj): transient – טֶפַח (pl): handbreadth – חֶלֶד (1 sg sf): life span – אַיִן: nothing – נֶגֶד (2 sg sf): before – הֶבֶל: breath – נָצַב (niph ptcp): stand – סֶלָה: unknown musical term

---

1 Corinthians 7:29-31

29 Τοῦτο δέ φημι, ἀδελφοί, ὁ καιρὸς συνεσταλμένος ἐστίν·
τὸ λοιπόν, ἵνα καὶ οἱ ἔχοντες γυναῖκας ὡς μὴ ἔχοντες ὦσιν
30 καὶ οἱ κλαίοντες ὡς μὴ κλαίοντες καὶ οἱ χαίροντες ὡς μὴ
χαίροντες καὶ οἱ ἀγοράζοντες ὡς μὴ κατέχοντες, 31 καὶ οἱ
χρώμενοι τὸν κόσμον ὡς μὴ καταχρώμενοι· παράγει γὰρ τὸ
σχῆμα τοῦ κόσμου τούτου.

συστέλλω (pf pass ptcp): shorten – τὸ λοιπόν: from now on – κλαίω (pres ptcp pl): weep – ἀγοράζω (pres ptcp pl): buy – κατέχω (pres ptcp pl): possess – χράομαι (pres ptcp pl): use – καταχράομαι (pres ptcp pl): make full use of – παράγω (pres 3 sg): pass away – σχῆμα: form

---

Large Catechism I 252-253

So we are to be richly compensated for all that we do for our neighbor's good and from friendship. King Solomon also teaches this in Prov 19:17, "Whoever is generous to the poor lends to the Lord, and He will repay him for his deed."

October 5

Exodus 23:20

הִנֵּה אָנֹכִי שֹׁלֵחַ מַלְאָךְ לְפָנֶיךָ לִשְׁמָרְךָ בַּדָּרֶךְ וְלַהֲבִיאֲךָ
אֶל־הַמָּקוֹם אֲשֶׁר הֲכִנֹתִי׃

שָׁלַח (qal ptcp): send – מַלְאָךְ: messenger, angel – שָׁמַר (qal inf cst + 2 sg sf): guard – דֶּרֶךְ: way – בּוֹא (hiph inf cst + 2 sg sf): bring – כּוּן (hiph pf 1 sg): prepare

Revelation 2:1

Τῷ ἀγγέλῳ τῆς ἐν Ἐφέσῳ ἐκκλησίας γράψον· Τάδε λέγει ὁ κρατῶν τοὺς ἑπτὰ ἀστέρας ἐν τῇ δεξιᾷ αὐτοῦ, ὁ περιπατῶν ἐν μέσῳ τῶν ἑπτὰ λυχνιῶν τῶν χρυσῶν·

ἐκκλησία: church – γράφω (aor imv): write – κρατέω (pres ptcp): hold – ἑπτά: seven – ἀστήρ (pl): star – δεξιός (f): right hand – περιπατέω (pres ptcp): walk – ἐν μέσῳ: among – λυχνία: lampstand – χρυσοῦς: golden

Large Catechism II 12

But for the learned and those who are somewhat advanced, these three articles may all be expanded and divided into as many parts as there are words. But now for young scholars let it suffice to make the most necessary points, as we have said, that this *[first]* article refers to the Creation. We emphasize the words “Creator of heaven and earth.”

October 6

Deuteronomy 32:6

הֲ־לַיְהוָה תִּגְמְלוּ־זֹאת עַם נָבָל וְלֹא חָכָם
הֲלוֹא־הוּא אָבִיךָ קָּנֶךָ הוּא עָשְׂךָ וַיְכֹנְנֶךָ׃

הֲ: interrog ה – גָּמַל (qal impf 2 pl m): repay – עַם: people – נָבָל: foolish – חָכָם (adj): wise – קָנָה (qal pf 3 sg + 2 sg sf): create – כּוּן (polel v-c impf 3 sg): make, form

---

Luke 15:18-19

18ἀναστὰς πορεύσομαι πρὸς τὸν πατέρα μου καὶ ἐρῶ αὐτῷ·
πάτερ, ἥμαρτον εἰς τὸν οὐρανὸν καὶ ἐνώπιόν σου, 19οὐκέτι
εἰμὶ ἄξιος κληθῆναι υἱός σου· ποίησόν με ὡς ἕνα τῶν
μισθίων σου.

ἀνίστημι (aor ptcp): rise – πορεύομαι (fut ind 1 sg): go – ἐρῶ (fut ind of λέγω/εἶπον): say – ἁμαρτάνω (aor ind 1 sg): sin – οὐρανός: heaven – ἐνώπιον: against – ἄξιος: worthy – καλέω (aor pass inf): call – υἱός: son – ποιέω (aor imv): make – μίσθιος: hired man

---

Large Catechism I 13

So you can easily understand what and how much this *[first]* commandment requires. A person's entire heart and all his confidence must be placed in God alone and in no one else.

OCTOBER 7

Isaiah 40:5

וְנִגְלָה כְּבוֹד יְהוָה וְרָאוּ כָל־בָּשָׂר יַחְדָּו כִּי פִּי יְהוָה דִּבֵּר׃

נִגְלָה (niph v-c pf 3 sg): be revealed – כָּבוֹד (cst sg): glory – רָאָה (qal v-c pf 3 pl): see – בָּשָׂר: flesh – יַחְדָּו: together – פֶּה (cst sg): mouth – דִּבֶּר (pi pf 3 sg): speak

---

Luke 3:21-22

21 Ἐγένετο δὲ ἐν τῷ βαπτισθῆναι ἅπαντα τὸν λαὸν καὶ
Ἰησοῦ βαπτισθέντος καὶ προσευχομένου ἀνεῳχθῆναι τὸν
οὐρανὸν 22 καὶ καταβῆναι τὸ πνεῦμα τὸ ἅγιον σωματικῷ
εἴδει ὡς περιστερὰν ἐπ' αὐτόν, καὶ φωνὴν ἐξ οὐρανοῦ
γενέσθαι· Σὺ εἶ ὁ υἱός μου ὁ ἀγαπητός, ἐν σοὶ εὐδόκησα.

βαπτίζω (aor pass inf/aor pass ptcp): baptize – ἅπας: all – λαός: people – προσεύχομαι (pres ptcp): pray – ἀνοίγω (aor pass inf): open – καταβαίνω: (aor inf): come down – σωματικός (adj): bodily – εἶδος: form – περιστερά: dove – φωνή: voice – γίνομαι (aor inf): come – ἀγαπητός: beloved – εὐδοκέω (aor 1 sg): take delight

---

Formula of Concord SD XI 6

His foreknowledge preserves order also in wicked acts or works, since a limit and measure is fixed by God for the evil that God does not will. He limits how far it should go, how long it should last, and when and how He will hinder and punish it. God the Lord rules over all [Ps 103:19] of this so that it must flow to the glory of the divine name and to the salvation of His elect, and for that reason the godless must be astonished [1 Cor 2:7-8].

OCTOBER 8

Psalm 107:8-9

8 יוֹדוּ לַיהוָה חַסְדּוֹ וְנִפְלְאוֹתָיו לִבְנֵי אָדָם׃
9 כִּי־הִשְׂבִּיעַ נֶפֶשׁ שֹׁקֵקָה וְנֶפֶשׁ רְעֵבָה מִלֵּא־טוֹב׃

יָדָה (hiph juss 3 pl): give thanks for – פָּלָא (niph ptcp pl): be extraordinary = marvelous deeds – אָדָם: man – שָׂבַע (hiph pf 3 sg): satisfy – נֶפֶשׁ: soul, person – שָׁקַק (qal ptcp): thirsty – רָעֵב (adj f): hungry – מָלֵא (pi pf 3 sg): fill

---

Ephesians 1:5-7

5 προορίσας ἡμᾶς εἰς υἱοθεσίαν διὰ Ἰησοῦ Χριστοῦ εἰς
αὐτόν, κατὰ τὴν εὐδοκίαν τοῦ θελήματος αὐτοῦ, 6 εἰς
ἔπαινον δόξης τῆς χάριτος αὐτοῦ ἧς ἐχαρίτωσεν ἡμᾶς
ἐν τῷ ἠγαπημένῳ. 7 Ἐν ᾧ ἔχομεν τὴν ἀπολύτρωσιν διὰ
τοῦ αἵματος αὐτοῦ, τὴν ἄφεσιν τῶν παραπτωμάτων, κατὰ
τὸ πλοῦτος τῆς χάριτος αὐτοῦ.

προορίζω (aor ptcp): predestine – υἱοθεσία: adoption – εὐδοκία: pleasure – θέλημα: will – ἔπαινος: praise – δόξα: (gen = adj): glorious – χάρις: grace – ἧς for ἥν: gen by attraction – χαριτόω (aor ind 3 sg): give freely – ἀγαπάω (pf pass ptcp): beloved – ἀπολύτρωσις: redemption – αἷμα: blood – ἄφεσις: forgiveness – παράπτωμα: sin – πλοῦτος: riches

---

Formula of Concord SD XI 5

God's eternal election, or predestination, means God's preordaining to salvation. It does not include both the godly and the wicked, but only God's children, who were elected and ordained to eternal life before the world's foundation was laid. As Paul says in Eph 1:4-5, "He chose us in Him. . . . He predestined us for adoption through Jesus Christ."

October 9

Jeremiah 32:18

עֹשֶׂה חֶסֶד לַאֲלָפִים וּמְשַׁלֵּם עֲוֺן אָבוֹת אֶל־חֵיק בְּנֵיהֶם אַחֲרֵיהֶם הָאֵל הַגָּדוֹל הַגִּבּוֹר יְהוָה צְבָאוֹת שְׁמוֹ׃

עָשָׂה (qal ptcp sg): show – חֶסֶד: faithful love – אֶלֶף (pl): thousand – שָׁלֵם (pi ptcp): repay – עָוֺן: sin (as guilt) – אָב (pl): father – חֵיק: bosom, lap – בֵּן (pl): son – אַחֲרֵי (3 pl sf): after – גָּדוֹל: great – גִּבּוֹר: powerful – צָבָא (pl): army, host

1 Corinthians 4:5

ὥστε μὴ πρὸ καιροῦ τι κρίνετε ἕως ἂν ἔλθῃ ὁ κύριος, ὃς καὶ φωτίσει τὰ κρυπτὰ τοῦ σκότους καὶ φανερώσει τὰς βουλὰς τῶν καρδιῶν· καὶ τότε ὁ ἔπαινος γενήσεται ἑκάστῳ ἀπὸ τοῦ θεοῦ.

καιρός: appointed time – κρίνω (pres imv 2 pl): judge – ἔρχομαι (aor subj 3 sg): come – φωτίζω (fut ind 3 sg): bring to light – κρυπτός: hidden – σκότος: darkness – φανερόω (fut ind 3 sg): expose – βουλή (pl): motive – καρδία: heart – ἔπαινος: praise – ἕκαστος: each

Smalcald Articles III VII 1

It is not in our power to judge which, how great, and how many the sins *[of a person]* are. This belongs to God alone.

OCTOBER 10

Ecclesiastes 4:9-10

9 טוֹבִים הַשְּׁנַיִם מִן־הָאֶחָד
אֲשֶׁר יֵשׁ־לָהֶם שָׂכָר טוֹב בַּעֲמָלָם׃
10 כִּי אִם־יִפֹּלוּ הָאֶחָד יָקִים אֶת־חֲבֵרוֹ
וְאִילוֹ הָאֶחָד שֶׁיִּפּוֹל וְאֵין שֵׁנִי לַהֲקִימוֹ׃

טוֹב + מִן of comparison: better – שְׁנַיִם: two – אֶחָד: one – יֵשׁ: there is – שָׂכָר: reward, return – עָמָל (3 pl sf): toil – נָפַל (qal impf 3 pl/3 sg): fall – קוּם (hiph impf 3 sg): help up – חָבֵר (3 sg sf): companion – אִילוֹ = אִי: alas + לוֹ: pity the man – שֶׁ = אֲשֶׁר – שֵׁנִי: a second person

---

Hebrews 10:24-25

24καὶ κατανοῶμεν ἀλλήλους εἰς παροξυσμὸν ἀγάπης καὶ καλῶν ἔργων, 25μὴ ἐγκαταλείποντες τὴν ἐπισυναγωγὴν ἑαυτῶν, καθὼς ἔθος τισίν, ἀλλὰ παρακαλοῦντες, καὶ τοσούτῳ μᾶλλον ὅσῳ βλέπετε ἐγγίζουσαν τὴν ἡμέραν.

κατανοέω (pres subj 1 pl): consider – παροξυσμός: inciting – ἐγκαταλείπω (pres ptcp): abandon – ἐπισυναγωγή: meeting together – ἔθος: habit – τίς (dat pl): some – παρακαλέω (pres ptcp): encourage – τοσούτῳ μᾶλλον ὅσῳ: by so much more as = all the more as – βλέπω (pres ind 2 pl): see – ἐγγίζω (pres ptcp): approach

---

Large Catechism II 51-52

This group *[the Church]* is called together by the Holy Spirit in one faith, one mind, and understanding, with many different gifts, yet agreeing in love, without sects or schisms [Eph 4:5-8,11]. I am also a part and member of this same group, a sharer and joint owner of all the goods it possesses [Rom 8:17].

OCTOBER 11

Psalm 34:2-3

2 אֲבָרְכָה אֶת־יְהוָה בְּכָל־עֵת תָּמִיד תְּהִלָּתוֹ בְּפִי׃
3 בַּיהוָה תִּתְהַלֵּל נַפְשִׁי יִשְׁמְעוּ עֲנָוִים וְיִשְׂמָחוּ׃

בָּרַךְ (pi coh 1 sg): praise – עֵת: time – תָּמִיד (adv): always – תְּהִלָּה (3 sg sf): praise – פֶּה (1 sg sf): mouth – הָלַל (hithp impf 3 sg f): boast – שָׁמַע (qal juss 3 pl): hear – עָנָו (pl): afflicted – שָׂמַח (qal juss 3 pl): rejoice

---

Acts 16:25

Κατὰ δὲ τὸ μεσονύκτιον Παῦλος καὶ Σιλᾶς προσευχόμενοι ὕμνουν τὸν θεόν, ἐπηκροῶντο δὲ αὐτῶν οἱ δέσμιοι.

μεσονύκτιον: midnight – προσεύχομαι (pres ptcp pl): pray – ὑμνέω (impf ind 3 pl): sing hymns of praise – ἐπακροάομαι (impf ind 3 pl): listen to – δέσμιος (pl): prisoner

---

Augsburg Confession XX 36-37

For without faith, human nature cannot, in any way, do the works of the First or Second Commandment [1 Cor 2:14]. Without faith, human nature does not call upon God, nor expect anything from Him, nor bear the cross [Matt 16:24].

October 12

Psalm 119:145

קָרָ֣אתִי בְכָל־לֵ֭ב עֲנֵ֥נִי יְהוָ֗ה חֻקֶּ֥יךָ אֶצֹּֽרָה׃

קָרָא (qal pf 1 sg): call – עָנָה (qal imv + 1 sg sf): answer – חֹק (pl + 2 sg sf): decree – נָצַר (qal coh 1 sg): obey

Romans 8:12-14

12 Ἄρα οὖν, ἀδελφοί, ὀφειλέται ἐσμὲν οὐ τῇ σαρκὶ τοῦ κατὰ
σάρκα ζῆν, 13 εἰ γὰρ κατὰ σάρκα ζῆτε, μέλλετε ἀποθνῄσκειν·
εἰ δὲ πνεύματι τὰς πράξεις τοῦ σώματος θανατοῦτε,
ζήσεσθε. 14 ὅσοι γὰρ πνεύματι θεοῦ ἄγονται, οὗτοι υἱοὶ
θεοῦ εἰσιν.

ὀφειλέτης (pl): one who has an obligation – σάρξ: flesh, sinful nature – ζάω (pres inf/pres ind 2 pl/fut ind 2 pl): live – μέλλω (pres ind 2 pl): be about to – ἀποθνῄσκω (pres inf): die – πνεῦμα: Spirit – πράξις (pl): deed – σῶμα: body – θανατόω (pres ind 2 pl): put to death – ἄγω (pres pass 3 pl): lead

Large Catechism II 11

The child could say, "This is my God: first, the Father, who has created heaven and earth. Besides this One only, I regard nothing else as God. For there is no one else who could create heaven and earth."

October 13

Isaiah 42:8

אֲנִי יְהוָה הוּא שְׁמִי
וּכְבוֹדִי לְאַחֵר לֹא־אֶתֵּן וּתְהִלָּתִי לַפְּסִילִים׃

שֵׁם (1 sg sf): name – כָּבוֹד (1 sg sf): glory – אַחֵר: other, another – נָתַן (qal impf 1 sg): give – תְּהִלָּה (1 sg sf): praise – פָּסִיל (pl): idol

Matthew 4:10

τότε λέγει αὐτῷ ὁ Ἰησοῦς,Ὕπαγε, Σατανᾶ· γέγραπται γάρ· Κύριον τὸν θεόν σου προσκυνήσεις καὶ αὐτῷ μόνῳ λατρεύσεις.

ὑπάγω (pres imv 2 sg): go away – γράφω (pf pass 3 sg): be written – κύριος: Lord – προσκυνέω (fut ind 2 sg): worship – μόνος: alone – λατρεύω (fut ind 2 sg): serve

Large Catechism I 35

He *[God]* has also made this known in all history, as the Scriptures abundantly show and daily experience still teaches. From the beginning, he has utterly uprooted all idolatry. Because of idolatry, He has uprooted both heathen people and Jewish people. To this day, He overthrows all false worship, so that all who remain therein must finally perish [2 Chron 7:19-20].

October 14

Psalm 34:19-20

19קָרוֹב יְהוָה לְנִשְׁבְּרֵי־לֵב וְאֶת־דַּכְּאֵי־רוּחַ יוֹשִׁיעַ׃
20רַבּוֹת רָעוֹת צַדִּיק וּמִכֻּלָּם יַצִּילֶנּוּ יְהוָה׃

קָרוֹב: near – שָׁבַר (niph ptcp cst pl) + לֵב: broken-hearted – דַּכָּא (adj cst pl): crushed – רוּחַ: spirit – יָשַׁע (hiph impf 3 sg): save – רַב (adj pl): many – רָעָה (cst pl): troubles – צַדִּיק: righteous – נָצַל (hiph impf 3 sg + 3 sg sf): deliver

---

Philippians 4:19-20

19ὁ δὲ θεός μου πληρώσει πᾶσαν χρείαν ὑμῶν κατὰ τὸ
πλοῦτος αὐτοῦ ἐν δόξῃ ἐν Χριστῷ Ἰησοῦ. 20τῷ δὲ θεῷ
καὶ πατρὶ ἡμῶν ἡ δόξα εἰς τοὺς αἰῶνας τῶν αἰώνων, ἀμήν.

πληρόω (fut ind 3 sg): fill – χρεία: need – πλοῦτος: riches – δόξα: glory – αἰών: age, eternity

---

Large Catechism II 13

He *[God]* has given and constantly preserves [Ps 36:6] for me my body, soul, and life, my members great and small, all my senses, reason, and understanding, and so on.

October 15

Psalm 86:11

הוֹרֵנִי יְהוָה דַּרְכֶּךָ אֲהַלֵּךְ בַּאֲמִתֶּךָ יַחֵד לְבָבִי לְיִרְאָה שְׁמֶךָ׃

יָרָה (hiph imv + 1 sg sf): teach – דֶּרֶךְ (2 sg sf): way – הָלַךְ (pi impf 1 sg): walk – אֱמֶת (2 sg sf): truth – יָחַד (pi imv): unite – לֵבָב (1 sg sf): heart – יָרֵא (qal inf cst): fear – שֵׁם (2 sg sf): name

---

Galatians 6:14-15

14’Εμοὶ δὲ μὴ γένοιτο καυχᾶσθαι εἰ μὴ ἐν τῷ σταυρῷ τοῦ
κυρίου ἡμῶν ’Ιησοῦ Χριστοῦ, δι’ οὗ ἐμοὶ κόσμος ἐσταύρωται
κἀγὼ κόσμῳ. 15οὔτε γὰρ περιτομή τί ἐστιν οὔτε ἀκροβυστία
ἀλλὰ καινὴ κτίσις.

μὴ γένοιτο (aor optative): God forbid! – καυχάομαι (pres inf): boast – σταυρός: cross – κόσμος: world – σταυρόω (pf pass 3 sg): crucify – περιτομή: circumcision – τι: anything – ἀκροβυστία: uncircumcision – καινός: new – κτίσις: creation

---

Smalcald Articles III XIII 2

The entire individual, both his person and his works, is declared to be righteous and holy from pure grace and mercy, shed upon us and spread over us in Christ.

October 16

Proverbs 1:33

וְשֹׁמֵ֣עַ לִ֭י יִשְׁכָּן־בֶּ֑טַח וְ֝שַׁאֲנַ֗ן מִפַּ֥חַד רָעָֽה׃

שֹׁמֵעַ (qal ptcp): the one who listens – שָׁכַן (qal impf 3 sg): live – בֶּטַח (adv): safely – שַׁאַן (palal v-c pf): be secure – פַּחַד (cst sg): fear – רָעָה: evil, harm

---

Matthew 14:26-27

26οἱ δὲ μαθηταὶ ἰδόντες αὐτὸν ἐπὶ τῆς θαλάσσης
περιπατοῦντα ἐταράχθησαν λέγοντες ὅτι φάντασμά
ἐστιν, καὶ ἀπὸ τοῦ φόβου ἔκραξαν. 27εὐθὺς δὲ ἐλάλησεν
[ὁ Ἰησοῦς] αὐτοῖς λέγων· Θαρσεῖτε, ἐγώ εἰμι· μὴ φοβεῖσθε.

μαθητής (pl): disciple – ἰδόντες (aor ptcp pl of ὁράω): see – θάλασσα: sea – περιπατέω (pres ptcp): walk – ταράσσω (aor pass ind 3 pl): be terrified – φάντασμα: ghost – φόβος: fear – κράζω (aor ind 3 pl): cry out – λαλέω (aor ind 3 sg): speak – θαρσέω (pres imv 2 pl): be courageous – φοβέομαι (pres imv 2 pl): fear

---

Large Catechism I 3

If your faith and trust is right, then your god is also true. On the other hand, if your trust is false and wrong, then you do not have the true God. For these two belong together, faith and God [Heb 11:6]. Now, I say that whatever you set your heart on and put your trust in is truly your god.

OCTOBER 17

Psalm 96:8

הָבוּ לַיהוָה כְּבוֹד שְׁמוֹ שְׂאוּ־מִנְחָה וּבֹאוּ לְחַצְרוֹתָיו׃

יָהַב (qal imv pl): give – כָּבוֹד (cst sg): glory – שֵׁם (3 sg sf): name – נָשָׂא (qal imv pl): bring – מִנְחָה: offering – בּוֹא (qal imv pl): come – חָצֵר (pl + 3 sg sf): court

---

James 2:15-17

15 ἐὰν ἀδελφὸς ἢ ἀδελφὴ γυμνοὶ ὑπάρχωσιν καὶ λειπόμενοι
τῆς ἐφημέρου τροφῆς 16 εἴπῃ δέ τις αὐτοῖς ἐξ ὑμῶν·
ὑπάγετε ἐν εἰρήνῃ, θερμαίνεσθε καὶ χορτάζεσθε, μὴ δῶτε
δὲ αὐτοῖς τὰ ἐπιτήδεια τοῦ σώματος, τί τὸ ὄφελος; 17 οὕτως
καὶ ἡ πίστις, ἐὰν μὴ ἔχῃ ἔργα, νεκρά ἐστιν καθ' ἑαυτήν.

γυμνός: without clothes – ὑπάρχω (pres subj 3 pl): be – λείπω (pres pass ptcp): lack – ἐφήμερος: daily – τροφή: food – εἶπον (aor subj 3 sg): say – ὑπάγω (pres imv 2 pl): go – εἰρήνη: peace – θερμαίνομαι (pres imv 2 pl): keep warm – χορτάζω (pres pass imv 2 pl): eat one's fill – δίδωμι (aor subj 2 pl): give – ἐπιτήδειος: what is necessary – σῶμα: body – ὄφελος: benefit, good – πίστις: faith – ἔχω (pres subj 3 sg): have – ἔργον (pl): work – νεκρός: dead

---

Large Catechism I 190

If, therefore, you send away someone who is naked when you could clothe him, you have caused him to freeze to death. If you see someone suffer hunger and do not give him food, you have caused him to starve. So also, if you see anyone innocently sentenced to death or in similar distress, and do not save him, although you know ways and means to do so, you have killed him.

October 18

Psalm 36:8,10

8 מַה־יָּקָר חַסְדְּךָ אֱלֹהִים
וּבְנֵי אָדָם בְּצֵל כְּנָפֶיךָ יֶחֱסָיוּן׃
10 כִּי־עִמְּךָ מְקוֹר חַיִּים בְּאוֹרְךָ נִרְאֶה־אוֹר׃

יָקָר (adj): priceless – חֶסֶד (2 sg sf): faithful love – אֱלֹהִים (voc): God – צֵל (cst sg): shadow – כָּנָף (pl + 2 sg sf): wing – חָסָה (qal impf 3 pl): seek refuge – מָקוֹר (cst): fountain – חַיִּים: life – אוֹר: light – רָאָה (qal impf 1 pl): see

---

John 1:48-49

48λέγει αὐτῷ Ναθαναήλ· πόθεν με γινώσκεις; ἀπεκρίθη
Ἰησοῦς καὶ εἶπεν αὐτῷ· πρὸ τοῦ σε Φίλιππον φωνῆσαι
ὄντα ὑπὸ τὴν συκῆν εἶδόν σε. 49ἀπεκρίθη αὐτῷ Ναθαναήλ·
ῥαββί, σὺ εἶ ὁ υἱὸς τοῦ θεοῦ, σὺ βασιλεὺς εἶ τοῦ Ἰσραήλ.

πόθεν: how? – γινώσκω (pres ind 2 sg): know – πρό: before – φωνέω (aor inf): call – ὄντα (pres ptcp of εἰμί): be – συκή: fig tree – εἶδον (aor of ὁράω): see – υἱός: Son – βασιλεύς: King

---

Large Catechism I 300

This last *[the tenth]* commandment, therefore, is given not for cheaters in the eyes of the world. It is for the most pious, who want to be praised and to be called honest and upright people.

Psalm 103:3-4

3 הַסֹּלֵחַ לְכָל־עֲוֺנֵכִי הָרֹפֵא לְכָל־תַּחֲלֻאָיְכִי׃

4 הַגּוֹאֵל מִשַּׁחַת חַיָּיְכִי הַמְעַטְּרֵכִי חֶסֶד וְרַחֲמִים׃

סָלַח (qal ptcp): forgive – עָוֺן (sg + 2 sg sf): sin (as guilt) – כִי: poetic 2 sg f sf referring to the soul (נֶפֶשׁ) of the writer – רָפָא (qal ptcp): heal – תַּחֲלֻאִים (2 sg sf): diseases – גָּאַל (qal ptcp): redeem – שַׁחַת: pit – חַיִּים (2 sg sf): life – עָטַר (pi ptcp + 2 sg sf): crown – חֶסֶד: faithful love – רַחֲמִים: compassion

Galatians 5:1

Τῇ ἐλευθερίᾳ ἡμᾶς Χριστὸς ἠλευθέρωσεν· στήκετε οὖν καὶ μὴ πάλιν ζυγῷ δουλείας ἐνέχεσθε.

ἐλευθερία: freedom – ἐλευθερόω (aor ind 3 sg): set free – στήκω (pres imv 2 pl): stand – ζυγόν: yoke – δουλεία: slavery – ἐνέχω (pres pass imv 2 pl): be subject to

Formula of Concord SD X 10-11

We also believe, teach, and confess that at a time of confession, when the enemies of God's Word want to suppress the pure doctrine of the Holy Gospel, God's entire church, indeed, every single Christian, but especially the ministers of the Word, as the directors of the community of God ‹God's church›, is bound by God's Word to confess the doctrine freely and openly. They are bound to confess every aspect of ‹pure› religion, not only in words, but also in works and actions. . . . For it is written: "For freedom Christ has set us free; stand firm therefore, and do not submit again to a yoke of slavery" (Gal 5:1).

October 20

Deuteronomy 8:5-6

5 וְיָדַעְתָּ עִם־לְבָבֶךָ כִּי כַּאֲשֶׁר יְיַסֵּר אִישׁ אֶת־בְּנוֹ יְהוָה
אֱלֹהֶיךָ מְיַסְּרֶךָּ׃ 6 וְשָׁמַרְתָּ אֶת־מִצְוֹת יְהוָה אֱלֹהֶיךָ
לָלֶכֶת בִּדְרָכָיו וּלְיִרְאָה אֹתוֹ׃

יָדַע (qal v-c pf 2 sg): know – עִם־לְבָבֶךָ: in your heart – יָסַר (pi impf 3 sg/pi ptcp + 2 sg sf): discipline – שָׁמַר (qal v-c pf 2 sg): observe – מִצְוָה (pl): command – הָלַךְ (qal inf cst): walk – דֶּרֶךְ (pl + 3 sg sf): way – יָרֵא (qal inf cst): fear

Romans 12:2

καὶ μὴ συσχηματίζεσθε τῷ αἰῶνι τούτῳ, ἀλλὰ μεταμορφοῦσθε τῇ ἀνακαινώσει τοῦ νοὸς εἰς τὸ δοκιμάζειν ὑμᾶς τί τὸ θέλημα τοῦ θεοῦ, τὸ ἀγαθὸν καὶ εὐάρεστον καὶ τέλειον.

συσχηματίζω (pres pass imv 2 pl): conform to – αἰών: world – μεταμορφόω (pres pass imv 2 pl): be transformed – ἀνακαίνωσις: renewing – νοῦς: mind – δοκιμάζω (pres inf): approve – θέλημα: will – ἀγαθός: good – εὐάρεστος: pleasing – τέλειος: perfect

Formula of Concord SD VI 12

Thereafter, the Holy Spirit uses the Law in order to teach the regenerate from it and to point out and show them in the Ten Commandments what is the "will of God, what is ‹good and› acceptable and perfect" (Rom 12:2) in what "good works, which God prepared beforehand, that we should walk" (Eph 2:10).

OCTOBER 21

Psalm 147:19-20

19 מַגִּיד דְּבָרוֹ [דְּבָרָיו] לְיַעֲקֹב חֻקָּיו וּמִשְׁפָּטָיו
לְיִשְׂרָאֵל׃
20 לֹא עָשָׂה כֵן לְכָל־גּוֹי וּמִשְׁפָּטִים בַּל־יְדָעוּם
הַלְלוּ־יָהּ׃

נָגַד (hiph ptcp): tell, make known – דָּבָר (qere: pl + 3 sg sf): word – חֹק (pl + 3 sg sf): decree – מִשְׁפָּט (pl + 3 sg sf): law – גּוֹי: nation – בַּל: not – יָדַע (qal pf 3 pl + 3 pl sf): know – הָלַל (pi imv): praise

---

Romans 3:1-2

1Τί οὖν τὸ περισσὸν τοῦ Ἰουδαίου ἢ τίς ἡ ὠφέλεια τῆς
περιτομῆς; 2πολὺ κατὰ πάντα τρόπον. πρῶτον μὲν [γὰρ]
ὅτι ἐπιστεύθησαν τὰ λόγια τοῦ θεοῦ.

περισσόν: advantage – ὠφέλεια: value – περιτομή: circumcision – τρόπος: way – πιστεύω (aor pass 3 pl): be entrusted with – λόγιον: saying, oracle

---

Large Catechism II 42

Through the Word He *[the Spirit]* reveals and preaches, He illumines and enkindles hearts, so that they understand, accept, cling to, and persevere in the Word [1 Cor 2:12].

OCTOBER 22

Psalm 37:5-6

[5]גּוֹל עַל־יְהוָה דַּרְכֶּךָ וּבְטַח עָלָיו וְהוּא יַעֲשֶׂה׃
[6]וְהוֹצִיא כָאוֹר צִדְקֶךָ וּמִשְׁפָּטֶךָ כַּצָּהֳרָיִם׃

גָּלַל (qal imv sg): roll – דֶּרֶךְ (2 sg sf): way – בָּטַח (qal imv sg): trust – עָשָׂה (qal impf 3 sg): do – יָצָא (hiph v-c pf 3 sg): bring out – אוֹר: light, dawn – צֶדֶק (2 sg sf): righteousness – מִשְׁפָּט (2 sg sf): judgment = the justice of your cause – צָהֳרַיִם: noon

Matthew 7:7-8

[7]Αἰτεῖτε καὶ δοθήσεται ὑμῖν, ζητεῖτε καὶ εὑρήσετε, κρούετε καὶ ἀνοιγήσεται ὑμῖν· [8]πᾶς γὰρ ὁ αἰτῶν λαμβάνει καὶ ὁ ζητῶν εὑρίσκει καὶ τῷ κρούοντι ἀνοιγήσεται.

αἰτέω (pres imv pl/pres ptcp): ask – δίδωμι (fut pass 3 sg): give – ζητέω (pres imv pl/pres ptcp): seek – εὑρίσκω (fut 2 pl): find – κρούω (pres imv pl/pres ptcp): knock – ἀνοίγω (fut pass 3 sg): be opened

Large Catechism III 4

But before we explain the Lord's Prayer part by part, it is most necessary first to encourage and stir people to prayer, as Christ and the apostles also have done [Matt 6:5-15].

October 23

Ecclesiastes 3:10

רָאִיתִי אֶת־הָעִנְיָן אֲשֶׁר נָתַן אֱלֹהִים לִבְנֵי הָאָדָם לַעֲנוֹת
בּוֹ׃

רָאָה (qal pf 1 sg): see – עִנְיָן: burden – נָתַן (qal pf 3 sg): place – עָנָה (qal inf cst): be concerned, troubled

---

1 Corinthians 2:9

ἀλλὰ καθὼς γέγραπται· ἃ ὀφθαλμὸς οὐκ εἶδεν καὶ οὖς οὐκ ἤκουσεν καὶ ἐπὶ καρδίαν ἀνθρώπου οὐκ ἀνέβη, ἃ ἡτοίμασεν ὁ θεὸς τοῖς ἀγαπῶσιν αὐτόν.

γράφω (pf pass 3 sg): written – ὀφθαλμός: eye – εἶδεν (aor ind of ὁράω): see – οὖς: ear – ἀκούω (aor ind 3 sg): hear – καρδία: heart – ἀναβαίνω (aor act 3 sg): enter – ἑτοιμάζω (aor ind 3 sg): prepare – ἀγαπάω (pres ptcp pl): love

---

Formula of Concord SD XI 23

God has prepared salvation not only in general in this counsel, purpose, and ordination. In grace He has considered and chosen to salvation each and every one of the elect who are to be saved through Christ.

October 24

Psalm 31:15-16

15וַאֲנִי עָלֶיךָ בָטַחְתִּי יְהוָה אָמַרְתִּי אֱלֹהַי אָתָּה׃
16בְּיָדְךָ עִתֹּתָי הַצִּילֵנִי מִיַּד־אוֹיְבַי וּמֵרֹדְפָי׃

בָּטַח (qal pf 1 sg): trust – אָמַר (qal pf 1 sg): say – יָד (2 sg sf): hand – עֵת (pl + 1 sg sf): time – נָצַל (hiph imv + 1 sg sf): deliver – אוֹיֵב (pl + 1 sg sf): enemy – רָדַף (qal ptcp pl + 1 sg sf): pursuer

---

1 Peter 5:6-7

6Ταπεινώθητε οὖν ὑπὸ τὴν κραταιὰν χεῖρα τοῦ θεοῦ,
ἵνα ὑμᾶς ὑψώσῃ ἐν καιρῷ, 7πᾶσαν τὴν μέριμναν ὑμῶν
ἐπιρίψαντες ἐπ’ αὐτόν, ὅτι αὐτῷ μέλει περὶ ὑμῶν.

ταπεινόω (aor pass imv 2 pl): humble – κραταιός: mighty – χείρ: hand – ὑψόω (aor subj 3 sg): exalt – καιρός: the right/proper time – μέριμνα: anxiety – ἐπιρίπτω (aor ptcp pl): cast – αὐτῷ μέλει: it is a concern to him

---

Small Catechism Table of Duties

Likewise, you who are younger, be subject to the elders. Clothe yourselves, all of you, with humility toward one another, for "God opposes the proud but gives grace to the humble." Humble yourselves, therefore, under the mighty hand of God so that at the proper time he may exalt you (1 Pet 5:5-6).

October 25

Psalm 126:1-2

1 בְּשׁוּב יְהוָה אֶת־שִׁיבַת צִיּוֹן הָיִינוּ כְּחֹלְמִים׃
2 אָז יִמָּלֵא שְׂחוֹק פִּינוּ וּלְשׁוֹנֵנוּ רִנָּה
אָז יֹאמְרוּ בַגּוֹיִם הִגְדִּיל יְהוָה לַעֲשׂוֹת עִם־אֵלֶּה׃

שׁוּב (qal inf cst): return – שִׁיבָה: restoration – חָלַם (qal ptcp pl): dream – מָלֵא (niph impf 3 sg): be filled – שְׂחוֹק: laughter – פֶּה (1 pl sf): mouth – לָשׁוֹן (sg + 1 pl sf): tongue – רִנָּה: song of joy – אָמַר (qal impf 3 pl): say – גּוֹי (pl): nation – גָּדַל (hiph pf 3 sg): do great things – עָשָׂה (qal inf cst): do

---

2 Thessalonians 2:13-14

13 Ἡμεῖς δὲ ὀφείλομεν εὐχαριστεῖν τῷ θεῷ πάντοτε περὶ
ὑμῶν, ἀδελφοὶ ἠγαπημένοι ὑπὸ κυρίου, ὅτι εἵλατο ὑμᾶς
ὁ θεὸς ἀπαρχὴν εἰς σωτηρίαν ἐν ἁγιασμῷ πνεύματος
καὶ πίστει ἀληθείας, 14 εἰς ὃ [καὶ] ἐκάλεσεν ὑμᾶς διὰ
τοῦ εὐαγγελίου ἡμῶν εἰς περιποίησιν δόξης τοῦ κυρίου
ἡμῶν Ἰησοῦ Χριστοῦ.

ὀφείλω (pres ind 1 pl): ought – εὐχαριστέω (pres inf): thank – ἀγαπάω (pf pass ptcp pl): beloved – εἵλατο (aor mid 3 sg of αἱρέω): choose – ἀπαρχή: firstfruits – σωτηρία: salvation – ἁγιασμός: sanctifying work – ἀλήθεια: truth – περιποίησις: obtaining, acquiring possession

---

Formula of Concord SD XI 12

There is no question that lack of repentance or despair should not in any way be caused or strengthened by the sound sense or right use of this teaching about God's eternal foreknowledge.

OCTOBER 26

Isaiah 40:7-8

7יָבֵשׁ חָצִיר נָבֵל צִיץ כִּי רוּחַ יְהוָה נָשְׁבָה בּוֹ
אָכֵן חָצִיר הָעָם׃
8יָבֵשׁ חָצִיר נָבֵל צִיץ
וּדְבַר־אֱלֹהֵינוּ יָקוּם לְעוֹלָם׃

יָבֵשׁ (qal pf 3 sg): wither – חָצִיר: grass – נָבֵל (qal pf 3 sg): wither and fall – צִיץ: flower – רוּחַ: breath – נָשַׁב (qal pf 3 sg f): blow – אָכֵן: surely – עַם: people – קוּם (qal impf 3 sg): stand – לְעוֹלָם: forever

---

1 Peter 1:23-25

23ἀναγεγεννημένοι οὐκ ἐκ σπορᾶς φθαρτῆς ἀλλὰ ἀφθάρτου
διὰ λόγου ζῶντος θεοῦ καὶ μένοντος.
24διότι πᾶσα σὰρξ ὡς
χόρτος καὶ πᾶσα δόξα αὐτῆς ὡς ἄνθος χόρτου· ἐξηράνθη
ὁ χόρτος καὶ τὸ ἄνθος ἐξέπεσεν·
25τὸ δὲ ῥῆμα κυρίου μένει
εἰς τὸν αἰῶνα. τοῦτο δέ ἐστιν τὸ ῥῆμα τὸ εὐαγγελισθὲν
εἰς ὑμᾶς.

ἀναγεννάω (pf pass ptcp pl): be born again – σπορά: seed – φθαρτός: perishable – ἄφθαρτος: imperishable – ζάω (pres ptcp sg): live – μένω (pres ptcp sg): endure – σάρξ: flesh – χόρτος: grass – ἄνθος: flower – ξηραίνω (aor pass 3 sg): wither – ἐκπίπτω (aor ind 3 sg): fall – ῥῆμα: word – αἰών: eternity – εὐαγγελίζω (aor pass ptcp): proclaim

---

Apology XXIII (XI) 70

You will discern that in God's judgment no lies against God's Word remain standing, as Isaiah says, "All flesh is grass, and all its beauty is like the flower of the field" (40:6).

OCTOBER 27

Psalm 18:40

וַתְּאַזְּרֵנִי חַיִל לַמִּלְחָמָה תַּכְרִיעַ קָמַי תַּחְתָּי׃

אָזַר (pi v-c impf 2 sg + 1 sg sf): equip, arm – חַיִל: strength – מִלְחָמָה: battle – כָּרַע (hiph impf 2 sg): force to bow down – קוּם (qal ptcp pl + 1 sg sf): rise against = my adversaries – תַּחַת (1 sg sf): under

Ephesians 6:13

διὰ τοῦτο ἀναλάβετε τὴν πανοπλίαν τοῦ θεοῦ, ἵνα δυνηθῆτε ἀντιστῆναι ἐν τῇ ἡμέρᾳ τῇ πονηρᾷ καὶ ἅπαντα κατεργασάμενοι στῆναι.

ἀναλαμβάνω (aor imv 2 pl): take up – πανοπλία: full armor – δύναμαι (aor dep subj 2 pl): be able – ἀνθίστημι (aor inf): resist, withstand – ἡμέρα: day – πονηρός: evil – κατεργάζομαι (aor ptcp pl): accomplish – ἵστημι (aor inf): stand

Large Catechism III 65

If we would be Christians, therefore, we must surely expect and count on having the devil with all his angels and the world as our enemies [Matt 25:41; Rev 12:9]. They will bring every possible misfortune and grief upon us. For where God's Word is preached, accepted, or believed and produces fruit, there the holy cross cannot be missing [Acts 14:22].

October 28

Isaiah 6:1-3

[1]בִּשְׁנַת־מוֹת הַמֶּלֶךְ עֻזִּיָּהוּ וָאֶרְאֶה אֶת־אֲדֹנָי יֹשֵׁב עַל־
כִּסֵּא רָם וְנִשָּׂא וְשׁוּלָיו מְלֵאִים אֶת־הַהֵיכָל׃ [2]שְׂרָפִים
עֹמְדִים מִמַּעַל לוֹ שֵׁשׁ כְּנָפַיִם שֵׁשׁ כְּנָפַיִם לְאֶחָד
בִּשְׁתַּיִם יְכַסֶּה פָנָיו וּבִשְׁתַּיִם יְכַסֶּה רַגְלָיו וּבִשְׁתַּיִם
יְעוֹפֵף׃ [3]וְקָרָא זֶה אֶל־זֶה וְאָמַר קָדוֹשׁ קָדוֹשׁ קָדוֹשׁ
יְהוָה צְבָאוֹת מְלֹא כָל־הָאָרֶץ כְּבוֹדוֹ׃

יָשַׁב (qal ptcp sg): sit – כִּסֵּא: throne – רוּם (qal ptcp): be high – נָשָׂא (niph ptcp): lifted up – שׁוּל (pl + 3 sg sf): train (of a robe) – מָלֵא (qal ptcp pl): fill – הֵיכָל: temple – עָמַד (qal ptcp pl): stand – שֵׁשׁ: six – כָּנָף (du used for pl): wing – כָּסָה (pi impf 3 sg): cover – רֶגֶל (pl + 3 sg sf): foot – עוּף (polel impf 3 sg): fly – קָדוֹשׁ: holy – מְלֹא: fulness

1 John 3:2

ἀγαπητοί, νῦν τέκνα θεοῦ ἐσμεν, καὶ οὔπω ἐφανερώθη τί ἐσόμεθα. οἴδαμεν ὅτι ἐὰν φανερωθῇ, ὅμοιοι αὐτῷ ἐσόμεθα, ὅτι ὀψόμεθα αὐτὸν καθώς ἐστιν.

τέκνον (pl): child – εἰμί (pres 1 pl/fut 1 pl): be – φανερόω (aor pass ind/subj 3 sg): be made known – ὅμοιος: like – ὁράω (fut ind 1 pl): see

Formula of Concord SD VI 25

Just as people will see God face-to-face, so they will—through the power of God's indwelling Spirit—do the will of God with unmingled joy, voluntarily, unconstrained, without any hindrance, and with entire purity and perfection.

October 29

Psalm 119:72-73

72 טֽוֹב־לִ֥י תֽוֹרַת־פִּ֑יךָ מֵ֝אַלְפֵ֗י זָהָ֥ב וָכָֽסֶף׃
73 יָדֶ֣יךָ עָ֭שׂוּנִי וַיְכוֹנְנ֑וּנִי הֲ֝בִינֵ֗נִי וְאֶלְמְדָ֥ה מִצְוֺתֶֽיךָ׃

טוֹב + מִן of comparison: better – תּוֹרָה (cst sg): law, teaching – פֶּה (2 sg sf): mouth – אֶ֫לֶף (cst pl): thousand – זָהָב: gold – כֶּ֫סֶף: silver – יָד (pl + 2 sg sf): hand – עָשָׂה (qal pf 3 pl + 1 sg sf): make – כּוּן (polel v-c impf 3 pl + 1 sg sf): form – בִּין (hiph imv + 1 sg sf): give understanding – לָמַד (qal coh 1 sg): learn – מִצְוָה (pl + 2 sg sf): command

John 6:68-69

68ἀπεκρίθη αὐτῷ Σίμων Πέτρος· Κύριε, πρὸς τίνα
ἀπελευσόμεθα; ῥήματα ζωῆς αἰωνίου ἔχεις, 69καὶ
ἡμεῖς πεπιστεύκαμεν καὶ ἐγνώκαμεν ὅτι σὺ εἶ ὁ
ἅγιος τοῦ θεοῦ.

ἀποκρίνομαι (aor ind 3 sg): answer – ἀπέρχομαι (fut ind 1 pl): go – ῥῆμα (pl): word – ζωή: life – αἰώνιος: eternal – πιστεύω (pf ind 1 pl): believe – γινώσκω (pf ind 1 pl): know – ἅγιος: Holy One

Formula of Concord SD VI 9

Because of these fleshly lusts, God's truly believing, elect, and regenerate children need the daily instruction and admonition, warning, and threatening of the Law in this life. But they also need frequent punishments. So they will be roused, ‹the old man driven out of them,› and they will follow God's Spirit, as it is written: "It is good for me that I was afflicted, that I might learn Your statutes" (Ps 119:71).

October 30

Psalm 46:2-3

2 אֱלֹהִים לָנוּ מַחֲסֶה וָעֹז עֶזְרָה בְצָרוֹת נִמְצָא מְאֹד׃
3 עַל־כֵּן לֹא־נִירָא בְּהָמִיר אָרֶץ וּבְמוֹט הָרִים בְּלֵב
יַמִּים׃

מַחֲסֶה: refuge – עֹז: strength – עֶזְרָה: help – צָרָה (pl): trouble – מָצָא (niph ptcp): be found = be – יָרֵא (qal impf 1 pl): fear – מוּר (hiph inf cst): change – מוֹט (qal inf cst): totter – הַר (pl): mountain – לֵב: heart – יָם (pl): sea

---

John 16:33

ταῦτα λελάληκα ὑμῖν ἵνα ἐν ἐμοὶ εἰρήνην ἔχητε. ἐν τῷ κόσμῳ θλῖψιν ἔχετε· ἀλλὰ θαρσεῖτε, ἐγὼ νενίκηκα τὸν κόσμον.

λαλέω (pf ind 1 sg): tell – εἰρήνη: peace – ἔχω (pres subj 2 pl): have – κόσμος: world – θλῖψις: trouble – θαρσέω (pres imv 2 pl): have courage – νικάω (pf ind 1 sg): conquer

---

Apology V (III) 242-243

"There is laid up for me the crown of righteousness, which the Lord, the righteous judge, will award to me" (2 Tim 4:8). The justified are due the crown because of the promise. Saints should know this promise, not that they may labor for their own profit, for they ought to labor for God's glory. But saints should know it so they may not despair in troubles. They should know God's will: He desires to aid, to deliver, and to protect them.

OCTOBER 31

Psalm 31:2

בְּךָ֣ יְהוָ֣ה חָ֭סִיתִי אַל־אֵב֣וֹשָׁה לְעוֹלָ֑ם בְּצִדְקָתְךָ֥ פַלְּטֵֽנִי׃

חָסָה (qal pf 1 sg): take refuge – בּוֹשׁ (qal coh 1 sg): be ashamed, put to shame – עוֹלָם: eternity – צְדָקָה: righteousness – פָּלַט (pi imv + 1 sg sf): rescue

Romans 1:16-17

16Οὐ γὰρ ἐπαισχύνομαι τὸ εὐαγγέλιον, δύναμις γὰρ
θεοῦ ἐστιν εἰς σωτηρίαν παντὶ τῷ πιστεύοντι, Ἰουδαίῳ
τε πρῶτον καὶ Ἕλληνι. 17δικαιοσύνη γὰρ θεοῦ ἐν αὐτῷ
ἀποκαλύπτεται ἐκ πίστεως εἰς πίστιν, καθὼς γέγραπται·
ὁ δὲ δίκαιος ἐκ πίστεως ζήσεται.

ἐπαισχύνομαι (pres ind 1 sg): be ashamed – εὐαγγέλιον: gospel – δύναμις: power – πιστεύω (pres ptcp sg): believe – δικαιοσύνη: righteousness – ἀποκαλύπτω (pres pass 3 sg): reveal – γράφω (pf pass 3 sg): written – ζάω (fut ind 3 sg): live

Formula of Concord Ep II 4

God the Holy Spirit, however, does not bring about conversion without means. For this purpose He uses the preaching and hearing of God's Word, as it is written in Rom 1:16, the Gospel "is the power of God for salvation to everyone who believes."

Ezekiel 18:23

הֶחָפֹץ אֶחְפֹּץ מוֹת רָשָׁע נְאֻם אֲדֹנָי יְהוִה הֲלוֹא בְּשׁוּבוֹ מִדְּרָכָיו וְחָיָה׃

הֲ: interrog ה – חָפֵץ (qal inf abs/qal impf 1 sg): take pleasure – מָוֶת (cst sg): death – רָשָׁע: wicked – נְאֻם: utterance – הֲלוֹא: is not? = surely – שׁוּב (qal inf cst): turn – דֶּרֶךְ (pl + 3 sg sf): way – חָיָה (qal v-c pf 3 sg): live

2 Peter 3:9

οὐ βραδύνει κύριος τῆς ἐπαγγελίας, ὥς τινες βραδύτητα ἡγοῦνται, ἀλλὰ μακροθυμεῖ εἰς ὑμᾶς, μὴ βουλόμενός τινας ἀπολέσθαι ἀλλὰ πάντας εἰς μετάνοιαν χωρῆσαι.

βραδύνω: delay, be slow in keeping – ἐπαγγελία: promise – βραδύτης: slowness – ἡγέομαι (pres ind 3 pl): understand – μακροθυμέω (pres ind 3 sg): have patience – βούλομαι (pres ptcp sg): want – ἀπόλλυμι (aor mid inf): perish – μετάνοια: repentance – χωρέω (aor inf): come

Formula of Concord Ep XI 10

The true judgment about predestination must be learned alone from the Holy Gospel about Christ, in which it is clearly testified, "For God has consigned all to disobedience, that He may have mercy on all [Rom 11:32]; not wishing that any should perish, but that all should reach repentance" [2 Pet 3:9], and believe in the Lord Christ. (See also Ezek 18:23; 33:11,18; 1 John 2:2.)

November 2

Psalm 73:23-24

23 וַאֲנִי תָמִיד עִמָּךְ אָחַזְתָּ בְּיַד־יְמִינִי׃
24 בַּעֲצָתְךָ תַנְחֵנִי וְאַחַר כָּבוֹד תִּקָּחֵנִי׃

תָּמִיד: always – עִם (prep + 2 sg sf): with – אָחַז (qal pf 2 sg): hold – יָמִין (1 sg sf): right hand – עֵצָה (2 sg sf): counsel, advice – נָחָה (hiph impf 2 sg + 1 sg sf): guide – אַחַר: afterwards – כָּבוֹד: glory – לָקַח (qal impf 2 sg + 1 sg sf): take

---

Galatians 2:20

ζῶ δὲ οὐκέτι ἐγώ, ζῇ δὲ ἐν ἐμοὶ Χριστός· ὃ δὲ νῦν ζῶ ἐν σαρκί, ἐν πίστει ζῶ τῇ τοῦ υἱοῦ τοῦ θεοῦ τοῦ ἀγαπήσαντός με καὶ παραδόντος ἑαυτὸν ὑπὲρ ἐμοῦ.

ζάω (pres ind 1 sg/pres ind 3 sg): live – σάρξ: flesh – πίστις: faith – ἀγαπάω (aor ptcp): love – παραδίδωμι (aor ptcp): give

---

Formula of Concord SD IV 19-20

Regarding the unwilling and rebellious flesh, Paul says, “I discipline my body and keep it under control” (1 Cor 9:27) and “those who belong to Christ Jesus have crucified [slain] the flesh with its passions and desires” (Gal 5:24). (See also Rom 8:13.) When it is asserted and taught that good works are free to believers in the sense that they are optional for them to do or not to do, this is false, and must be rejected. It is false to say that believers might or could act against ‹God’s Law› and still have faith and God’s favor and grace.

NOVEMBER 3

Ecclesiastes 9:10

כֹּל אֲשֶׁר תִּמְצָא יָדְךָ לַעֲשׂוֹת בְּכֹחֲךָ עֲשֵׂה
כִּי אֵין מַעֲשֶׂה וְחֶשְׁבּוֹן וְדַעַת וְחָכְמָה בִּשְׁאוֹל
אֲשֶׁר אַתָּה הֹלֵךְ שָׁמָּה׃

מָצָא (qal impf 3 sg f): find – יָד (2 sg sf): hand – עָשָׂה (qal inf cst/qal imv sg): do – כֹּחַ (2 sg sf): strength – אַיִן (cst): nonexistence – מַעֲשֶׂה: work – חֶשְׁבּוֹן: planning – דַּעַת: knowledge – חָכְמָה: wisdom – שְׁאוֹל: the grave – אֲשֶׁר ... שָׁמָּה: where – הָלַךְ (qal ptcp): go

2 Thessalonians 3:10

καὶ γὰρ ὅτε ἦμεν πρὸς ὑμᾶς, τοῦτο παρηγγέλλομεν ὑμῖν, ὅτι εἴ τις οὐ θέλει ἐργάζεσθαι μηδὲ ἐσθιέτω.

εἰμί (impf ind 1 pl): be – παραγγέλλω (impf ind 1 pl): instruct – θέλω (pres ind 3 sg): desire – ἐργάζομαι (pres inf): work – ἐσθίω (pres imv 3 sg): eat

Augsburg Confession XX 1-2

Our teachers are falsely accused of forbidding good works. Their published writings on the Ten Commandments, and other similar writings, bear witness that they have usefully taught about all estates and duties of life. They have taught well what is pleasing to God in every station and vocation in life.

November 4

Psalm 116:1-2

1אָהַבְתִּי כִּי־יִשְׁמַע יְהוָה אֶת־קוֹלִי תַּחֲנוּנָי׃
2כִּי־הִטָּה אָזְנוֹ לִי וּבְיָמַי אֶקְרָא׃

אָהֵב (qal pf 1 sg): love – שָׁמַע (qal impf 3 sg): hear – קוֹל (1 sg sf): voice – תַּחֲנוּן (pl + 1 sg sf): cry for mercy – נָטָה (hiph pf 3 sg): turn – אֹזֶן (3 sg sf): ear – יוֹם (pl + 1 sg sf): day + בְּ: as long as I live – קָרָא (qal impf 1 sg): call on

---

Romans 8:26

ὡσαύτως δὲ καὶ τὸ πνεῦμα συναντιλαμβάνεται τῇ ἀσθενείᾳ ἡμῶν· τὸ γὰρ τί προσευξώμεθα καθὸ δεῖ οὐκ οἴδαμεν, ἀλλὰ αὐτὸ τὸ πνεῦμα ὑπερεντυγχάνει στεναγμοῖς ἀλαλήτοις·

ὡσαύτως: in the same way – πνεῦμα: Spirit – συναντιλαμβάνομαι (pres ind 3 sg): help – ἀσθένεια: weakness – προσεύχομαι (aor subj 1 pl): pray – καθὸ δεῖ: as we ought to – ὑπερεντυγχάνω (pres ind 3 sg): intercede – στεναγμός: groaning – ἀλάλητος: too deep for words

---

Large Catechism III 2

Nothing is more necessary than that we should continually turn towards God's ear, call upon Him, and pray to Him. We must pray that He would give, preserve, and increase faith in us and the fulfillment of the Ten Commandments [2 Thess 1:3].

NOVEMBER 5

Genesis 5:24

וַיִּתְהַלֵּךְ חֲנוֹךְ אֶת־הָאֱלֹהִים וְאֵינֶנּוּ כִּי־לָקַח אֹתוֹ אֱלֹהִים׃

הָלַךְ (hithp v-c impf 3 sg): walk about – אֵת (prep): with – אַיִן (3 sg m sf): nonexistence

---

1 John 1:5-6

5Καὶ ἔστιν αὕτη ἡ ἀγγελία ἣν ἀκηκόαμεν ἀπ' αὐτοῦ καὶ
ἀναγγέλλομεν ὑμῖν, ὅτι ὁ θεὸς φῶς ἐστιν καὶ σκοτία ἐν
αὐτῷ οὐκ ἔστιν οὐδεμία. 6Ἐὰν εἴπωμεν ὅτι κοινωνίαν
ἔχομεν μετ' αὐτοῦ καὶ ἐν τῷ σκότει περιπατῶμεν,
ψευδόμεθα καὶ οὐ ποιοῦμεν τὴν ἀλήθειαν·

ἀγγελία: message – ἀκούω (pf ind 1 pl): hear – ἀναγγέλλω (pres ind 1 pl): declare – φῶς: light – σκοτία: darkness – οὐδείς (f sg): none = no – εἶπον (aor subj 1 pl): say – κοινωνία: fellowship – περιπατέω (pres subj 1 pl): walk – ψεύδομαι (pres ind 1 pl): lie – ἀλήθεια: truth

---

Formula of Concord SD VI 11

The Law indeed says it is God's will and command that we should walk in a new life [Rom 6:4]. But it does not give the power and ability to begin and to do it. The Holy Spirit renews the heart. He is given and received, not through the Law, but through the preaching of the Gospel (Gal 3:14).

NOVEMBER 6

Genesis 3:19

בְּזֵעַת אַפֶּיךָ תֹּאכַל לֶחֶם
עַד שׁוּבְךָ אֶל־הָאֲדָמָה כִּי מִמֶּנָּה לֻקָּחְתָּ
כִּי־עָפָר אַתָּה וְאֶל־עָפָר תָּשׁוּב׃

זֵעָה (cst sg): sweat – אַפַּיִם (2 sg sf): face – אָכַל (qal impf 2 sg): eat – שׁוּב (qal inf cst + 2 sg sf): return – אֲדָמָה: ground – לָקַח (pu pf 2 sg): be taken – עָפָר: dust

Hebrews 2:14-15

14 Ἐπεὶ οὖν τὰ παιδία κεκοινώνηκεν αἵματος καὶ σαρκός, καὶ
αὐτὸς παραπλησίως μετέσχεν τῶν αὐτῶν, ἵνα διὰ τοῦ
θανάτου καταργήσῃ τὸν τὸ κράτος ἔχοντα τοῦ θανάτου,
τοῦτ᾽ ἔστιν τὸν διάβολον, 15 καὶ ἀπαλλάξῃ τούτους, ὅσοι
φόβῳ θανάτου διὰ παντὸς τοῦ ζῆν ἔνοχοι ἦσαν δουλείας.

παιδίον: child – κοινωνέω (pf ind 3 sg): share – αἷμα: blood – σάρξ: flesh – παραπλησίως: similarly – μετέχω (aor ind 3 sg): share – θάνατος: death – καταργέω (aor subj 3 sg): destroy – κράτος: power – ἔχω (pres ptcp): have – διάβολος: devil – ἀπαλλάσσω (aor subj 3 sg): free (from slavery) – φόβος: fear – τὸ ζῆν (pres inf of ζάω): life – ἔνοχος: subject to – δουλεία: slavery

Smalcald Articles III I 1

Here we must confess, as Paul says in Rom 5:12, that sin originated from one man, Adam. By his disobedience, all people were made sinners and became subject to death and the devil. This is called original or the chief sin.

NOVEMBER 7

Joshua 21:44-45

44 וַיָּנַח יְהוָה לָהֶם מִסָּבִיב כְּכֹל אֲשֶׁר־נִשְׁבַּע לַאֲבוֹתָם
וְלֹא־עָמַד אִישׁ בִּפְנֵיהֶם מִכָּל־אֹיְבֵיהֶם אֵת כָּל־אֹיְבֵיהֶם
נָתַן יְהוָה בְּיָדָם׃ 45 לֹא־נָפַל דָּבָר מִכֹּל הַדָּבָר הַטּוֹב
אֲשֶׁר־דִּבֶּר יְהוָה אֶל־בֵּית יִשְׂרָאֵל הַכֹּל בָּא׃

נוּחַ (hiph v-c impf 3 sg): give rest – מִסָּבִיב: on every side – שָׁבַע (niph pf 3 sg): swear – אָב (pl + 3 pl sf): ancestors – עָמַד (qal pf 3 sg): stand – פָּנִים (3 pl sf): face + בְּ: against them – אֹיֵב (pl + 3 pl sf): enemy – נָתַן (qal pf 3 sg): give – יָד (3 pl sf): hand – נָפַל (qal pf 3 sg): fall, fail – בּוֹא (qal pf 3 sg): come to pass

Matthew 24:35

ὁ οὐρανὸς καὶ ἡ γῆ παρελεύσεται, οἱ δὲ λόγοι μου οὐ μὴ παρέλθωσιν.

οὐρανός: heaven – γῆ: earth – παρέρχομαι (fut ind 3 sg/aor subj 3 pl): pass away

Apology V (III) 59-60

The promise should always be in sight. Because of His promise, God wishes to be gracious and to justify for Christ's sake, not because of the Law or our works. In this promise timid consciences should seek reconciliation and justification. By this promise they should sustain themselves and be confident that they have a gracious God for Christ's sake, because of His promise. So works can never make a conscience peaceful. Only the promise can.

November 8

Isaiah 64:7

וְעַתָּה יְהוָה אָבִינוּ אָתָּה
אֲנַחְנוּ הַחֹמֶר וְאַתָּה יֹצְרֵנוּ וּמַעֲשֵׂה יָדְךָ כֻּלָּנוּ׃

אָב (1 pl sf): father – חֹמֶר: clay – יֹצֵר (qal ptcp sg + 1 pl sf): potter – מַעֲשֶׂה (cst sg): work – יָד (2 sg sf): hand – כֹּל (1 pl sf): all

---

Romans 9:20-21

20ὦ ἄνθρωπε, μενοῦνγε σὺ τίς εἶ ὁ ἀνταποκρινόμενος τῷ
θεῷ; μὴ ἐρεῖ τὸ πλάσμα τῷ πλάσαντι· τί με ἐποίησας
οὕτως; 21ἢ οὐκ ἔχει ἐξουσίαν ὁ κεραμεὺς τοῦ πηλοῦ ἐκ
τοῦ αὐτοῦ φυράματος ποιῆσαι ὃ μὲν εἰς τιμὴν σκεῦος
ὃ δὲ εἰς ἀτιμίαν;

ἄνθρωπος (voc): man – μενοῦνγε: on the contrary – ἀνταποκρίνομαι (pres ptcp): answer back – ἐρεῖ (fut ind 3 sg of λέγω/εἶπον): say – πλάσμα: what is formed – πλάσσω (aor ptcp dat sg): form – ποιέω (aor ind 2 sg): make – ἐξουσία: the right – κεραμεύς: potter – πηλός: clay – φύραμα: lump – τιμή: honorable purpose – σκεῦος: vessel – ἀτιμία: dishonorable use

---

Formula of Concord SD XI 9

This eternal election or ordination of God to eternal life must not be considered in God's secret, mysterious counsel in a simple-minded way. It is not as though election included nothing further, or nothing more belonged to it, or nothing more were to be considered in it, than that God foresaw who and how many were to be saved and who and how many were to be damned.

NOVEMBER 9

Psalm 115:1-3

1לֹא לָנוּ יְהוָה לֹא לָנוּ כִּי־לְשִׁמְךָ תֵּן כָּבוֹד
עַל־חַסְדְּךָ עַל־אֲמִתֶּךָ׃
2לָמָּה יֹאמְרוּ הַגּוֹיִם אַיֵּה־נָא אֱלֹהֵיהֶם׃
3וֵאלֹהֵינוּ בַשָּׁמָיִם כֹּל אֲשֶׁר־חָפֵץ עָשָׂה׃

כִּי: after negative = but – שֵׁם (sg + 2 sg sf): name – נָתַן (qal imv sg): give – כָּבוֹד: glory – חֶסֶד (2 sg sf): faithful love – אֱמֶת (2 sg sf): faithfulness – לָמָּה: why? – אָמַר (qal impf 3 pl): say – גּוֹי (pl): nation – אַיֵּה: where? – חָפֵץ (qal pf 3 sg): please – עָשָׂה: do

---

Acts 11:26

καὶ εὑρὼν ἤγαγεν εἰς Ἀντιόχειαν. ἐγένετο δὲ αὐτοῖς καὶ ἐνιαυτὸν ὅλον συναχθῆναι ἐν τῇ ἐκκλησίᾳ καὶ διδάξαι ὄχλον ἱκανόν, χρηματίσαι τε πρώτως ἐν Ἀντιοχείᾳ τοὺς μαθητὰς Χριστιανούς.

εὑρίσκω (aor ptcp): find (when Barnabas found Saul) – ἄγω (aor ind 3 sg): bring – γίνομαι (aor ind 3 sg): be, happen – ἐνιαυτός: year – ὅλος: whole – συνάγω (aor pass inf): come together, meet – ἐκκλησία: church – διδάσκω (aor inf): teach – ὄχλος: multitude, number – ἱκανός: considerable – χρηματίζω (aor inf): be called – πρώτως: for the first time

---

Apology V (III) 188

This faith *[in Christ's atoning sacrifice]* gives God the honor, gives God that which is His own. By receiving the promises, it obeys Him.

NOVEMBER 10

Isaiah 6:5-7

5וָאֹמַר אוֹי־לִי כִי־נִדְמֵיתִי כִּי אִישׁ טְמֵא־שְׂפָתַיִם אָנֹכִי
וּבְתוֹךְ עַם־טְמֵא שְׂפָתַיִם אָנֹכִי יוֹשֵׁב כִּי אֶת־הַמֶּלֶךְ יְהוָה
צְבָאוֹת רָאוּ עֵינָי׃ 6וַיָּעָף אֵלַי אֶחָד מִן־הַשְּׂרָפִים וּבְיָדוֹ
רִצְפָּה בְּמֶלְקַחַיִם לָקַח מֵעַל הַמִּזְבֵּחַ׃ 7וַיַּגַּע עַל־פִּי
וַיֹּאמֶר הִנֵּה נָגַע זֶה עַל־שְׂפָתֶיךָ וְסָר עֲוֺנֶךָ וְחַטָּאתְךָ
תְּכֻפָּר׃

אוֹי: woe! – דָּמָה (niph pf 1 sg): be ruined – טָמֵא (adj cst): unclean – שָׂפָה (du): lip – תָּוֶךְ (cst): midst – עוּף (qal v-c impf 3 sg): fly – יָד (3 sg sf): hand – רִצְפָּה: hot coal – מֶלְקָחַיִם: tongs – מִזְבֵּחַ: altar – נָגַע (hiph v-c impf 3 sg): touch – פֶּה (1 sg sf): mouth – שָׂפָה (pl + 2 sg sf): lip – סוּר (qal v-c pf): turn aside – עָוֺן (2 sg sf): sin – חַטָּאת (2 sg sf): sin – כָּפַר (pu impf 3 sg f): be atoned for

---

John 6:19-20

19ἐληλακότες οὖν ὡς σταδίους εἴκοσι πέντε ἢ τριάκοντα
θεωροῦσιν τὸν Ἰησοῦν περιπατοῦντα ἐπὶ τῆς θαλάσσης καὶ
ἐγγὺς τοῦ πλοίου γινόμενον, καὶ ἐφοβήθησαν.
20ὁ δὲ λέγει αὐτοῖς· ἐγώ εἰμι· μὴ φοβεῖσθε.

ἐλαύνω (pf ptcp pl): advance – στάδιον: measure of distance (25 or 30 = 3 miles) – θεωρέω (pres ind 3 pl): see – περιπατέω (pres ptcp): walk – θάλασσα: sea – ἐγγύς: near – πλοῖον: boat

---

Apology V (III) 14

This veil *[of human opinion about the Law]* is removed from us . . . when God shows to our hearts our uncleanness and the hatefulness of sin.

November 11

Psalm 145:18-19

18קָרוֹב יְהוָה לְכָל־קֹרְאָיו לְכֹל אֲשֶׁר יִקְרָאֻהוּ בֶאֱמֶת׃
19רְצוֹן־יְרֵאָיו יַעֲשֶׂה וְאֶת־שַׁוְעָתָם יִשְׁמַע וְיוֹשִׁיעֵם׃

קָרוֹב: near – קָרָא (qal ptcp pl + 3 sg sf/qal impf 3 pl + 3 sg sf): call on – אֱמֶת: truth – רָצוֹן (cst sg): desire – יָרֵא (qal ptcp pl + 3 sg sf): fear – עָשָׂה (qal impf 3 sg): do, fulfill – שַׁוְעָה (3 pl sf): cry – יָשַׁע (hiph impf 3 sg + 3 pl sf): save

---

Acts 14:17

καίτοι οὐκ ἀμάρτυρον αὑτὸν ἀφῆκεν ἀγαθουργῶν, οὐρανόθεν ὑμῖν ὑετοὺς διδοὺς καὶ καιροὺς καρποφόρους, ἐμπιπλῶν τροφῆς καὶ εὐφροσύνης τὰς καρδίας ὑμῶν.

καίτοι: yet – ἀμάρτυρος: without witness – ἀφίημι (aor ind 3 sg): leave – ἀγαθουργέω (pres ptcp sg): show kindness – οὐρανόθεν: from heaven – ὑετός: rain – δίδωμι (pres ptcp sg): give – καιρός: season – καρποφόρος: fruit-bearing – ἐμπιπλάω (pres ptcp sg): fill – τροφή: food – εὐφροσύνη: joy – καρδία: heart

---

Large Catechism I 4

The purpose of this *[first]* commandment is to require true faith and trust of the heart, which settles upon the only true God and clings to Him alone. It is like saying, "See to it that you let Me alone be your God, and never seek another." In other words, "Whatever you lack of good things, expect it from Me."

NOVEMBER 12

Isaiah 46:4

וְעַד־זִקְנָה אֲנִי הוּא וְעַד־שֵׂיבָה אֲנִי אֶסְבֹּל
אֲנִי עָשִׂיתִי וַאֲנִי אֶשָּׂא וַאֲנִי אֶסְבֹּל וַאֲמַלֵּט׃

זִקְנָה: old age – שֵׂיבָה: gray hair – סָבַל (qal impf 1 sg): carry, sustain – נָשָׂא (qal impf 1 sg): carry – מָלַט (pi impf 1 sg): rescue

Philippians 1:3-6

[3]Εὐχαριστῶ τῷ θεῷ μου ἐπὶ πάσῃ τῇ μνείᾳ ὑμῶν
[4]πάντοτε ἐν πάσῃ δεήσει μου ὑπὲρ πάντων ὑμῶν,
μετὰ χαρᾶς τὴν δέησιν ποιούμενος, [5]ἐπὶ τῇ κοινωνίᾳ
ὑμῶν εἰς τὸ εὐαγγέλιον ἀπὸ τῆς πρώτης ἡμέρας ἄχρι
τοῦ νῦν, [6]πεποιθὼς αὐτὸ τοῦτο, ὅτι ὁ ἐναρξάμενος ἐν
ὑμῖν ἔργον ἀγαθὸν ἐπιτελέσει ἄχρι ἡμέρας Χριστοῦ Ἰησοῦ·

εὐχαριστέω (pres 1 sg): thank – μνεία: remembrance – δέησις: prayer – χαρά: joy – ποιέω (pres mid ptcp): make – κοινωνία: fellowship – πείθω (pf act ptcp): be convinced – ἐνάρχομαι (aor ptcp): begin – ἔργον: work – ἀγαθός: good – ἐπιτελέω (fut ind 3 sg): bring to completion – ἡμέρα: day

Formula of Concord SD XI 8

God's eternal election does not just foresee and foreknow the salvation of the elect. From God's gracious will and pleasure in Christ Jesus, election is a cause that gains, works, helps, and promotes our salvation and what belongs to it.

NOVEMBER 13

Hosea 13:4

וְאָנֹכִי יְהוָה אֱלֹהֶיךָ מֵאֶרֶץ מִצְרָיִם
וֵאלֹהִים זוּלָתִי לֹא תֵדָע וּמוֹשִׁיעַ אַיִן בִּלְתִּי׃

זוּלָה (1 sg sf): except – יָדַע (qal impf 2 sg): acknowledge – יָשַׁע (hiph ptcp): Savior – אַיִן: nonexistence – בִּלְתִּי: except me

---

1 Timothy 2:5-6

5εἷς γὰρ θεός, εἷς καὶ μεσίτης θεοῦ καὶ ἀνθρώπων, ἄνθρωπος
Χριστὸς Ἰησοῦς, 6ὁ δοὺς ἑαυτὸν ἀντίλυτρον ὑπὲρ πάντων,
τὸ μαρτύριον καιροῖς ἰδίοις.

εἷς: one – μεσίτης: mediator – δίδωμι (aor ptcp sg): give – ἀντίλυτρον: ransom – μαρτύριον: testimony – καιρός: time – ἴδιος: proper

---

Large Catechism I 1-2

You shall have Me alone as your God. What is the meaning of this, and how is it to be understood? What does it mean to have a god? Or, what is God? Answer: A god means that from which we are to expect all good and in which we are to take refuge in all distress.

November 14

1 Samuel 3:9-10

9וַיֹּאמֶר עֵלִי לִשְׁמוּאֵל לֵךְ שְׁכָב וְהָיָה אִם־יִקְרָא אֵלֶיךָ
וְאָמַרְתָּ דַּבֵּר יְהוָה כִּי שֹׁמֵעַ עַבְדֶּךָ וַיֵּלֶךְ שְׁמוּאֵל וַיִּשְׁכַּב
בִּמְקוֹמוֹ׃ 10וַיָּבֹא יְהוָה וַיִּתְיַצַּב וַיִּקְרָא כְפַעַם־בְּפַעַם
שְׁמוּאֵל שְׁמוּאֵל וַיֹּאמֶר שְׁמוּאֵל דַּבֵּר כִּי שֹׁמֵעַ עַבְדֶּךָ׃

שָׁכַב (qal imv sg/qal v-c impf 3 sg): lie down – קָרָא (qal impf 3 sg): call – שָׁמַע (qal ptcp sg): is listening – עֶבֶד (2 sg sf): servant – מָקוֹם (3 sg sf): place – יָצַב (hithp v-c impf 3 sg): stand – כְּפַעַם־בְּפַעַם: as the other times

---

Luke 19:5-6

5καὶ ὡς ἦλθεν ἐπὶ τὸν τόπον, ἀναβλέψας ὁ Ἰησοῦς εἶπεν
πρὸς αὐτόν· Ζακχαῖε, σπεύσας κατάβηθι, σήμερον γὰρ
ἐν τῷ οἴκῳ σου δεῖ με μεῖναι. 6καὶ σπεύσας κατέβη καὶ
ὑπεδέξατο αὐτὸν χαίρων.

τόπος: place – ἀναβλέπω (aor ptcp): look up – σπεύδω (aor ptcp): hurry – καταβαίνω (aor imv 2 sg/aor ind 3 sg): come down – σήμερον: today – οἶκος: house – δεῖ: it is necessary – μένω (aor inf): stay – ὑποδέχομαι (aor ind 3 sg): welcome – χαίρω (pres ptcp sg): rejoice

---

Smalcald Articles III VIII 3

In issues relating to the spoken, outward Word, we must firmly hold that God grants His Spirit or grace to no one except through or with the preceding outward Word.

NOVEMBER 15

Amos 8:11

הִנֵּה יָמִים בָּאִים נְאֻם אֲדֹנָי יְהוִה
וְהִשְׁלַחְתִּי רָעָב בָּאָרֶץ
לֹא־רָעָב לַלֶּחֶם וְלֹא־צָמָא לַמַּיִם
כִּי אִם־לִשְׁמֹעַ אֵת דִּבְרֵי יְהוָה׃

יוֹם (pl): day – בּוֹא (qal ptcp pl): come – נְאֻם (cst sg): utterance – שָׁלַח (hiph v-c pf 1 sg): send – רָעָב: famine – לֶחֶם: bread – צָמָא: thirst – שָׁמַע (qal inf cst): hear

---

Acts 13:46

παρρησιασάμενοί τε ὁ Παῦλος καὶ ὁ Βαρναβᾶς εἶπαν· ὑμῖν ἦν ἀναγκαῖον πρῶτον λαληθῆναι τὸν λόγον τοῦ θεοῦ· ἐπειδὴ ἀπωθεῖσθε αὐτὸν καὶ οὐκ ἀξίους κρίνετε ἑαυτοὺς τῆς αἰωνίου ζωῆς, ἰδοὺ στρεφόμεθα εἰς τὰ ἔθνη.

παρρησιάζομαι (aor ptcp): speak boldly – εἶπαν (aor ind 3 pl of εἶπον): speak – ἀναγκαῖος: necessary – πρῶτον: first – λαλέω (aor pass inf): speak – ἐπειδή: since – ἀπωθέω (pres mid 2 pl): push aside – ἄξιος: worthy – κρίνω (pres ind 2 pl): consider – αἰώνιος: eternal – ζωή: life – στρέφω (pres pass dep 1 pl): turn – ἔθνη: Gentiles

---

Formula of Concord SD II 9

First, mankind's reason or natural intellect does still have a dim spark of the knowledge that there is a God. It also knows about the doctrine of the Law (Rom 1:19-21,24,32). Yet it is so ignorant, blind, and perverted that even when the most ingenious and learned people on earth read or hear the Gospel of God's Son and the promise of eternal salvation, they cannot by their own powers perceive, apprehend, understand, or believe and regard it as true.

November 16

Daniel 12:13

וְתָנוּחַ וְתַעֲמֹד לְגֹרָלְךָ לְקֵץ הַיָּמִין׃

נוּחַ (qal impf 2 sg): rest – עָמַד (qal impf 2 sg): stand, rise – גּוֹרָל (2 sg sf): allotted inheritance – קֵץ: end = at the end – יוֹם (Aramaic form of pl): day

Matthew 25:34

τότε ἐρεῖ ὁ βασιλεὺς τοῖς ἐκ δεξιῶν αὐτοῦ· δεῦτε οἱ εὐλογημένοι τοῦ πατρός μου, κληρονομήσατε τὴν ἡτοιμασμένην ὑμῖν βασιλείαν ἀπὸ καταβολῆς κόσμου.

ἐρεῖ (fut ind of λέγω/εἶπον): say – βασιλεύς: king – δεξιός: right – δεῦτε (interj): come! – εὐλογέω (pf pass ptcp): blessed – κληρονομέω (aor imv 2 pl): inherit – ἑτοιμάζω (pf pass ptcp): prepared – βασιλεία: kingdom – καταβολή: beginning

Formula of Concord SD XI 18

The Spirit will justify all those who in true repentance receive Christ by a true faith. He will receive them into grace, the adoption of sons, and the inheritance of eternal life [Gal 3:19].

November 17

Isaiah 61:10

שׂוֹשׂ אָשִׂישׂ בַּיהוָה תָּגֵל נַפְשִׁי בֵּאלֹהַי
כִּי הִלְבִּישַׁנִי בִּגְדֵי־יֶשַׁע מְעִיל צְדָקָה יְעָטָנִי

שִׂישׂ (qal inf abs/qal impf 1 sg): rejoice – גִּיל (qal juss 3 sg f): rejoice – נֶפֶשׁ (1 sg sf): soul – לָבַשׁ (hiph pf + 1 sg sf): clothe – בֶּגֶד (cst pl): garment – יֶשַׁע: salvation – מְעִיל: robe – צְדָקָה: righteousness – יָעַט (qal pf + 1 sg sf): wrap, cover

---

Revelation 1:5-6

5Τῷ ἀγαπῶντι ἡμᾶς καὶ λύσαντι ἡμᾶς ἐκ τῶν ἁμαρτιῶν
ἡμῶν ἐν τῷ αἵματι αὐτοῦ, 6καὶ ἐποίησεν ἡμᾶς βασιλείαν,
ἱερεῖς τῷ θεῷ καὶ πατρὶ αὐτοῦ, αὐτῷ ἡ δόξα καὶ τὸ κράτος
εἰς τοὺς αἰῶνας [τῶν αἰώνων]· ἀμήν.

ἀγαπάω (pres ptcp): love – λύω (aor ptcp): set free – ἁμαρτία: sin – αἷμα: blood – βασιλεία: kingdom – ἱερεύς (pl): priest – δόξα: glory – κράτος: power – αἰών: eternity

---

Apology VII-VIII (IV) 5

The Church is not only the fellowship of outward objects and rites, as other governments, but at its core, it is a fellowship of faith and of the Holy Spirit in hearts. Yet this fellowship has outward marks so that it can be recognized. These marks are the pure doctrine of the Gospel and the administration of the Sacraments in accordance with the Gospel of Christ. This Church alone is called Christ's body, which Christ renews, sanctifies, and governs by His Spirit.

NOVEMBER 18

Exodus 19:6

וְאַתֶּם תִּהְיוּ־לִי מַמְלֶכֶת כֹּהֲנִים וְגוֹי קָדוֹשׁ אֵלֶּה הַדְּבָרִים אֲשֶׁר תְּדַבֵּר אֶל־בְּנֵי יִשְׂרָאֵל׃

מַמְלָכָה (cst sg): kingdom – כֹּהֵן (pl): priest – גּוֹי: nation – קָדוֹשׁ: holy

Revelation 5:9-10

[9]καὶ ᾄδουσιν ᾠδὴν καινὴν λέγοντες· ἄξιος εἶ λαβεῖν τὸ
βιβλίον καὶ ἀνοῖξαι τὰς σφραγῖδας αὐτοῦ, ὅτι ἐσφάγης
καὶ ἠγόρασας τῷ θεῷ ἐν τῷ αἵματί σου ἐκ πάσης φυλῆς καὶ
γλώσσης καὶ λαοῦ καὶ ἔθνους [10]καὶ ἐποίησας αὐτοὺς τῷ θεῷ
ἡμῶν βασιλείαν καὶ ἱερεῖς, καὶ βασιλεύσουσιν ἐπὶ τῆς γῆς.

ᾄδω (pres ind 3 pl): sing – ᾠδή: song – καινός: new – ἄξιος: worthy – εἰμί (pres ind 2 sg): be – λαμβάνω (aor inf): take – βιβλίον: scroll – ἀνοίγω (aor inf): open – σφραγίς (pl): seal – σφάζω (aor pass 2 sg): slay – ἀγοράζω (aor ind 2 sg): purchase – αἷμα: blood – φυλή: tribe – γλῶσσα: tongue – λαός: people – ἔθνος: nation – βασιλεία: kingdom – ἱερεύς: priest – βασιλεύω (fut ind 3 pl): reign

Smalcald Articles III XII 3

For the children pray, "I believe in one holy Christian Church." This holiness does not come from albs, tonsures, long gowns, and other ceremonies they made up without Holy Scripture, but from God's Word and true faith.

Isaiah 60:19

לֹא־יִהְיֶה־לָּךְ עוֹד הַשֶּׁמֶשׁ לְאוֹר יוֹמָם
וּלְנֹגַהּ הַיָּרֵחַ לֹא־יָאִיר לָךְ
וְהָיָה־לָךְ יְהוָה לְאוֹר עוֹלָם וֵאלֹהַיִךְ לְתִפְאַרְתֵּךְ׃

לֹא עוֹד: no longer – **שֶׁמֶשׁ**: sun – **אוֹר**: light – **יוֹמָם** (adv): by day – **נֹגַהּ**: brightness – **יָרֵחַ**: moon – **אוֹר** (hiph impf 3 sg): shine – **עוֹלָם**: eternity – **תִּפְאֶרֶת** (2 sg sf): glory

---

Colossians 1:12-13

12εὐχαριστοῦντες τῷ πατρὶ τῷ ἱκανώσαντι ὑμᾶς εἰς τὴν
μερίδα τοῦ κλήρου τῶν ἁγίων ἐν τῷ φωτί· 13ὃς ἐρρύσατο
ἡμᾶς ἐκ τῆς ἐξουσίας τοῦ σκότους καὶ μετέστησεν εἰς
τὴν βασιλείαν τοῦ υἱοῦ τῆς ἀγάπης αὐτοῦ . . .

εὐχαριστέω (pres ptcp pl): give thanks – ἱκανόω (aor ptcp dat sg): empower, qualify – μερίς: share – κλῆρος: inheritance – ἅγιος: saint – φῶς: light – ῥύομαι (aor ind 3 sg): rescue – ἐξουσία: dominion – σκότος (gen sg): darkness – μεθίστημι (aor ind 3 sg): transfer

---

Smalcald Articles II I 1-4

Jesus Christ, our God and Lord, died for our sins and was raised again for our justification (Rom 4:24-25). He alone is the Lamb of God who takes away the sins of the world (John 1:29), and God has laid upon Him the iniquities of us all (Isa 53:6). All have sinned and are justified freely, without their own works or merits, by His grace, through the redemption that is in Christ Jesus, in His blood (Rom 3:23-25). This is necessary to believe. This cannot be otherwise acquired or grasped by any work, law, or merit.

November 20

Psalm 145:15-16

15 עֵינֵי־כֹל אֵלֶיךָ יְשַׂבֵּרוּ וְאַתָּה נוֹתֵן־לָהֶם אֶת־אָכְלָם
בְּעִתּוֹ׃
16 פּוֹתֵחַ אֶת־יָדֶךָ וּמַשְׂבִּיעַ לְכָל־חַי רָצוֹן׃

עַיִן (cst pl): eye – שָׂבַר (pi impf 3 pl): wait, hope – נָתַן (qal ptcp): give – אֹכֶל (3 pl sf): food – עֵת (3 sg sf): time – פָּתַח (qal ptcp): open – יָד (2 sg sf): hand – שָׂבַע (hiph ptcp): satisfy – חַי: living – רָצוֹן: desire

Matthew 7:9-11

9 ἢ τίς ἐστιν ἐξ ὑμῶν ἄνθρωπος, ὃν αἰτήσει ὁ υἱὸς αὐτοῦ
ἄρτον, μὴ λίθον ἐπιδώσει αὐτῷ; 10 ἢ καὶ ἰχθὺν αἰτήσει,
μὴ ὄφιν ἐπιδώσει αὐτῷ; 11 εἰ οὖν ὑμεῖς πονηροὶ ὄντες
οἴδατε δόματα ἀγαθὰ διδόναι τοῖς τέκνοις ὑμῶν, πόσῳ
μᾶλλον ὁ πατὴρ ὑμῶν ὁ ἐν τοῖς οὐρανοῖς δώσει ἀγαθὰ
τοῖς αἰτοῦσιν αὐτόν.

αἰτέω (fut ind 3 sg): ask for – ἄρτος: bread – λίθος: stone – ἐπιδίδωμι (fut ind 3 sg): give – ἰχθύς: fish – ὄφις: snake – πονηρός: evil – οἶδα: know – δόμα (pl): gift – ἀγαθός: good – δίδωμι (pres inf): give – οὐρανός: heaven

Large Catechism III 72

If God did not cause food to grow and He did not bless and preserve it in the field, we could never take bread from the oven or have any to set upon the table.

November 21

Ezekiel 48:35

וְשֵׁם־הָעִיר מִיּוֹם יְהוָה שָׁמָּה׃

שֵׁם: name – עִיר: city – מִיּוֹם: from that time on – שָׁמָּה (adv): there

Revelation 22:5

καὶ νὺξ οὐκ ἔσται ἔτι καὶ οὐκ ἔχουσιν χρείαν φωτὸς λύχνου καὶ φωτὸς ἡλίου, ὅτι κύριος ὁ θεὸς φωτίσει ἐπ' αὐτούς, καὶ βασιλεύσουσιν εἰς τοὺς αἰῶνας τῶν αἰώνων.

νύξ: night – ἔχω (pres ind 3 pl): have – χρεία: need – φῶς: light – λύχνος: lamp – ἥλιος: sun – κύριος: Lord – φωτίζω (fut ind 3 sg): give light – βασιλεύω (fut ind 3 pl): reign – αἰών: eternity

Augsburg Confession XVII 5

Our churches also condemn those who are spreading certain Jewish opinions, that before the resurrection of the dead the godly shall take possession of the kingdom of the world, the ungodly being everywhere suppressed.

NOVEMBER 22

Psalm 89:2

חַסְדֵי יְהוָה עוֹלָם אָשִׁירָה לְדֹר וָדֹר אוֹדִיעַ אֱמוּנָתְךָ בְּפִי׃

שִׁיר (qal coh 1 sg): sing – דּוֹר: generation – יָדַע (hiph impf 1 sg): make known – אֱמוּנָה (2 sg sf): faithfulness – פֶּה (1 sg sf): mouth

---

Colossians 3:16-17

16 Ὁ λόγος τοῦ Χριστοῦ ἐνοικείτω ἐν ὑμῖν πλουσίως,
ἐν πάσῃ σοφίᾳ διδάσκοντες καὶ νουθετοῦντες ἑαυτούς,
ψαλμοῖς ὕμνοις ᾠδαῖς πνευματικαῖς ἐν [τῇ] χάριτι
ᾄδοντες ἐν ταῖς καρδίαις ὑμῶν τῷ θεῷ·
17 καὶ πᾶν ὅ τι
ἐὰν ποιῆτε ἐν λόγῳ ἢ ἐν ἔργῳ, πάντα ἐν ὀνόματι κυρίου
Ἰησοῦ, εὐχαριστοῦντες τῷ θεῷ πατρὶ δι᾽ αὐτοῦ.

ἐνοικέω (pres imv 3 sg): dwell – πλουσίως: richly – νουθετέω (pres ptcp pl): admonish – ᾠδή (pl): song – πνευματικός: spiritual – χάρις: grace, gratitude – ᾄδω (pres ptcp pl): sing – ποιέω (pres subj 2 pl): do

---

Smalcald Articles III IV

We will now return to the Gospel, which does not give us counsel and aid against sin in only one way. God is superabundantly generous in His grace: First, through the spoken Word, by which the forgiveness of sins is preached in the whole world [Luke 24:45-47]. This is the particular office of the Gospel. Second, through Baptism. Third, through the holy Sacrament of the Altar. Fourth, through the Power of the Keys. Also through the mutual conversation and consolation of brethren, "Where two or three are gathered" (Matt 18:20) and other such verses [especially Rom 1:12].

NOVEMBER 23

Isaiah 63:15-16

15אַיֵּה קִנְאָתְךָ וּגְבוּרֹתֶךָ הֲמוֹן מֵעֶיךָ
וְרַחֲמֶיךָ אֵלַי הִתְאַפָּקוּ׃ 16כִּי־אַתָּה אָבִינוּ
כִּי אַבְרָהָם לֹא יְדָעָנוּ וְיִשְׂרָאֵל לֹא יַכִּירָנוּ
אַתָּה יְהוָה אָבִינוּ גֹּאֲלֵנוּ מֵעוֹלָם שְׁמֶךָ׃

אַיֵּה: where? – קִנְאָה (2 sg sf): zeal – גְּבוּרָה (2 sg sf): might – הָמוֹן (cst sg): abundance – מֵעִים (2 sg sf): pity – רַחֲמִים (2 sg sf): compassion – אָפַק (hithp pf 3 pl): be withheld – יָדַע (qal pf + 1 pl sf): know – נָכַר (hiph impf 3 sg + 1 pl sf): acknowledge – גָּאַל (qal ptcp): Redeemer

---

Romans 7:24-25

24Ταλαίπωρος ἐγὼ ἄνθρωπος· τίς με ῥύσεται ἐκ τοῦ
σώματος τοῦ θανάτου τούτου; 25χάρις δὲ τῷ θεῷ διὰ
Ἰησοῦ Χριστοῦ τοῦ κυρίου ἡμῶν. ἄρα οὖν αὐτὸς ἐγὼ τῷ
μὲν νοῒ δουλεύω νόμῳ θεοῦ τῇ δὲ σαρκὶ νόμῳ ἁμαρτίας.

ταλαίπωρος: wretched – ῥύομαι (fut ind 3 sg): rescue – σῶμα: body – θάνατος: death – χάρις: thanks – νοῦς (dat sg): mind – δουλεύω: be a slave to – νόμος: law

---

Formula of Concord SD II 11

A person who is physically dead cannot from his own powers prepare or make himself come back to life again. So the person who is spiritually dead in sins cannot by his own strength make or apply himself to acquire spiritual and heavenly righteousness and life. This is true unless he is delivered and brought to life by God's Son from the death of sin.

NOVEMBER 24

Deuteronomy 29:28

הַנִּסְתָּרֹת לַיהוָה אֱלֹהֵינוּ וְהַנִּגְלֹת לָנוּ וּלְבָנֵינוּ עַד־עוֹלָם
לַעֲשׂוֹת אֶת־כָּל־דִּבְרֵי הַתּוֹרָה הַזֹּאת׃

סָתַר (niph ptcp pl f): the secret/hidden things – גָּלָה (niph ptcp pl f): the revealed things – עוֹלָם: forever – עָשָׂה (qal inf cst): do – תּוֹרָה: law, teaching

John 15:14-15

14ὑμεῖς φίλοι μού ἐστε ἐὰν ποιῆτε ἃ ἐγὼ ἐντέλλομαι ὑμῖν.
15οὐκέτι λέγω ὑμᾶς δούλους, ὅτι ὁ δοῦλος οὐκ οἶδεν τί ποιεῖ αὐτοῦ ὁ κύριος· ὑμᾶς δὲ εἴρηκα φίλους, ὅτι πάντα ἃ ἤκουσα παρὰ τοῦ πατρός μου ἐγνώρισα ὑμῖν.

φίλος (pl): friend – ποιέω (pres subj 2 pl): do – ἐντέλλομαι: command – δοῦλος: slave – οἶδα (3 sg): know – κύριος: master – εἴρηκα (pf ind of λέγω/εἶπον): call – ἀκούω (aor ind 1 sg): hear – γνωρίζω (aor ind 1 sg): make known

Augsburg Confession V 4

Our churches condemn the Anabaptists and others who think that through their own preparations and works the Holy Spirit comes to them without the external Word.

November 25

Jeremiah 33:16

בַּיָּמִים הָהֵם תִּוָּשַׁע יְהוּדָה וִירוּשָׁלִַם תִּשְׁכּוֹן לָבֶטַח וְזֶה אֲשֶׁר־יִקְרָא־לָהּ יְהוָה צִדְקֵנוּ׃

יוֹם (pl): day – יָשַׁע (niph impf 3 sg f): be saved – שָׁכַן (qal impf 3 sg): dwell – בֶּטַח: safety – יִקְרָא־לָהּ: one will call it = it will be called – צֶדֶק (sg + 1 pl sf): righteousness

---

Revelation 3:12

Ὁ νικῶν ποιήσω αὐτὸν στῦλον ἐν τῷ ναῷ τοῦ θεοῦ μου, καὶ ἔξω οὐ μὴ ἐξέλθῃ ἔτι, καὶ γράψω ἐπ' αὐτὸν τὸ ὄνομά τοῦ θεοῦ μου καὶ τὸ ὄνομα τῆς πόλεως τοῦ θεοῦ μου, τῆς καινῆς Ἰερουσαλήμ, ἡ καταβαίνουσα ἐκ τοῦ οὐρανοῦ ἀπὸ τοῦ θεοῦ μου, καὶ τὸ ὄνομα μου τὸ καινόν.

νικάω (pres ptcp sg): be victorious – ποιέω (fut ind 1 sg): make – στῦλος: pillar – ναός: temple – ἔξω: outside – ἐξέρχομαι (aor subj 3 sg): go out – καινός: new

---

Formula of Concord Ep III 1

It is unanimously confessed in our churches, in accordance with God's Word and the meaning of the Augsburg Confession, that we poor sinners are justified before God and saved alone through faith in Christ.

NOVEMBER 26

Psalm 96:1

שִׁירוּ לַיהוָה שִׁיר חָדָשׁ שִׁירוּ לַיהוָה כָּל־הָאָרֶץ׃

שִׁיר (qal imv pl): sing – שִׁיר: song – חָדָשׁ (adj): new

Revelation 7:9-10

9Μετὰ ταῦτα εἶδον, καὶ ἰδοὺ ὄχλος πολύς, ὃν ἀριθμῆσαι
αὐτὸν οὐδεὶς ἐδύνατο, ἐκ παντὸς ἔθνους καὶ φυλῶν καὶ
λαῶν καὶ γλωσσῶν ἑστῶτες ἐνώπιον τοῦ θρόνου καὶ ἐνώπιον
τοῦ ἀρνίου, περιβεβλημένους στολὰς λευκὰς καὶ φοίνικες
ἐν ταῖς χερσὶν αὐτῶν, 10καὶ κράζουσιν φωνῇ μεγάλῃ
λέγοντες· Ἡ σωτηρία τῷ θεῷ ἡμῶν τῷ καθημένῳ ἐπὶ
τῷ θρόνῳ καὶ τῷ ἀρνίῳ.

εἶδον (aor ind 1 sg of ὁράω): see, look – ὄχλος: multitude – πολύς: great – ἀριθμέω (aor inf): count – δύναμαι (impf ind 3 sg): be able – ἔθνος: nation – φυλή: tribe – λαός: people – γλῶσσα: tongue, language – ἵστημι (pf ptcp with pres meaning): stand – ἐνώπιον: before – ἀρνίον: Lamb – περιβάλλω (pf mid ptcp): wear – στολή: festive robe – λευκός: white – φοίνιξ (pl): palm branch – χείρ (pl): hand – κράζω (pres ind 3 pl): call out – σωτηρία: salvation – κάθημαι (pres ptcp): sit

Large Catechism III 39

Since we call God our Father in this *[Lord's]* prayer, it is our duty always to act and behave ourselves as godly children, that He may not receive shame, but honor and praise from us.

NOVEMBER 27

Isaiah 66:13

כְּאִישׁ אֲשֶׁר אִמּוֹ תְּנַחֲמֶנּוּ כֵּן אָנֹכִי אֲנַחֶמְכֶם וּבִירוּשָׁלַ͏ִם
תְּנֻחָמוּ׃

אֵם (3 sg sf): mother – נָחַם (pi impf 3 sg + 3 sg sf/pi impf 1 sg + 2 pl sf): comfort – נָחַם (pu impf 2 pl): be comforted

Luke 8:47-48

47ἰδοῦσα δὲ ἡ γυνὴ ὅτι οὐκ ἔλαθεν τρέμουσα ἦλθεν καὶ
προσπεσοῦσα αὐτῷ δι' ἣν αἰτίαν ἥψατο αὐτοῦ ἀπήγγειλεν
ἐνώπιον παντὸς τοῦ λαοῦ καὶ ὡς ἰάθη παραχρῆμα. 48ὁ δὲ
εἶπεν αὐτῇ, Θυγάτηρ, ἡ πίστις σου σέσωκέν σε· πορεύου
εἰς εἰρήνην.

ἰδοῦσα (2 aor ptcp sg f of ὁράω): see – λανθάνω (aor ind 3 sg): escape notice – τρέμω (pres ptcp sg f): tremble – προσπίπτω (aor ptcp sg f): fall down before – δι' ἥν αἰτίαν: for what reason, why – ἅπτω (aor mid 3 sg): touch – ἀπαγγέλλω (aor 3 sg): tell – ἰάομαι (aor pass 3 sg): heal – παραχρῆμα (adv): instantly – θυγάτηρ (voc): daughter – σῴζω (pf ind 3 sg): save – πορεύομαι (pres imv 2 sg): go

Small Catechism Seventh Petition

But deliver us from evil.

What does this mean?

And finally, when our last hour shall come, we pray that He would grant us a blessed end and graciously take us from this vale of tears to Himself into heaven.

Isaiah 1:18

לְכוּ־נָא וְנִוָּכְחָה יֹאמַר יְהוָה
אִם־יִהְיוּ חֲטָאֵיכֶם כַּשָּׁנִים כַּשֶּׁלֶג יַלְבִּינוּ
אִם־יַאְדִּימוּ כַתּוֹלָע כַּצֶּמֶר יִהְיוּ׃

הָלַךְ (qal imv pl): come – יָכַח (niph coh 1 pl): decide/debate a case in court – אָמַר (qal impf 3 sg): say – הָיָה (qal impf 3 pl): be – חֵטְא (pl + 2 pl sf): sin (as missing the mark) – שָׁנִי (pl): scarlet – שֶׁלֶג: snow – לָבֵן (hiph impf 3 pl): be white – אָדֵם (hiph impf 3 pl): be red – תּוֹלָע: crimson – צֶמֶר: wool

1 John 1:7

καὶ τὸ αἷμα Ἰησοῦ τοῦ υἱοῦ αὐτοῦ καθαρίζει ἡμᾶς ἀπὸ πάσης ἁμαρτίας.

αἷμα: blood – καθαρίζω (pres ind 3 sg): cleanse – ἁμαρτία: sin

Smalcald Articles II I 1

The first and chief article is this: Jesus Christ, our God and Lord, died for our sins and was raised again for our justification (Rom 4:24-25).

NOVEMBER 29

Genesis 3:22-24

22וַיֹּאמֶר יְהוָה אֱלֹהִים הֵן הָאָדָם הָיָה כְּאַחַד מִמֶּנּוּ
לָדַעַת טוֹב וָרָע וְעַתָּה פֶּן־יִשְׁלַח יָדוֹ וְלָקַח גַּם מֵעֵץ
הַחַיִּים וְאָכַל וָחַי לְעֹלָם׃ 23וַיְשַׁלְּחֵהוּ יְהוָה אֱלֹהִים
מִגַּן־עֵדֶן לַעֲבֹד אֶת־הָאֲדָמָה אֲשֶׁר לֻקַּח מִשָּׁם׃ 24וַיְגָרֶשׁ
אֶת־הָאָדָם וַיַּשְׁכֵּן מִקֶּדֶם לְגַן־עֵדֶן אֶת־הַכְּרֻבִים וְאֵת
לַהַט הַחֶרֶב הַמִּתְהַפֶּכֶת לִשְׁמֹר אֶת־דֶּרֶךְ עֵץ הַחַיִּים׃

אֶחָד (cst sg): one – יָדַע (qal inf cst): know – פֶּן: lest – שָׁלַח (qal impf 3 sg): reach out – שָׁלַח (pi v-c impf 3 sg + 3 sg sf): banish – גַּן: garden – עָבַד (qal inf cst): work – לָקַח (pu pf): be taken – גָּרַשׁ (pi v-c impf 3 sg): drive out – שָׁכַן (hiph v-c impf 3 sg): place – לַהַט: flame – חֶרֶב: sword – הָפַךְ (hithp ptcp): turn this way and that

---

Revelation 22:14

Μακάριοι οἱ πλύνοντες τὰς στολὰς αὐτῶν, ἵνα ἔσται ἡ ἐξουσία αὐτῶν ἐπὶ τὸ ξύλον τῆς ζωῆς καὶ τοῖς πυλῶσιν εἰσέλθωσιν εἰς τὴν πόλιν.

μακάριος: blessed – πλύνω (pres ptcp pl): wash – στολή (pl): robe – ἐξουσία: the right – ξύλον: tree – ζωή: life – πυλών (dat pl): gate – εἰσέρχομαι (aor subj 3 pl): enter – πόλις: city

---

Formula of Concord Ep I 2

We believe, teach, and confess that there is a distinction between man's nature and original sin.

NOVEMBER 30

Zephaniah 3:15

הֵסִיר יְהוָה מִשְׁפָּטַיִךְ פִּנָּה אֹיְבֵךְ
מֶלֶךְ יִשְׂרָאֵל יְהוָה בְּקִרְבֵּךְ לֹא־תִירְאִי רָע עוֹד׃

סוּר (hiph pf 3 sg): take away – מִשְׁפָּט (pl + 2 sg sf): punishment – פָּנָה (pi pf 3 sg): turn back – אֹיֵב (2 sg sf): enemy – מֶלֶךְ (cst sg): King – קֶרֶב (2 sg sf): midst – יָרֵא (qal impf 2 sg): fear – רַע: harm – עוֹד: again

Revelation 21:3

καὶ ἤκουσα φωνῆς μεγάλης ἐκ τοῦ θρόνου λεγούσης· ἰδοὺ ἡ σκηνὴ τοῦ θεοῦ μετὰ τῶν ἀνθρώπων, καὶ σκηνώσει μετ' αὐτῶν, καὶ αὐτοὶ λαοὶ αὐτοῦ ἔσονται, καὶ αὐτὸς ὁ θεὸς μετ' αὐτῶν ἔσται . . .

ἀκούω (aor ind 1 sg): hear – φωνή: voice – λέγω (pres ptcp): say – σκηνή: dwelling – σκηνόω (fut ind 3 sg): dwell – λαός: people – εἰμί (fut ind 3 pl): be

Smalcald Articles III III 37-38

A person who confesses that everything in him is nothing but sin includes all sins, excludes none, forgets none. Neither can the satisfaction *[won by Christ]* be uncertain, because it is not our uncertain, sinful work. Rather, it is the suffering and blood of the innocent Lamb of God, who takes away the sin of the world [John 1:29].

Psalm 24:9-10

9 שְׂא֤וּ שְׁעָרִ֨ים ׀ רָֽאשֵׁיכֶ֗ם וּ֭שְׂאוּ פִּתְחֵ֣י עוֹלָ֑ם וְ֝יָבֹ֗א מֶ֣לֶךְ הַכָּבֽוֹד׃
10 מִ֤י ה֣וּא זֶה֮ מֶ֤לֶךְ הַכָּ֫ב֥וֹד יְהוָ֥ה צְבָא֑וֹת ה֤וּא מֶ֖לֶךְ הַכָּב֣וֹד סֶֽלָה׃

נָשָׂא (qal imv pl): lift up – שַׁ֫עַר (pl): gate – רֹאשׁ (pl + 2 pl sf): head – פֶּ֫תַח (cst pl): door – בּוֹא (qal impf 3 sg): enter – כָּבוֹד: glory – צָבָא (pl): army, host

---

Matthew 3:1-3

1Ἐν δὲ ταῖς ἡμέραις ἐκείναις παραγίνεται Ἰωάννης ὁ
βαπτιστὴς κηρύσσων ἐν τῇ ἐρήμῳ τῆς Ἰουδαίας 2[καὶ]
λέγων· μετανοεῖτε· ἤγγικεν γὰρ ἡ βασιλεία τῶν οὐρανῶν.
3οὗτος γάρ ἐστιν ὁ ῥηθεὶς διὰ Ἠσαΐου τοῦ προφήτου
λέγοντος· φωνὴ βοῶντος ἐν τῇ ἐρήμῳ· ἑτοιμάσατε τὴν
ὁδὸν κυρίου, εὐθείας ποιεῖτε τὰς τρίβους αὐτοῦ.

παραγίνομαι (pres dep 3 sg): arrive – κηρύσσω (pres ptcp): proclaim – ἔρημος: wasteland – μετανοέω (pres imv 2 pl): repent – ἐγγίζω (pf ind 3 sg): come near – βασιλεία: kingdom – οὐρανός: heaven – ῥηθείς (aor pass ptcp of λέγω/εἶπον): speak – φωνή: voice – βοάω (pres ptcp): call out – ἑτοιμάζω (aor imv 2 pl): prepare – ὁδός: way – εὐθύς: straight – τρίβος (pl): path

---

Augsburg Confession XII 3-5

Now, strictly speaking, repentance consists of two parts. One part is contrition, that is, terrors striking the conscience through the knowledge of sin. The other part is faith, which is born of the Gospel [Rom 10:17] or the Absolution and believes that for Christ's sake, sins are forgiven.

DECEMBER 2

Malachi 3:23-24

23 הִנֵּה אָנֹכִי שֹׁלֵחַ לָכֶם אֵת אֵלִיָּה הַנָּבִיא
לִפְנֵי בּוֹא יוֹם יְהוָה הַגָּדוֹל וְהַנּוֹרָא׃
24 וְהֵשִׁיב לֵב־אָבוֹת עַל־בָּנִים וְלֵב בָּנִים עַל־אֲבוֹתָם
פֶּן־אָבוֹא וְהִכֵּיתִי אֶת־הָאָרֶץ חֵרֶם׃

שָׁלַח (qal ptcp): send – נָבִיא: prophet – לִפְנֵי (prep): before – בּוֹא (qal inf cst/qal impf 1 sg): come – יָרֵא (niph ptcp): fearful – שׁוּב (hiph v-c pf 3 sg): turn – לֵב: heart – אָב (pl): father – בֵּן (pl): son, child – פֶּן: lest – נָכָה (hiph v-c pf 1 sg): strike – חֵרֶם: curse (literally: ban for utter destruction)

John 1:6-7

6 Ἐγένετο ἄνθρωπος, ἀπεσταλμένος παρὰ θεοῦ, ὄνομα αὐτῷ
Ἰωάννης· 7 οὗτος ἦλθεν εἰς μαρτυρίαν ἵνα μαρτυρήσῃ περὶ
τοῦ φωτός, ἵνα πάντες πιστεύσωσιν δι᾽ αὐτοῦ.

ἀποστέλλω (pf pass ptcp): send out – ὄνομα: name – ἔρχομαι (aor ind 3 sg): come – μαρτυρία: testimony – μαρτυρέω (aor subj 3 sg): testify – φῶς: light – πιστεύω (aor subj 3 pl): believe

Formula of Concord SD V 1

The distinction between the Law and the Gospel is a particularly brilliant light. It serves the purpose of rightly dividing God's Word [2 Tim 2:15] and properly explaining and understanding the Scriptures of the holy prophets and apostles.

Jeremiah 23:5-6

5 הִנֵּה יָמִים בָּאִים נְאֻם־יְהוָה וַהֲקִמֹתִי לְדָוִד צֶמַח צַדִּיק
וּמָלַךְ מֶלֶךְ וְהִשְׂכִּיל וְעָשָׂה מִשְׁפָּט וּצְדָקָה בָּאָרֶץ׃
6 בְּיָמָיו תִּוָּשַׁע יְהוּדָה וְיִשְׂרָאֵל יִשְׁכֹּן לָבֶטַח
וְזֶה־שְּׁמוֹ אֲשֶׁר־יִקְרְאוֹ יְהוָה צִדְקֵנוּ׃

נְאֻם (cst): utterance – קוּם (hiph v-c pf 1 sg): raise up – צֶמַח: branch – צַדִּיק: righteous – מָלַךְ (qal v-c pf 3 sg): reign – שָׂכַל (hiph v-c pf 3 sg): act wisely – מִשְׁפָּט: justice – יָשַׁע (niph impf 3 sg): be saved – שָׁכַן (qal impf 3 sg): dwell – בֶּטַח: safety

---

John 18:37

εἶπεν οὖν αὐτῷ ὁ Πιλᾶτος· οὐκοῦν βασιλεὺς εἶ σύ; ἀπεκρίθη ὁ Ἰησοῦς· σὺ λέγεις ὅτι βασιλεύς εἰμι. ἐγὼ εἰς τοῦτο γεγέννημαι καὶ εἰς τοῦτο ἐλήλυθα εἰς τὸν κόσμον, ἵνα μαρτυρήσω τῇ ἀληθείᾳ· πᾶς ὁ ὢν ἐκ τῆς ἀληθείας ἀκούει μου τῆς φωνῆς.

οὐκοῦν: so then – βασιλεύς: king – ἀποκρίνομαι (aor ind): answer – γεννάω (pf pass 1 sg): be born – ἔρχομαι (pf ind 1 sg): come – μαρτυρέω (aor subj 1 sg): bear witness

---

Formula of Concord Ep III 1

Christ alone is our Righteousness, who is true God and man, because in Him the divine and the human natures are personally united with each other (Jer 23:6; 1 Cor 1:30; 2 Cor 5:21).

December 4

1 Samuel 2:1,2

1 וַתִּתְפַּלֵּל חַנָּה וַתֹּאמַר עָלַץ לִבִּי בַּיהוָה
2 אֵין־קָדוֹשׁ כַּיהוָה כִּי אֵין בִּלְתֶּךָ וְאֵין צוּר כֵּאלֹהֵינוּ׃

פָּלַל (hithp v-c impf 3 sg f): pray – עָלַץ (qal pf 3 sg): rejoice – אַיִן (cst): there is no one – קָדוֹשׁ: holy – בִּלְתִּי (particle of negation + 2 sg sf): besides you – צוּר: Rock

---

Luke 1:46-49

46Καὶ εἶπεν Μαριάμ· Μεγαλύνει ἡ ψυχή μου τὸν κύριον,
47καὶ ἠγαλλίασεν τὸ πνεῦμά μου ἐπὶ τῷ θεῷ τῷ σωτῆρί
μου, 48ὅτι ἐπέβλεψεν ἐπὶ τὴν ταπείνωσιν τῆς δούλης
αὐτοῦ. ἰδοὺ γὰρ ἀπὸ τοῦ νῦν μακαριοῦσίν με πᾶσαι αἱ
γενεαί, 49ὅτι ἐποίησέν μοι μεγάλα ὁ δυνατός. καὶ ἅγιον
τὸ ὄνομα αὐτοῦ . . .

μεγαλύνω (pres ind 3 sg): praise – ψυχή: soul – ἀγαλλιάω (aor ind 3 sg): be glad – πνεῦμα: spirit – σωτήρ: Savior – ἐπιβλέπω (aor ind 3 sg): care about – ταπείνωσις: humble state – δούλη: female slave – ἰδού: behold! – μακαρίζω (fut ind 3 pl): call/consider blessed – γενεά (pl): generation – ποιέω (aor ind 3 sg): do – μέγας (pl): great – δυνατός: the powerful one – ἅγιος: holy – ὄνομα: name

---

Large Catechism III 45-46

In this *[first]* petition we pray for exactly what God demands in the Second Commandment. . . . So this point is easy and clear if only the language is understood: to hallow means the same as to praise, magnify, and honor both in word and deed.

DECEMBER 5

Deuteronomy 18:15

נָבִיא מִקִּרְבְּךָ מֵאַחֶיךָ כָּמֹנִי יָקִים לְךָ יְהוָה אֱלֹהֶיךָ אֵלָיו תִּשְׁמָעוּן׃

נָבִיא: prophet – קֶרֶב (2 sg sf + prep מִן): midst – אָח (pl + 2 sg sf + prep מִן): brother – כְּ (prep + 1 sg sf): like – קוּם (hiph impf 3 sg): raise up – שָׁמַע (qal impf 2 pl): listen

---

Acts 3:22-23

22Μωϋσῆς μὲν εἶπεν ὅτι προφήτην ὑμῖν ἀναστήσει κύριος
ὁ θεὸς ὑμῶν ἐκ τῶν ἀδελφῶν ὑμῶν ὡς ἐμέ· αὐτοῦ ἀκούσεσθε
κατὰ πάντα ὅσα ἂν λαλήσῃ πρὸς ὑμᾶς. 23ἔσται δὲ πᾶσα
ψυχὴ ἥτις ἐὰν μὴ ἀκούσῃ τοῦ προφήτου ἐκείνου
ἐξολεθρευθήσεται ἐκ τοῦ λαοῦ.

ἀνίστημι (fut ind 3 sg): raise up – ἀδελφός (gen pl): brother – ἀκούω (fut dep 2 pl/aor subj 3 sg): hear – λαλέω (aor subj 3 sg): speak – ψυχή: person – ἐξολεθρεύω (fut pass 3 sg): destroy utterly – λαός (gen sg): people

---

Formula of Concord Ep V 7

The Law and the Gospel are also contrasted with each other. Likewise also, Moses himself as a teacher of the Law and Christ as a preacher of the Gospel are contrasted with each other [John 1:17].

December 6

Isaiah 24:18-20

18 כִּֽי־אֲרֻבּוֹת מִמָּרוֹם נִפְתָּחוּ וַֽיִּרְעֲשׁוּ מוֹסְדֵי אָֽרֶץ׃
19 רֹעָה הִתְרֹעֲעָה הָאָרֶץ פּוֹר הִתְפּוֹרְרָה אֶרֶץ
מוֹט הִתְמוֹטְטָה אָֽרֶץ׃
20 נוֹעַ תָּנוּעַ אֶרֶץ כַּשִּׁכּוֹר וְהִתְנוֹדְדָה כַּמְּלוּנָה
וְכָבַד עָלֶיהָ פִּשְׁעָהּ וְנָפְלָה וְלֹא־תֹסִיף קֽוּם׃

אֲרֻבָּה (pl): floodgates – מָרוֹם (+ prep מִן): sky, heavens – פָּתַח (niph pf): be opened – רָעַשׁ (qal v-c impf 3 pl): shake – מוֹסָד (cst pl): foundation – רָעַע (qal inf abs/hithpoel pf 3 sg): break up – פָּרַר (qal inf abs/hithpoel pf 3 sg): split – מוֹט (qal inf abs/hithpolel pf 3 sg): shake – נוּעַ (qal inf abs/qal impf 3 sg): totter – שִׁכּוֹר: drunkard – נוד (hithpolel v-c pf 3 sg): sway – מְלוּנָה: hut – כָּבֵד (qal v-c pf 3 sg): be heavy – פֶּשַׁע: sin (as rebellion) – יָסַף (hiph impf 3 sg) + inf: again – קוּם (qal inf cst): rise

2 Peter 3:7

οἱ δὲ νῦν οὐρανοὶ καὶ ἡ γῆ τῷ αὐτῷ λόγῳ τεθησαυρισμένοι εἰσὶν πυρὶ τηρούμενοι εἰς ἡμέραν κρίσεως καὶ ἀπωλείας τῶν ἀσεβῶν ἀνθρώπων.

θησαυρίζω (pf pass ptcp): reserve – πῦρ: fire – τηρέω (pres pass ptcp): keep – κρίσις: judgment – ἀπώλεια: destruction – ἀσεβής: ungodly

Formula of Concord SD XI 58

In part, we should recognize God's judgment. They are well-deserved penalties for sins when God punishes a land or nation for despising His Word.

December 7

Joel 4:15-16

15 שֶׁמֶשׁ וְיָרֵחַ קָדָרוּ וְכוֹכָבִים אָסְפוּ נָגְהָם׃
16 וַיהוָה מִצִּיּוֹן יִשְׁאָג וּמִירוּשָׁלַםִ יִתֵּן קוֹלוֹ
וְרָעֲשׁוּ שָׁמַיִם וָאָרֶץ
וַיהוָה מַחֲסֶה לְעַמּוֹ וּמָעוֹז לִבְנֵי יִשְׂרָאֵל׃

שֶׁמֶשׁ: sun – יָרֵחַ: moon – קָדַר (qal pf 3 pl): be dark – כּוֹכָב (pl): star – אָסַף (qal pf 3 pl): remove – נֹגַהּ (3 pl sf): brightness – שָׁאַג (qal impf 3 sg): roar – נָתַן קוֹל: utter his voice – רָעַשׁ (qal v-c pf 3 pl): tremble – מַחֲסֶה: shelter – מָעוֹז: refuge

---

Matthew 24:30

καὶ τότε φανήσεται τὸ σημεῖον τοῦ υἱοῦ τοῦ ἀνθρώπου ἐν οὐρανῷ, καὶ τότε κόψονται πᾶσαι αἱ φυλαὶ τῆς γῆς καὶ ὄψονται τὸν υἱὸν τοῦ ἀνθρώπου ἐρχόμενον ἐπὶ τῶν νεφελῶν τοῦ οὐρανοῦ μετὰ δυνάμεως καὶ δόξης πολλῆς·

φαίνομαι (fut ind): appear – σημεῖον: sign – υἱός: Son – οὐρανός: heaven – κόπτω (fut mid 3 pl): mourn – φυλή: nation, people – ὄψονται (fut 3 pl of ὁράω): see – ἔρχομαι (pres ptcp): come – νεφέλη: cloud – δύναμις: power – δόξα: glory

---

Formula of Concord Ep VII 17

Although they *[unbelievers]* thrust Christ as a Savior away from themselves, yet they must receive Him, even against their will, as a strict Judge.

December 8

Psalm 110:1

נְאֻם יְהוָה לַאדֹנִי שֵׁב לִימִינִי
עַד־אָשִׁית אֹיְבֶיךָ הֲדֹם לְרַגְלֶיךָ׃

נְאֻם (cst sg): utterance – יָשַׁב (qal imv sg): sit – יָמִין (1 sg sf): right hand – שִׁית (qal impf 1 sg): make – אֹיֵב (pl + 2 sg sf): enemy – הֲדֹם: stool – רֶגֶל (pl + 2 sg sf): foot

---

Matthew 25:31-33

31 Ὅταν δὲ ἔλθῃ ὁ υἱὸς τοῦ ἀνθρώπου ἐν τῇ δόξῃ αὐτοῦ καὶ
πάντες οἱ ἄγγελοι μετ᾽αὐτοῦ, τότε καθίσει ἐπὶ θρόνου
δόξης αὐτοῦ· 32 καὶ συναχθήσονται ἔμπροσθεν αὐτοῦ πάντα
τὰ ἔθνη, καὶ ἀφορίσει αὐτοὺς ἀπ᾽ ἀλλήλων, ὥσπερ ὁ ποιμὴν
ἀφορίζει τὰ πρόβατα ἀπὸ τῶν ἐρίφων, 33 καὶ στήσει τὰ μὲν
πρόβατα ἐκ δεξιῶν αὐτοῦ, τὰ δὲ ἐρίφια ἐξ εὐωνύμων.

ἔρχομαι (aor subj 3 sg): come – δόξα: glory – καθίζω (fut ind 3 sg): sit – συνάγω (fut pass 3 pl): gather – ἔμπροσθεν: before – ἔθνος (pl): nation – ἀφορίζω (fut ind 3 sg): separate – ποιμήν: shepherd – πρόβατον (pl): sheep – ἔριφος/ἐρίφιον: goat – ἵστημι (fut ind 3 sg): put – δεξιός: right hand – εὐώνυμος: the left

---

Formula of Concord SD VIII 92

Christ—by His divine omnipotence—wherever He will, can be present with His body, which He has placed at the right hand of God's majesty and power.

DECEMBER 9

Isaiah 40:3

קוֹל קוֹרֵא בַּמִּדְבָּר פַּנּוּ דֶּרֶךְ יְהוָה
יַשְּׁרוּ בָּעֲרָבָה מְסִלָּה לֵאלֹהֵינוּ׃

קוֹל: voice – קָרָא (qal ptcp): call – מִדְבָּר: wild wasteland – פָּנָה (pi imv): prepare – דֶּרֶךְ: way – יָשַׁר (pi imv): make straight – עֲרָבָה: desert – מְסִלָּה: highway

---

Mark 1:4

ἐγένετο Ἰωάννης [ὁ] βαπτίζων ἐν τῇ ἐρήμῳ καὶ κηρύσσων βάπτισμα μετανοίας εἰς ἄφεσιν ἁμαρτιῶν.

ἔρημος: barren wasteland – κηρύσσω (pres ptcp): preach – μετάνοια: repentance – ἄφεσις: forgiveness – ἁμαρτία: sin

---

Apology XXIV (XII) 17

Baptism is not a work that we offer to God. It is a work in which God baptizes us. In other words, a minister baptizes us on God's behalf. God here offers and presents the forgiveness of sins, and so forth, according to the promise "Whoever believes and is baptized will be saved" (Mark 16:16). A sacrifice, on the contrary, is a ceremony or work that we give to God in order to provide Him honor.

December 10

Jeremiah 10:10

וַיהוָה אֱלֹהִים אֱמֶת הוּא־אֱלֹהִים חַיִּים וּמֶלֶךְ עוֹלָם
מִקִּצְפּוֹ תִּרְעַשׁ הָאָרֶץ וְלֹא־יָכִלוּ גוֹיִם זַעְמוֹ׃

אֱמֶת (adj): true – חַי (adj pl): living – עוֹלָם (adj): eternal – קֶצֶף (3 sg sf): anger – רָעַשׁ (qal impf 3 sg): tremble – כּוּל (hiph impf 3 pl): endure – גּוֹי (pl): nation – זַעַם (3 sg sf): wrath

---

Revelation 6:15-16

15Καὶ οἱ βασιλεῖς τῆς γῆς καὶ οἱ μεγιστάνες καὶ οἱ
χιλίαρχοι καὶ οἱ πλούσιοι καὶ οἱ ἰσχυροὶ καὶ πᾶς δοῦλος
καὶ ἐλεύθερος ἔκρυψαν ἑαυτοὺς εἰς τὰ σπήλαια καὶ εἰς
τὰς πέτρας τῶν ὀρέων. 16καὶ λέγουσιν τοῖς ὄρεσιν καὶ
ταῖς πέτραις, πέσετε ἐφ' ἡμᾶς καὶ κρύψατε ἡμᾶς ἀπὸ
τοῦ προσώπου τοῦ καθημένου ἐπὶ τοῦ θρόνου καὶ ἀπὸ τῆς
ὀργῆς τοῦ ἀρνίου.

βασιλεύς (pl): king – μεγιστάν (pl): great one – χιλίαρχος (pl): military officer – πλούσιος (pl): rich – ἰσχυρός (pl): mighty – δοῦλος: slave – ἐλεύθερος: free – κρύπτω (aor ind 3 pl/aor imv 2 pl): hide – σπήλαιον (pl): cave – πέτρα (pl): rock – ὄρος (pl): mountain – πίπτω (aor imv 2 pl): fall – πρόσωπον: face – κάθημαι (pres ptcp): sit – θρόνος: throne – ὀργή: wrath – ἀρνίον: Lamb

---

Formula of Concord Ep XII 20

All those who regard Christ as a creature according to the flesh have no true knowledge of Christ as the reigning King of heaven.

DECEMBER 11

Psalm 98:8-9

[8]נְהָרוֹת יִמְחֲאוּ־כָף יַחַד הָרִים יְרַנֵּנוּ׃
[9]לִפְנֵי־יְהוָה כִּי בָא לִשְׁפֹּט הָאָרֶץ
יִשְׁפֹּט־תֵּבֵל בְּצֶדֶק וְעַמִּים בְּמֵישָׁרִים׃

נָהָר (pl): river – מָחָא (qal juss 3 pl): clap – כַּף: hand – יַחַד (adv): together – הַר (pl): mountain – רָנַן (pi juss 3 pl): sing – בּוֹא (qal ptcp sg): come – שָׁפַט (qal inf cst/qal impf 3 sg): judge – תֵּבֵל: world – מֵישָׁרִים: uprightness

---

Jude 14-15

[14]Προεφήτευσεν δὲ καὶ τούτοις ἕβδομος ἀπὸ Ἀδὰμ
Ἑνὼχ λέγων· ἰδοὺ ἦλθεν κύριος ἐν ἁγίαις μυριάσιν
αὐτοῦ [15]ποιῆσαι κρίσιν κατὰ πάντων καὶ ἐλέγξαι πᾶσαν
ψυχὴν περὶ πάντων τῶν ἔργων ἀσεβείας αὐτῶν ὧν
ἠσέβησαν καὶ περὶ πάντων τῶν σκληρῶν ὧν ἐλάλησαν
κατ᾽ αὐτοῦ ἁμαρτωλοὶ ἀσεβεῖς.

προφητεύω (aor ind 3 sg): prophesy – ἕβδομος: seventh – ἰδού: behold – ἔρχομαι (aor ind 3 sg): come – ἅγιος: holy – μυριάς: myriad, 10,000 (God's holy myriads = the angels) – κρίσις: judgment + ποιεῖν: to bring – ἐλέγχω (aor inf): convict – ψυχή: soul, person – ἀσέβεια: ungodly action – ἀσεβέω (aor ind 3 pl): act impiously – σκληρός: harsh (words) – λαλέω (aor ind 3 pl): speak – ἀσεβής: godless

---

Augsburg Confession III 6

The same Christ will openly come again to judge the living and the dead, and so forth, according to the Apostles' Creed.

December 12

Jeremiah 29:11

כִּי אָנֹכִי יָדַעְתִּי אֶת־הַמַּחֲשָׁבֹת אֲשֶׁר אָנֹכִי חֹשֵׁב עֲלֵיכֶם
נְאֻם־יְהוָה מַחְשְׁבוֹת שָׁלוֹם וְלֹא לְרָעָה לָתֵת לָכֶם
אַחֲרִית וְתִקְוָה׃

יָדַע (qal pf 1 sg): know – מַחֲשָׁבָה (pl): plan – חָשַׁב (qal ptcp): plan – נְאֻם (cst): utterance – רָעָה: harm – נָתַן (qal inf cst): give – אַחֲרִית: future – תִּקְוָה: hope

---

Revelation 21:4

καὶ ἐξαλείψει πᾶν δάκρυον ἐκ τῶν ὀφθαλμῶν αὐτῶν, καὶ ὁ θάνατος οὐκ ἔσται ἔτι οὔτε πένθος οὔτε κραυγὴ οὔτε πόνος οὐκ ἔσται ἔτι, [ὅτι] τὰ πρῶτα ἀπῆλθαν.

ἐξαλείφω (fut ind 3 sg): wipe away – δάκρυον: tear – ὀφθαλμός: eye – θάνατος: death – οὐκ ἔτι: no more – πένθος: grief, mourning – κραυγή: crying – πόνος: pain, labor, toil – πρῶτος: first, former – ἀπέρχομαι (aor ind 3 pl): pass away

---

Formula of Concord SD II 50

Out of His immense goodness and mercy, God provides for the public preaching of His divine eternal Law and His wonderful plan for our redemption, that of the holy, only saving Gospel of His eternal Son, our only Savior and Redeemer, Jesus Christ.

December 13

Isaiah 55:6-7

6 דִּרְשׁוּ יְהוָה בְּהִמָּצְאוֹ קְרָאֻהוּ בִּהְיוֹתוֹ קָרוֹב׃
7 יַעֲזֹב רָשָׁע דַּרְכּוֹ וְאִישׁ אָוֶן מַחְשְׁבֹתָיו
וְיָשֹׁב אֶל־יְהוָה וִירַחֲמֵהוּ וְאֶל־אֱלֹהֵינוּ כִּי־יַרְבֶּה לִסְלוֹחַ׃

דָּרַשׁ (qal imv pl): seek – מָצָא (niph inf cst + 3 sg sf): be found – קָרָא (qal imv pl + 3 sg sf): call on – הָיָה (qal inf cst + 3 sg sf): be – קָרוֹב: near – עָזַב (qal juss 3 sg): forsake – רָשָׁע: wicked – דֶּרֶךְ (3 sg sf): way – אָוֶן: wickedness – מַחֲשָׁבָה (pl + 3 sg sf): thought – שׁוּב (qal juss 3 sg): return – רָחַם (pi impf 3 sg + 3 sg sf): have mercy – רָבָה (hiph impf 3 sg) + inf: freely – סָלַח (qal inf cst): pardon

2 Corinthians 6:1-2

1 Συνεργοῦντες δὲ καὶ παρακαλοῦμεν μὴ εἰς κενὸν τὴν χάριν τοῦ θεοῦ δέξασθαι ὑμᾶς· 2 λέγει γάρ· καιρῷ δεκτῷ ἐπήκουσά σου καὶ ἐν ἡμέρᾳ σωτηρίας ἐβοήθησά σοι. ἰδοὺ νῦν καιρὸς εὐπρόσδεκτος, ἰδοὺ νῦν ἡμέρα σωτηρίας.

συνεργέω (pres ptcp pl): work together – παρακαλέω (pres ind 1 pl): urge – κενός: without result – δέχομαι (aor inf): receive – καιρός: time – δεκτός: acceptable – ἐπακούω (aor ind 1 sg): hear – βοηθέω (aor ind 1 sg): help – εὐπρόσδεκτος: what is acceptable

Large Catechism I 15

To cling to Him with the heart is nothing else than to trust in Him entirely. For this reason God wishes to turn us away from everything else that exists outside of Him and to draw us to Himself [John 6:44].

DECEMBER 14

Exodus 15:1-2

1 אָז יָשִׁיר־מֹשֶׁה וּבְנֵי יִשְׂרָאֵל אֶת־הַשִּׁירָה הַזֹּאת לַיהוָה
וַיֹּאמְרוּ לֵאמֹר אָשִׁירָה לַיהוָה כִּי־גָאֹה גָּאָה סוּס וְרֹכְבוֹ
רָמָה בַיָּם׃ 2 עָזִּי וְזִמְרָת יָהּ וַיְהִי־לִי לִישׁוּעָה זֶה אֵלִי
וְאַנְוֵהוּ אֱלֹהֵי אָבִי וַאֲרֹמְמֶנְהוּ׃

שִׁיר (qal impf 3 sg/qal coh 1 sg): sing – שִׁירָה: song – גָּאָה (qal inf abs/qal pf 3 sg): be exalted – רָכַב (qal ptcp + 3 sg sf): rider – רָמָה (qal pf 3 sg): hurl – עֹז (1 sg sf): strength – זִמְרָת: song – יְשׁוּעָה: salvation – נָוָה (hiph impf 1 sg + 3 sg sf): praise – רוּם (polel impf 1 sg + 3 sg sf): exalt

---

Revelation 15:3

καὶ ᾄδουσιν τὴν ᾠδὴν Μωϋσέως τοῦ δούλου τοῦ θεοῦ καὶ τὴν ᾠδὴν τοῦ ἀρνίου λέγοντες· μεγάλα καὶ θαυμαστὰ τὰ ἔργα σου, κύριε ὁ θεὸς ὁ παντοκράτωρ· δίκαιαι καὶ ἀληθιναὶ αἱ ὁδοί σου, ὁ βασιλεὺς τῶν ἐθνῶν·

ᾄδω (pres ind 3 pl): sing (subject: the saints) – ᾠδή: song – ἀρνίον: the Lamb – μέγας: great – θαυμαστός: marvelous – ἔργον: deed – παντοκράτωρ: Almighty – δίκαιος: just – ἀληθινός: true – ὁδός (pl): way

---

Large Catechism I 84

On this day of rest (since we can get no other chance), we have the freedom and time to attend divine service. We come together to hear and use God's Word, and then to praise God, to sing and to pray [Col 3:16].

DECEMBER 15

Isaiah 65:17

כִּי־הִנְנִי בוֹרֵא שָׁמַיִם חֲדָשִׁים וָאָרֶץ חֲדָשָׁה
וְלֹא תִזָּכַרְנָה הָרִאשֹׁנוֹת וְלֹא תַעֲלֶינָה עַל־לֵב׃

בָּרָא (qal ptcp): create – חָדָשׁ: new – זָכַר (niph impf 3 pl): be remembered – רִאשׁוֹן (pl): former – עָלָה (qal impf 3 pl): come – לֵב: heart = to mind

---

2 Peter 3:13

καινοὺς δὲ οὐρανοὺς καὶ γῆν καινὴν κατὰ τὸ ἐπάγγελμα αὐτοῦ προσδοκῶμεν, ἐν οἷς δικαιοσύνη κατοικεῖ.

καινός: new – ἐπάγγελμα: promise – προσδοκάω (pres ind 1 pl): look for – δικαιοσύνη: righteousness – κατοικέω (pres ind 3 sg): dwell

---

Augsburg Confession XVII 1

[At the judgment, Christ] will give the godly and elect eternal life and everlasting joys, but He will condemn ungodly people and the devils to be tormented without end [Matt 25:31-46].

DECEMBER 16

Psalm 23:5-6

[5]תַּעֲרֹךְ לְפָנַי שֻׁלְחָן נֶגֶד צֹרְרָי דִּשַּׁנְתָּ בַשֶּׁמֶן רֹאשִׁי כּוֹסִי
רְוָיָה׃ [6]אַךְ טוֹב וָחֶסֶד יִרְדְּפוּנִי כָּל־יְמֵי חַיָּי וְשַׁבְתִּי
בְּבֵית־יְהוָה לְאֹרֶךְ יָמִים׃

עָרַךְ (qal impf 2 sg): prepare – שֻׁלְחָן: table – נֶגֶד: among – צָרַר (qal ptcp pl + 1 sg sf): show hostility to – דָּשֵׁן (pi pf 2 sg): anoint – שֶׁמֶן: oil – כּוֹס (1 sg sf): cup – רְוָיָה: saturation = is well-filled, overflowing – חֶסֶד: faithful love – רָדַף (qal impf 3 pl + 1 sg sf): follow – שַׁבְתִּי (qal v-c pf 1 sg of שׁוּב): turn, return; LXX reads שִׁבְתִּי (qal inf cst of יָשַׁב + 1 sg sf): dwell

---

John 14:1-3

[1]Μὴ ταρασσέσθω ὑμῶν ἡ καρδία· πιστεύετε εἰς τὸν θεὸν
καὶ εἰς ἐμὲ πιστεύετε. [2]ἐν τῇ οἰκίᾳ τοῦ πατρός μου
μοναὶ πολλαί εἰσιν· εἰ δὲ μή, εἶπον ἂν ὑμῖν ὅτι πορεύομαι
ἑτοιμάσαι τόπον ὑμῖν· [3]καὶ ἐὰν πορευθῶ καὶ ἑτοιμάσω
τόπον ὑμῖν, πάλιν ἔρχομαι καὶ παραλήμψομαι ὑμᾶς πρὸς
ἐμαυτόν, ἵνα ὅπου εἰμὶ ἐγὼ καὶ ὑμεῖς ἦτε.

ταράσσω (pres pass imv): trouble – μονή (pl): room – πορεύομαι (pres ind 1 sg/aor subj 1 sg): go – ἑτοιμάζω (aor inf/aor subj 1 sg): prepare – τόπος: place – παραλαμβάνω (fut mid 1 sg): take

---

Formula of Concord SD XI 23

He *[God]* has also ordained that in the way just mentioned He will, by His grace, gifts, and efficacy, bring them *[the elect]* to salvation. He will aid, promote, strengthen, and preserve them.

DECEMBER 17

Psalm 130:7-8

7 יַחֵל יִשְׂרָאֵל אֶל־יְהוָה כִּי־עִם־יְהוָה הַחֶסֶד וְהַרְבֵּה
עִמּוֹ פְדוּת׃
8 וְהוּא יִפְדֶּה אֶת־יִשְׂרָאֵל מִכֹּל עֲוֹנֹתָיו׃

יָחַל (pi imv sg): hope – חֶסֶד: faithful love – רָבָה (hiph inf abs used as adj): full – פְּדוּת: redemption – פָּדָה (qal impf 3 sg): redeem – עָוֹן (pl + 3 sg sf): sin (as guilt)

Matthew 1:21

τέξεται δὲ υἱόν, καὶ καλέσεις τὸ ὄνομα αὐτοῦ Ἰησοῦν· αὐτὸς γὰρ σώσει τὸν λαὸν αὐτοῦ ἀπὸ τῶν ἁμαρτιῶν αὐτῶν.

τίκτω (fut ind 3 sg): give birth to – καλέω (fut ind 2 sg): call – σῴζω (fut ind 3 sg): save – λαός: people – ἁμαρτία: sin

---

Smalcald Articles III III 8

On the other hand, the Gospel brings consolation and forgiveness. It does so not just in one way, but through the Word and the Sacraments and the like, as we will discuss later. As Ps 130:7 says against the dreadful captivity of sin, "with the LORD is . . . plentiful redemption."

DECEMBER 18

Psalm 147:11-12

¹¹רוֹצֶה יְהוָה אֶת־יְרֵאָיו אֶת־הַמְיַחֲלִים לְחַסְדּוֹ׃
¹²שַׁבְּחִי יְרוּשָׁלַםִ אֶת־יְהוָה הַלְלִי אֱלֹהַיִךְ צִיּוֹן׃

רָצָה (qal ptcp): be pleased with – יָרֵא (qal ptcp pl + 3 sg sf): fear – יָחַל (pi ptcp pl): wait for, hope – חֶסֶד (3 sg sf): faithful love – שָׁבַח (pi imv sg): laud – הָלַל (pi imv sg): praise

---

Revelation 3:5

Ὁ νικῶν οὕτως περιβαλεῖται ἐν ἱματίοις λευκοῖς καὶ οὐ μὴ ἐξαλείψω τὸ ὄνομα αὐτοῦ ἐκ τῆς βίβλου τῆς ζωῆς καὶ ὁμολογήσω τὸ ὄνομα αὐτοῦ ἐνώπιον τοῦ πατρός μου καὶ ἐνώπιον τῶν ἀγγέλων αὐτοῦ.

νικάω (pres ptcp sg): conquer, overcome – περιβάλλω (fut mid 3 sg): clothe oneself – ἱμάτιον: robe – λευκός: white – ἐξαλείφω (aor subj 1 sg): wipe out, erase – βίβλος: book – ζωή: life – ὁμολογέω (fut ind 1 sg): acknowledge

---

Large Catechism I 325

So then all the Scriptures have everywhere preached and taught this *[first]* commandment, aiming always at these two things: fear of God and trust in Him. The prophet David especially does this throughout the Psalms, as when he says "the LORD takes pleasure in those who fear Him, in those who hope in His steadfast love" [Ps 147:11]. He writes as if the entire commandment were explained by one verse, as if to say, "The Lord takes pleasure in those who have no other gods."

DECEMBER 19

Exodus 12:11

וְכָ֫כָה תֹּאכְלוּ אֹתוֹ מָתְנֵיכֶם חֲגֻרִים נַעֲלֵיכֶם בְּרַגְלֵיכֶם וּמַקֶּלְכֶם בְּיֶדְכֶם וַאֲכַלְתֶּם אֹתוֹ בְּחִפָּזוֹן פֶּ֫סַח הוּא לַיהוָה׃

כָּ֫כָה (adv): thus – אָכַל (qal impf 2 pl): eat – מָתְנַ֫יִם (2 pl sf): loins – חָגַר (qal pass ptcp): gird – נַ֫עַל (pl + 2 pl sf): sandal – רֶ֫גֶל (pl + 2 pl sf): foot – מַקֵּל (2 pl sf): staff – יָד (2 pl sf): hand – חִפָּזוֹן: haste – פֶּ֫סַח: Passover

Luke 12:35-37

35 Ἔστωσαν ὑμῶν αἱ ὀσφύες περιεζωσμέναι καὶ οἱ λύχνοι καιόμενοι· 36 καὶ ὑμεῖς ὅμοιοι ἀνθρώποις προσδεχομένοις τὸν κύριον ἑαυτῶν πότε ἀναλύσῃ ἐκ τῶν γάμων, ἵνα ἐλθόντος καὶ κρούσαντος εὐθέως ἀνοίξωσιν αὐτῷ. 37 μακάριοι οἱ δοῦλοι ἐκεῖνοι, οὓς ἐλθὼν ὁ κύριος εὑρήσει γρηγοροῦντας·

εἰμί (pres imv 3 pl): be – ὀσφῦς: loins – περιζώννυμι (pf pass ptcp): gird about – λύχνος: lamp – καίω (pres pass ptcp): light – ὅμοιος: like – προσδέχομαι (pres ptcp): wait for – ἀναλύω (aor subj 3 sg): return – γάμος: wedding celebration – κρούω (aor ptcp): knock – εὐθέως: immediately – ἀνοίγω (aor subj 3 pl): open – γρηγορέω (pres act ptcp): keep watch

Large Catechism IV 63

Therefore, we must be watchful and well armed [2 Cor 10:4]. We must not allow ourselves to be directed or turned away from the Word, in order that we may not think of Baptism as a mere empty sign, like the fanatic's dream [Jer 23:25].

DECEMBER 20

Jeremiah 50:20

בַּיָּמִים הָהֵם וּבָעֵת הַהִיא נְאֻם־יְהוָה יְבֻקַּשׁ אֶת־עֲוֺן
יִשְׂרָאֵל וְאֵינֶנּוּ וְאֶת־חַטֹּאת יְהוּדָה וְלֹא תִמָּצֶאינָה כִּי
אֶסְלַח לַאֲשֶׁר אַשְׁאִיר׃

יוֹם (pl): day – עֵת: time – נְאֻם (cst sg): utterance – בָּקַשׁ (pu impf 3 sg): search will be made – עָוֺן: sin (as guilt) – אַיִן (sf): nonexistence – חַטָּאת (pl): sin (as missing the mark) – מָצָא (niph impf 3 pl): be found – סָלַח (qal impf 1 sg): forgive – שָׁאַר (hiph impf 1 sg): leave over = the remnant I spare

---

2 Corinthians 8:9

γινώσκετε γὰρ τὴν χάριν τοῦ κυρίου ἡμῶν Ἰησοῦ Χριστοῦ, ὅτι δι᾽ ὑμᾶς ἐπτώχευσεν πλούσιος ὤν, ἵνα ὑμεῖς τῇ ἐκείνου πτωχείᾳ πλουτήσητε.

γινώσκω (pres ind 2 pl): know (by experience) – χάρις: grace – πτωχεύω (aor ind 3 sg): become poor – πλούσιος: rich – πλουτέω (aor subj 2 pl): become rich

---

Large Catechism II 26

Here we learn to know the Second Person of the Godhead. We see what we have from God over and above the temporal goods mentioned before. We see how He has completely poured forth Himself [Matt 26:28] and withheld nothing from us [2 Cor 8:9].

DECEMBER 21

Genesis 15:5-6

וַיּוֹצֵא אֹתוֹ הַחוּצָה וַיֹּאמֶר הַבֶּט־נָא הַשָּׁמַיְמָה וּסְפֹר[5]
הַכּוֹכָבִים אִם־תּוּכַל לִסְפֹּר אֹתָם וַיֹּאמֶר לוֹ כֹּה יִהְיֶה
זַרְעֶךָ׃ [6]וְהֶאֱמִן בַּיהוָה וַיַּחְשְׁבֶהָ לּוֹ צְדָקָה׃

יָצָא (hiph v-c impf 3 sg): lead out – חוּץ: (+ directional ה): outside – נָבַט (hiph imv sg): look at – סָפַר (qal imv sg/qal inf cst): count – כּוֹכָב (pl): star – יָכֹל (qal impf 2 sg): be able – אָמַן (hiph pf 3 sg): believe – חָשַׁב (qal v-c impf 3 sg + 3 sg sf): credit

Romans 4:20-22

[20]εἰς δὲ τὴν ἐπαγγελίαν τοῦ θεοῦ οὐ διεκρίθη τῇ ἀπιστίᾳ
ἀλλ' ἐνεδυναμώθη τῇ πίστει, δοὺς δόξαν τῷ θεῷ [21]καὶ
πληροφορηθεὶς ὅτι ὃ ἐπήγγελται δυνατός ἐστιν καὶ
ποιῆσαι. [22]διὸ [καὶ] ἐλογίσθη αὐτῷ εἰς δικαιοσύνην.

ἐπαγγελία: promise – διακρίνω (aor pass 3 sg): doubt, waver – ἀπιστία: unbelief – ἐνδυναμόω (aor pass 3 sg): strengthen – δίδωμι (aor ptcp): give – πληροφορέω (aor pass ptcp): convince fully – ἐπαγγέλλομαι (pf ind): promise – δυνατός: able – λογίζομαι (aor pass): credit

Formula of Concord SD III 33

Here belongs also what St. Paul writes in Rom 4:3. Abraham was justified before God through faith alone, for the sake of the Mediator, without the cooperation of his works. This was true not only when Abraham was first converted from idolatry and had no good works, but also afterward, when he had been renewed by the Holy Spirit and adorned with many excellent good works (Gen 15:6; Heb 11:8).

DECEMBER 22

Malachi 3:1

הִנְנִי שֹׁלֵחַ מַלְאָכִי וּפִנָּה־דֶרֶךְ לְפָנָי
וּפִתְאֹם יָבוֹא אֶל־הֵיכָלוֹ הָאָדוֹן אֲשֶׁר־אַתֶּם מְבַקְשִׁים
וּמַלְאַךְ הַבְּרִית אֲשֶׁר־אַתֶּם חֲפֵצִים הִנֵּה־בָא אָמַר יְהוָה
צְבָאוֹת׃

שָׁלַח (qal ptcp): send – מַלְאָךְ (1 sg sf): messenger – פָּנָה (pi v-c pf 3 sg): prepare – דֶּרֶךְ: way – פִּתְאֹם: suddenly – בּוֹא (qal impf 3 sg): come – הֵיכָל (3 sg sf): temple – אָדוֹן: the Lord – בָּקַשׁ (pi ptcp pl): seek – מַלְאָךְ (cst sg): messenger – בְּרִית: covenant – חָפֵץ (adj pl): delighting in – צָבָא (pl): army, host

Luke 1:76

Καὶ σὺ δέ, παιδίον, προφήτης ὑψίστου κληθήσῃ· προπορεύσῃ γὰρ ἐνώπιον κυρίου ἑτοιμάσαι ὁδοὺς αὐτοῦ . . .

παιδίον: child – ὕψιστος: the most high – καλέω (fut pass 2 sg): call – προπορεύομαι (fut ind 2 sg): go on before – ἐνώπιον: before – ἑτοιμάζω (aor inf): prepare – ὁδός: way

Smalcald Articles III III 5

John the Baptist (preceding Christ) is called a preacher of repentance, but this is for the forgiveness of sins. That is, John was to accuse all and convict them of being sinners. This is so they can know what they are before God and acknowledge that they are lost. So they can be prepared for the Lord [Mark 1:3] to receive grace and to expect and accept from Him the forgiveness of sins.

DECEMBER 23

Micah 5:1

וְאַתָּה בֵּית־לֶחֶם אֶפְרָתָה צָעִיר לִהְיוֹת בְּאַלְפֵי יְהוּדָה מִמְּךָ לִי יֵצֵא לִהְיוֹת מוֹשֵׁל בְּיִשְׂרָאֵל וּמוֹצָאֹתָיו מִקֶּדֶם מִימֵי עוֹלָם׃

צָעִיר: little, insignificant – אֶלֶף (cst pl): thousand – יָצָא (qal impf 3 sg): come out – מָשַׁל (qal ptcp): rule – מוֹצָאָה (pl + 3 sg sf): act of going out, origin – קֶדֶם: ancient time – יוֹם (cst pl): day – עוֹלָם: eternity

---

Matthew 2:4-5

4καὶ συναγαγὼν πάντας τοὺς ἀρχιερεῖς καὶ γραμματεῖς τοῦ λαοῦ ἐπυνθάνετο παρ' αὐτῶν ποῦ ὁ χριστὸς γεννᾶται. 5οἱ δὲ εἶπαν αὐτῷ· ἐν Βηθλέεμ τῆς Ἰουδαίας· οὕτως γὰρ γέγραπται διὰ τοῦ προφήτου·

συνάγω (aor ptcp sg): call together (subject is King Herod) – ἀρχιερεύς: chief priest – γραμματεύς (pl): teacher of the law – λαός: people – πυνθάνομαι (impf 3 sg): inquire – γεννάω (pres pass ind 3 sg): be born – γράφω (pf pass ind 3 sg): write

---

Augsburg Confession III 2-3

There are two natures—the divine and the human—inseparably joined in one person. There is one Christ, true God and true man, who was born of the Virgin Mary, truly suffered, was crucified, died, and was buried. He did this to reconcile the Father to us and to be a sacrifice, not only for original guilt, but also for all actual sins of mankind [John 1:29].

DECEMBER 24

Isaiah 7:14

לָכֵן יִתֵּן אֲדֹנָי הוּא לָכֶם אוֹת הִנֵּה הָעַלְמָה הָרָה וְיֹלֶדֶת
בֵּן וְקָרָאת שְׁמוֹ עִמָּנוּ אֵל׃

נָתַן (qal impf 3 sg): give – אוֹת: sign – עַלְמָה: virgin – הָרָה (adj): pregnant – יָלַד (qal ptcp f): give birth to – קָרָא (qal v-c pf 2 sg): call – שֵׁם (3 sg sf): name – עִם (prep + 1 pl sf): with us – אֵל: God

---

Luke 1:34-35

34 εἶπεν δὲ Μαριὰμ πρὸς τὸν ἄγγελον· πῶς ἔσται τοῦτο, ἐπεὶ
ἄνδρα οὐ γινώσκω; 35 καὶ ἀποκριθεὶς ὁ ἄγγελος εἶπεν αὐτῇ·
πνεῦμα ἅγιον ἐπελεύσεται ἐπὶ σέ, καὶ δύναμις ὑψίστου
ἐπισκιάσει σοι· διὸ καὶ τὸ γεννώμενον ἅγιον κληθήσεται,
υἱὸς θεοῦ.

πῶς: how? – ἀνήρ: man – γινώσκω: know (by experience) – ἀποκρίνομαι (aor pass ptcp): answer – πνεῦμα: Spirit – ἐπέρχομαι (fut ind 3 sg): come upon – δύναμις: power – ὕψιστος: the Most High – ἐπισκιάζω (fut ind 3 sg): overshadow – διό: therefore – γεννάω (pres pass ptcp): be born – ἅγιος: holy – καλέω (fut pass 3 sg): call

---

Formula of Concord Ep VIII 12

So we believe, teach, and confess that Mary conceived and bore not merely a man and no more, but God's true Son. Therefore, she also is rightly called and truly is "the mother of God."

DECEMBER 25

Isaiah 9:5

כִּי־יֶלֶד יֻלַּד־לָנוּ בֵּן נִתַּן־לָנוּ וַתְּהִי הַמִּשְׂרָה עַל־שִׁכְמוֹ
וַיִּקְרָא שְׁמוֹ פֶּלֶא יוֹעֵץ אֵל גִּבּוֹר אֲבִיעַד שַׂר־שָׁלוֹם׃

יֶלֶד: child – יָלַד (pu or qal pass pf): be born (prophetic perfect) – נָתַן (niph pf): be given – מִשְׂרָה: rule, dominion – שְׁכֶם (3 sg sf): shoulder – שֵׁם (3 sg sf): name – פֶּלֶא: miracle, wonder – יָעַץ (qal ptcp): counselor – גִּבּוֹר: mighty – עַד: perpetuity (past and future) – שַׂר: prince

---

Luke 2:10-12

10καὶ εἶπεν αὐτοῖς ὁ ἄγγελος· μὴ φοβεῖσθε, ἰδοὺ γὰρ
εὐαγγελίζομαι ὑμῖν χαρὰν μεγάλην ἥτις ἔσται παντὶ τῷ
λαῷ, 11ὅτι ἐτέχθη ὑμῖν σήμερον σωτὴρ ὅς ἐστιν χριστὸς
κύριος ἐν πόλει Δαυίδ. 12καὶ τοῦτο ὑμῖν τὸ σημεῖον,
εὑρήσετε βρέφος ἐσπαργανωμένον καὶ κείμενον ἐν φάτνῃ.

φοβέομαι (pres imv 2 pl): fear – εὐαγγελίζω (pres mid 1 sg): announce good news – λαός: people – τίκτω (aor pass 3 sg): be born – σήμερον: today – σωτήρ: Savior – πόλις: city – σημεῖον: sign – βρέφος: infant – σπαργανόω (pf pass ptcp): wrapped in cloths – κεῖμαι (pres ptcp): lie – φάτνη: manger

---

Formula of Concord Ep I 5

Furthermore, God's Son has received this human nature [John 1:14], but without sin. Therefore, He did not receive a foreign nature, but our own flesh in the unity of His person. In this way He has become our true Brother.

DECEMBER 26

Psalm 148:1-2

1 הַֽלְלוּ יָהּ הַלְלוּ אֶת־יְהוָה מִן־הַשָּׁמַיִם הַלְלוּהוּ
בַּמְּרוֹמִים׃
2 הַֽלְלוּהוּ כָל־מַלְאָכָיו הַלְלוּהוּ כָּל־צְבָאוֹ [צְבָאָיו]׃

הָלַל (pi imv pl): praise – יָהּ (proper name contracted from יְהוָה): the LORD – שָׁמַיִם: heaven – מָרוֹם (pl): height – מַלְאָךְ (pl + 3 sg sf): angel – **צָבָא** (qere: pl + 3 sg sf): host

---

Luke 2:13-14

13 καὶ ἐξαίφνης ἐγένετο σὺν τῷ ἀγγέλῳ πλῆθος στρατιᾶς οὐρανίου αἰνούντων τὸν θεὸν καὶ λεγόντων· 14 δόξα ἐν ὑψίστοις θεῷ καὶ ἐπὶ γῆς εἰρήνη ἐν ἀνθρώποις εὐδοκίας.

ἐξαίφνης: suddenly – πλῆθος: great company – στρατιά: host – οὐράνιος: heavenly – αἰνέω (pres act ptcp): praise – δόξα: glory – ὕψιστος: highest – γῆ: earth – εἰρήνη: peace – εὐδοκία: favor

---

Apology V (III) 188

This faith gives God the honor, gives God that which is His own. By receiving the promises, it obeys Him. Just as Paul also says, "No distrust made him waver concerning the promise of God, but he grew strong in his faith as he gave glory to God" (Rom 4:20).

DECEMBER 27

Isaiah 9:1

הָעָם הַהֹלְכִים בַּחֹשֶׁךְ רָאוּ אוֹר גָּדוֹל
יֹשְׁבֵי בְּאֶרֶץ צַלְמָוֶת אוֹר נָגַהּ עֲלֵיהֶם׃

עַם: people – הָלַךְ (qal ptcp pl): walk – חֹשֶׁךְ: darkness – רָאָה (qal pf 3 pl): see – אוֹר: light – גָּדוֹל: great – יָשַׁב (qal ptcp cst pl): dwell – צַלְמָוֶת: death-shadow – נָגַהּ (qal pf 3 sg): shine

---

Ephesians 5:8

ἦτε γάρ ποτε σκότος, νῦν δὲ φῶς ἐν κυρίῳ· ὡς τέκνα φωτὸς περιπατεῖτε.

εἰμί (impf 2 pl): be – ποτέ: once – σκότος: darkness – φῶς: light – κύριος: Lord – τέκνον (pl): child – περιπατέω (pres imv 2 pl): walk, live

---

Apology XXIV (XII) 32

The preaching of the Gospel produces faith in those who receive the Gospel [Rom 10:17]. They call upon God, give thanks to God, bear troubles for their confession, and produce good works for Christ's glory. So the name of the Lord becomes great among the Gentiles [Mal 1:11].

DECEMBER 28

Psalm 98:1-2

[1]שִׁירוּ לַיהוָה שִׁיר חָדָשׁ כִּי־נִפְלָאוֹת עָשָׂה
הוֹשִׁיעָה־לּוֹ יְמִינוֹ וּזְרוֹעַ קָדְשׁוֹ׃
[2]הוֹדִיעַ יְהוָה יְשׁוּעָתוֹ לְעֵינֵי הַגּוֹיִם גִּלָּה צִדְקָתוֹ׃

שִׁיר (qal imv pl): sing – שִׁיר: song – חָדָשׁ: new – פָּלָא (niph ptcp pl): be extraordinary = marvelous things – יָשַׁע (hiph pf 3 sg f): work salvation – יָמִין (3 sg sf): right hand – זְרוֹעַ (cst sg): arm – קֹדֶשׁ (3 sg sf): holiness – יָדַע (hiph pf 3 sg): make known – גָּלָה (pi pf 3 sg): reveal – צְדָקָה (3 sg sf): righteousness

---

Luke 1:68-69

[68]Εὐλογητὸς κύριος ὁ θεὸς τοῦ Ἰσραήλ, ὅτι ἐπεσκέψατο
καὶ ἐποίησεν λύτρωσιν τῷ λαῷ αὐτοῦ, [69]καὶ ἤγειρεν κέρας
σωτηρίας ἡμῖν ἐν οἴκῳ Δαυὶδ παιδὸς αὐτοῦ.

εὐλογητός: blessed – κύριος: Lord – ἐπισκέπτομαι (aor ind 3 sg): come to help – ποιέω (aor ind 3 sg): bring about – λύτρωσις: redemption – λαός: people – ἐγείρω (aor ind 3 sg): raise up – κέρας: horn – σωτηρία: salvation – οἶκος: house – παῖς: servant

---

Apology V (III) 4

Therefore, when we have been justified by faith and regenerated, we begin to fear and love God, to pray to Him, to expect aid from Him, to give thanks and praise Him.

December 29

Isaiah 8:13-14

[13] אֶת־יְהוָה צְבָאוֹת אֹתוֹ תַקְדִּישׁוּ וְהוּא מוֹרַאֲכֶם וְהוּא
מַעֲרִצְכֶם׃
[14] וְהָיָה לְמִקְדָּשׁ וּלְאֶבֶן נֶגֶף וּלְצוּר מִכְשׁוֹל

צָבָא (pl): army, host – קָדַשׁ (hiph impf 2 pl): regard as holy – מוֹרָא (2 pl sf): object of reverence – עָרַץ (hiph ptcp + 2 pl sf): cause fear – מִקְדָּשׁ: sanctuary – אֶבֶן: stone – נֶגֶף: striking – צוּר: rock – מִכְשׁוֹל: stumbling

---

Luke 2:34-35

[34]καὶ εὐλόγησεν αὐτοὺς Συμεὼν καὶ εἶπεν πρὸς Μαριὰμ τὴν
μητέρα αὐτοῦ· ἰδοὺ οὗτος κεῖται εἰς πτῶσιν καὶ ἀνάστασιν
πολλῶν ἐν τῷ Ἰσραὴλ καὶ εἰς σημεῖον ἀντιλεγόμενον [35]καὶ
σοῦ [δὲ] αὐτῆς τὴν ψυχὴν διελεύσεται ῥομφαία, ὅπως ἂν
ἀποκαλυφθῶσιν ἐκ πολλῶν καρδιῶν διαλογισμοί.

εὐλογέω (aor ind 3 sg): bless – μήτηρ: mother – κεῖμαι (pres ind 3 sg): lie, be appointed, be destined – πτῶσις: fall – ἀνάστασις: rising – σημεῖον: sign – ἀντιλέγω (pres pass ptcp): speak against, contradict – σοῦ αὐτῆς: your own – ψυχή: soul – διέρχομαι (fut ind 3 sg): pierce – ῥομφαία: sword – ὅπως (purpose): that – ἀποκαλύπτω (aor pass subj 3 pl): reveal – διαλογισμός (pl): thought

---

Apology V (III) 273

So there have always been some who have taught this earthly righteousness alone to the exclusion of the righteousness of faith. Such teachers will always exist.

DECEMBER 30

Psalm 100:4-5

4 בֹּאוּ שְׁעָרָיו בְּתוֹדָה חֲצֵרֹתָיו בִּתְהִלָּה הוֹדוּ־לוֹ בָּרְכוּ
שְׁמוֹ׃
5 כִּי־טוֹב יְהוָה לְעוֹלָם חַסְדּוֹ וְעַד־דֹּר וָדֹר אֱמוּנָתוֹ׃

בּוֹא (qal imv pl): enter – שַׁעַר (pl + 3 sg sf): gate – תּוֹדָה: thanksgiving – חָצֵר (pl + 3 sg sf): court – תְּהִלָּה: praise – יָדָה (hiph imv pl): give thanks – בָּרַךְ (pi imv pl): bless – עוֹלָם: eternity – חֶסֶד (3 sg sf): faithful love – דּוֹר: generation – אֱמוּנָה (3 sg sf): faithfulness

Luke 1:49-50

49ὅτι ἐποίησέν μοι μεγάλα ὁ δυνατός. καὶ ἅγιον τὸ ὄνομα
αὐτοῦ, 50καὶ τὸ ἔλεος αὐτοῦ εἰς γενεὰς καὶ γενεὰς τοῖς
φοβουμένοις αὐτόν.

ποιέω (aor ind 3 sg): do – μέγας (n pl): great – ὁ δυνατός: Mighty One – ἅγιος: holy – ὄνομα: name – ἔλεος: mercy – γενεά (pl): generation – φοβέομαι (pres ptcp pl): fear

Apology XXI (IX) 4

Our Confession approves honoring the saints in three ways. The first is thanksgiving. We should thank God because He has shown examples of mercy, because He wishes to save people, and because He has given teachers and other gifts to the Church.

DECEMBER 31

Psalm 90:10,12

10 יְמֵי־שְׁנוֹתֵינוּ בָהֶם שִׁבְעִים שָׁנָה וְאִם בִּגְבוּרֹת
שְׁמוֹנִים שָׁנָה וְרָהְבָּם עָמָל וָאָוֶן כִּי־גָז חִישׁ וַנָּעֻפָה׃
12 לִמְנוֹת יָמֵינוּ כֵּן הוֹדַע וְנָבִא לְבַב חָכְמָה׃

שִׁבְעִים: seventy – גְּבוּרָה (pl): strength – שְׁמוֹנִים: eighty – רֹהַב (3 pl sf): (object of) pride – עָמָל: trouble – אָוֶן: sorrow – גּוּז (qal pf 3 sg): pass – חִישׁ: quickly – עוּף (qal v-c impf 1 pl): fly away, vanish – מָנָה (qal inf cst + לְ): count – כֵּן: so – יָדַע (hiph imv sg): teach – בּוֹא (hiph impf 1 pl): gain – לֵבָב (cst sg): heart – חָכְמָה: wisdom

---

Philippians 3:8-9

8 ἀλλὰ μενοῦνγε καὶ ἡγοῦμαι πάντα ζημίαν εἶναι διὰ τὸ ὑπερέχον τῆς γνώσεως Χριστοῦ Ἰησοῦ τοῦ κυρίου μου, δι' ὃν τὰ πάντα ἐζημιώθην, καὶ ἡγοῦμαι σκύβαλα, ἵνα Χριστὸν κερδήσω
9 καὶ εὑρεθῶ ἐν αὐτῷ, μὴ ἔχων ἐμὴν δικαιοσύνην τὴν ἐκ νόμου ἀλλὰ τὴν διὰ πίστεως Χριστοῦ, τὴν ἐκ θεοῦ δικαιοσύνην ἐπὶ τῇ πίστει.

μενοῦνγε: indeed – ἡγέομαι (pres ind 1 sg) consider – ζημία: loss – ὑπερέχω: (pres ptcp n sg as substantive): surpassing greatness – ζημιόω (aor pass 1 sg): lose – σκύβαλον (pl): garbage – κερδαίνω (aor subj 1 sg): gain – εὑρίσκω (aor pass subj 1 sg): find

---

Formula of Concord SD III 4

Therefore, the righteousness of faith is the forgiveness of sins, reconciliation with God, and our adoption as God's children only on account of Christ's obedience.

Old Testament Selections

Genesis

Exodus

Leviticus

Numbers

Deuteronomy

Jeremiah

Lamentations

Ezekiel

New Testament Selections

John

Acts

Romans

1 Corinthians

1 John

Jude

Revelation

Lutheran Confessions Selections

Small Catechism

Large Catechism

Smalcald Articles

Power and Primacy

Formula of Concord